THE MI'KMAW GRAMMAR OF FATHER PACIFIQUE

NEW EDITION

BERNIE FRANCIS AND JOHN HEWSON

Copyright © 2016 Cape Breton University Press

All rights reserved. No part of this work may be reproduced or used in any form or by any means, electronic or mechanical, including photocopying, recording or any information storage or retrieval system, without the prior written permission of the publisher. Cape Breton University Press recognizes fair dealing uses under the *Copyright Act* (Canada). Responsibility for the research and permissions obtained for this publication rests with the authors/editors.

Cover design: Cathy MacLean Design, Chéticamp, NS.
Layout: Mike Hunter, West Bay and Sydney, NS.
First printed in Canada.

Library and Archives Canada Cataloguing in Publication
Pacifique, père, 1863-1943
[Leçons grammaticales théoriques et pratiques de la langue micmaque. English]
    The Mi'kmaw grammar of father Pacifique / Bernie Francis and John Hewson. -- New edition.
Translation of: Leçons grammaticales théoriques et pratiques de la langue micmaque.
"First edition: Leçons grammaticales théoriques et pratiques de la langue micmaque
    of Rev. Father Pacifique Buisson (1939)."
"Second edition: Translated, transcribed and edited by Bernard Francis and John
    Hewson (1990)."
"New edition updated, 2016."
Includes bibliographical references and index.
Issued in print and electronic formats.
ISBN 978-1-897009-50-5 (paperback).--ISBN 978-1-77206-074-4 (pdf).--
ISBN 978-1-77206-075-1 (epub).--ISBN 978-1-77206-076-8 (kindle)

    1. Micmac language--Grammar. I. Francis, Bernard, 1948-, translator, editor
II. Hewson, John, 1930-, translator, editor III. Title. IV. Title: Leçons grammaticales théoriques et pratiques de la langue micmaque. English.

PM1792.P313 2016   497'.3435   C2016-905470-5
                                                                                    C2016-905471-3

Cape Breton University Press
PO Box 5300
Sydney, Nova Scotia B1P 6L2
Canada

Distributed by
Nimbus Publishing
3731 MacKintosh St
Halifax, Nova Scotia B3K 5A5
Canada

THE MI'KMAW GRAMMAR OF FATHER PACIFIQUE

NEW EDITION

BERNIE FRANCIS AND JOHN HEWSON

First edition: *Leçons grammaticales théoriques et pratiques de la langue micmaque* of Rev. Father Pacifique Buisson (1939)

Second edition: Translated, transcribed and edited by Bernard Francis and John Hewson (1990)

New edition updated, 2016

Cape Breton University Press
Sydney, Nova Scotia

TABLE OF CONTENTS

Preface to the (2016) Edition — vii
Preface (1990) — xvi

Lesson 1. The Mi'kmaw Alphabet — 1
Lesson 2. Simple Syllables — 7
Lesson 3. Syllables — 11
Lesson 4. Syllables from Diphthongs — 13
Lesson 5. Vowels or Diphthongs with consonants — 20
Lesson 6. Nouns and adjectives — 26
Lesson 7. Nouns and Adjectives (continuation) — 33
Lesson 8. Nouns and Adjectives (continuation) — 38
Lesson 9. The Verb — 42
Lesson 10. First Conjugation (Intransitive) in -i — 48
Lesson 11. Examples of the First Conjugation — 58
Lesson 12. Second Conjugation (intransitive) in -ai (diphthong) — 66
Lesson 13. Examples of the Second Conjugation — 75
Lesson 14. Third Conjugation (intransitive) in -ei (diphthong) — 80
Lesson 15. Examples of the Third Conjugation — 87
Lesson 16. Fourth Conjugation (active inanimate) in -m and other consonants — 95
Lesson 17. Examples of the Fourth Conjugation — 103
Lesson 18. Fifth Conjugation (active inanimate) in -u — 110
Lesson 19. Examples of the Fifth Conjugation — 119
Lesson 20. TO HAVE and TO BE — 125
Lesson 21. Animate (TA) Verbs — 131

Lesson 22. Sixth Conjugation (TA Verbs)   135
Lesson 23. Sixth Conjugation (continued)   142
Lesson 24. Seventh Conjugation (Two goal TA Verbs)   149
Lesson 25. Seventh Conjugation (continued)   155
Lesson 26. Examples of the Sixth and Seventh Conjugations   163
Lesson 27. Examples of the Sixth and Seventh Conjugations (continued) 170
Lesson 28. Classification of Verbs   180
Lesson 29. Numbers   188
Lesson 30. Pronouns and Adjectives   195
Lesson 31. Possession   202
Lesson 32. Adverbs   207
Lesson 33. Prepositions, Conjunctions, Interjections   225

List of Mi'kmaw Words   231

PREFACE TO THIS NEW EDITION

The original edition of the translation and re-transcription of Father Pacifique's *Leçons grammaticales* was published more than twenty years ago, in 1990. It was Memoir 7, one of the early volumes published by Algonquian and Iroquoian Linguistics at the University of Manitoba, under the Editorship of John D. Nichols and H.C. Wolfart. It was given the title *The Micmac Grammar of Father Pacifique*.

Within a decade it was out of print, and the development of a new edition was undertaken. When the original edition was prepared, computerized printing was still in its infancy, and instead of the italics that Father Pacifique had used for the Mi'kmaw words in the text these words were underlined in the translation, which resulted in large quantities of underlining on every page. The underlining has now been eliminated, through the tireless industry of Lawrence Greening, and entirely replaced by italics, which gives the whole presentation of the text a much more pleasant aspect.

Towhid bin Muzzafar, at the time a graduate student at Memorial University, also read the text in its entirety to check the translation for coherence and lucidity, so that over a period of a year or so there were adjustments on almost every page. The details of the Preface were also checked and some additions and corrections made, especially paying attention to the comments of Paul Proulx in his review of the work in the *Canadian Journal of Linguistics/Revue Canadienne de Linguistique* 37: 461-63.

It was also thought more suitable to publish a second edition closer to Cape Breton and Newfoundland, where so much of the work of translation and transcription had been done. Cape Breton University Press, with its forty-plus year history of publishing texts connected to Cape Breton and Maritime history, economics and culture, was approached and the possibility emerged of having the second edition produced at a locale where it could be immediately accessible to first language Mi'kmaw speakers in a university environment. Cape Breton University has had a long relationship with the Mi'kmaw communities of Cape Breton Island (Unama'ki) with more that 250 Mi'kmaw students attending the university annually.

The title was also changed: the English term *Micmac* has been largely replaced in everyday usage with the Indigenous terms *Mi'kmaw* (singular) and *Mi'kmaq* (plural). Some of the original French of Father Pacifique's title was maintained in the new title, and a secondary explanatory title added to indicate that this was a traditional grammar, begun by Father Maillard in the early 18th century, and completed, in remarkable detail by Father Pacifique early in the 20th century. The text, in fact, is so complete and so well organized that it was frequently possible, in the translation, to use modern technical terms such as *conjunct, obviative, subordinative*, as one would in a modern grammar.

Bernie Francis and John Hewson

PREFACE OF THE EDITORS TO 1990 EDITION

The *Leçons grammaticales théoriques et pratiques de la langue micmaque* of Rev. Father Pacifique Buisson, ofmcap, published in 1939, is a vast and important collection of information on the Mi'kmaw language. It represents a tradition of Mi'kmaw grammatical studies by missionary priests that spans 200 years from the days of Father Maillard, who died in 1762, to Father Pacifique, who, although he intended his grammar to be a guide to other priests who wanted to learn the language, seems to have been the last priest to speak the language fluently.

Father Pacifique's important study is now unfortunately out of print. Those Mi'kmaq who own a copy also find it difficult to use because their second language is normally English. And because of the "abbreviated" alphabet (as Fr. Pacifique calls it, p. 1) that was used, it is next to impossible to tell how words are to be pronounced. What was needed, therefore, was a translation with a complete retranscription of the Mi'kmaw words into an accurate orthography. Such an enterprise would give Fr. Pacifique's work a wide audience, which would include not only the Mi'kmaw people themselves, but also students, researchers and others interested in the Mi'kmaw language.

The enterprise of translating the *Leçons grammaticales* was first undertaken by James Fidelholtz at about the time when he was preparing his doctoral thesis entitled *Micmac Morphophonemics* (1968). We were able to obtain a copy of this manuscript, but it was obvious for several reasons that a totally new translation and transcription was needed. The translator's very solid knowledge of French was not adequate for handling some of the idiomatic usage in the text, and almost every Mi'kmaw word needed either adjustment or complete retranscription. Fidelholtz, for example, had made certain minimal adjustments to the orthography used by Pacifique, but had otherwise followed the original faithfully. The original normally fails to mark vowel length, and also uses the spelling *e* not only for mid front vowels, but also for schwa, and adds it to the spelling of the syllabic sonorants, so that one cannot tell from the spelling *el*, for example, whether one should pronounce [l.], [el], or [e'l].

Fr. Pacifique's grammatical forms represent an older form of the language, which has undergone considerable reshaping in the modern dialects. It is clear that Fr. Pacifique also incorporated words from his predecessors, items that are no longer known even to the older speakers of the present day, but may be found in the grammar of Father Maillard, written in the 1740's. Occasionally, therefore, there are items of specialized vocabulary in the text whose exact phonetic shape is not necessarily absolutely certain. As far as the grammatical forms are concerned, we have taken care to report the older usage as reported by Fr. Pacifique, even though it is no longer in use. The whole question of the historical differences of usage will be discussed in the grammar of the modern language that we are now preparing.

We thought at first that the early section on sound should be left out, because of the inconsistency and incoherence in some of the detail. Since this section contains some valuable lexical commentary, however, we decided to keep it, but the reader must be warned that at times the examples used do not coherently match the text because items spelled in the under-differentiated orthography used by Fr. Pacifique may no longer be appropriate when they are spelled exactly: long vowels are given as illustrations of short vowels, and so on.

The purpose of using the new orthography is of course to give the reader who does not know the language exact information on the pronunciation of each Mi'kmaw word. This was not an important goal for Pacifique, since he recommends that the pronunciation should be obtained from a native speaker. Now that the language has been lost on many reserves, so that native speakers are not as available as they were, it has become crucially important to use the new exact orthography, so that the written word can be used to convey as much information as possible on the accepted pronunciations.

We may take almost any word from Fr. Pacifique's original text to illustrate the kind of transcription that had to be done. When he writes *oigoèg* (1939: 220), for example, we write *wi'kue'k*, a spelling which adds four items of detail. It indicates (1) that the initial element (spelled *o*) is not a vowel, is non-syllabic; (2) that the vowel of the initial syllable is long; (3) that the fourth element (also spelled *o*) **is** syllabic, but is [u] not [o]; and (4) that the final vowel is long. When one appreciates that Fr. Pacifique's *o* can be syllabic or non-syllabic, and can represent the vowels *o* and *o'* as well as *u* and *u'*, it is obvious that one cannot learn pronunciation from such spelling.

NOTES ON THE NEW ORTHOGRAPHY

In the early 1970's, the Nova Scotia Mi'kmaw chiefs instructed Doug Smith and Bernard Francis to develop a suitable orthography for the Mi'kmaw language that would be useful for teaching the language. It is this orthography, that uses a separate letter for each distinctive sound that has been used in the retranscription.

Mi'kmaw has five long vowels, spelled *a'*, *e'*, *i'*, *o'*, *u'*, five corresponding short vowels *a*, *e*, *i*, *o*, *u*, and a schwa represented thus: *i-*.

Mi'kmaw also has eleven consonants, written as follows: *p*, *t*, *k*, *q*, *kw*, *qw*, *j*, *s*, *l*, *m*, *n*. Of these *q*, *qw*, are post velars, the latter with labialization, and *j* is a simple affricate as in English *church* when unvoiced, or English *judge* when voiced.

The sonorants *l*, *m*, *n*, may be either syllabic or non-syllabic; they are always syllabic when they follow obstruents in the same word, so that *atlasmit* "s/he rests" has five syllables [a-dl.-a-zm.-it], and *kmtn* "hill" is [km.-dn.]. When the sonorants *l*, *m*, *n*, are unpredictably syllabic, they are spelled *l'*, *m'*, *n'*, being longer than their non-syllabic alternants.

The high vowels *i*, *u*, may also be non-syllabic, and in such cases are written *y*, *w*. Using the different symbols allows us to distinguish *-kw* from *-ku* in words such as *nsiskw* "my face" and *sisku* "mud ." If one were to form a plural of *nsiskw*, there is a good argument for writing *nsiskwl* "my faces," where /l/ is predictably syllabic after /kw/, as noted above. Consequently, we write such forms as *nutmu'kwl* "we (incl.) hear them (inan)," the latter having four syllables [nu-dm.-u'-gwl.], where the /l/ has been added as an inanimate plural marker.

When two sonorants occur in succession, the second is normally syllabic, so that *mntu* "devil" has two syllables [mn.-du], and *mu kelusiwn* "you are not speaking" is pronounced [mu ge-lu-zi-wn.]. If the first of the two sonorants is syllabic, it has to be marked; in such cases the second sonorant is today non-syllabic in everyday speech: *l'mu'j* "dog" is normally heard as two syllables [l.-mu'j].

Since the editors of the translation presented here are now engaged in the production of a further extensive manual which will contain a full chapter on the phonology of the language, the purpose of these few brief notes is only to give the reader the necessary information to interpret the retranscription of Fr. Pacifique's spellings.

NOTES ON THE ORIGINAL LEÇONS GRAMMATICALES

The original version of the *Leçons grammaticales* was published in two separate fascicules in the *Annales de l'ACFAS*, the Journal of the Association Canadienne-Française pour l'Avancement des Sciences. The first seventeen chapters were published in 1938 (*AACFAS* 4.211-333) and the remaining sixteen in 1939 (*AACFAS* 5.157-276). Both of these publications carried a secondary pagination in brackets which became the pagination of the subsequent single volume printed in the Office of the Mi'kmaw Messenger at Fr. Pacifique's home parish of Ste-Anne-de-Restigouche. This single volume is printed from the same typesetting as the ACFAS publications, by simply removing the AACFAS pagination and setting up the bracketed pagination as definitive.

There was also a *Supplement* of six further Lessons (34-39), published in 1940 (*AACFAS* 6.271-277). We have translated and retranscribed these Lessons, but they are not included in the present publication because they constitute a separate book of exercises on their own: they are not a continuation or completion of the original grammar. Lesson 34, for example, goes back to practising the sounds that are introduced in Lessons 1-4 of the original volume.

Because each lesson is short, and has a clear-cut paradigmatic internal layout, and because the author numbers each sub-section systematically as he proceeds, we found that it is not necessary to add the pagination of the original to each page of the translation, because it is easier to follow the numbering of the Lessons and the numbering of the subsections, which is much more detailed than the pagination. We have therefore given the pagination of the original only in the Table of Contents.

NOTES ON THE REFERENCES

Fr. Pacifique makes many references to manuscripts and publications, some of which he explains in his Preface, others of which he seemingly expects his audience to be aware of.

In his Preface, for example, he mentions the various manuscript copies of the grammar of Fr. Maillard, of which he made his own copy, which he sometimes refers to as the *Manuscript grammar*, but generally uses the abbreviation *Gr. Ma.* He also refers to the published grammar of Fr. Maillard, for which we have used the abbreviation *Pub. Gr.* This is the 1864 publication *Grammaire de la language micmaque*, New York: Cramoisy Press (John Gilmary Shea, pub.), which was reprinted in 1970 (New York: AMS Press). He also refers to a notebook of Fr. Maillard's grammatical comments, collated by Fr. Bellenger early in the 19th Century, under the abbreviation *Rem. gr.* (i.e. *Remarques grammaticales*), or just *Rem*. Maillard's Catechism mentioned in the Preface is referred to as *Cat*.

Fr. Pacifique also mentions Rev. Silas Tertius Rand's *Dictionary of the Language of the Micmac Indians* (Halifax: Nova Scotia Printing Company, 1888) as "E.-M. Dict" (i.e. English-Mi'kmaw), and *Rand's Micmac Dictionary* (ed. J.S. Clark, Charlottetown: The Patriot Publishing Company, 1902) as "M.-E. Dict" (i.e. Micmac-English Dictionary). There are also references to "Rand's Reading Book," which is *A First Reading Book in the Micmac Language*, Halifax: Nova Scotia Printing Company, 1875, also referred to as *Rea*.

Elsewhere, he refers to the *Souvenir* of the 1910 Tercentenary celebration of the baptism of the Mi'kmaw Chief Membertou, the first Native Indian to be baptised on this continent (24 June 1610). He also refers to the Proceedings (1907) of the International Congress of Americanists which was held at Quebec in 1906, using sometimes the simple abbreviation *Congress*, and sometimes *Amer.* and even *Am*.

His references to the Scriptures, and to the translations of the liturgy are presumably from the translations of Fr. Maillard that he mentions in the prefix. These have been maintained with the standard references to book, chapter, and verse. He quotes, too, from Rand's translation of the Scriptures, retranscribing from Rand's orthography into his own. He assumes that the reader will be familiar with the *Jesuit Relations*, as shown by his reference, on page 21, to the Relation of 1611, where, although he gives pagination, he makes no reference to the publication or edition.

The reference on p. 21 to "M. Maillard, letter, p.302," as Paul Proulx notes (Canadian Journal of Linguistics 37: 462) refers to Maillard's famous letter, written in 1755, and published long after his death in *Les Soirées Canadiennes* 3: 289-426 (1863) under the title *Lettre à Madame de Drucourt*. This letter of nearly 140 pages is an invaluable resource document for eighteenth century Mi'kmaw customs, for the history of the area, and is full of Mi'kmaw language quotations.

The references to *Hier.* are obviously to Fr. Maillard's celebrated Mi'kmaw hieroglyphic prayer book, originally copied on birch bark, then on paper, and finally printed in Vienna in 1866, with a second edition published in Restigouche by Fr. Pacifique. Details of the history of this intriguing book are given in Hewson "An 18th Century Mi'kmaw Grammarian: the Mi'kmaw studies of Fr. Maillard" in *Historiographia Linguistica* XXI: 65-76 (1994), especially pages 66-70. The most common and important prayers of this book have now been gathered into a small volume complete with Mi'kmaw written texts and English translations: David L. Schmidtand Murdena Marshall, *Mi'kmaq Hieroglyphic Prayers*, Halifax: Nimbus 1995.

One of the mysterious references is "Par.," which is apparently an abbreviation for *Parossien*, for which he gives no bibliographical references at all. This is, in fact, his own publication: R. P. Pacifique, Capucin, *ALASOTMAMGEWEL. Le Paroissien micmac. Prayer-Book in Micmac*. Ste-Anne-de-Ristigouche. There are two volumes (1re Partie, 2^e Partie), and more than one edition. A new edition, considerably enlarged, for example, was produced in 1912. Another mysterious reference is "Jo.," which, to judge by the subject matter, is presumably *Journal*, a monthly newspaper, the *Micmac Messenger*, mentioned briefly at the bottom of p. 3 (p. 12 in the original).

There are other references that are a complete mystery. We cannot tell, for example, not having access to the original, whether the reference *Ms.* refers to Maillard's manuscript grammar (normally *Gr. Ma.*) Or to some other manuscript. The references to *Doc. C. F.*, *7 pr.*, *S. F.*, and *Leg.* (Legends?) that are scattered throughout the text are completely mysterious. The two references *Ch. B.* on p. 205-206 are presumably to Charles Bernard, mentioned briefly in Lesson Ten (p. 48).

NOTES ON EDITORIAL PRACTICE

We have silently corrected the typographical errors in Fr. Pacifique's text, and apologize, in turn, for any that have crept into our own text and somehow avoided the scrutiny of several edits. There were many puzzles, some of which also baffled the elders, uncertainties that led to inconsistencies in the first drafts. Almost all of these have now been clarified, and the text searched for consistency, but in such an enormous collection of information, there is always the danger that an occasional detail has escaped correction.

We have kept much of Fr. Pacifique's original terminology, and have made no attempt to rewrite it. Where it was possible, and did not intrude, we have also introduced the standard terminology and abbreviations now used universally by students of Algonquian languages, as a helpful secondary guide. Certain terms, which might be misleading when translated into everyday English, we have translated directly into the standard terminology; in this way *Complément* has become *Obviative Forms*, and *Subjonctif* has become *Subordinative*, for example.

Where editorial comment was necessary to clarify the text or explain confusions, such commentary has been added in square brackets. The very first paragraph of Lesson One, for example, is an extended editorial comment on the presentation of speech sounds in the early chapters.

There is a certain amount of variation in the morphology of the Inanimate Subject forms of the first five conjugations. These variations, which were not noted by Father Pacifique, have been silently added in brackets, indicating that these formative elements are optional. They represent regional variation: forms that are normally heard in certain communities, but not everywhere.

ABBREVIATIONS

As well as the abbreviations used by Fr. Pacifique for his references, we have also used the following abbreviations for grammatical categories, especially in the Index of Mi'kmaw Words.

NA Noun, animate
NI Noun, inanimate
N Nominal element of no fixed gender
AI Animate Intransitive verb
II Inanimate Intransitive verb
TA Transitive Animate verb
TI Transitive Inanimate verb
PV Preverb
XP Particle or adverbial element

Verbs in the index have been quoted in their third person singular forms.

We would like to thank Stephanie Inglis, without whose insistence on the importance of this project it would probably not have been undertaken. Our thanks for material help go to Ann-Marie White, Audrey Dawe-Sheppard, and especially to Wendy Sheppard, who spent long hours preparing the Index, adjusting to the various changes, and conscientiously concentrating on the production of a coherent text.

The work was supported by a Research Grant from the Social Sciences and Humanities Research Council of Canada. The Grammar of Father Pacifique will unquestionably be an important reference point for any future grammar of Mi'kmaw, and its presentation in English, along with the phonemicisation of the orthography, will make its contents available to a wide audience. We thank the SSHRC for their assistance in this work.

Finally, we would like to express special thanks to elder Wilfred Prosper of the Eskasoni Reserve, and Pauline Bernard from the Membertou Reserve in Sydney, for their invaluable help with all kinds of puzzles and thorny details. Mr. Wallace Bernard, husband of Pauline was also of great assistance to us until his untimely death during the early stages of this project. His passing reminds us that there is so much that remains to be done, and that the opportunity to do it must not be lost.

Bernie Francis, John Hewson

THEORETICAL AND PRACTICAL GRAMMATICAL LESSONS IN THE MI'KMAW LANGUAGE

PREFACE TO THE 1939 EDITION

We owe to the abbé Maillard, a priest of the Seminary of Foreign Missions of Paris, a missionary among the Mi'kmaq from 1735 to 1762, the first and in fact the only Mi'kmaw grammar which we have. Even so we have not been able so far to find the original manuscript of the author. What comes closest to it is a copy made by M. Bellenger, parish priest of Carleton and missionary at Restigouche from 1814 to 1819, preserved in the library of the Archbishops of Quebec. Another copy, or rather the beginning of the same work, made by abbé Huot, is preserved in the Seminary of Nicolet. It is the former which I have transcribed myself, and it is the pages of my notebook which I cite in my writings, where they occur, under the abbreviation Gr. Ma.

Another copy, as well as an English translation, made in 1766 by the Rev. Thos. Wood, an Anglican minister from Halifax, was recently found by Dr. Webster Shediac, acquired by him and placed in the St. John Museum, N.B., with a long critical analysis made by me. Unfortunately, this text contains only about a third of what is in M. Bellenger's, and it was also rather clumsily done by the translator copyist, insufficiently knowledgeable for such work.

M. Bellenger, for his part, studied this text and others of abbé Maillard with rare energy and great success. He very rapidly ascertained that this work, immense in itself, greatly lacks order, method, and therefore, practical utility. It is an inexhaustible mine, but one which is in great need of exploitation. The zealous missionary felt that M. Maillard should have revised his grammar, and, no doubt, such was his intention; but he postponed it so as to leave fewer gaps. A typical example, which is a proof of imperfection and equally so of authenticity, is found on pages 31 and 152: "I have forgotten," says the author about his first conjugation, "to give the future with the negative."

Here is an omission which is repeated in all our copies and is corrected in none. But if M. Maillard did not revise, correct, and complete the text itself of his grammar, he never ceased working on the language, developing rules, gathering examples, increasing the analysis and conjugations, with regard to everything, with no increase in methodology, it is true, but also without respite. M. Bellenger has gathered together quite a large manuscript, likewise preserved in Quebec. The copy which I have made of it, under the title "Grammatical Remarks," fills up a ms. of 233 pages. Besides this valuable collection and his copy of the grammar, this indefatigable missionary undertook furthermore the immense task of putting this work in the best possible order. Without completely succeeding, because his stay among the Mi'kmaq was too short, he left in manuscript form a work so well edited that it was possible to produce a quite respectable publication long after his death and, it may be added, without the aid of anyone who knew the language.

M. Maillard also drafted all the liturgical offices, the usual prayers, the catechisms, numerous pages of Scripture, long sermons and other instructions, and finally a detailed questionnaire for confession (130 pages) in French and in Mi'kmaw, which can also be used for the study of the language as well as for the ministry. Such was the achievement of this great man. And if anyone should think that it cost him little, let him read this passage of a letter written in 1755 to M. de Lalanne, his superior, of the Foreign Missions: "What it costs, Sir, in work, in struggle, and in burning the midnight oil, to learn these sorts of languages by oneself, and to finally manage to pronounce the words: I dare not say the number of years spent on this work. Eight years devoted almost solely to this have not been enough."

Another important worker on the Mi'kmaw language, who cannot be disregarded today is Dr. S. T. Rand, a Baptist minister in Nova Scotia, who spent a half century in working assiduously with the Indians, and died in 1890. His religious successes were mediocre, but his linguistic work was considerable. He himself published, in 1888, an English-Mi'kmaw dictionary. He also wrote or undertook to write a very extensive grammar. Unfortunately, it was destroyed, with a large number of other manuscripts, in a fire at Wellesley College in Massachusetts, where they were kept. Another misfortune is that his Mi'kmaw-English dictionary, left in manuscript and sold to the Federal Government, was published in 1902 by an editor who did not know the language, and who thought he should refuse the free co-operation which I offered him. The result was that this part can hardly be used without other aids which are not within reach of everybody. Besides these two volumes, Dr. Rand translated and published all the New Testament and several books of the Old, with the aid of an exceptionally gifted Frenchman who had adopted the life and the language of the Mi'kmaq, without whom, says he, it would have been impossible for him to undertake this work. He acknowledges, furthermore, that he was greatly helped by using an essay on Mi'kmaw grammar which had belonged to Fr. Sigogne and was published by Mr. Thomas Irwin in the Charlottetown Gazette (about 1832). Now I know, by certain details of the correspondence of this Mr. Irwin with Fr. Sigogne, that this essay was none other than the first part of M. Maillard's grammar. Which comes back to saying finally that we still do not have any other grammatical text; and however imperfect it may be, it gives us the theory of the language; it is quite a creation. The innumerable applications which he made of it afterwards, with all his other writings, constitutes a first class literature.

But I hasten to say that it would be of little use today without my lessons, whether for the Whites, because the language has evolved, especially in pronunciation, or for the Mi'kmaq, who never made use of his alphabet. M. Maillard in 1815 published a small pamphlet in which it can be found, along with a quite extensive syllabary and the principal daily prayers. He was able to be of service to the missionaries who learned the modern pronunciation from the Mi'kmaq themselves, but not in any way to the latter. They copied and recopied many liturgical texts but always with their little alphabet. The same can be said for the English alphabet of Mr. Rand, which nevertheless several people learned in the schools; they made use of it and make use of it to write in English, but never in Mi'kmaw. Those who read or tried to read his scriptural writings, mostly guessed at them, and if they had wanted to copy them, they would have retranscribed them as best they could into their own little alphabet.

It seems to me, therefore, that the best means of learning the language of the Mi'kmaq, with good hope of success and without danger of discouragement, is to make use of my Mi'kmaw "lessons" while being sure to keep in contact with the Indians, from the outset pronouncing in front of them some words or expressions, and noting their manner, often different, of pronouncing them or using them. One reads sometimes that the Mi'kmaq boast of always having two ways of pronouncing the same thing. This is partly true. They have sometimes more than two; but usually there are differences or nuances, not always easy to grasp. We add, for the consolation of novices (and one remains such for a long time in this enterprise) that it is not necessary to know everything to speak Mi'kmaw, even very passably. There is a big difference between speaking and telling someone how to speak and why. From the very first lesson, the learner will be surprised that he can already say something.

As for the directors of the ACFAS who have undertaken to include it in their Annals, they will find in the letter which follows the thanks which my own inadequate acknowledgements were unable to express.

30 June 1935

Bishopric of Gaspé

Rev. Father Pacifique, O.M. Cap.

Ste-Anne-de-Ristigouche.

Dear Reverend Father,

I am very happy to learn that "The French-Canadian Association for the Advancement of Science" has offered to publish in their Annals your texts of the studies which you have prepared on the theory and practice of the Mi'kmaw language, under the title: "Theoretical and Practical Treatise on the Mi'kmaw Language." Your long ministry among the Mi'kmaq of Restigouche; the well-known love that you have for them and which caused you to study their language with an avid apostolic zeal both to penetrate more deeply into their soul and in turn to deliver your soul to them; the meticulous care with which you scrutinize the questions which are submitted to you: these are the many reasons that give us a guarantee of the competence which you bring to your "Grammatical Lessons."

The Association will live up to its goal by making these extensive studies available to linguists, and it will render an inestimable service to the missionaries who must learn this language, which, I am told, possesses a remarkable degree of perfection. Please offer the directors my personal thanks, and accept my sincere congratulations and my heartiest good wishes for the continuation of your ministry among the Indians of my diocese, the devotion and charity of which I have been in a position to appreciate for almost half a century.

François-Xavier

Bishop of Gaspé

LESSON ONE

THE MI'KMAW ALPHABET

[Note from the editors: in his opening paragraphs, Fr. Pacifique reported that Mi'kmaw was traditionally written with an "abbreviated" alphabet of only thirteen letters - five vowels and eight consonants. Fr. Pacifique was aware of many of the inadequacies of this "abbreviated" alphabet, and added what he described as "some very simple signs which indicate the pronunciation" so that he could, for example, distinguish *peska'lik*, "I lead him off the trail," from *pesqa'lik*, "I skin an animal," and distinguish short vowels from long vowels (when he felt it necessary - but note that in his text vowel length is mostly ignored). He also sometimes wrote *ö* where we use *w*, but had difficulty making clear the distinction between *i* and *y* that we see in such pairs as *welei*, "I am well" (3rd person *wele'k*), vs. *pemiey*, "I walk, move" (3rd person *pemiet*), where the difference in the first person forms indicates what the third person forms will be. The three different vowels *e'*, *e*, and *i*, furthermore, are all spelled *e* by Fr. Pacifique, which leads to very serious difficulties for the reader. For the details see the Editors' Preface. This brief note replaces the first two paragraphs of Fr. Pacifique's text, which now follows beginning at paragraph three].

The **vowels** are named as in French: *a*, as in *a'-papi*, "thread," the *babiche* of the early settlers; *e*, *e'-pite's*, "girl"; *i*, *i-la'skw*, "card"; *o* [used here to replace Fr. Pacifique's *ô*], *wqosi*, "(finger)-nail, claw"; *u* [used here to replace Pacifique's *o*] represents this very frequent sound in Mi'kmaw, as in *u-tan* (pronounced udan), "village."

The **consonants** are all pronounced with *e* or *e'*: *ke*, *ke-wisin*, "be hungry"; *le*, *Le-mi*, Rémi; *me*, *me-ko'tik*, "dear, expensive"; *ne*, *net*, "this"; *pe*, *pe-wat-m*, "want"; *se*, *Se'-sus*, Jesus; *te*, *te-ke'k*, "it is cold"; *je*, *je-nu*, "hero, giant" [earlier spelled as *tj*], which is pronounced as the first syllable of the English word *cherish*.

Several vowels together form a **diphthong**, if they are pronounced by a single utterance of the voice, as *ey*, "I say," *waw*, "egg." but several vowels which follow one another do not always form a diphthong; thus in *welei*, "I am well," *we* is a diphthong, but *lei* comprises two syllables, *le-i*. When it is the same vowel that is repeated, one hears a small aspiration made between the two; *e'e* (pron. ehe), "yes"; *a'a* (aha), "ah." But often there is only the lengthening of the same sound, and in writing only a single vowel was used: *tpi'i* or *tpi'*, "give me a share"; *tpi* (*i* short) means, "give him his share." All the vowels can be long or short, and this is often very important; long vowels will be marked as follows [in the new orthography: *a'*, *e'*, *i'*, *o'* and *u'*]. There is also *w*, which is pronounced as short or voiceless /u/. For *wa*, *we*, *wi*, pronounce the last as *oui* in French and the others in an analogous manner; there is also *wo*, *wu*, pronounced as in English *woe*, *woo*.

E [in the original orthography] represents *e*, *e'*, or *i*, since the latter sound is spelled *e* in French; [in the new orthography the vowel heard in French *le*, *me* is spelled as the letter *i* with a transverse bar]. The vowels *e* and *e'* are found in *wele'k*, "he goes well"; in the past of this verb we find all three of these vowels: *we-le'k-sip*, "he was well."

O is pronounced as in Fr. *pot*; when it is short, it will be indicated by the symbol *o* and pronounced as in Fr. *botte*; ex.: *pot-lo-tek*, "Indian island at Cape Breton"; *ne'po'ss*, "he was killed." They are easily recognized in practice.

Final unstressed *w* when preceded by a *k* which follows a long vowel, has a voiceless sound which is hard to explain; one has to hear it from the mouth of the Indians; Mr. Rand calls it explosive *ikw* (M.-E. Dict. X); M. Bellenger, in a note in his copy (page 154) unsuccessfully tried to make it clear by saying: "it is pronounced with a barely detectable accent, if one is careful, as in (Fr.) *Angélique*, while pronouncing the *que* a little too strongly." I add, without hesitation, that if you haven't heard it, you won't be able to pronounce it. [Fr. Pacifique writes this *w* as *o* in the older orthography; in the new, *w* is used]. For example: *ke-lu-si'kw*, "we speak"; this is the example given by M. Bellenger.

We now come to the consonants.

K, which is with *u* the most common letter in Mi'kmaw, has three pronunciations: 1. That of French *g* before *a*, *o*, *u*, and it is always hard, even before *e*, *i*. It is ordinarily pronounced this way, when it is between two vowels; ex.: *Se-su-ku-li*, "Jesus Christ." 2. That of k, mainly at the beginning and at the end of words, or when it precedes or follows another consonant; ex.: *ke'*, "let's go, courage, try, it's your turn"; *kti-kik* (pron. as in placing a French mute *e* or a small aspiration before the double consonant), "the others." 3.

Finally it has a slightly guttural articulation, [a post-velar spelled as a *q* in the new orthography]. M. Maillard (*Grammaire*, page 8) says that it is "crushed" in pronouncing it roughly at the back of the throat; that is why he calls it "crushed *k*." Rand calls it "aspirated *k*" (loc. cit.); the closest sound to it is Fr. *k* followed by a uvular *r*; thus Fr. *agrès*, pronounced in this manner, is quite close to the interjection *aqai*, "alas!" English *wh* is also like it; for example, the exclamation *O what*! is almost exactly the verb *oqwa't*, "he lands." It would nevertheless be a great mistake to wish to represent it by French *r*, which does not exist in any way in Mi'kmaw. *Q* is regularly pronounced this way before and after *a* and *o*; ex.: *aqq*, "and"; *toqu*, "then"; *aqay*, "alas!"; *oqoj*, "for"; I use [i.e. the earlier orthography used] a circumflex accent over *g*, which resembles the symbol which M. Maillard put above the *k* he used. In the spelling, say: *ke'-a-qa, ke'-e-ke, ke'-i-ki, ke'-o-qo, ke'-u-ku*.

L presents no difficulty; it replaces *r* in the words which come from French, as *Ma'li* (long *a*), "Mary, the blessed Virgin"; *Mali* (short *a*) "for other Maries." The Mi'kmaq almost always double this consonant in their writings, very unnecessarily; thus they write "Malli," from which comes the anglicized family name, Malley. *Pi-e'l*, "Pierre." *Mal-kl-it*, "Marguerite."

M is pronounced as in English; so is *N*. *Kn* is pronounced separately; ex.: *a-kn-u-tm-a-qn*, "news" (pron. a-gn-u-dm-a-qan); Fr. Agnès becomes in Mi'kmaw *A-ni-e's*, Fr. Angelique *A-se-lik*.

P, s, t are pronounced *b, z, d* between two vowels; in this case they are still written *p, s, t*; but *s* must not be hissed as in French; formerly it was pronounced and written *ch* and *g* (soft) as in Fr. *changer*, and indeed this word became Mi'kmaw, in this form: *sa'-se'-wa'-tu*, which was formerly written and pronounced *chageouadou* (as in French). *S* is pronounced as if it were double when it takes the place of another letter; ex.: *Nis-kam*, "God," pron. Niss-kam, for *Nik-skam*. Sometimes it is *s* itself which is suppressed, as in the French word *apôtre*; then it is the following consonant which is doubled in pronunciation; ex. *Nuj-jinen*, "our father," which was formerly written *nusjinen*, is today pronounced *nuj-jinen*.

J is pronounced as English *ch* in *church* or, between two vowels, as *j* in *just*; in the latter case, it will still be spelled *j*; ex.: *ji-ju-a-qa*, "sometimes." [In the earlier orthography *tj* was used, that is two letters for only a single sound; *j* was never found by itself].

Mr. Rand (M.-E. Dict., xi) says that *b* and *p*, *d* and *t* easily change places; he himself wrote for whale *boot-up* (*pu-tip*) and *poot-up*; the strangest thing being that the *t* in this word, is certainly pronounced *d*. He says the same thing in his dictionary (E.-M., pp. 33, 63, and 71): "It is impossible to be always able to distinguish the sounds *b* and *p* as the Indians utter them; these sounds are often interchanged in the same word, and by the same and different speakers. Many words may begin with *p* or *b*." It is the same for *ch* and *j*, *s* and *z*, *k* and *g*. "G and k are the same to them (33)" Also the Mi'kmaq use only a single letter for each pair; for *p* and *b* the majority use only the *p*, and those who prefer *b*, as in Cape Breton, never use *p*. In the proceedings of the Congress of Americanists, held at Quebec in 1906 (pp. 87-124), there are ten legends published by Mr. J.D. Prince, based on a manuscript of Peter Googoo, a Mi'kmaw of Cape Breton; in this document of 37 octavo pages, there is not a single *p*, whereas there are one or more *b*'s on each line, a great number of which are surely pronounced *p*. This was the universal usage at that time. Moreover, there were in the manuscript two other characters, the first a *v* with a dot over it; the editor says *n*, but I am certain that it is a *v*, used to replace the *k* or *q* of Restigouche; he was notified of its pronunciation and substituted *k* for it; there are a certain number of them on each page, of which perhaps half are pronounced *k* or *q*; otherwise there are no more *k*'s than *p*'s in this document as it is printed. The other character he chose to use was *ch*; it is this which is now replaced by *j* in print. This manuscript symbol is not at all peculiar to Mr. Googoo, nor even to his companions in Cape Breton, but universal. Today it is replaced by *j* even in writing. I consider this document a valuable monument of authentic modern Mi'kmaw literature, without other outside interference. There are a number of other documents of theMi'kmaq themselves, published in their "Journal," which was published regularly every month for twenty-two years, but with the modifications characteristic of the old orthography.

P replaces moreover *f* and *v* in words of foreign origin, as *Pikto'l*, "Victor"; *Plansue, Plansua* or *Plassua*, Fr. *François*; *Pessa*, Fr. *Vincent*; *pestie'wimk*, "feast"; *te'pine'klewey*, "vinegar"; *te'plma'sewey*, "cheese" (Fr. *fromage*); *lesui'p*, "a Jew" (Fr. *le juif*). On the other hand one hears the Indians saying in English *few* for *pew*, *site* for *side*, *gold* for *cold*, even *goat* for *colt*, which one day on a farm caused the destruction of a colt, when an Indian had been instructed to kill a goat.

We should note that examples of consonants with several pronunciations are not lacking in other languages, even in French: thus c = k in *second*; t = s in *nation, patience* and many others. In the "Abenaki Dialogues" (p. 10), it is said that, in this language, b and d at the end of words are always pronounced *p* and *t*, respectively, without a change in the spelling. Likewise, in a small manual of the Cree language (p. 8) one reads this note: "Sometimes one uses *B* in the place of *P*." Finally Rand himself had only eight words beginning with *d* in his dictionary (M.-E., p. 35), putting the rest under *t*.

An example will indicate the near impossibility of changing a letter, when the pronunciation changes. Thus the final letter of the word *e'-pit*, "woman" is pronounced *t*; now in its diminutive *e'-pi-te's*, "girl," it must absolutely be pronounced *d*. Moreover, if the preposition *ik-tuk*, which means "with" or "at the house of," is added to the same word, *e'-pi-te-wik-tuk*, this *t* becomes pronounced *d*; likewise in *e-pit* (short *e*), "he is seated," *p* is pronounced *b*; if we adjoin it to the prefix *wel*, "good," it gets pronounced *p*: *wel-pit*, "he is well seated."

There is moreover in the majority of Mi'kmaw words a stress, which normally falls on the last syllable, as in French, or on a preceding long vowel. [Stress in general tends to go to long vowels and then to every alternate syllable].

Dialects

There are not, properly speaking, any dialects among the Mi'kmaq, but one finds some regular differences between different centres in the usage of certain words or expressions, especially in pronunciation and in spelling. At Restigouche, particularly, they sometimes depart from what is the general usage elsewhere, which certainly conforms better to the roots or to the regular formation of words. Thus, to give two or three examples, it is easy to understand that the verbs in *-ey* should make their imperative in *e*, as those in *-ay* make theirs in *a*; now at Restigouche they say *a* in both cases, which is as unknown elsewhere as *e* is at Restigouche; likewise "no" is said *moqwa'j* or *moqwa* at Restigouche, elsewhere it is *moqwe'j*, *moqwe*. Now as this word is composed of *mu koqoey*, it is evident that the latter is the proper spelling. These differences are to be expected, and one should conform to the local usages. These differences will be mentioned in the lessons, when it is worthwhile. It is also particularly at Restigouche that *n* is doubled in the plural instead of adding *l*, that one omits this syllable in the third person of verbs of the animate gender, or that *jl* is changed to *tl*. Moreover one says *alasutmay* for *elasutmay* or *i'alasutmay*, although there is a slight difference in meaning; moreover *apune'k* for *epune'k*, *eksitpu'k* for *eskitpu'k*, *wksitqamu'k* for *wskitqamu'k*, *wi'sis* for *waisis*, *etu'kutewek* for *etu'kmi-kewek*, *wejku'ey* for *wejkuiey*, *juku'a* or *jukuia* for *jukuie*, *qajue'wj* for *mia'wj*, *lamukuom* for *lamikuom*, *mi'watm* for *mui'watm*, *mlakejk* (plural for the word for milk) and *mlakeju'mi* "butter," for *tepu'lewey*, *nme'ji'j*, "herring," for *akoqmaw* (or *akoqmekw*), *Niskam*, "God," for *Nikskam*, *pessmkewe'k* for *peskmkewe'k*, "image, relic of a saint," *pukwelk* for *pikwelk*, *sunmink*, "rosary," for *semuimink*, *tapatan* for *tapatat*, *tliaj* for *teliej* or *nteliej*, *jipji'j* for *sisip*, "bird," etc.

Text to Read and Translate

Niskam Se'sus ne'po'ss. Ma'li pejili-sape'wit. Pie'l Malli wele'ksɨp. Teke'k jijuaqa Potlotek pestie'wimk. E'pitewiktuk aknutmaqn nutmɨk (*one hears*).

Pikto'l oqwa't toqu e't: Kewisin aqq wa'w pewatm kuluk (*with*) pipnaqn (*bread*). Aqai! me' meko'tik nike' (*now*). Ke', Plassua, u't (*this*) sa'se'wa'tu, toqu tpi Pessa aqq Malklit, Lemi, Anie's aqq ktɨkik, ni'n nkutey (*me too*) tpi'i.

Nemitmk (*one sees a thing*) utan, wa'w, te'pine'klewey, te'plma'sewey; e'e. Katu (*but*) a'papi, e'pite's, ila'skw, wqosi, nme'j, putɨp, jenu, Lesui'p, na (*that*) nemu't (*one sees a person or thing of the animate gender*); a'a; teli- (*thus*) klusi'kw oqoj.

Remarks: 1. This lesson was written for the first time on 13 May 1905; it was recopied several times afterwards, for the benefit of individuals who wished to begin the study of the Mi'kmaw language; the final draft, for publication, was completed, by curious coincidence, exactly on 13 May 1935.

2. This lesson must be mastered before proceeding to the following ones. It is important to do the same for the other chapters. This is the only way to sustain interest in this work, and to avoid confusion and discouragement.

3. It is a good idea to make a list, in alphabetical order, of all the words met with, noting the page or the pages where they are analyzed and translated.

LESSON TWO

FIRST EXERCISE
ON SPELLING AND PRONUNCIATION

Simple Syllables

formed of a **single vowel**, preceded or followed by a **single consonant** or another vowel.

[**Remark**: In this table the vowels may be long or short, and for the sake of simplicity, no vowel length is marked. There are no examples using the consonants *q/qw/kw* or the vowel *i*].

A	aa	–(or else long *a*)			ae	ai	ao	au		
E	ea	ee	–(or else long *e*)			ei	eo	eu		
I	ia	ie	ii	–(or else long *i*)			io	iu		
O	oa	oe	oi	oo	–(or else long *o*)			ou		
U	ua	ue	ui	uo	uu	–(or else long *u*)				
K	ka	ke	ki	ko	ku	ak	ek	ik	ok	uk
L	la	le	li	lo	lu	al	el	il	ol	ul
M	ma	me	mi	mo	mu	am	em	im	om	um
N	na	ne	ni	no	nu	an	en	in	on	un
P	pa	pe	pi	po	pu	ap	ep	ip	op	up
S	sa	se	si	so	su	as	es	is	os	us
T	ta	te	ti	to	tu	at	et	it	ot	ut
J	ja	je	ji	jo	ju	aj	ej	ij	oj	uj

Pronunciation, Analysis and Translation

1. A, long or short, the first letter of the alphabet, *aa* (pron. aha), "ah! well! all right (Rand)"; *ae* (/ahe/), "a sigh from the Mi'kmaw song *Nskawaqn*"; *a-i*, in *we-ka-i, -in, -ik*, "I get angry, you get angry, he ..."; *au, a-wi-a*! "the final exclamation of the same song"; *aw-ti*, "road"; the end of many words: *pi'-taw, saq-maw*, etc.

Aqq, "and"; *al*, in *a-la*, "that"; *am* in *ti-a'm*, "moose," *an*, in *A-ni-e's*, "Agnes"; *app*, "again"; *a-po-qn-mu-ey, -en, -et*, "I help, you help, he helps"; *a'-pi* (long *a*), "net"; *a-pi* (short *a*), "bow"; also, "to have just done": *a-pi a-la'-si*, "I have just been for a walk"; *a-pu* in composition, "juice, gravy"; *wi-u-sa-pu*, "broth"; *wi'-ki-kn-a-pu*, "ink"; *as* in *a's-u'n*, "outergarment, blanket"; *at*, in *A-ta*, "Adam"; *aj*, in *a-ja'-si, -sin, -sit*, "to progress" (these are the first three persons of the verb, I, you s., he); I will give these forms in the other instances, while translating by the infinitive, barring indication to the contrary.

2. *E*, the second letter; *e'e* (*e'he*), "yes"; *e'y* (a diphthong, pronounced as in Fr. *Eiffel*), "I say," *e'n* "you say," *e't*, "he says"; *e'w* (with *ma'*), "I will not say"; in normal discourse, a compound *te-lu-ey, -en, -et*, "to speak thus," is used; *e'y-oq* (exclamation, mark of distressed surprise), "is that right? you don't say!"

Ek, in *ek-su-ey, -en, -et*, "to tell a lie"; *mu ek-su-ew*, "I'm not lying"; *ma' ek-su-ew*, "I will not lie"; *e'l*, added to a word, signifies toward: *ma-la*, "over yonder," *ma-la-e'l*, (pron. ma-la-he'l), "in that direction"; *ta-mi*, "where? in what place?"; *ta-mi-e'l* (ta-mi-he'l), "towards what place?"; *ela*, in *e-la-sn-i-ka*, "he said to them": *te-li-aq e'y-oq*, "what you say is true"; *e-li-ey, -en, -et*, "to go"; *e-lu-e'-wi, -win, -wit*, "to be wicked, a sinner"; *l'-nu-i, -in, -it*, "to be a man, Indian"; *l'-nu-a'-si, -sin, -sit*, "to become a man," *-siss*, "he became a man"; *l'-pa*, "truly, really"; *e'n*, "you say"; *en-tu*, "I lose something"; *E'p*, "Eve"; *e-pa'-si*, "I sit down"; *ep-si, -sin, -sit*, "be warm, have a fever"; *e's*, "shellfish, clam"; *e't*, "he says"; *e-ta* (affirmative particle, corresponding to *ta*, below), "yes, in truth, that's it, it is me, you, him, etc."; *ej*, in *e-je-la'-tu*, "I can't do that, that is impossible for me."

3. *I*, the third letter; *i'* (long) at the beginning of a word indicates frequency, custom; *pu-si*, "I set out in a boat"; *i'-pu-si*, "I set out often, I make many trips by water"; *i'-a*, "oh! dear me, oh dear!"; *i'-e'n*, "be there!"; *i'k*, "be there, if he is there"; *i'pa-ji*, "humbly"; *i'ss*, "he should be there"; *is-te-ke*, "as"; *i'j*, "let him be there"; *a-ij* or *a-yej*, "something or other, so-and-so."

4. *O*, the fourth letter [P.'s *ô*]; also an interjection, *o*, oh! long *o* is added to public calls, for example, to announce the beginning of prayers, before they had bells: *a-la-sut-ma-i-ku-p o o o*! "to prayer!; lit., we have to pray ..."; *ow*, in *we'k-ow*, "and so on, until, as far as"; *oq-wa't*, "he lands"; *w-qo-si*, "nail,

claw"; *o-qo-tey*, "friend, companion, husband, wife"; *ol-i-pie*, "(the Mount of) Olives"; *o'p-la'-te-key*, "I do evil, bad"; *te'-si-pow*, "horse"; *kuj-ju-ow*, "your (pl.) father."

5. *U* [P.'s *o*], the fifth letter [and also *w*]; *wa-ql-a*, "those"; *we-kl-a*, "these"; *we-ka-i, -in, -ik*, "to get angry"; *we-le-i, -in, -e'k*, "be well, happy"; *ku-le-in*, "greetings! literally, may you be well, happy"; also *w-le-ie'n*, "be well"; *we-le-in ta*, "are you well?"; *we-le-y eta*, "yes I am well"; *we-li* (adv.), "well"; *we-ji-ey, -en, -et*, "come from"; *ma-la te'-si-pow we-ji-et*, "the horse comes from over yonder."

W, *u*, and *u'*, in *w-su-ku-ni*, "tail"; *u-la*, "this one, here"; *um*, in *e'-um*, "I use it"; *u'n*, "fog"; *Un-a-ma'-ki*, "Cape Breton"; *w-na-qa-ni'-kn*, "capital"; *w-na-qa'-si*, "get up!"; *w-pit-ney*, "sleeve"; *u-si, -sin, -sit*, "warm oneself"; *we-li-u-sit*, "he warms himself well"; *u't*, "this one (in front of one)"; *u'j*, "fly"; *wujjl*, "his father."

6. *K* (*ke*), the sixth letter, [P.'s *g*], the first consonant; *ke'* is an interjection for *ke'j* and *ke'-sik*, "let's go, courage!, try, it's your turn"; *ka*, in *ka-qa-mi*, "stand up"; *kqa-ma'-si*, "get up and stand up straight"; *ka-tu* or *ska-tu*, "but"; *ke* (again) in *ke-sa-lu-et*, "he loves, he is loving"; *ki* in *ki-lu*, "your food"; *ki-nu*, "we (you s. or you pl. and I)"; *ki-ju'*, "mother (in addressing her), mommy"; *kki-ji-nu*, "our mother"; *ku-jji-nu*, "our father."

7. *L* (*le*), the seventh letter; *la* in *la-ssi-et*, "plate," *a-la-me's*, "mass"; *La-mu-li*, Fr. "*Lamorue*"; *le* in *Le-su-i'p*, "Jew"; *li* and *e-li* (from *e-li-ey*, "to go") a prefix giving a verb a sense of going; *pa'-si*, "sit down!," *li-pa'-si*, "go and sit down!"; *e-li-pu-si*, "I am going to embark"; *e-li-u-si*, "I am going to warm myself"; *l'u* in *L'u-i*, *L'u-i's*, "Louis, Louise."

8. *M* (*me*), the eighth letter; also an adverb for *me'j*, "always, moreover, more"; *ma'* (with the future), "not"; see above (2) *ma'e'w*; and *Ma'-li* (first lesson); *ma* in *ma-ja'-si, -sin, -sit*, "move, depart"; *mi* in *mi-ta* or *mu-ta*, "because"; *me-tu-e'k*, "it is hard, sad, difficult"; *me'ka-tu me-tu-e'k*, "that's awful"; *me-tu-e'k i-ka'y*, "I fall into misfortune"; *mi* in *Mi-li*, "Emily"; *mi'-so-qo*, "as far as"; *mi'-so-qu ma-la-e'l*, "right up to there"; *mi-ti*, "poplar"; *mu*, "not (present and past)"; *mu-in*, "bear"; *Mo-is*, "Moses."

9. *N* (*ne*), the ninth letter; *na*, "this, there is, isn't that so?," used superabundantly in Mi'kmaw conversations; *na-la-iw*, "late, far," with *me'*, "later, farther on"; *ne* in *ne-na-qi-ta-si, -sin, -sit*, "to make an object for myself quickly"; *ne-kl-a*, "these, these things"; *ni* in *ni-lu, ki-lu, wi-lu*, "my, your s., his food"; *ni-pi*, "leaf, cabbage"; *nu'*, "father, my father (in addressing him), daddy"; otherwise one says *nujj*; *Nu-el*, "Christmas"; *nu-ji*, adverb meaning of the nature of: *nu-ji-a-po-qn-mu-et* (cf. (1)), "assistance, relief, helper."

10. *P* (*pe*), the tenth letter, also an interjection for *pe'l*, "stop! wait!"; *pa* (pron. ba, as Eng. *bah* or Fr. *bas*), "certainly"; *mu pa*, "certainly not"; *pa-pi, -pin, -pit*, "play"; *pa-ji-ji*, "above," and *pe-ji-li*, "most"; *pa-ji-ji w-le-in*, "you are very happy"; *pe-ji-li ksa-lu-et*, "the most loving (Jesus)"; *pe-mi-ey, -en, -et*, "walk"; *pe-mi-aq*, "that goes"; *pe-ma'-la-ji*, "he carries them"; *pi*, "stay seated"; *Pi-e'l*, "Pierre"; *Pi-o*, "Pius"; *pi'-kun*, "feather"; *qa-li-pu*, "caribou"; *qa-li-pu-ti*, "shovel."

11. *S* (*se*), the eleventh letter; *sa'*, "order him out," imp. of *e-sa'q*, "I expel him"; *sa'-se'-wa'-tu*, "change that thing! or else, I change it (see the first lesson)"; the only real example which retains the former pronunciation of *sh* (replaced by *s*) is *shat* or *chatte*, used to shoo cats; *sa'-qa-ti*, "needle"; *se* in *Se-su-ku-li*, "Jesus Christ"; *si* in *si-pe-li-w*, "often"; *si-pu*, "river"; *Sop-pi*, "Sophie"; *ni-sa'-si, ni-sa'-tu*, "go down."

12. *T* (*te*), the twelfth letter; *ta* (pron. da), "question particle, used in second position"; *ta-li*, "how?"; *ta-mi*, "where?"; *tami ta* "where ever?"; *na'-ta-mi*, "somewhere, in the vicinity, approximately"; *ta-lu-en* "what are you saying?"; *te-lu-ey, -en, -et*, "I say that, I speak thus, you ..., he ..."; *te-li*, "thus"; *te-li-aq*, "that is true, it is so"; *te-pi-aq*, "that is enough, there is enough of it"; *ti-a'm*, "moose"; *to-qu*, "then"; *tu-oq*, "I don't know [short for *mu kejituoq*?]"; *Tu-ma*, "Thomas"; *ta'-pu*, "two, twice."

13. *J* (*je*), the thirteenth and final letter, [*tj* in the earlier orthography, but now *j*]; *ja-qa-li*, "rapidly, briskly, quick"; *ja-ji-ke-i, -in, -e'k*, "to be vigorous"; *je-nu*, "giant"; *ji-le-i, -in, -e'k*, "to be wounded"; *ji-kl-a'-si*, "go away, go back, withdraw," from *e-ji-kl-a-si*, "I withdraw"; *Jo'*, "nickname for Joseph (anglicized)"; *ju-ku'-wa*, "come here" (*ku-ia, ku-ie*).

Text or Readings to Translate into English

Sesukuli kesaluet aqq kkijinu Ma'li nuji-apoqnmuet. Ke', nu', ula sa'se'wa'tu nenaqita'si. Ke', kiju', pa'si aqq usi; toqu Mili i'j. Pie'l, pusi, u't sipu (*here is the river*). Muin pemiet, aqq mala te'sipow wejiet; na wilu, nipi eta. Me' welein, Soppi? E'e, jajikei. Eksuen ta? Mu pa eksuew; ala eksuet; a'a. Aij wekaik; e'yoq, me' katu metue'k. U't Ata, toqu ula me' nalaiw E'p. Nuel kujjinu aqq L'ui's kkijinu. Tami ta elien, Muis? Tuoq; maja'si, eliey mi'soqo na'tami; malae'l eli-pusi; miti me' nutaiw; sipu me' nalaiw. U't ta Miti sipu (*is that the Metis River?*) Tuoq; katu miti tepiaq; na l'pa teliaq. Tia'm ta'pu mala wejiet. L'nuin ta, Lemi? L'nui eta, aqq Jo' wijey. L'nuit ta Se'sus? e'e, l'nuit pa, mita l'nua'siss. Ula a'pi aqq ala tapi: na Pio teluet. Sa'qati wsua'l (*take it*), Mili, toqu maja'si.

LESSON THREE

SECOND EXERCISE
ON SPELLING AND PRONUNCIATION

Syllables

formed of a **simple vowel** preceded and followed by a **single consonant**.

[**Remark**: To form these syllables, consonants have been added to the syllables of the preceding table. This is only a representative set: vowels may by long or short, and other combinations of *k* and *q* are possible; *i*, *kw*, and *qw* are not used].

TABLE									
kaq	kek	kik	koq	kuk	laq	lek	lik	loq	luk
kal	kel	kil	kol	kul	lal	lel	lil	lol	lul
kam	kem	kim	kom	kum	lam	lem	lim	lom	lum
kan	ken	kin	kon	kun	lan	len	lin	lon	lun
kap	kep	kip	kop	kup	lap	lep	lip	lop	lup
kas	kes	kis	kos	kus	las	les	lis	los	lus
kat	ket	kit	kot	kut	lat	let	lit	lot	lut
kaj	kej	kij	koj	kuj	laj	lej	lij	loj	luj
maq	mek	mik	moq	muk	naq	nek	nik	noq	nuk
mal	mel	mil	mol	mul	nal	nel	nil	nol	nul
mam	mem	mim	mom	mum	nam	nem	nim	nom	num
man	men	min	mon	mun	nan	nen	nin	non	nun
map	mep	mip	mop	mup	nap	nep	nip	nop	nup
mas	mes	mis	mos	mus	nas	nes	nis	nos	nus
mat	met	mit	mot	mut	nat	net	nit	not	nut
maj	mej	mij	moj	muj	naj	nej	nij	noj	nuj
paq	pek	pik	poq	puk	saq	sek	sik	soq	suk
pal	pel	pil	pol	pul	sal	sel	sil	sol	sul
pam	pem	pim	pom	pum	sam	sem	sim	som	sum
pan	pen	pin	pon	pun	san	sen	sin	son	sun
pap	pep	pip	pop	pup	sap	sep	sip	sop	sup
pas	pes	pis	pos	pus	sas	ses	sis	sos	sus

The monosyllables of this list which make words are: *Kaq* (in composition), "completely": *kaq-kim*, "recite all"; *kal* (a French word), "one fourth"; *kas* (English word), "train, wagons"; *ka't*, "eel," *ka-taq*, "eels"; *ke'n*, "thank you"; *kess* (to a dog), "go away"; *ke'j*, "for example, let's see, try"; *ki'k* (long *i*), "your house"; *ki'kk*, "sharp"; *ki'l*, "you"; *kim*, "recite, count"; *ki's*, "already"; *kij*, "let him recite, count"; *Kop* (proper noun), "Cope"; *Kuk*, "Cook"; *Ku'l*, "Gould"; *kujj*, "your father."

La'l, "carry it"; *Le'n*, "diminutive of Helen"; *Loq*, "Roch"; *lo'q*, "very, many"; *Lo's*, "Rose"; *Lat*, "Lot"; *Luk*, "Luke"; *Lo'm*, "Rome."

Me'j, "moreover, always, more."

Na'n, "five, five times"; *naj*, *nass*, "if he loses, if he lost (his soul)"; *na's*, "I will lose it"; *na't*, "these things"; *nep*, "I die"; *nej*, *ness*, "if he dies, if he died"; *net*, "this"; *net-na*, "that's it, all right"; *ni'k*, "my house"; *ni'n*, "I, me"; *nujj*, "my father."

Pe'l, "listen! stop!"; *pis*, "flea"; *pij*, "let him remain seated"; *Po'l*, "Paul"; *Po's*, "Pontius (Pilate)."

Sa'k, "Jacques"; *Sa'n*, "John"; *sa'l*, "shawl"; *sa's*, "I will order him out"; *sa'j*, "let him expel him"; *so'q*, "banish him!"; *se'k*, "in vain"; *sik*, "only"; *sikw*, "(the) spring"; *sm*, "feed him"; *so'j*, "let him be banished"; *Suk*, *Sul*, "(proper nouns), Sook, Sewell."

Tam, "ask him for it"; *ta'n*, "which, that which, that, when"; *ta's*, "how many times?"; *te's*, "so many times"; *tett*, "here"; *te'j*, "either"; *to'q*, "therefore"; *tu's*, "my daughter"; *tu's-tut*, "my daughters" [vocative].

Jel, "and, and even"; *Jim*, "Jim"; *Jo'j*, "George"; *ji'j* (ending), "small."

Remark: Look for the other syllables in the two following lessons.

LESSON FOUR

THIRD EXERCISE
ON SPELLING AND PRONUNCIATION

Syllables

Formed from Diphthongs

preceded or followed by a **single** consonant

Remarks: 1. With regard to the spelling, pronounce all the separately marked syllables with a single emission of the voice, as in *wa'w*, *ewk*, *wow*. In these words and in others in *-aw*, *-ew*, *-iw*, *-ow*, these syllables are cut very short, almost *o*, especially in Nova Scotia and Newfoundland.

2. It is necessary to recall here what we have said about the *w* that goes with *k* and *q*: *-kw* and *-qw* make only a single syllable with the long vowels and even the consonant which precedes them; as *i-ka'ta'qw*, "we put it in for him"; but when final *-ku* or *-qu* is accented it is pronounced clearly and forms a distinct syllable, as in *i-ka'-ta-qu*, "I am a farmer." This final short *w* can be found before the *k*, without noticeable difference between *ne-mi'kw*, "we see him," and *mu ne-mi'wk*, "he does not see me," apart from the negative particle.

3. In the following list we group together vowels which follow other vowels, even when they form distinct syllables, not separated by consonants.

List of Diphthongs

Examples, Translation and Analysis
1. Ai, aie, aiei, aiw, ao, au, awa, awe, awei, awi, awia', awie, awiei, awiu', awiwei, awo, awow.

Examples: *a-ij, a-yej*, "so-and-so"; *a-qa-y*, "alas"; *i-ka'y, -ka'n, -ka't, -ka'q*, "arrive"; *a-lu'-say, -san, -sat*, "to be thin"; *wet-ta-qa-iey, -en, -et*, "to belong to a party"; *n-qa-saiw*, "immediately"; *ta'n n-qa-saiw*, "as soon as."

Aw in *aw-na*, "on the contrary"; *ne'-kaw*, "straight ahead"; *maw*, "together"; *saq-maw*, "chief, lord"; *pi'-taw*, "higher up, up river"; *pi'-ta-wa'-si, -sin, -sit*, "to go up"; *pi'-ta-wa'm, -wa'-mn, -wa'q*, "row, swim against the current"; *kl-i-taw*, "raspberry"; *ta-ul-tn-a'-si, -sin, -sit*, "open the mouth"; *ji'-ka'w*, "bass, achigan."

Awa in *a-wa-ne-i, -in, -e'k*; *a-wa-ni-tu, -tu'n, -toq*, "be ignorant of, forget"; "neglect"; *ka-wat-ku-pi*, "beer"; *Mi'k-ma-wa'j*, "a Mi'kmaw"; *sa-qm-a-wa'-ki*, "district, organized territory (with a chief)"; *Kan'-ta-wa'-ki*, "Caughnawaga, Canada"; *U-ta-wa*, "Ottawa"; they also say: *A-ttua*; *a-mal-kawa-qn*, "a dance."

Awe in *ma'-wen*, "no one"; *ma'-wen kpil-si-maw*, "do not bear false witness against anyone"; *awey* in *new-tis-ka'-qa-wey*, "tenth"; *sa'-qa-wey*, "old"; *sa-la-wey*, "salt"; *tm-a-wey*, "tobacco"; *Na-wey*, "Noah"; *na-wi-aq*, "impossible"; *ta-wey*, "former nickname to call an Indian"; it probably comes from *e-ta-wey*, "I ask, I collect; beggar"; *wi-sa-wey*, "yellow"; *kwe-sa-wey*, "point."

Awi, a-wiw, "around"; *a-wi-siw*, "rarely"; *a-wi-o* in *ma-wi-o'-mi*, "assembly, group"; *san-te-wi Ma-wi-o'-mi*, "the Church"; one also says *a-la-sut-me-wi-nui Ma-wi-o'-mi*, "assembly of those who pray"; *a-wi-we* in *Wes-ta-wi'-wet*, "he saves," *Nuji-Wsi--ta-wi'-wet*, "the Savior"; *awi-je'-jit*, "s/he is rare"; *ma-wi*, "very, much."

Awo in *qa-sa-wo'q*, "iron"; *qa-sa-wo'-qwey*, "instrument of iron"; *qa-sa-wo'-qwey aw-ti*, "railroad"; *qa-sa-wo'-qapi*, "iron wire."

2. Ei', eia, eie, eio, eiwa, eo, ewa, ewai', ewe, ewei, eweiei, ewi, ewia, ewie, ewiei, ewiw, ewiwei, ewo, ewow, ewowei.

Examples: *e'y, e'n, e't*, "to say"; *e'-yikw, e'-yek, e'-yoq, e'-jik*, "we, you pl., they say"; *eym, ei-mn, eyk, ei-mu'kw, ei-mek, ei-moq, ey-kik*, "to be, I, you, he, ..."; *mi-mey*, "oil"; *o-qo-tey* and *tey*, "friend, companion, husband, wife (in addressing them)."

E'w (with *ma'*), "I will not say"; *a-li-kew*, "thing, linen"; *qas-kew*, "whoa, stop!"; *ki-lew*, "you pl."; *ma-tew*, "never"; *mal'-tew*, "blood"; *i't-ti-tew na'-kwek*, "a day will come"; *kun'-tew*, "stone"; *ki'l kun'-te-win*, "you are Peter"; *puk-tew*, "fire"; *puk-te-wey*, "of fire"; *puk-te-we'-ji'j*, "match"; *eu-le'-jit*, "a pauper"; *e'um, e'u-mn, e'uk*, "to use"; *eu-na-siet*, "deranged, crazy"; *ew-sa-mi*, "too much"; *ne'w*, "four"; *ne-wi-jik, new-kl*, "four persons, four things"; *kew-ji, -jin, -jit*, "be cold"; *neu-ku-na'q, neu-ku-nit*, "four days"; *a-la-sut-mewk*, "to lead in prayer"; *a-la-sut-mel-sewk*, "to pray for someone"; *a-la-sut-mel-se-win*, "pray for us"; *a-la-sut-mel-sewi-tes-nen*, "you will pray for us"; *te-lui-sun-keuss*, s/he was so named.

Ewa in *e-wa-i, -in, -it*, "have possess"; *pe-way, -wan, -wat*, "to dream"; *pe-wa'm, -wa'mn, -wa'q*, "to sweep"; in the imperative *pua'-e'n* (pua'-he'n), "sweep that!"; *pe-wa-tm, -wa-t-mn, -watk*, "to want"; *pe-wat-kiss*, "he wanted."

Ewe, ewey, in *e-we-ke'k, mu e-we-ke'-nuk*, "there is room, there is no room"; *tm-ke-wey*, "first of all, firstly, first (in position)"; *am-skwe-se-wey*, "first (in time)"; *ta'-puo-wey*, "second"; *si's-te-wey*, "third"; *ne'-wo-wey*, "fourth"; *na'-ne-wey*, "fifth"; *a-su-ko-me-wey*, "sixth"; *l'ui-kne-ke-wey*, "seventh"; *u-ku-mul-ji-ne-wey*, "eighth"; *pes-qu-na-te-ke-wey*, "ninth"; *w-tej-ke-wey*, "last"; *ni'ne-wey*, "mine"; *ki'-le-wey*, "yours"; *ne-kme-wey*, "his"; *kalku-ne-wey*, "biscuit"; *te'-pi-ne'-kle-wey*, "vinegar"; *te'-pi-se-wey*, "pepper"; *tu-li'-je-we'l*, "rice"; *mi-jip-je-wey*, "food"; *na'ku'setewey*, "watch"; *tepknusetewey*, "calendar"; *pitewey*, "tea"; *pitewey-o'q*, "teapot"; *ket-lewey, ket-lewei-wa-qn*, "truth"; *a-la-sut-mam-kewe'l*, "prayer book"; *Ap-ji'-tim-kewey*, "the Eucharist"; *ap-ji'-tim-kewey-ey*, "of the Eucharist"; *te-pu'-lewey*, "butter."

Ewi, ewiey in *e-lue'-wi, -win, -wit*, "to be nasty, quick-tempered, a sinner"; *a-la-sut-mel-se-win e-lue'-ul-tiyek*, "pray for us sinners"; *e-lue'-wi-ey, -en, -et*, "to be crazy"; *Nis-ka-me-wit*, "he is God"; *nis-ka-meu-ti*, "divinity," *-me-ewi*, "divine," *-me-we-i, -in, -e'k*, "to be pious, consecrated to God"; *Nis-ka-me-wi-kia*, "Mother of God"; it is better to say *Nis-kam w-kwi-jl* or *We-kwi-sin Wes-ta-u'l-kup*; *an-sa-le'-wit*, "angel"; *pa'-pe'-wit*, "the Pope"; *e-le-ke'-wit*, "the king."

Ewo, ewowey in *puk-te-wo'-kuom*, "(fiery) furnace"; *ne'-wo-wey* (above-mentioned); *ki-lew*, "you pl."; *ki-le-wo-wey*, "your."

3. Ia, iaw, iawey, – ie, iey, iew, iewey, ieweyey, ieweyo – iw, iwe, iwey.

Examples: *i'-a*, "oh dear!"; *ia-muj, mi-a-muj*, or simply *a-muj*, "certainly, assuredly, indeed"; it is used also to say *yes*; *te-li-aq*, "it's true"; *te-lia-qa-wey, -we'l*, "the truth, true things"; *Mu-li-an*, "Montreal"; *tli-aj*, "let it be so"; *iaj*, "especially"; *iap, ia-paq*, "male"; *iap-jiw*, "always," *ap-jiw*, "usually"; *iap-ji-wo-wey*, "eternal"; *tmi-pias*, "50 cents"; *ti-a'm*, "moose"; *li-a, li-e*, "go on!," all the imperatives of verbs in *-iey* have the same *-ia* at Restigouche, *-ie* everywhere else; *mi-a'wj*, "cat"; at Restigouche one says *qa-ju-e'wj*; *sia-wiw*, "continually."

Ie, iey in *i'-e'n*, "be there"; *kal-kie*, "one fourth"; *em-pie*, "one foot (measure)"; *Pi-e'l*, "Pierre, Peter"; *e-li-ey, -en, -et*, "to go"; *pe-mi-ey, -en, -et*, "walk"; *el-mi-ey, -en, -et*, "to go away"; *we-na-qi-ey, -en, -et*, "jump, leap"; *kes-mi-ey*, "push ahead, advance, progress"; *ks-ma'-tu*, "push! (a button or a bell)"; *a-ji-ey*, "advance, increase"; *ne'w a-ji-et*, "four hours"; *ket-ki-ey*, "to be drunk"; *aq-la-si-e'w*, "English(man)"; *su-lie-wey*, "silver"; *su-lie-we-yey*, "of silver"; *wi-sa-wi-su-lie-wey*, "gold"; *su-lieweyo'-kuom*, "bank"; *a-jiaq su-li-ewey*, "interest"; *kul-jiewey* or *klu-jjiewey*, "cross."

Io, iw in *Pio*, "Pius"; *kiw-to'-qiw*, "around"; *kiw-na-qaj*, "especially"; *kiw-nik*, "otter"; *kiw-ni-ke-wey*, "of the otter"; *ki-wkw*, "earthquake"; *si-pe-liw*, "often"; *an-km-iw* or *nan-km-iw*, "immediately"; *kul'-piw*, "forthwith"; *ki'k-we-su*, "musk-rat"; *si-wei, -wein, -we'k*, "to be bored, tired"; *tu-jiw*, "then."

4. Wa, wae, waei, wai, wao, waw, wawe, wawei.

Examples: *wa* in *wa-qa-sit*, "wild animal"; *wan-sit*, "servant"; *wa'q-aj*, "barely"; *wa-lam-kew*, "fishing hole"; *wal-ney*, "bay"; *wal-po'q*, "pond"; *wal-tes*, "wooden dish, for the game of dice," *wal-tes-ta-qn*; *wan-pi*, *wan-taq-pi*, "keep still!"; *was-sa-mi*, *wes-sa-mi* or *aw-sa-mi*, "too much"; *wa-pus*, "rabbit, hare"; *was-pu*, "seal"; *wa'-so'q*, "sky"; *was-tew*, "snow"; *wa-ju'-pin*, "full" (of graces, *sa-pe'wu-ti'l*); *ji-ji-kwa-qaj* and *ji-jua-qa*, "sometimes"; *e-lu-kwalk, -kwa-tm*, "shape, mold"; *ki-po-qwa'-si, -sin, -sit*, "to be inclined"; *mas-qwa'-tu*, "hide, put aside," from *mas-kwi*, "bark (of a tree)"; *mo-qwaj*, *mo-qwa* (at Restigouche; elsewhere *mo-qwej*, *mo-qwe*), "no"; *pua-qn*, "dream"; *pa-pua-qn*, "game."

Way, "his property, his wealth"; *way-wal*, "their wealth"; see the seventh and tenth commandments, little used elsewhere; one says more properly: *wu-tap-sun, w-ta-li-kam*; *ma'-wen way km-sn-muaw*, "do not take anyone's property"; *ktap-tn-muaw*, "don't keep it"; *kpu-a-tm-uaw*, "do not covet it"; *wa-ij*, "imp, sorcerer's doll"; *wai-juey mun'-ti*, "medicine bag"; *wai-sis* (at Restigouche *wi'-sis*), "animal"; *wai-si-se-mo'-kuom*, "den, lair"; *o-qwa'y, -a'n, -a't, -a'q*, "to land"; *ke-si-nu-kway, -an, -at, -aq*, "to be sick"; *ke-si-nu-kwam-kl*, "sicknesses"; *pis-kwa'y, -a'n, -a't, -a'q*, "to enter"; *we-si-mu-kway, -an, -at, -aq*, "to flee."

Wa'w, "egg"; *wa'-wl*, "eggs"; *wa'-we'-key, -ken, -ket*, "to gather eggs"; *wa'-wey*, "made of eggs"; *te-pa-te*, "meat or fish pie"; *pe-ta-qn*, "tart"; *wa'wk* or *wa'-kw*, "louse."

5. We, wei, wew, wewei, wewi, wewiei.

Examples: *We* in *we-kwi-si, -sin, -sit*, "to have a son"; *We-kwi-sit Nis-kam*, "God the Father"; *pe-ji-li sa-pe'-win Ma'-li we-kwi-sin Wes-ta-u'l-kup, ni-ke'j a-la-sut-mel-se-win e-lue'-ul-ti-ek*, "holy Mary, ..."; *we-kwi-ji, -jin, -jit*, "to have as a mother"; *we-li-kis-kik*, "a pretty day, good day"; *wmi-t-ki, -kin, -kit*, "to have a native land"; *wen*, "who?"; *wen ta Nis-kam*, "who is God?" *wen u't*, "who is this?," hence *We-nuj*, "Frenchman," the first whites who saw the Mi'kmaq; *wen'-ji'-kuom*, "house"; *wen'-ju'-su'n*, "apple"; *wen'-ju-tia'm*, "cow"; *wen'-ju-tia'-muey*, "beef"; *wen'-ju-tia'-mu'j*, "calf"; *we-nis-ka-mi*, "to have as God"; *we-ni-ja-ni*, "to have children"; *wep-tn-i, -nin, -nit*, "to have hands"; *we-saq-ma-mi*, "to have as a lord"; *we-saq-ma-mul-ti'kw*, "he is Our Lord"; *Wes-ta-u'lkw, -ul-kup*, "our Saviour"; *we-tu-si, -sin, -sit*, "to have a daughter"; *wet-me-y, -me-in, -me'k*, "to be busy"; *we-ji*, "from there"; *we-ji-ey, -en, -et*, "to come from"; *We-ji-wli Nis-kam*, "the Holy Ghost." Again, *we* in *ke'-kwe'k*, "above, upstairs"; *na'-kwek, na'-kwe-kl*, "day"; *an-sue'k*, "that is unfortunate"; *su-el*, "almost, as it were"; *Et-ue'l*, "Edward"; *wej-kwa'-tu, -tu'n, -toq*, "bring"; *we-ji-ma-nit*, "fruit"; *nas-kwet*, "virgin"; *we-li Nas-kwet*, "the Blessed Virgin"; *kwet-mat*, "he smokes"; *Mi'k-muesu*, "the nymph of the forest"; *ma-tues*, "porcupine"; *pues-su*, "bushel," pl. *pue-su-aq*.

Wey in *kwey*, "greetings! hello!"; *e-lu-kwey, -kwen, -kwet*, "work"; *ko-qoey*, "what?"; *na't ko-qoey*, "something"; *ko-qoey w-jit*, "why? what for?"; *ko-qoe'-ji'j*, "a little thing"; *ko-qoe'-juey*, "a trifle"; *pu-kwey*, "half"; *pi-luey*, "something else"; *pi-luey wen*, "someone else"; *i-la's-ku-kwey, -en, -et*, "to play cards"; *pa'-qa-pu-kuey, -en, -et*, "to confess one's sins"; *ikn-muey, -en, -et*, "to give"; *ikn-mui-ek*, "you s. give to us"; *ikn-muin*, "give us"; *pne-kn-muin ni-lu'-nen*, "give us our food from on high"; *ik-n-maq, -mat, -mua-jl*, "to give to someone"; *se's-kwey, -en, -et*, "to shout (in a disorderly manner)"; *ne-tawey*, "to shout out (appropriately), to sell by auction."

Wew, wewi, in *jij-kl-ue'w-ji'j*, "lamb"; *e-lue'wi-nu*, "a wicked person, a sinner"; *e-lue'wi-et*, "a madman."

6. Wi, wia, wie, wiey, wiu, wiwey.

Examples: *wi'k* (long), "his house, his place"; *wi-kuow*, "their house"; *wi-kuaq*, "at their place"; *wi-kuom*, "a house"; *wi-ku-omk*, "in the house"; *wikk* (short *i*), "sweet, tasty," *wik-kl* (plural); *wi-ka-pu'k*, "what tastes good"; *wi-kwa-je'j-kl*, "pleasures"; *wi-kew*, "fat"; *wi-ke-wi, -win, -wit*, "to be fat"; *wik-pey*, "to like to drink"; *wi-lu*, "his food"; *wi'n, wip*, "marrow, sap"; *wi's*, "den, lair [beaver lodge, rathouse]"; *wis-qew*, and *wis-qi*, "quickly, suddenly"; *wis-kui*, "astonishingly"; *ta-puis-ka'q*, "twenty"; *kul-kwi's*, "pig"; *kul-kwi's-uey*, "bacon"; *kul-kwi's-uo'-kuom*, "pigsty"; *l'uik-nek*, "seven."

Tal-ui-sin? "what is your name?"; *a-ij te-lui-si, -sin, -sit*, "I, you (s.), he is named so-and-so"; *ta'n te-lui-sin*, "your name"; *te-lui-si'kw, -siyek, -siyoq*,

-si-jik, -sul-ti'kw, -tiyek, -tiyoq, -ti-jik, "we incl., we excl., you, they, ... are called"; *pu-ne-wis-tu,* "be quiet!"; *wi't,* "name him!"; *ke'-sɨk wi't,* "go ahead and name him"; *wi-jey,* "the same thing, likewise"; *me-luij,* "rather"; *pi-tui,* "lengthened, raised, further off," hence *pi-tui mtl-na-qn,* "a thousand"; *pi-tui nis-ka-mij,* "great grandfather"; *pi-tui-wuji'-ji,* "great grandchildren"; *pil-tui,* "new, first, peculiar"; *pil-tui km-nie'u-ti,* "first communion"; *kwi-lm, kwi-laq,* "to search for"; *w-kwi-sl,* "his son"; *w-kwi-jl,* "his mother."

Wia in *wia-qiw,* "pell-mell, mixed-up, confused"; *a-le-luia,* "hallelujah"; *wi'-kwi-a-tiyek,* "we are failing, we are at death's door, dying"; *tu-ia, tu-ie, tu'-a,* "out!"; *pi-suiw,* "in vain, uselessly, (consequently) freely"; *u-yus* or *wi-us,* "meat," (also) a family name, which the English changed to *Weush* and the French to *Voyouche*; *ki-si-kui, -kuit,* "to be old"; *ki-si-kui-ey,* "to grow old."

7. Wo, ow, owey, wow, wowa, wowe, wowey, wowi.

Examples: *uo* in *tu-oq,* "it is not known"; *wo'-ke-jij,* "spider"; *wo'-ke-jij-a'-pi,* "cobweb, spider's web"; *ow,* in *ne-k-mow,* "they"; *ne-k-mo-wey,* "their"; *e-lu-kowk,* "to work for someone."

Wow, "pot, boiler, cauldron, kettle"; *kuow, kuaq,* "pine (-tree)"; *kuo-wip-kw,* "pine balm, turpentine"; *kuo-wa'-qa-mitk,* "a grove of pine trees"; *wow-kwis,* "fox"; *wej-uow,* "near"; *wej-uo-wa'-si, -sin, -sit,* "to approach"; *ki-nuo-wey,* "our"; *puo-win,* "sorcerer, wizard"; *kl-o-qo-wej,* "star."

Text to Read and Translate

Sign of the Cross. Ta'n teluisit Wekwisit Niskam, aqq Ewjit Niskam, aqq Weji-wli Niskam. Amen kisna tliaj.

Nujjinen wa'so'q epin, jiptuk teluisin mekite'tmek. Wen ta Niskam? Ta'n eta kisitoqsɨp (*he made*) wa'so'q aqq maqmikew.

Pejili-sape'win Ma'li ki'l wekwisin Westau'lkup, nike'j alasutmelsewin elue'ultiyek aqq api's (*especially*) wi'kwiatiyek (*at death*) alasutmelsewitesnen. Ki'l welein, e'pijik pajiji-wleinik. Nujɨwsi-tawi'wet wkwijl nekm Ma'li teluisit. Eleke'wit etuk me' Jo'j na'newey teluisit? Moqwa, ta'n kiskuk eleke'witewit Jo'j asukomewey, na nekm wkwisl.

Wen ta ki'l? Ni'n eta mijua'ji'j kisna teluey l'pa'tuj mi'kmawa'j, Ta'pit teluisi, wejiey Puksɨk; nmis eta Lo's, Plna'l wte'piteml. Wiktm wa'wey tepate aqq petaqn. Nemi'k jijklue'wji'j a'sɨk eyk; nipi ketui-iknmaq. Pi'taw ni'n eliey, ki'l papke'k elien, katu pe'l qaskew, nitapji'j, kijka' piskwa' ni'k; ki's kujj eyk aqq etuk asukom te'sijik ji'nmuk aklasie'wk. Awije'jit aklasie'w alasutmewinu (*Catholic*). Sm te'sipow aqq wen'jutia'mu'j.

Koqoey ta pewatmn (*what do you want*)? Mijipjewey pewatm, pipnaqn aqq wius, wen'jutia'muey kisna kulkwi'suey, pitewey aqq salawey, qamu kisna mimey. Oqotey, mesta wikapu'k. Kopit wikewit. Tami ta eyk? Wi's eyk. Wen ta teluet? Mise'l teluet, Sa'k nkutey, aqq ni'n; ki's sa'q nemi'k.

LESSON FIVE

FOURTH EXERCISE
ON PRONUNCIATION AND SPELLING

Vowels Or Diphthongs

preceded or followed by **several** consonants

Remarks: 1. To pronounce two or even three consonants at the beginning of a word, the Indians often add a very short *i* or mute *e*; ex.: *nti*, almost *in-ti*, "my dog"; *kti*, almost *ik-ti*, "your dog"; but these three or four letters make only a single syllable. They introduce into the words themselves, between two consonants, a break difficult to distinguish from mute *e*. Thus the *m* in *nik-ma'j*, "my neighbor," and *nekmow*, "they," is syllabic, and is pronounced as if it were *im*. Likewise in English one cannot get them to say *twelve*, one hears instead *tweleve* (tuelip), and *tweleve times* (tuelip taymis).

2. In the spelling, *q* normally appears with *a* or *o*, as in *nqa*, *sqa*, *aqt*, *tqo*, *jqo*, *oqt*; but, when these syllables occur in words, it often happens that the sound is *k* not *q* as in *nkam-la-mun*, "my heart."

Exercise

1. *Kl* in *Kle'*, "Gray," *Kle'l*, "Claire"; *lak-klem*, "cream"; *lak-kla'ns*, "barn." *Ks* in *ksal*, "love him!"; *pe-ji-li-ksa-luet*, "the very loving (Jesus)"; *pe-ji-li-ksal-ku-sit*, "beloved"; *nu-luks*, "my nephew."

Kt in *ktik* (ĭk-tik), *kti-kik*, "the other, the others"; *Kta-qm-kuk*, "Newfoundland"; *a-paqt*, "the sea"; *kji-a-paqt*, "the ocean"; *mu kti-ka'-li-nen*, "lead us not"; *newt*, "one, an"; the Indians often write *ne-kut*; *ni-pukt*, "forest"; *ktl-a-mi-luk*, "your entrails."

Kj in *Kji-nis-kam*, "the great God"; *Kji-saq-maw*, "the supreme Lord"; *Kji-sa-pe'-wit*, "the most Holy One"; *kji-sa-pe'wu-ti'l*, "the theological virtues"; *kji-l'ue'wu-ti'l*, "the deadly sins"; *kji-a-la-sut-ma-qn*, "a sacrament"; *kji-pa'-tli-a's*, "the bishop"; *qa-ju-e'wj*, "cat"; *wi-pukj, u-pukj, u-puk-jik* and *wi-kupj*, "soon, before long."

2. *Lk* in *ji-palk, -palt, -pa-la-jl*, "to fear someone"; *ji-patk*, "he fears it"; *ke-salk, -salt, -sa-la-jl*, "to love"; *ke-satk*, "he loves it"; *elk, eɫp*, "also"; *pi-kwelk, pu-kwelk*, "several"; *kwilk*, "he looks for something"; *ke-lu'lk*, "good"; *Ki-su'lkw*, "the Creator."

L'm in *l'mu'j*, "dog"; *l'mi-a, l'mi-e*, "go home!."

Ln in *l'n*, "for, because"; also *eln*, "I tell you (s.)"; *el-noq*, "I tell you (pl.)"; *l'nim*, "too"; *l'nu*, "man, Indian"; *Saln*, "Charles"; *Salnot*, "Charlotte, also Jeannotte"; *eln-ta-na*, contracted to *enntana*, "as a matter of fact."

Ls in *mals*, "flint"; *L'si-puk-tuk*, "Richibouctou."

Lt in *alt*, "some people, those, there are some who"; *alt ... alt*, "some ... others."

3. *Mk* in *emk, te-luemk*, "one says"; *nis-kamk*, "the gods"; *tmk*, "firstly."

Ms in *msa'l, msa'-tu*, "swallow"; *msit*, "all"; *msaq-taqt*, "floor."

Mt in *mta-we-kn*, "flag"; *mt-lui-kn*, "finger"; *mtln*, "ten"; *mtl-ne-wey*, "tenth"; *Pio mtl-ne-wey jel newt*, "Pius XI"; *mte-san*, "baby, the last child (even an adult)"; *mte's-km*, "serpent"; *mtia'-qa-tes-ta-qn*, "collection"; *mti-jin*, "thumb, inch"; *mtu-kwa-pe'-kn*, "chin"; *mtu-kwe-jan*, "forehead"; *mto-qn*, "garment"; *mtu'-noqt*, "bad weather, storm."

Mj in *mji-jaq-mij*, "the soul."

4. *Nk*, in *nkam-la-mun, kkam-la-mun, wkwam-la-mun*, "my, your, his heart"; *nqa-no'-pa-ti*, "well"; *nqa-ni'p-sm-un*, "chalice"; *nkl-ni-kn*, "god-child"; *nqa-nui-sun*, "family name"; *nkat*, "my foot"; *nkij, kkij, wkwi-jl*, "my, your s., his mother"; *nkwe'-ji'j, kkwe'-ji'j, wkwe'-ji'-jl*, "my your s., his (younger) sister"; *nkwis, kkwis, wkwi-sl*, "my, your s., his son"; *Nki-su'lkum, Kki-su'l-kum, Wkwi-su'l-ku-ml*, "my, your s., his God (Creator)"; *nki-si-kum, -kwi's-kom*, "my husband, my wife."

Np in *npa'-tlia'-sm, kpa'-tlia'-sm, w-pa'-tlia'-s-ml,* "my, your sg, his priest (parish priest)"; *npi-tn*, "my hand"; *npa'-tlia'-si'skom*, "my schoolmistress (nun)."

Ns in *nsaq-mam*, "my chief, my Lord"; *nsm*, "my niece, cousin"; *nsɨt-na-qn*, "orphan"; *nsi'l*, "my lips"; *nsis*, "my (elder) brother"; *nsis-kw*, "my face"; *nska-wa-qn*, "the Mi'kmaw song"; *nspɨtk*, "at the same time."

Nt in *nta-qo'-qn*, "(sense of) shame"; *nta-qo'-qn-ey*, "ashamed"; *nt-la-mi-luk*, "my entrails"; *ntl-i-ta'-nen*, "that we may go"; *nti-pil-ja-qn*, "my glove"; *nte'-pi-tem*, "my wife"; *kte'-pi-tem, w-te'-pi-te-ml,* "your sg., his"; *nte-pluk*, "armies"; *nti, kti, w-ti'l,* "my, your, his dog"; *nti-nin, kti-nin, w-ti-nin,* "my, your, his body"; *ntu-e'm, ktu-e'm, w-tue'-ml,* "my, your, his work animal"; *ntul, ktul, wtul,* "my, your, his dingy, open boat, canoe"; *ntu-kwe-jan*, "my forehead"; *ntun*, "my mouth"; *ntus*, "my daughter"; *ntlu'-sue's-kom* (*n-tlu* ...), "my daughter-in-law"; *lu'-sue'skw*, "a daughter-in-law"; *ntl-u'-suk*, "my son-in-law."

Nj in *nji-kn-am*, "my (younger) brother"; *njilj, kjilj, w-jil-jl,* "my, your, his father-in-law"; *nji'-n-mum*, "my husband"; *nji-ja-qa-mij*, "my soul (my shadow)"; *nju-kwi'-ji'j*, "my mother-in-law."

5. *Pk* in *wapk*, "morning, the dawn"; *wa-pn-a'-ki*, "land of the dawn, land of the Abenaquis"; *e-wipk*, "the sea is calm"; *nipk*, "summer"; *pqan*, "nut"; *pqanj, pqan-ji'j, ma-li-pqanj,* "hazel-nuts"; *pku*, "gum, incense"; *kpu-kum*, "your quid (of tobacco)"; *tual-qa'l*, "take it out!"; *pku-o'q*, "incense-box"; *pku-ma-qn*, "weapon, whip"; *pqo-tn-anj*, "bastard," it is better to say *se-ke-wey mi-jua'-ji'j*, "found infant"; *pqo-ju*, "fugitive"; *pqo'qt*, "bump, bruise, lump."

Pl in *pla-wej*, "partridge"; *Pla-sit*, "Placide"; *pla-sulk*, "schooner"; *Pli-sit*, "Brigitte"; *plos*, "brush."

Pm in *pmi* (contracted form of *pe-mi*) indicates walking, carrying on; *pmi-an-ki-te'-te'n*, "keep thinking about it; reflect with mature consideration"; *i-pa-ji-kpmi-te'l-mul*, "I humbly honor you" (*p* is almost not heard).

Ps and *pt* in *pip-to-qop-ska'-la-snl*, "he has formed, shaped it"; *Te-waps-kik*, "Port-Royal, Annapolis."

Pj in *apj*, "again, afresh"; *pji-liw*, "especially."

6. *Sk* in *ska-tu* or *ka-tu*, "but"; *te-li sqa-tas-kik*, "as they obey you"; *te-li sqa-tu-lek*, "that we obey you thus"; *skmt-tuk* or *smt-tuk*, "immediately"; *Ksaq-ma-minu te-kwe-yask*, "Our Lord is with you"; *e'sk* or *ke'sk*, "while"; *e'sk mnaq* or *e's-ku m-naq*, "before"; *sku*, "leech"; *skwew*, "hen"; *skus*, "weasel." See *Nis-kam* and *nska-wa-qn* below.

Sn in *sna-wey*, "maple"; *sna-wey-ey*, "of maple"; *sna-wey-e'l puk-su-kul*, "maple wood (for burning)."

St in *si'st*, "three"; *kwas-ta-le* "(interjection of astonishment) ah! really!."

7. *Tk* in *tkey*, "a cold"; *tki-poq*, "spring"; *tku*, "wave"; *tqoq*, "last autumn"; *tqo'-nuk*, "next autumn"; *to-qwa'q*, "autumn"; *tko'tj*, "let him be present, attend"; *tkwe-yu-loqj*, "let him be with you"; *we-tqolk*, "I forbid him"; *we-tqol-tim-ke-wey*, "forbidden" (see *mi-nijk* below); *tqo-pe'j*, "twin"; *pe-watk*, "he wants"; *kitk*, "both"; *tqam*, "hit him!"; *L'-sit-kuk*, "Bear River."

Tl in *tlant-su* (trente sous) "25 cents"; *tley, tle'l, tle'k*, "to belong, to be from"; one says also *tett tley-awi, -win, -wit*: *Kta-qm-kuk tley* or *tett tley-awit*, "he is from Newfoundland"; *tla-mu'k-tij*, "let it be the same colour"; *tli* (contracted from *te-li*), "thus"; *tli-aj*, "let it be so"; *tlim*, "tell him!"; *tlui-ta-ten*, "he will be called that"; *tlui-siass*, "if my name were that"; *tli-sip*, "then"; *to-qu tli-sip*, "next"; *ta'n tli'-sip*, "when."

Tp in *tpa'q* (in compounds), "during the night"; *aq-ta-tpa'q*, "at midnight"; *new-ti-tpa'q*, "a night, all night"; *po-qn-i-tpa'q*, "darkness, gloom, gloomy night"; *tpi'i*, "give me a share"; *tpuk*, "the night (just after midnight)"; *tpu'-nuk*, "during the night (which is beginning)"; *w-lo'-nuk*, "tonight."

Jk in *Kwe-tejk*, "Iroquois"; *wi-ne'j-kl*, "evil things, lewdness"; *wi-kwa-je'j-kl*, "pleasures, agreeable things," this does not mean shameful things, for the latter, one uses *nta-qo'-qnl*; *puk-te-wijk*, "intoxicating beverage (fire water)"; *mi-nijk*, "fruit"; *mi-nij-kek we-qol-tim-ke-we-yek*, "the forbidden fruit (in the past)"; *jij-ka-wi-kn-e'jk*, "grapes" [oranges]; *jqolj*, "toad"; *jqol-je-wi-ku's*, "former name of the month of November"; *ej-kujk*, "pumpkin, melon, cucumbers"; *ej-kuj-ke-wey te-pa-te*, "pumpkin pie"; *jij-kl-ue'w-ji'j*, "lamb"; *Kji-nis-kam w-jij-kl-ue'w-ji'-jml*, "the Lamb of God."

Niskam or **Niks-kam** (Nik-skam), "God," as the universal ancestor (118, 2); *niks-kam* is certainly the true spelling; M. Maillard writes *nix-skam*; that is how it is pronounced in Cape Breton; at Restigouche the first *k* is not pronounced, but the *s*, which is strongly pronounced, is redoubled. *Nis-ka-mij* or *nij-ka-mij*, "grandfather," is the diminutive of it; *A-ta-o'q kmel-ta-mi nis-ka-mi-ji-nu-aq*, Adam, our first ancestor (Rem. gr. 230). "The name under which God revealed himself to Abraham, *El-saddai*, which is translated as Almighty God, can also be interpreted as God the Father (Christus p. 857)." Fathers Biard and Leclercq state that the pagan Mi'kmaq worshipped the sun, which they called *Niscaminou* (Rel. 1611, p.20), but their concept was more vague and mysterious; they invoked him rather *in* the sun, which has another name in Mi'kmaw, or by turning in the direction of the rising sun. Nevertheless they must have considered the latter as the Father of light (M. Maillard, letter, p. 302) and source of life. *N-nis-kam, k-nis-kam, w-nis-ka-ml*, "my your, his God," *w-nis-ka-mu-al*, "their"; *nis-kamk w-nis-ka-mu-al*, "God of gods" (Ms. 9, 188). *Nis-ka-me-wi, -win, -wit, -wik*, "to be God"; *we-nis-ka-mi, -min, -mit*, "to have as God"; *we-nis-ka-mi-yek kti-nin*, "you are our God," this word includes the sense of "to treat as God." *Nis-ka-me-we-i, -we-in, -we'k*, "to be pious, holy" (1 Cor. 7, 34); also *nis-ka-me-we-y, -we-yaq, -wo'-tm*, "to hold as God"; *nis-ka-me-wey, -we'l, -we'k* (adjective), "divine"; *nis-ka-me-wi wi'-ka-ti-kn*, "the Scripture"; *nis-ka-me-wa'-si, -wa'-lik, -wa'-tu, -wa'l-si*, "to make God, to become God, to be worshipped"; *nis-ka-me-wi-ta'-si, -te'-lmk, -te'l-key, -te'-tm, -te'-te-key*, "to believe in someone, something, oneself, as a god." *Nis-ka-me-u-ti*, "divinity"; *w-nis-ka-me-u-ti-wow*, "their divinity"; *Nis-ka-me-wi-kia*, "Mother of God." *We-nis-ka-mi-ji, -jin, -jit*, "to have as a grandfather"; *n-nis-ka-mij, k-, w-*, "my, your, his grandfather"; *w-nis-ka-mi-jl Pe-ju'l*, "his grandfather Lamorue" (Jo. 310).

Nskawa-qn (n-skawa-qn), a Mi'kmaw song (response) with gestures and sighs, composed of meaningless syllables, to which one responds with a sigh, approximately like this: *Ku'-na'-li'-o kwa'-nu'-te' e-i-ke kwa'-nu'-tan na he*; response: *a-e* (a-he, strongly aspirated); final sigh: *a-wi-a* (ha-wi-ha)! Another text, interspersed with directions, and which makes some sense, was published in the proceedings of the Congress of 1906 (1 p. 119).

1. *Wai-sis-tu-ku-li'-ti'-tij ke-tu'-ma-qi-k a*, "I want to sing for the hunters" (twice); *wai-sis-tu-ku-li'-ti'-tij ula ke-tu'-ma-qi-k a*, "I want to sing for these hunters here" (twice).

2. Direction: *ka-qi w-na-qi-ta'-tij u-la a-mal-kal'-ti-p-nik*, then you rise for the dance; *tli-sip ki-si-ku te-li ntoq sta-qe* (*is-te-ke*) *u't*; then the elder sings as follows:

3. *E-i-ko e-li-lo ku-ko a-i-o e-li-lo, a-wi-a*!

4. *Wai-sis-tu-ku-nik we-kl-a ke-tu'-ma-qi'k*? "It is perhaps good for the animals that I wanted to sing"; *ka-tu mu wai-si-si-kwi'k, pa-sik ne-kl-a wai-si-sa ke-ta-na'-ti-ta*, "but no, it wasn't for the animals, but for the people who were hunting them."

Here is another stanza of equally undramatic verse: *Na'-ta-qa-ma'-sian ja-ji-ka'-si-tess*, "if I go across I will follow the shore, which is repeated endlessly, while involving no commitment."

Text to Read and Translate Literally

Remark: We now have all the syllables and even all the words necessary to read intelligently the whole of the Lord's Prayer, the Hail Mary and the Creed.

Nujjinen wa'so'q epin, jiptuk teluisin mekite'tmek, wa'so'q ntlita'nen jiptuk iknmuiek ula (*there*) nemu'lek wle'tesnen; na'te'l wa'so'q eykik teli-sqataskik jiptuk elp ninen teli-sqatulek maqmikek eymek. Telamu'kɨpnikl esmie'kl apj nike'j kiskuk tlamu'ktij pneknmuin nilu'nen; teli-apiksiktaqajik (*as we forgive*) wekaiwinamɨtɨpnik (*those who trespass against us*), tli-apiksiktuin (*so forgive us*) elue'wultiyek; ml'knin me'j winsuti'l (*evil things*) mu ktika'linen; kesinukwamkl winjikl koqoe'l jikla'tuin (*remove from us*).

Kulein, Ma'li, sapewuti'l waju'pinl, Ksaqmaminu tekweyask, e'pijik pajiji-wleinik, aqq wele'k ta'n ktlamiluk wejimanit Se'sus. Pejili-sape'win Ma'li, wekwisin Westau'lkup, nike'j alasutmelsewin elue'wultiyek, aqq api's wi'kwiatiyek alasutmelsewitesnen. Amen.

Apostle's Creed. Weli-ketla'msɨta'si Kjiniskam Wekwisit msɨt koqoe'l ta'n telite'tkl tela'tikl, netna nekm kisitoqsɨp wa'so'q aqq maqmikew. Weli-ketla'msɨta'si elp Se'sukulial wkwisl newtikilijl (*only, unique*); netna nekm wesaqmamulti'kw. Weji-wli Niskam piptoqopska'lasnl l'nua'lasnl ke'sk Ma'li naskwetek (*being a virgin*) wtlamiluk weji-wskijinuilisnl (*he was born from her*). Amaskwiplnutaq Po's Pilato'q saqmawitek, klujjiewto'taq, nepkaq, utqutalutaq. Lamqamu'k eli-pkewietaq, tapukuna'qek weji-minu'nsisni neplipni. Wa'so'q eli-wnaqietaq (*he ascended*). Wujjl wtinaqnk (*locative, on his right*) epijl (*he was seated*). Apj pkisintew wa'so'q wjietew ta'n telite'lmaj (*what he thinks of them*) tle'lita (*they will be such, that is to say, he will decide their destiny*) weskijinuultiliji aqq iapji neliji (*the living and the dead*).

Weli-ketla'msɨtasi Weji-wli Niskam, santewi mesta Mawio'mi, *kisna* Te'si'tij alasutmajik newte'jilijl saqtua'tijl napkuajl Se'susl; sape'wuti'l mawiaj (*communion of saints*), elue'wuti'l mniaj, ma'qe'l apijipetal (*word by word: the sins are taken away, the flesh will be restored*), iapji-wskijinuuti (*eternal life*).

LESSON SIX

NOUNS AND ADJECTIVES

In nouns and adjectives we have to distinguish gender, number, tense, case, agreement and the degrees of comparison.

I. Gender

There are two genders in Mi'kmaw: the animate gender and the inanimate gender, that M. Maillard also calls noble and ignoble. Men and animals belong to the former. The same is true for a great number of things for which the Indians seem to have had a superstitious reverence. Such are: *na'ku'set, tepknuset, kloqoejk, nipi, a'pi, lassiet, klitaw*, etc. The others are of the inanimate gender. The list of the principal things of animate gender will be found in the following section.

This list will show that the reason given by Father Lemoine for the Algonkin language (Congress 1906, 2, 228), is hardly relevant to the Mi'kmaw language: "In the first gender, says he, are collected whatever has animal life or which has a special value in the eyes of the Indians, such as trees, certain fruits, crosses, rosaries, thunder, ice, snow, the stars, skins, pipes, etc...." In Mi'kmaw all that is of the inanimate gender except for stars and rosaries, certain trees and certain fruits. Likewise, Mr. Rand says that the animate gender "includes, besides animals, growing trees, the heavenly bodies, household utensils and weapons used in war and in the chase; ... it is worthy of note that a tree when growing is animate and inanimate as soon as it dies or is cut down (M-E Dictionary XVII)." This is only true in part: so that *tmoqta'w*, "log," and *naskoplaw*, "plank," are of the animate gender; similarly carts, balls for playing games, dolls, etc.; whereas *tmi'kn, wlaqn, pe'skewey*, are inanimate; and for the parts of the body, the heart, the head, the blood, the entrails, the hands, the feet, the chest, the back, the flesh, the body itself, etc., are inanimate, whereas the veins, the lungs, even the nails, etc., are of the animate gender; *l'noqm*, "greenwood," and *mljoqm*, "dry wood," are both of inanimate gender. The real truth is to be found in this affirmation of Father Maillard (Grammar 202): "This gender includes animate beings and what it has pleased the Mi'kmaq to put in the category of the noble and animate gender."

On the other hand there is not, in the nouns and the adjectives, any distinction of sex, apart from the ending *-skw* and *-skwa'q*, added to certain nouns of persons to express the feminine sex, and from which the white man has made the ridiculous name of *squaw* or *sqwah* that they take to mean Indian woman. In reality *-skw* is only an ending, which is added to the masculine noun, in words which express state, rank, occupation; just like *-esse* in French in the word *sauvagesse, comtesse, princesse*, etc. To it an *-a* is joined at the end of sentences and *-aq* in the plural. For young people *-skwa* becomes *-skwe'j* and *-skwe'ji'j*. Examples: *l'nu*, "man, Indian"; *l'nu'skw*, "Indian woman"; *l'nu'skwe'j*, "Indian girl." Notice that man, as distinct from woman, is *ji'nm*, and has no more feminine form than does the word *homme* in French; woman, *e'pit*; while those which express race, etc., have their feminine ending, as in *mi'kmawa'j*, "a Mi'kmaw"; *mi'kmawi'skw*, "a Mi'kmaw woman"; *mi'kmawi'skwe'j*, "a young Mi'kmaw girl." *Nuji-kina'muet*, "a teacher," *nuji-kina'mueti'skw*, "a female teacher"; *nuji-kina'mueti'skwe'j*, "a young, new woman teacher, or teacher's aide." We even have *pa'tlia's*, "priest"; *pa'tlia'si'skw*, "a nun"; and *pa'tlia'si'skwe'j*, "a novice." *Kisiku*, "old man, old gaffer"; *kisikui'skw*, "old woman, or simply married woman." *Nkutapew*, *nkutapewi'skw*, "a bachelor, old maid," but it is not found in good usage; it is better to say *kisiku-l'pa'tu's, kisiku-e'pite's*, or even *nqani-l'pa'tus, nqani-e'pite's*. We find *l'pa'tu'skwaq* for girls, in an anthem of Father Maillard's (Manuscript 9, p. 183). *Eleke'wit*, "king"; *eleke'wi'skw*, "queen"; *eleke'wi'skwe'j*, "princess"; *eleke'witji'j*, "prince"; *nteleke'wi'skwom*, "my queen." *Wenuj*, "a Frenchman"; *wen'jui'skw*, "a French woman"; *wen'jui'skwe'j*, "a French girl." *Aklasie'w*, "an Englishman"; *aklasie'wi'skw*, "an English woman"; *aklasie'wi'skwe'j*, "an English girl," not married; *aklasie'wi'skwe'ji'j*, "a little English girl," and by extension, a little Protestant girl.

Other names of persons, with their plural, will be found in the supplementary exercises.

This ending *-skw* seems to be reserved for persons. It is found however applied to a few names of animals, such as *putip*, "whale," *putipe'skw*; *muin*, "bear," *muine'skw*; *wijik*, "a sort of partridge," that Rand calls "spruce partridge," *wijiki'skw*; but only when they are treated as legendary personages; for as animals they have their own feminine designation. And so it is that Mr. Rand, in the legends (p.46), translates this feminine form by "Weechuk's wife, or in English phraseology, Mrs. Weechuk"; in French must admit that it is not expressible, for which there is no cause for regret. For the true animals, even for the bear and others of its size, we have *nape'skw* for the male, *nuse'skw* for the female; that is to say that these words are joined to the generic name, when one wishes to express whether it is male or female; the expression for the brood or litter is derived from the special name of the female; here it is *pneskwit*. For the whale, the seal, etc., we say *napiaq* and *skwewiaq*, with *pniaskwit*; for other fish *napeme'kw* and *skweme'kw*. For the canine race, *napesm* and *skwesm*. For the moose, the caribou, the ox, the sheep, we use *iap* and *l'kwetu*; however, after the introduction of the cow, *wen'jutia'm*, the Frenchman's moose, it was thought important to keep in Mi'kmaw the French name of the bull, *latto'law*, as also that of the horse, *te'sipow*, and for the mare we have this charming Mi'kmaw creation *te'sipow-l'kwetu*, "a female horse." For the smaller animals (otter, fox, etc.) we have *nape'kwik* and *skwe'kwik*; for the beaver *plmskw* and *nusumskw*; for chickens, *napew* and *skwew*, which becomes *pnet*, when the hen lays. It is certainly this latter which resembles the word *squaw*; the ladies, *saqma'skwaq*, would certainly not be flattered by having the title applied to them.

But since neither the adjectives, nor the pronouns, nor the verbs vary in agreement with the sex of the animate beings, there is no other way to represent it from a grammatical point of view. On the other hand, the essential distinction between animate and inanimate gender is the basis of the whole grammatical system, especially in the verbs.

II. Number

There are three numbers in Mi'kmaw: the singular, the plural and the dual. This latter is used, not only for two persons or two things, but for a larger number of a single category. In nouns, the plural is not distinguished from the dual except when they take the form of a verb, which happens very frequently. Thus, *ji'nm*, "man," becomes *ji'nmuk*, in the plural as in the dual; but we are able to make such words as *ji'nmuijik* (dual) and *ji'nmultijik* (plural), from the verb *ji'nmui*, "I am a man."

The plural in the nouns, the adjectives and some pronouns, is formed by adding *k* to the singular for the animate gender and *l* for the inanimate gender, with or without vowel, according to usage and euphony. And so we have *kisiku*, "old man," which becomes *kisiku'k*, "old men"; *skus*, "weasel," *skusk*; for things of animate gender, *eptaqn*, "dish," *eptaqnk*; *wow*, "pot," *wowk*; for the inanimate gender, *wa'w*, "egg," *wa'wl*; *sipu*, "river," *sipu'l*; *mun'ti*, "pocket, bag," *mun'ti'l*; *awti*, "path, road," *awti'l*; *elue'wuti*, "sin," *elue'wuti'l*; *sape'wuti*, "virtue," *sape'wuti'l*.

Nouns in *-aw*, *-ew*, ordinarily give *-aq*, *-al*, such as *saqmaw*, "gentleman," *saqmaq*, "gentlemen"; *latto'law*, "bull," *latto'laq*; *klitaw*, "raspberry," *klitaq*;

alikew, "cloth," *alikal*, "clothes"; *maqmikew*, "land," *maqmikal*; *kun'tew*, "stone," *kun'tal*. *Aklasie'w*, "English," regularly becomes *Aklasie'wk*; *malike'w*, "barrel," *malike'wk*; and *napew*, *napewk*, "male bird." Likewise *Wenuj*, "Frenchman," *Wenujk*; *Talian*, "Italian," *Taliank*. But *Spanio'l*, "Spaniard," becomes *Spanio'laq*, *Alma*, "German," *Almaq*; *L'nate*, "Irishman," *L'nateaq*; *Mi'kmawa'j*, "Mi'kmaw," *Mi'kmaq*; *Kanipewa'j*, "Abenaki," *Kanipewaq*; *kiplno'l*, "governor," *kiplno'laq*; *tia'm*, "moose," *tia'muk*; *kiwnik*, "otter," *kiwnikik*; *sinumkw*, "wild goose," *sinumkwaq*; *muin*, *muinaq*, "bear"; *te'sipow*, "horse," *te'sipowk*; *mia'wj*, *qajue'wj*, "cat," *mia'wjik*, *qajue'wjik*; *nme'j*, "fish," *nme'jik*; *jijklue'wj*, "sheep," *jijklue'wjik*; *iap*, "male," *iapaq*; *iapaq jijklue'wjik*, "rams"; the diminutive *jijklue'wji'jk*, "lambs," is regular; *jqolj*, "toad," *jqoljik*. The names of women in -*skw* become -*skwaq*; those in -*skwe'j* regularly become -*skwe'jk*. *Kopit*, "beaver," becomes *kopitaq*; but in general names in -*t* become -*jik* in the plural, such as *e'pit*, "woman," *e'pijik*; *eleke'wit*, "king," *eleke'wijik*; *ansale'wit*, "angel," *ansale'wijik*; *tepknuset*, "month, moon," *tepknusejik*. Similarly for the adjectives: *wikapuksit klitaw*, "a raspberry of good flavour," *wikapuksijik klitaq*; *melkiknat kinap*, "a strong giant," *melkiknajik kinapaq*; *pukwelk*, *pukwelkik*; *meskilk*, *meskilkik*, etc.

Names of birds in -*i* take -*aq*: *apaqtuiaq*, "marsh bittern"; *klopskiaq*, "falcon"; *muiaq*, "sea duck"; *tma'qaniaq*, "shell bird"; similarly the generic name *meljekuiaq*, "bird without feathers."

Certain names of fish in -*me'kw* become in the plural -*maq*: *amlmekw*, *amlmaq*, "mackerel"; *aqoqme'kw*, *aqoqma'q*, "herring"; in Restigouche this word is not used, we simply say *nme'jij*, "small fish"; *wipetme'kw*, *wipetmaq*, "shark"; *wapnme'kw*, *wapnmaq*, "white porpoise"; *sapetime'kw*, *sapetimaq*, "grampus"; similarly the generic name of male and female, *napeme'kw*, and *skweme'kw*, become *napema'q* and *skwema'q*.

Here now are the principal names of things personified or of animate gender, with their plural: *aqm*, *aqmk*, "snow shoes," also *nasawkwaw*, *nasawkwaq*. *Emqwanji'j*, "spoon"; *emqwan*, "soup spoon." *Apoqoksit*, *apoqoksijik* (or *lapa'y*), "cauldron, boiler, kettle." *A'papi*, *a'papi'k*, "thread, line"; *kjia'papi*, "the equator." *A'pi*, *a'pi'k*, "nets." *Api* or *tapi*, *api'k* or *tapi'k*, "bow." *Apsute'kan*, *apsute'kank*, "doll." *Atuomkomin*, *atuomkomink*, "strawberries." *Ajioqjomin*, *ajioqjomink*, "blackberries, brambles." *L'no'qoqm*, *l'no'qoqmk*, "skates." *L'nuoqta'w*, *l'nuoqta'q*, "statue." *Epsaqtej*, *epsaqtejk*, "stove." *Etu'kutewe'k* or *etu'kmikewe'k*, "scapula" (no singular). *Ila'skw*, *ila'skuk*, "cards"; *ila'sku kesalaji*, "he likes cards, card games." *Wasiantej*, *wasiantejk*, "lamp (glass)." *Wow*, *wowk*, "pot, vase, vessel." *Wskijipnekw*, *wskijipnekuk*, "hosts." *Wqosi*, *wqosi'k*, "nails"; *wqosi'muska'laji*, "he shows his claws."

Kawatkw, *kawatkuk*, "spruce"; *kawatkupi*, "spruce beer." *Kawi*, *kawi'k*, "porcupine quill." *Kawiksa'w*, *kawiksa'q*, "thorns." *Kawskusi*, *kawskusi'k*, "cedar." *Qamu, qamu'k,* "suet pudding." *Kaju, kaju'k,* "wild pepper." *Kloqoej, kloqoejk,* "stars." *Kmu'j, kmu'jik,* "tree (standing)"; *sape'wit kmu'j,* "Christmas tree." *Kikamkun, kikamkunk,* "perch." *Kmtn, kmtnk,* "mountain"; *pmtn, pmtnk,* "ridge"; *Kisu'lkw wpmtniktuk,* "on the mountain of God." *Kuow, kuaq,* "pine." *Ko'komin, ko'komink,* "sloes"; *wen'jui-ko'komink,* "plums, prunes"; *watapsit, watapsijik,* "yellow ones." *Kopji'j, kopji'jk* or *kopsiji'jk,* "cup." *Klujjiewta'sit, klujjiewta'sijik,* "crucifix." *Ksu'sk, ksu'skik,* "black spruce." *Kjikmuatkw, kjikmuatkuk,* "white pine."

Lakko'l, lakko'lk, "cord (of wood)"; almost all nouns with *la* are French nouns, that may be easily recognized. *Laklus, laklusk,* "jug"; *sa'qawey mimey etek,* "there is oil or rancid grease in it." *Lapa'y, lapa'yk,* "tub, bucket." *Lappelis, lappelisk,* "yard (measure)." *Lapilask,* "linen"; I have not heard it used in the singular. *Lapwel, lapwelk,* "hair." *Lapolji'j, lapolji'jk,* "bowl, cup"; *waju'pet, waju'pejik,* "full." *Lassiet, lassietk,* "plate." *La'taqsun, la'taqsunk,* "pail or bucket (for carrying)"; *nqapaqsun, nqapaqsunk,* "a dipper": *e'pit elajl: Saqmaw, nqapaqsun moqwe kekkunawkw aqq nqano'pati pitalqek,* "the woman says to Jesus: Master, you have no bucket to draw water and the well is deep." *Letqa'mun, letqa'munk,* "arrow." *Lipqatamun, lipqatamunk,* "lady's slipper (plant)"; *lipqomutaqn, lipqomutaqnk,* "top"; *kiwto'qwa'jijit,* "turns"; *mimntet,* "while spinning."

Malike'w, malike'wk, "barrel." *Missemin, missemink,* "blackcurrants." *Mlakej* or *molakej, molakejk,* "milk, breasts"; at Restigouche always used in the plural for milk: *molakejk kwejaqmiejik,* "boiled milk." *Mkisn,* "shoe, footware, mocassin," has two plurals, but with a different sense; M. Maillard only uses the inanimate plural *mkisnl* (Grammar p. 9), but the other that the Indians pronounced *mokasnk,* is just as sure, and means shoes with a sole, boots; the first means the original ancient mocassins and also modern slippers and worn-out shoes; the difference is accentuated in the possessive: *nmkisnl, kmkisnl, wmkisnl; nmuksnk, kmuksnk, wmuksn,* "my, your, his footware"; for the animate gender, Mr. Rand only uses *wen'juksnank* (animate), "French footware," and *mkisnl* (inanimate), "Indian shoe," and makes an attempt at humour by asking if this difference is to be considered as a compliment for the French (see dictionary p. 233); well, no, there is neither compliment nor mockery; but it was newer, and, for the Indians, more mysterious; today they are proud to wear them, just as White men are quite happy to use Indian shoes in Winter in the woods and elsewhere.

Napui'kikn, napi'kiknk, "portrait, photograph." *Naskoplaw, naskoplaq,* "planks." *Nimnoqn, nimnoqnk,* "birch." *Nipi, nipi'k,* "leaves, cabbages"; Mr. Rand gives *nipi'l,* inanimate plural, to indicate a cabbage; I have never met this distinction in the usage of the Indians. *Nalko'n, nalko'nk, nukwaltuko'n, nukwaltuko'nk,* "comb." *Nqani'psmun, nqani'psmunk,* "chalice."

Pakusi, pakusi'k, "lily." *Pekilew, pekilewk,* "glass"; *pekilewiktuk teli ksike'lmuksin,* "vas honorabile." *Pesmkewey* or *peskmkewey, peskmkewe'k,* "any object of piety, images, medals, relics, etc." *Pito'qn, pito'qnk,* "cloak, shroud."

Kpijoqosuti, kpijoqosuti'k, "pin, button." *Puessu, puessuaq,* "bushel." *Pui'kn, pui'knk,* "broom." *Pu'tay, pu'tayk,* "bottle." *Pqaw, pqaq* or *pqwaq,* "spruce bark"; *pqawikan, pqawikanl,* "cabin covered with spruce bark." *Pku, pku'k,* "gum, resin, incense, wax"; for the latter *lasi'l* is also used for sealing wax, which is also of animate gender, but has no plural; *pkuo'q, pkuo'qok,* "incense box"; *npukum, kpukum, wpukuml,* "my, your, his gum, chewing gum."

Sa'qati, sa'qati'k, "needle." *Sekepen* or *sikapun, sekapenk,* "artichoke"; *wen'ju'sukapun,* "turnips." *Ksispanikn* or *suspanikn, suspaniknk,* "soap"; *musapoqjat,* "soft (soap)." *Suppin, suppink,* "cup"; *stoqnamuksijik suppink,* "green cups." *Stoqn, stoqnk,* "fir, branches of fir, palms"; *stoqnk kewkunujik,* "Palm Sunday." *Sunmink* or *semuimink,* "rosary"; these have no singular.

Tapatat, tapatatk; in Restigouche *tapatan, tapatank,* "potatoes." *Tmelet, tmeletk,* "glass (tumbler)." *Tlako'pn, tlako'pnk,* "hellebore, hemlock, poisonous plant." *Tmoqta'w, tmoqta'q,* "trunk of a tree." *Tu'aqn, tu'aqnk,* "ball (for games)." *Tupi* or *tutupi, tutupi'k,* "spruce root"; *ketanaji tutupi'-a,* "he is collecting roots."

For the inanimate gender, words ending in a vowel which is not a diphthong simply take *-l* (see the examples below); those in *-aw, -ew,* the diphthongs, become *-al*; those that end in a consonant take *-l* (syllabic *l*); those in *-aq* and in *-uk*, become phonetically *-aqal* and *-ukul*, such as *puksuk, puksukul,* "fire wood"; *jikuksuk, jikuksukul,* "tinder"; the same is true for adjectives: *telamu'k, telamu'kul,* "equal, such"; *telamu'kipnikl* (past); *wikapu'k, wikapu'kul,* "tasting good"; *melkiknaq, melkiknaqal,* "strong." Most of the others take *l*; examples: *A'kwesn, a'kwesnl,* "headgear"; *kelu'lk, kelu'lkl,* "beautiful, good." *Alame's, alame'sl* (from French), "mass"; *meski'k, meski'kl,* "for high mass"; *apje'jk, apje'jkl,* "for low mass." *Alawey* (not used), *alawe'l,* "peas"; *wikk,* "sweet, tasty," becomes *wikkl*. *Su'n, su'nl,* "berry"; *sewk, sewkl* or *sewkul,* "sweet"; *sewkewey, sewkewe'l,* "tid bits"; *mimi'l* (which has no singular), "sugared almond or sugar-covered pill"; *wen'ju'su'n, wen'ju'su'nl,* "apples"; *wataptek, wataptekl,* "yellow ones"; *eule'jk, eule'jkl,* "poor ones"; *suklikaq, suklikaql,* "rotten ones." *Awti,* "way or road," becomes *awti'l*; but *awti'j,* "path," becomes *awti'jl*; *wi'katikn, wi'katiknl,* "book, paper, letter"; *kwitn, kwitnl,* "canoe"; *wlaqn, wlaqnl,* "vase"; *topaqn, topaqnl*; likewise *nipit, nipitl,* "my teeth"; *na'kwek, na'kwekl,* "day"; *tepkik, tepkikl,* "night." *Nitu'l, kitu'l, witu'l,* "beard or side whiskers," has no singular; *kitu'linal,* "our beards"; *witu'lual,* "their beards." *Witui* or *wituay,* "to have a beard"; *maqtewi'tuat,* "he has a black beard"; *Pekitualuet,* (ancient chief of Cape Breton), "Long Beard."

In the words which end in *-n* in the singular, it is normally the practice to double this consonant to form the plural, instead of adding *-l*: *wen'ju'su'nn*, "apples"; *wlaqnn*, "vases"; *kjialasutmaqnn*, "sacraments"; *kwitnn*, "canoes"; *mkisnn*, "footwear," and in order to insist on it, a final *-a* is added, *mkisnn-a*.

Just like nouns, adjectives in *-ey*, which are numberless, have a plural in *-e'l*, but for these latter there is the important difference that the singular serves for both genders and that they have another plural in *-e'k*, when they relate to a noun or a pronoun of animate gender.

Examples: *amskwesewey*, "first"; *amskwesewey pukuales*, "first swallow"; *amskwesewey kekina'masuti*, "first lesson"; *amskwesewe'k pukualesk*; *amskwesewe'l kekina'masuti'l*; *wtejkewey, wtejkewe'k, wtejkewe'l*, "last." *Piley, pile'k, pile'l*, "new"; *piley musuey*, "new handkerchief"; *piley malsan*, "a new shopkeeper"; *pile'l wa'wl*, "fresh eggs"; *pile'k nipi'k*, "new cabbages, fresh cabbages." *Sa'qawey, sa'qawe'k, sa'qawe'l*, "old, ancient"; *sa'qawe'l koqoe'l*, "ancient things"; *sa'qawe'k puowinaq*, "old witches or sorcerers." *Piluey, pilue'k, pilue'l*, "other, different"; *ktik*, "other" (adjective and pronoun) becomes *ktikik, ktikl*; *ta'n, ta'nik, ta'nl*; *teken, tekenik, tekenl*, "which?" *Mitiey, mitie'k, mitie'l*, "of a poplar tree"; *mitie'k nipi'k*, "poplar leaves"; *mitie'l nipisoqnl* or *nipispaqnl*, "poplar shoots" (Genesis 30, 37); likewise *l'nuey*, "Indian"; *mi'kmawey*, "Mi'kmaw"; *ni'newey, ki'lewey, nekmewey*, etc.

The plural of the cardinal numbers is in *-jik* and *-al, -el, -ol*. Apart from *newte'jit*, "one," they have no singular.

Newte'jit, newte'jk, "a person, a thing"; *newte'jijik, newte'jkl*, "they are one."
Tapusijik, tapu'kl, "two persons, two things."
Ne'sisijik, ne'siskl, "three."
Newijik, newkl, "four."
Nanijik, nankl, "five."

From *asukom*, "six," *te'sijik*, and *te'sikl* are added.
L'uiknek, ukumuljin, pesqunatek, mtln te'sijik, te'sikl, "seven," "eight," "nine," "ten"; for the latter we also say *newtiskeksijik, newtiska'ql*, "ten persons," "ten things."
Tapuiskeksijik, tapuiska'qal or *tapuinska'ql*, "twenty."
Nesiskeksijik, nesiska'ql, "thirty."
Newiskeksijik, newiska'ql, "forty."
Naniskeksijik, naniska'ql, "fifty."
Beginning with sixty, we put, as above, *asukom, l'uiknek*, etc., with *te'siskeksijik, te'siska'ql* or *te'sinska'ql*.
Kaskmtlnaqnijik, kaskmtlnaqnl, "hundred"; *pitui-mtlnaqnijik, pitui-mtlnaqnl*, "thousand"; *kjipitui-mtlnaqnijik, kjipitui-mtlnaqnl*, "million."

LESSON SEVEN

NOUNS AND ADJECTIVES (CONTINUATION)

III. Tense

A distinction is also made, in the nouns, the adjectives and some pronouns, between present tense and past tense, and in some of them, the future. The past of the animate gender is formed by adding *-aq* to the present and *-o'q* for proper names; the inanimate gender takes *-ek*. The plural is in *-ik* or *-kik*, and *-kel* respectively.

Examples: *l'nu*, "man, Indian," past *l'nuaq*; *l'nu'k, l'nu'kik*, "men." *Ji'nm, ji'nmaq, ji'nmuk, ji'nmukik* or *ji'nmukwik*; this *w* that is added for vowel harmony is scarcely heard; it is the same in other words in *-uk*, even in *l'nu'k*, which could be written *l'nu'kwik*. *E'pit, e'pitaq*, "woman"; the plural of the past, and others like it, is formed on the present singular more easily than on the plural (*e'pijik*): *e'pitkik*. Proper names: *Ata, Atao'q*; *E'p, E'po'q*; *Nawey, Naweyo'q*; *E'li, E'lio'q*; *L'ui, L'uio'q*; *Misel, Miselo'q*; *Anie's, Anie'so'q*; *Mali, Malio'q*. This tells us that they are dead, or just simply absent. It is quite remarkable that we never put the name of Jesus in the past, nor that of Mary, *Ma'li*, the Blessed Virgin. The names of angels are put in the past, when we speak of a revelation or of a past fact: *ansale'wito'q, ansale'witkik*. We also say *Sosepo'q* for Saint Joseph. This ending in *-o'q* is still used for certain common nouns of people that end in *-skw*. For example: *kisikui'skw*, "an old lady"; *kisikui'skwo'q* (if she is dead or absent); *kisikui'skwaq*, "old ladies"; *kisikui'skwaqik*, "the female dead, feminine ancestors." *Kisikuaq*, "an old man"; *kisiku'kik*, "the ancients," and *sa'qawe'jkik*, the present of which is not used. *Pilat*, "Pilate," *Pilato'q, Po's Pilato'q saqmawitek*, "Pontius Pilate being in command"; if we wrote *saqmawito'q*, adjective form, that would mean that he was governor, the other form (verbal) means under his administration; *amaskwiplnutaq, klujjiewto'taq, nepkaq, utqotalutaq*, "Jesus suffered, literally was tormented, crucified, he died, was buried"; *lamqamu'k*, "under ground, under the earth"; *eli-pkewietaq*, "he descended"; *tapukuna'qek* (past inanimate), "two days later"; *tapukuna'q*, "two days"; *tapukuna'qek*, " two days having passed"; *weji-minu'nsisni neplipni* (see accusative case below), he rose again from the dead. *Pipnaqn*, "bread," *pipnaqnek, pipnaqnl, pipnaqnkl, pipnaqnek wesua'toqsi-pnek*, "he took bread." The seasons have a separate form of the past; see below.

There are adjectives which have the same root, but with a different ending for the two genders and for the two numbers. Examples: *meski'k*, "big," becomes *meskilk* in the animate gender, plurals *meski'kl* and *meskilkik*; past *meskilkaq, meskilknik, meski'kek, meski'kikl*; *meskilk saqmaw*, "an important gentleman," *meskilkik saqmaq*, "important gentlemen"; *meskilkaq saqmawaq, meskilknik saqmaqik*; *meski'k wen'ji'kuom*, "a large house," *meski'kl wen'ji'kuoml, meski'kek wen'ji'kuomek, meski'kikl wen'ji'kuomkl*. *Maqa'q*, "large"; *maqa'ql pipnaqnl, maqa'qek pipnaqnek, maqa'qikl pipnaqnkl*; *maqoqsit malike'w*, "a large barrel"; *maqoqsijik, maqoqsitaq, maqoqsitkik*. *Pita'q*, "long," *pitoqsit*; *pita'qawe'l*, "trousers." *Newta'q wasoqnmaqn*, "a candle"; *newtoqsit pu'tay*, "a bottle"; *newta'qek, newtoqsitaq*. *Kelu'lk, kelu'sit*, "good, beautiful"; *kelu'lkek, kelu'sitaq*. *Eule'jk, eule'jit*, "poor, wretched"; *eule'jkek, eule'jitaq*. *Welamu'k, welamkusit, welamuksit*, "good looking"; *welamu'kwek, welamkusitaq* or *welamuksitaq*.

The future is in *-uk*, but it is hardly used except for the seasons, in words which express time itself and for the interrogative adverb *ta'n*. Examples: *kesik*, "winter"; *ksin*, "last winter"; *ksinuk*, "next winter"; *-puk* is also used in compounds; *wejkwipuk*, "winter is coming, the winter which is coming"; *pejipuk*, "the winter which is close"; *pemipuk*, "during the winter"; *ktikipuk*, "the past winter"; *aqtapuk*, "in the depth of the winter"; *teknek na'kwe'k weskijinuiss?* "On what day was our Saviour born?" *Aqtatpa'qek eta aqtapukwek tlisip weskijinuiss*, "in the middle of the night, in the depth of the winter that was when he was born." *Nipk*, "summer," *nipn*, "last summer"; *nipnuk*, "next summer," *ktiki-nipn*, "the summer before." *Sikw*, "springtime"; *sikun*, "last spring"; *ktiki-sikun*, "springtime before"; *sikunuk*, "next spring"; we also say *paniaq, paniaqek, panianuk*. *Toqwa'q*, "autumn"; *tqoq*, "last autumn," *ktikitqoq*, "the autumn before"; *tqo'nuk*, "next autumn." *Ta'n, ta'nik, ta'nuk?* "When?" *Eskitpu'k* or *eksitpu'k*, "the morning"; *eksitpu'kwek*, "yesterday morning"; normally *wlaku*, "yesterday," is joined to it, *wela'kwek*, "yesterday evening"; *wlo'nuk*, "this evening"; *eksitpu'nuk*, "tomorrow morning": *sapo'nuk*, "tomorrow"; *ktiki-sapo'nuk*, "the day after tomorrow." *Sepey*, "this morning." *Wapk*, "the morning" (future sense); *wapn*, "the dawn"; *wapkek*, "at the break of day"; *wapna'ki*, "the land of the dawn, of the Abenaki." *Keket ketui-wla'kwek ktiki-wla'kw nepkaq Pie'lo'q kikmenuaq, Pie'lo'q eta ta'naq kilew weli-kjijioqsipnaq, ansma kinapewamuksisnaq*, "the day before yesterday towards evening Peter our brother died, this Peter that you have known so well, who had a truly martial appearance (Father Maillard, letter P. 295). *Kinap*, "giant, hero, warrior"; *kinapi'skw*, "Amazon"; *kinapaq, kinapi'skwo'q. Tpuk*, "this morning"; *tpuk kisakisiss*, "this morning or during the past night, there was a full moon" (10 words in two); *wlo'nuk kisakisitew*, "this evening it will be full"; *tpu'nuk*, "during the night which is beginning."

IV. The Cases

In Mi'kmaw there are four cases, besides the simple form of the nominative, or four distinct endings, according to the function of the noun and the adjective.

Father Maillard curiously begins this section, which is the first of his grammar (P. 5): "Among the Mi'kmaq he says, nouns are not declined"; and then right away he speaks of the accusative which is governed by the verbs, and further on of the nominative, and even elsewhere of genitives, datives and ablatives (Pp. 36 and 198). Likewise in his copy, M. Bellenger thought it necessary to add a note: "Contrary to M. Maillard I note an oblique case, which is the equivalent of the Latin accusative." Elsewhere he repeats, after the master, that nouns vary their endings and even their beginnings, according to the different tenses, numbers, persons, and according to their relation as subjects or objects of the verb. They also vary when they are affected by a negation or a contraction. This is what is meant when we speak of cases.

1. The accusative [i.e. the obviative] is found in nouns, pronouns and adjectives of the animate gender only, when they are used as a direct or indirect object of a verb or even of another noun or pronoun in the third person. It is formed, for the singular, by adding *-l* to the nominative, with or without a vowel, and in the plural, by contrast, by deleting the final *-k*.

Examples: *Kisu'lkw teplmajl l'nu'l*, "God judges man"; *Se'sus westawiaji l'nu'*, "Jesus saves men." Names in the singular past, which end in *-k*, delete it also, as in the plural (see *Ta'pito'q*, below). In nouns or verbal adjectives, the syllable *-li-* is inserted before the ending: *eleke'wit*, "king," *mimajuinu kepmite'lmajl eleke'wilijl*, "the individual respects the king"; *saqmaq elkimkwi'tij eleke'wiliji*, "the chiefs are appointed by the kings"; or else, *eleke'wit elkimajl saqmal*, "the king appoints the chief"; *eleke'wijik elkima'tiji saqma*, "the kings appoint the chiefs." *Kisu'lkw tali-ewlite'lmasnika Ata'l aqq E'pal knki'kwinaqa*? "How did the Creator take pity on Adam and Eve, our first parents?" *Telimasnika eta*: *elmiknik e'pit mte'skml wunuji paske'skmuatal*, "he said to them: later on the woman shall crush the serpent's head." *Wen ta ula e'pit*? "Who is this woman?" *Kkijinu Ma'li eta, ta'n wekwisisnl* *westau'lkwl*, "Our mother Mary, who had the Saviour as her son." *Wenl toqonasi'tisnl?* "Who was her spouse?" *Sape'wilijl eta Sosepal, kitk Ta'pito'q wejikitisna*, "it was Saint Joseph, both of them were descended from David."

It is the same thing for nouns and pronouns in the third person that depend on another in the same person, in the singular or the plural: Michael's cat becomes Michael his cat, *Misel wti'l*; the disciples of our Lord become in the same way, *kniskaminu wnaqapem*; although there is no -*k* here, the mark of the animate plural, there is no confusion as a result, because in the singular one would write *wnaqapeml*, "his disciple." If this noun or pronoun object is accompanied by a verb or a verbal adjective, this too is also put into the accusative with -*li*: *mijua'ji'j jipalajl maqoqsilijl muinal*, "the child is afraid of the big bear." When the verb or the noun or verbal adjective already has an -*l* in its ending, this -*li*- is changed into -*ni*-. And so in the preceding example, if one had had *meskilk*, big this would become in the accusative *meskilnijl muinal*, "the big bear." *Muin* is also the name of the constellation.

2. The second case is the terminative. It is an -*a* added to any word which ends a period of discourse. Thus in the preceding propositions, one would end by *elkimajl saqmal-a*, and even *elkima'tiji saqama-a*, with a little breath between the two *a*'s; likewise *meskilnijl muinal-a*. We take no note of this case in our lessons, because it entirely up to the speaker.

3. The third is the locative. It is a -*k* added to the end of words expressing a place, with or without modification of the final syllable. It is the abbreviation of *iktuk*, "in, on."

Examples: *maqmikew*, "the earth"; *maqmikek*, "on earth"; one could say: *maqmikew iktuk*, but that would more likely mean in the earth. When the word already ends by -*k*, nothing is added. Example: *nujjinen wa'so'q epin*, "our Father who art in heaven"; but if one wanted to insist on the name of the place, or by emphasis, one would write *wa'so'qiktuk*. In this case a real preposition is used, *iktuk*, but which is always placed after the word, as in *vobiscum* in Latin. For proper names the locative is in -*ek* and indicates the residence, the abode, as *Sosepek*, "at Joseph's"; *I'sni'skwek*, "at Mrs. Eason's house," Bloody Creek (Annapolis County, Nova Scotia); similarly *puowinek, klaptanek*, "at the sorcerer's, at the blacksmith's." In the possessives are found striking modifications. Thus: *Kniskaminu*, "Our Lord," to express: "in Our Lord," will be changed into *Kniskaminaq*; in this regard the Indians observed that it is as if one were speaking of several Lords; *wkutputimuaq*, "on their seats"; *wtawtiwaq*, "on their paths," (Ps. 1).

4. The fourth case is the vocative. It is only found in the singular in a few nouns expressing relationship, such as *nujj*, "my father," vocative *nu*, "Father, Dad, you my father"; this term expresses tenderness; it is rarely used in

speaking to the priest; one says *nujj*, and also and even more so *nujjinen*, "our Father." *Nkij*, "my mother"; *kiju'*, "mother, Mom, you my mother." *Nkwis*, "my son"; *kwis*, "you my son." *Ntus*, "my daughter"; *tus*, "you my daughter." *Niskami'* or *nijkami'*, "you grandfather"; *nukumi'* "grandmother"; *klamuksi'*, "uncle"; *sukwi'*, "aunt"; *kewkuni'*, *kewkuski'*, "god-father or god-mother," etc. In the plural these names of address are much more numerous, and the formation of them is simple and uniform: one has only to change the final *-k* of the simple plural into *-tut*. We can begin by *nujjtut*, "my fathers," as addressed to priests, and *nujjinenatut*, "our fathers"; *nsistut*, "my brothers"; *nmistut*, "my sisters"; *nijantut*, "my children"; this word or its diminutitive *nijanji'jtut*, "my little children," that is to say, "my dear children," replaces in the mouth of the priest the words "my brethren, my dear brethren," in the pulpit as in conversation.

Chief Lamorue, from Prince Edward Island, began his speech, at the Third Centenary in 1910 with these words: *kjipa'tlia'stut aqq pa'tlia'stut, aqq kilew aniapsuinutut* (religious) *nujjinatut* (our Fathers), *aqq kilew l'nu saqmatut aqq keptinetut* (an English word, captain), *aqq nkijtut ta'n te'sioq mi'kmawi'skwultioq* (all you Mi'kmaw mothers and ladies); and later on: *wijikmuloq mi'kmatut*, "Mi'kmaq my brothers" (Souvenir, p. 37).

Here are a few other examples, in constant use: *ji'nmutut*, "you men"; *e'pittut*, "you women"; *lpa'tu'stut, e'pite'stut*; *ni'kmatut*, "my allies, my brothers," (relations in general); *nitaptut, nitapji'jtut*, "friends, buddies"; with the most intimate: *oqotitut* from *oqoti*, shortened to *ti* is seldom used in the singular except between spouses; there is also *tutut*, from *tuey*, "comrades," but which, except in military style, sounds somewhat trivial. The heroic captain René at the siege of Louisbourg in 1745, gave his soldiers the order to attack with these words: *tutut matntinej*, "comrades, let us fight" (letter of M. Maillard, p. 372). Our Lord addressed his disciples with the words *naqapemtut* or *nijintut*.

LESSON EIGHT

NOUNS AND ADJECTIVES (CONTINUATION)

V. Diminutive and augmentative

To the cases we should also add the diminutive and the augmentative. The first of these is formed by adding *-ji'j*, or simply *-i'j*, if the word begins in *j*, or just *j* alone, if the preceding vowel is suitable. The second of these is formed by adding the prefix *kji-* (*kesi-* or *ksi-* with adjectives and verbs).

Examples: *eleke'wit,* "king"; *kji-eleke'wit,* "great king, emperor"; *pa'tlia's,* "priest"; *kji-pa'tlia's,* "bishop"; *pa'tlia'sji'j,* "cleric"; *kji-pa'tlia'sji'j,* "prelate." *E'pit,* "woman"; *e'pitji'j,* "little woman, dear creature"; *e'pite's,* "girl"; *e'pite'ji'j,* "little girl." *Eleke'wi'skw,* "queen"; *kji-eleke'wi'skw,* "empress"; *eleke'wi'skwe'j,* "princess"; *eleke'wi'skwe'ji'j,* "little princess." There is a double diminutive in these, a frequent occurrence. Likewise *saqmaw,* "chief, master, lord," becomes *kji-saqmaw,* "great lord, the proper name of the Lord"; *saqma'j,* "little chief, son of the chief"; *saqma'ji'j,* "baby chief"; *saqmatut,* "gentlemen"; for gentleman there is only *saqmaw*. *Saqma'skw,* "the chief's wife," or simply "a lady"; *saqma'skwe'j, saqma'skwe'ji'j,* "a miss"; *saqma'skwe'tut,* "ladies"; *saqama'skwe'jtut,* "mesdemoiselles." *Kji-saqmaw,* "great chief, great lord," is normally used only for God. *Niskam,* "God"; *kji-niskam,* "the great God"; *kji-sape'wit, kjikelu'sit,* "the holy, the good above all." *Niskamij,* "grandfather, ancestor"; *pitui-niskamijk,* "ancestors."

In the same way, for the inanimate gender, there is *pipnaqn,* "bread"; *pipnaqnji'j,* "roll," or rather "a little bread"; *pipnaqsikn,* "a piece of bread, a pancake"; *pipnaqsiknu'j,* "a little piece." *Samuqwan,* "water"; *samuqwanji'j,* "a drop of water." *Ni'k,* "my cabin"; *ni'kji'j,* "my little cabin, my dear little place of my own." *Koqoey,* "something"; *koqoe'ji'j,* "a little something"; and even *koqoe'juey, koqoe'jue'l,* "a trifle, trifles"; *talapankitulki-p?* "how were you paid?" *koqoe'jue'l eta iknmuimkisnl*, "they gave me a few trifles" (Grammar, Maillard, 62). *Sipu*, "river"; *kji-sipu*, "great river"; hence the name of *sisipu*, Weymouth; there, and in other regions, they soften the pronunciation of *j* in pronouncing the diminutives and some augmentatives after the fashion of the Maliseet, as *sipu'si's*, "stream," that the Mi'kmaq elsewhere pronounce *jipu'ji'j*; *e'pite'si's*, *lmu'si's*, etc.; *wlaqn*, "vase, recipient"; *kji-wlaqn, wlaqnji'j*; locative *wlaqnk, wlaqnji'jk*. *Apje'jk, apje'ji'jk*, "little, quite little, very little."

VI. Agreement of adjectives

They agree with the nouns to which they relate in gender, in number, in tense and in case.

Examples: *meskilk ansale'wit*, "a great angel"; *meskilkik ansale'wijik*; *meskilkaq ansale'witaq*; *meskilkipnik* (verbal form) or *meskilultitkik ansale'witkik*; for archangel there is *kji-ansale'wit*; a newly baptized child is called *ansale'witji'j*. *Meski'k alasutmo'kuom*, "great church"; *kji-alasutmo'kuom*, "cathedral"; *meski'kl alasutmo'kuoml*; *meski'kik alasutmo'kuomik*; *meski'kipnl* (verbal form) *alasutmo'kuoml*; *meski'kji'j alasutmo'kuomji'j*, "a somewhat large chapel"; *kesimsiki'k kji-alasutmo'kuom*, "an immense cathedral." *Teke'k, teke'ji'jk eskitpu'k*, "this morning is cold, a little cold"; *teke'kek, teke'ji'jkek ktikek eskitpukwek*, "it was cold, fresh, the other morning." *Sape'wuti*, "virtue"; *kaqai'skl sape'wuti'l*, "there are several virtues"; *kji-sape'wuti'l*, "the theological virtues"; *ne'siskl*, "they are three"; *elue'wuti*, "sin, evil"; *kji-l'ue'wuti'l*, "the deadly sins"; *l'uiknek te'sikl*, "there are seven of them"; *kji-alasutmaqn*, "sacrament"; *kji-alasutmaqnl elp l'uiknek te'sikl*, "there are also seven sacraments"; *alasutmaqnji'j*, "a short prayer, an invocation," *naqmaje'jk*, "is easy," *jel wjit mijua'ji'jk*, "even for the children." *Nemituapnek samuqwanek weji-tuiaqappnek alasutmo'kuomk inaqneke'l*, "vidi aquam ..."; *waqntew* "bone," *waqntal, waqntewe'k, waqntewe'kl*; *melke'k, melke'kl*, "hard." *Kun'tew, kun'tewe'k*, "stone, rock"; *kun'te'j*, "little stone, pebble"; *kun'te'jik*. *Kun'tew* is also a proper name of a family, "Condo"; in this form it becomes in the past *kun'tewaq, kun'tewi'skw, kun'tewi'sqwaq, kun'tewi'skwe'j, kun'tewi'skwe'jaq*, etc. *Kutputi*, "seat"; *mutputi*, "chair, bench"; *mujkajewey*, "well-made, excellent, pleasant, suitable"; *kutputiek, mujkajeweyek, kutputiekl, mujkajeweyekl*.

VII. Degrees of comparison

They can be found in adjectives, verbs and adverbs.

1. The comparative of equality is expressed in Mi'kmaw by *teli-*, and the second member becomes the first. Example: "Paul is as strong as Peter,"

Pie'l teli-melkiknat Po'l teli-melkiknat, and it can be shortened as follows: *Pie'l teliknat Po'l teliknat*, or expressed by *tetpi*, "equally"; *tetpiknajik*, "they are of equal strength." The Son is as great as his Father and the Holy Spirit, *Ewjit Niskam tetpikili'tijl Wujjl aqq Weji-wli-Niskaml*. "Thy will be done on earth as it is in heaven," *na'te'l wa'so'q eykik teli-sqataskik jiptuk elp ninen teli-sqatulek maqmikek eymek*; "the great God is as much at ease in hell as in paradise," *Kjiniskam wa'so'q teli-wle'k mntua'kik teli-wle'k*; *teli-wle'n teli-wlei*, "I am as well, as happy as you are"; one can also use *ki'l* and *ni'n*, or with *tetpi*, *tetpi-wlei'kw*, "we are equally happy."

2. The comparative of inferiority is expressed in the same way but putting *mu* or *moqwa'* in front of the first member, which in this case keeps its place. Example: Paul is not as strong as Peter, *Po'l moqwa' teliknaqw Pie'l teliknat*; *ni'n moqwa' teli-wleiw ki'l teli-wlein*.

3. The comparative of superiority is expressed by *me'j* or *me'*, *aji*, "more," and the "than" which follows *mu nkutey*, "it is not the same"; with *aji*, the "than" is better expressed by *aqq*. Example: "the angel is higher than the man," *ansale'wit me'espe'k mu nkutey l'nu*; or else *aji-espe'k aqq l'nu*. "More than" is expressed by *atelk*, *me'pukwelk*, inanimate gender in the singular, even when one speaks of people, plural *atelkl*, *atelkik*, *pukwelkl*, *pukwelkik*; than, *mu nkutey*; *apistane'wj mu meskiluk*, *lo'q kijka' atkilk aqq atu'tukwej*, "the marten is not big, it is hardly bigger than the squirrel" (Letter).

4. The absolute superlative is translated by *lo'q*, *mawi*, *kesi pukweli*, *ewsami*, "very," "much," "excessively," "too much," placed as prefixes before the adjective, the verb or the adverb. Example: "he shall be called the Son of the Most High," *mawi-espe'k Niskam Wkwisl tlui'tuksitew*. "He is too crazy to properly look after so many things," *awsami-l'ue'wiet teli-pukwelkl koqowe'l wwli-kwso'tmn*. "The devil is very harmful, and so he is called the great evil-doer," *mntu kesi-l'ue'wit, jel weji-wi'tut kji-winsit*; "you are very sick," *lo'q wisqisin*.

5. The relative superlative is expressed by *pejili-*, *pajiji-*, prefixes of preference. Example: *e'pijik pajiji-wleinik*, "blessed art thou among women"; *weli-naskultijik pejili-naskwenik*, "you are the virgin of virgins"; *u't pejili-msiki'k*, "that is the biggest of them"; *pejili-ksalkusit*, "the beloved, the favourite"; *pejili-pkitaik*, "to the highest degree, in excelsis." *Ma'wen kisi-pjili-pata'siwk*, "no one could commit a greater fault"; *kinu tapusi'kw wen pejiliknat*? "which of the two of us is the stronger?" *Pejila'si* means "to advance"; whenever someone appeared at the door of the cabin with the greeting *kwe'*, if the voice was recognized, the first thing that would be said was *piskwa'*, "come in," and then: *pjila'si*, "advance"; *nuji-ktanit pajijiknat ni'n*, "my adversary is much stronger than I am."

VIII. Contraction

It has been noted that there is often contraction or elision of a vowel in the first syllable of nouns and adjectives; it is the same thing as well in verbs, as we shall see. There is contraction, when these words are preceded by a prefix which modifies them, and also in compound words. In verbs it is found in the imperative, in the future of the indicative and in other moods. We have just seen it in *pejila'si* which becomes *pjila'si*; likewise *welein*, *pajiji-wleinik*. Often it consists only of the transposition of the *e* or of another vowel; thus *meskilk*, "big," becomes *mawi-msikilk*, "very big"; *nestmalsewet*, "he interprets," *nuji-nsitmalsewet*, "he is an interpreter"; *nekm wtuisunm kesite'tmik*, "his name is respected," *pajiji-ksite'tmik*, "very respected" or "very respectable"; in this latter case it would be useful to add *amuj*, "it is necessary." *Meselmul*, "I beg you"; *i'paji-mselmul*, "I humbly implore you, I earnestly implore you." The contraction rule however is not absolute; if it makes the words difficult to pronounce, it is omitted: *ketlamsitasi*, "I believe within myself"; *melki ketlamsitasi*, "strongly." In compound words, the first one ordinarily loses its last syllable and the second its first; as in *apatnmul*, "I hand over to you," composed of *apaji*, "in return," *iknmul*, "I give you"; *punulkwalul*, "I stop following you," for *puna'tu majulkwalul*.

LESSON NINE

THE VERB

Remark: Logical order would require us to place here that which concerns the negation of nouns and adjectives, then the numeral adjectives, and then the pronouns. But in a language that is essentially verbal, one must move quickly to become familiar with the verbal paradigms. Subsequently, what remains will be more intelligible, especially the numbers.

I. Persons and numbers

There are in the Mi'kmaw verb eleven fundamental persons or forms: three for the singular, as in French or English, then four for the dual and the same number for the plural, because the first person is quite different according to whether it responds to *kinu* or to *ninen*, "us," the first including, the second excluding, the one or the ones to whom one is speaking.

The verb agrees in number, gender and person with its subject. A collective subject in the singular requires, as in French, a verb in the singular: "a crowd was present," *pukwelk teko'tkip*. With "or," *kisna*, the verb is used in the singular, if the state or action is only affirmed of a single person: *Pie'l kisna Po'l nikanintutew*, "Peter or Paul will be the master cantor"; in the dual or in the plural, if the meaning can be applied to each of them: *Pie'l kisna Po'l me'j welite'lmujik*, "Peter or Paul are always welcome"; the same thing is done in the former case if the subjects are different persons and one uses the person who has priority: *ki'l kisna Williom nikanintutoqsip*, but it would be better to treat them separately: *ki'l nikanintutisk kisna Williom*. With "neither ... nor ...," *mu ... kisna ...*, the same thing is done, the verb is put in the plural and agrees with the person which has priority, if the subjects are different persons; in the singular, if they are the same person: *mu ki'l kisna nekm teleiwoq*, "it is neither you nor he who are so"; *moqwa'ki'l kisna ni'n kisewistukkw*, "neither you nor

I can speak"; *moqwa'ula kisna ala kisa'tukw*, "neither the latter nor the former will succeed." *Kitk*, "each," requires the verb in the plural and in the person which has priority: *kitk wejiki'tisna Ta'pito'*, "they were each descended from David"; *kitk la'titesnu*, "each of us (you and I) will go"; *la'titesnen*, "we, (he and I)," *la'titoqsip*, "you (you and he)" ...

But when a verb in the third person is the complement of another verb in this person, the syllable *-li-* is introduced between the root and the ending and the latter is also slightly modified. Thus in the first model which follows, *teluisi, teluisin, teluisit*, "to be called thus," *teluisit* will become in this case *teluisilijl*, in the dual and in the plural *teluisiliji, teluisultiliji*. If there is already an *l* in the verb which is a complement, *-li-* is changed into *-ni-*: *meskilk*, "he is big," *meskilnijl*, dual *meskilniji*; but in the plural *-li-* is again used, because of the extra syllable that is introduced, *meskilultiliji*; *wenuj pa'qalamajl l'nu'l etulnijl*, "the Frenchman looks with surprise at an Indian busy building a canoe"; if there is an *n*, *l* is placed in front of it: *na tle'tew l'nu wkwisl pkisilnij-a*, it will be thus when the Son of Man comes (Matthew 24, 39). Moreover when the subject is of the inanimate gender, the third person is in *-k, -kl*: *teluisik, teluisikl, teluisultikl*, "that is called so, those things are called thus." Finally when the third person, of which one is speaking, is gone, dead or absent, the verb becomes *itaq, itkik*, agreeing with the nouns or pronouns in the past (p. 42). Example: *ula ji'nm teluisit Klo't*, "this man's name is Claude"; *alaq ji'nmaq teluisitaq Klo'to'q*, "that man was called Claude." When it is the complement, this person will end in *silita, silitka, sultilitka*, and the final *q* is suppressed of names in *-aq* and in *-o'q*. There are likewise special forms for the past; we will note them, where there is need, under the title of supplementary forms, after the enumeration of the eleven fundamental forms.

II. Tenses and moods

There are three tenses, as in French, but the perfect, the pluperfect, and the past anterior are merely the imperfect, before which are put, when there is need, the prefixes *kisi-* or *ki's-kisi-*, "already" or "after." Example: *ki's kelusiss putu'suinu*, "(already) the orator has spoken"; when there is the sense of "after" it is better to use a special mood, which is called the conjunct; *kisiklusitek*, "when he had spoken"; *ki's-kisiklusitek*, "after he had finished speaking." In the future perfect *ki's* and *ki's-kisi* are also used, but with the present of the conjunct: *kisiklusijl*, "when he will have spoken"; *ki's-kisiklusijl*, "when he will have finished speaking." In Restigouche the *l* is not pronounced: *kelusij* [nor elsewhere in modern usage].

This special mood is nothing but the indicative with **when**, and it likewise replaces our present and past participles. There is another mood which we may call the reduced conjunct, to distinguish it from the conditional. This would be, in English, the indicative with **if**. To this should be added the dubitative or indicative with **perhaps**. See Section 7 below. But the forms of this mood that are known are not very numerous, and quite rare. I shall give with each conjugation the ones that I have been able to collect.

The infinitive is also conjugated impersonally in all tenses and all moods. It corresponds to the French verb conjugated with the pronoun *on*: *teluisimk*, *teluisultimk*, "to be named, one is named."

III. Indirect object with intransitive verbs

Intransitive verbs can have an indirect agreement with nouns in the plural, of either animate or inanimate gender. This agreement is expressed by a special ending in *-l*, in *-ik* or in *-i*. Thus for *teluisi*, "I am thus named," if I want to say that on all the reserves I carry this name, one would have to say: *msɨt l'nui-maqmikal tetuji-tluisianl*; or, that my name is above that of others, I will say: *ktikik pajijiaq ta'n teluisianik*. This requires two other conjugations in the present and in the past. In the future the modification applies only to the third persons. This form, on the other hand, is the same in all the verbs. In the transitive inanimate verbs, only the first kind of agreement is possible, that is, to a plural inanimate object, direct or indirect. When there is a second object, of animate gender, the verb belongs to the class of mixed or two-goal verbs.

IV. Contractions

In the future of the indicative and in the infinitive, as well as in the imperative and in all the tenses of the reduced conjunct and the conditional, there is a contraction in the initial syllable; that is to say that when there is an *e*, it is suppressed or transposed. In this way *teluisi* becomes in the future *tluisites* and in the imperative *tluisi*; in the same way *welei*, "I am well"; *wle'tes*, "I will be well"; *wleye'n*, "be well, be happy"; *wleian*, "if I am well"; *wleikk*, "I would be well"; *wekai*, "I get angry"; *wkwaites*, "I will get angry"; in the latter *w* is added after *k* by assimilation; the *k* itself is as if geminated in the pronunciations; *kewji*, "I am cold"; *ku'jites*, "I will be cold"; *wekwisi*, "I have a son"; *wkwisites*, "I will have a son," etc. However initial *e*, followed by *u* and a consonant, is not contracted: *eule'ji*, "I am poor"; *eule'jites*, "I will be poor"; *eulite'tekey*, "I have compassion"; *eulite'teka's*, "I will have compassion." But, if there is any other vowel after *w* it follows the general rule: *ewi'kikey*, "I write"; *wi'kika's*, "I will write"; *ewikmawi*, "I have a relative, an ally, a friend"; *wikmawites*, "I will have a friend." *A* and *o* also contract sometimes as does *e*; *paqasiet*, "he falls in the water"; *pqasietew*, "he will fall in the water"; *toqonasiek*, "we live together"; *tqonasitesnen*, "we will live together." In *nestm*, "understand," and other verbs, a vowel is inserted after the initial consonant cluster: *nsittes*, "I will understand that"; *nsite'n*, "understand it!"

V. Subordinative

The contraction also applies in the subordinative, but with another modification which is proper to this mood. In front of the root is placed the initial element of the corresponding personal pronoun of each person, except the third, for which one takes the initial element of *wt-*, *ula-*, instead of that of *nekm*. The ending is in *-an*, *-en*, *-in*, *-un* for the three persons of the singular, and *-nu*, *-nen*, *-ew* or *-wo* for those of the plural and the dual persons. Example: *nwi'kiken*, *kwi'kiken*, *wwi'kiken*, *kwi'kikennu*, etc., "that I write," "that you write," "that he writes," "that we write" and so forth. When the verb begins with a vowel other than *u*, and sometimes even with the latter, a *t* is introduced between the initial letter and the root of the verb. Example: *elue'wi*, "I am bad, a sinner"; *ntelue'win*, "that I am evil, that I am bad." In this case the *l* becomes syllabic. It is the same way and for the same reason, for example, with *teluisi*, which in the subordinative is softened to *ntluisin*, *e* disappearing and the *l* becoming syllabic. In fact the Indians write it this way: *ntluisin*. In the third person there is often introduced a euphonic *k*, which is hardly pronounced and resembles an aspiration: *wktluisin*, "that he is called thus"; *wkwi'kiken*, "that he writes." The Indians do not normally write this sound, although it is clearly heard in the pronunciation. [The *k* here is non-phonemic. It is a glottal catch which marks a syllabic boundary, and the presence of an extra-syllabic consonant.]

The euphonic *t* is also introduced in the same verbs in the second person of the negative imperative, also with a *k* preceding this consonant or that of the verb. Example: *tluisi*, "call yourself"; *mu ktluisiw*, *mu ktluisipp*, *mu ktluisultipp*; *alasutma*, "pray"; *mu ktalasutmaw*, *mu ktalasutmapp*, *mu ktalasutmatipp*, "do not pray."

VI. Intransitive verbs, and transitive inanimates

Intransitive verbs, and transitive verbs with an inanimate object are characterized by the first persons of the present of the indicative, in the three numbers, from which the other forms can be derived. It is necessary however to add the third person singular, which is sometimes in *-t*, sometimes in *-k* or *-oq*; we add the first person of the future and of the present subordinative and the second person of the imperative, because of the contraction and other modifications of the root. This is all that is needed in order to conjugate these verbs, their innumerable forms being developed in all verbs in the same way.

Information on the transitive animate verb and the two goal verbs will be found later.

VII. Negative and dubitative forms

There is in the verbs a negative form which affects the whole conjugation, and a dubitative form which modifies just certain persons. The former consists of putting in front of the verb *mu, moqwa, moqwe*, "not," and of introducing in the ending the sounds *u* and *a*; in the future *mu* is replaced by *ma'*, but the endings are the same as in the present, except that the contraction has to be made, when the verb is one that takes contractions. For example *pekisink*, "he comes"; *mu (moqwa, moqwe) pekisinuk*, "he doesn't come"; *ma' pkisinuk*, "he won't come."

The dubitative form is made by introducing the particle *etuk* or *jiptuk*, "perhaps," with the contraction, with just certain persons of the present and the past: *pkisinutuk*, "he perhaps came"; *msiki'ktnutuknek nekla na'kwek*, "this must have been a great day" (that of the baptism of the first Mi'kmaq: speech of Chief Lamorue, *Souvenir*, p. 37); *puni-i'mutuk*, "he is perhaps no longer there"; *alita'siktuk*, "I was perhaps distracted." We will quote, where appropriate, the forms that we have; they are not very numerous. There is a useful means of replacing them; one simply uses *etuk, jiptuk* as adverbs, without attempting to incorporate them into the verb. When one wishes to restrain one's approbation of what is assured by others, one has only to interject this little intervention, which is always useful: *jiptuk, etuk jel, etuk suel*. It is as if to say: I am inclined to believe that, or else the contrary, one can translate simply by: *ketlamsitmuk ni'n*; or else *moqwa'j etuk-a, moqwa'j suel-a*. But when one can use the dubitative, as in the examples given here or in the conjugation, it is curiously expressive.

VIII. Conjugations

There are in Mi'kmaw seven main conjugations: three for the intransitive verbs, two for the transitive inanimates, one for the transitive animates, and one for the mixed or two-goal verbs. The passive verbs, reflexives and reciprocals are all of the first conjugation.

The latter is in *-i*; principal model: *teluisi, teluisin, teluisit, teluisi'kw, teluisulti'kw*, "to call oneself thus"; *tluisites, tluisi, ntluisin*; let us add also the imperative negative: *mu ktluisiw, mu ktluisipp, mu ktluisultipp*.

To this main model must be added three secondary models, because of certain important peculiarities: the first for the verbs in *-a-i* which become *-ik* in the third person, and take -*ulti'kw* in the plural, without reducing the *i*; model: *wekai, wekain, wekaik, wekai'kw, wekaiulti'kw*, "to get angry"; *wkwaites, wkwai, nkwain, mu kkwaiw*; the second for verbs in -*e-i*, which by contrast suppress these two letters and form the plural in -*o'lti'kw*, the third person in -*e'k* and the imperative in -*ye'n*; model: *welei, welein, wele'k, welei'kw, welo'lti'kw*, "to be well, happy"; *wle'tes, wlein, nulein, mu kuleiw*: the third for the verbs of movement in -*a'si*, which change *s* to *t* in the dual, and form a plural in -*ita'yikw*; model: *ala'si, ala'sin, ala'sit, ala'ti'kw, alita'yikw*, "to go from side to side"; *ala'sites, ala'si, ntala'sin, mu ktala'siw*.

The second conjugation has the diphthong -*ay*; principal model: *alasutmay, alasutman, alasutmat, alasutmayikw, alasutma'ti'kw*, "to pray"; *alasutma's* or *alasutmates, alasutma, ntalasutman, mu ktalasutmaw*. Here there are also three secondary models, the modifications of which will be given in Lesson 13.

The third has the diphthong -*ey*; principal model: *ewi'kikey, ewi'kiken, ewi'kiket, ewi'kikeyikw, ewi'kikiti'kw*, "to write"; *wi'kika's* or *wi'kiketes, wi'kika* or *wi'kike, nui'kiken, mu kui'kikew*. Four secondary models.

The fourth conjugation (first of the transitive inanimates) is in -*m* or other consonants; principal: *nestm, nestmn, nestik, nestmu'kw, nestmu'ti'kw*, "to understand something"; *nsittes, nsite'n, nsitmn, mu knsitmu*. Two secondary models. There is a great number of these verbs, as well as of the following conjugation, which are intransitive in their sense; but that makes no difference to the conjugation.

The fifth is in -*u*: principal model: *mena'tu, mena'tu'n, mena'toq, mena'tu'kw, mena'tu'ti'kw*, "to remove or tear off"; *mna'tutes, mna'tu, nmna'tu'n, mu kmna'tu*. [Fr. Pacifique claims that there is no contraction in this verb, which does not appear to be the case].

The sixth conjugation (transitive animate verbs); these verbs are all in -*k* preceded by a vowel or another consonant. Principal model: *nemi'k, nemi't, nemiajl*, "see a person, animal or thing of the animate gender"; *nmias* or *nmiates, nmi, nnmian, mu knmiaw*.

The seventh (mixed or two-goal verbs); these verbs have two objects, of which at least one is animate; they are all in -*maq* or -*taq*; model: *kisitaq, kisitat, kisituajl*, "to do something for someone"; *kisitua's* or *kisituates, kisitu, nkisituan, mu kkisituaw*.

We shall give in a single lesson (two for the transitive animate verbs) the whole conjugation of the principal model of each, affirmative and negative. But one must not try to learn the whole paradigm at once. One must be satisfied with a single tense at a time, and practise conjugating in this tense several other verbs indicated in the lesson which follows each conjugation. The following tenses will then be much easier to study.

LESSON TEN

FIRST CONJUGATION (INTRANSITIVE) IN I

PRINCIPAL MODEL: TELUISI, I AM NAMED

Present indicative

teluisi, my name is
teluisin, your name is
teluisit, his name is
teluisi'kw, our (two) name is (incl.)
teluisiyek, our (two) name is (excl.)
teluisiyoq, your (two) name is
teluisijik, their (two) name is
teluisulti'kw, our (all) name is (incl.)
teluisultiyek, our (all) name is (excl.)
teluisultiyoq, your (all) name is
teluisultijik, their (all) name is

Negative Conjugation: *mu teluisiw*, "I am not called thus," etc., *mu teluisiwn, mu teluisiwk, mu teluisi'ukw, mu teluisiwek, mu teluisiwoq, mu teluisi'ti'wk, mu teluisultiukw, mu teluisultiwek, mu teluisultiwoq, mu teluisulti'ti'kw*.

Supplementary Forms: 1. If the subject is of the inanimate gender, in the third person, the verb becomes *teluisik, teluisikl, teluisultikl*, "its name is, these things are called so"; in the negative: *mu teluisinukw, mu teluisinukwl, mu teluisultinukwl*; those that have a future *-titew*, such as *meski'k*, "big," here become *-tnukw*: *mu meski'ktnukw, mu meski'ktnukwl*, "it is not big."

2. In the same way, in the third persons, the obviative forms are: *teluisilijl, teluisiliji, teluisultiliji*; in the negative *mu teluisilikwl, mu teluisilikwi, mu teluisultilikwi*.

3. For those who are unavailable, dead or absent, the following forms are used: *teluisitaq, teluisitkik, teluisultitkik*, "the dead or absent who are thus named"; and then in the negative, *mu teluisikwaq, mu teluisi'ti'wkwi'k, mu teluisulti'ti'wkwi'k*; and the obviative forms *teluisilita, teluisilitka, teluisultilitka*.

4. This verb although intransitive, may have an indirect agreement with things in the plural or with persons, the former being expressed by an ending in *-l*, the second in *-ik* or *-i*, as follows: *teluisianl, teluisinl, teluisijl, teluisi'kwl, teluisiyekl, teluisiyoql, teluisi'jikl, teluisulti'kwl, teluisultiyekl, teluisultiyoql, teluisulti'tijl*; *teluisianik, teluisinik, teluisiji, teluisi'kwik, teluisiyekik, teluisiyoqik, teluisi'tiji, teluisulti'kwik, teluisultiyekik, teluisultiyoqik, teluisulti'tiji*; in the negative: *mu teluisiwanl, mu teluisiwnl, mu teluisikwl, mu teluisiukwl, mu teluisiwekl, mu teluisiwoql, mu teluisi'tikwl, mu teluisultiukwl, mu teluisultiwekl, mu teluisultiwoql, mu teluisulti'tikwl*; and then *mu teluisiwanik, mu teluisiwnik, mu teluisikwi, mu teluisiukwik, mu teluisiwekik, mu teluisiwoqik, mu teluisi'tikwi, mu teluisultiukwik, mu teluisultiwekik, mu teluisultiwoqik, mu teluisulti'tikwi*. *-sijl* is also used for the complement in the obviative singular, as in *wejuowa'sijl pa'tlia'sl*, "he approaches the priest"; in the plural *wejuowa'siji pa'tlia's*.

Past indicative

teluisiep or *teluisiap*, my name was
teluisisip, teluisi'p, your name was
teluisiss, teluisip, teluisisp, his/her name was
teluisi'kuss, teluisi'kup, teluisi'kusp, our (incl.) name was
teluisiyeksip, teluisiyekip, teluisiyekiss, our (excl.) name was
teluisiyoqsip, teluisiyoqip, teluisiyoqiss, your name was
teluisisnik, teluisipnik, teluisipnik, their name was
teluisulti'kuss, teluisulti'kup, teluisulti'kusp, our (incl.) name was
teluisultiyeksip, teluisultiyekip, teluisultiyekiss, our (excl.) name was
teluisultiyoqsip, teluisultiyoqip, teluisultioqiss, your name was
teluisultisnik, teluisultipnik, teluisultisipnik, their name was

Negative Conjugation: *mu teluisiwep, mu teluisiwap*, "I wasn't named so," etc., *mu teluisiwsip, mu teluisiwksip, mu teluisiukup, mu teluisiweksip, mu teluisiwoqsip, mu teluisiwksipnik, mu teluisultiukup, mu teluisultiweksip, mu teluisultiwoqsip, mu teluisultiwksipnik*.

Remarks: 1. When there are two or more forms for one and the same person, the former is considered as the most common; in the third person *-pnik* is more expressive than *-snik*; the latter seems to include a doubt or a hesitation; the former is more affirmative; when in the plural or in the negative one reads "etc.," that means that one has to add the other corresponding endings to the dual or to the affirmative. With the endings *-isp*, *-usp*, and in the other conjugations *-asp*, *-esp*, these two consonants are only pronounced in the derived forms *-sipnl*, *-sipnik*.

2. In practice the first person of the past of this conjugation is *-iep*, while that of the third conjugation, in *-ei* diphthong, becomes *-ap*, as one can see in the Confiteor: *kaqais winita'siep, kaqais winapukuap, kaqais wina'siep*, "I have sinned several times in thought, word and deed"; the Indians still say *-ass* [reported past, not a conjunct, as Fr. Pacifique seems to have thought].

Supplementary Forms: 1. As in the present, there are third persons with inanimate subjects; *teluisiksip, teluisiksipnl, teluisultiksipnl*; in the negative: *mu teluisinuksip, mu teluisinuksipnl, mu teluisultinuksipnl*.

2. The obviative forms in the third person are as follows: *teluisilisnl, teluisilisni, teluisultilisni*; in the negative: *mu teluisiliwksipnl, mu teluisiliwksipni, mu teluisultiliwksipni*. But it would be better to use the conjunct. See below.

3. For the unavailable, dead or absent, one can use the absentative forms of the present which have a real past sense. There are however also the following forms of the past: *teluisisnaq, teluisisnika, teluisultisnika*; and also in the obviative: *teluisilisnika, teluisultilisnika*. These forms appear more difficult than they are in reality; one does not have to be very advanced to read and understand this reply in the catechism: "the apostles of Jesus Christ were twelve": *Westau'lkw wnaqapemka newtiske'ksilisnika jel tapusilisnika*. In the negative, we have: *teluisiwksipnika*; and in the obviative: *teluisiliwksipna, teluisiliwksipnika, teluisultiliwksipnika*. But it would be better to put off to later a study of these supplementary forms. It is the same for the following forms, which are only placed here with the goal of having as complete a table as follows.

Charles Bernard once gave me these examples, the real sense of which could only be grasped by a member of the tribe, educated as he was: *ji'nmaq poqtamka'sipnaq*, "the man has left" (and has not come back but will come back perhaps); if he is back one will say: *poqtamka'sip* or *poqtamka'siss*; if he has left definitively or is dead, *poqtamka'sitaq*; *wenijanipnaq*, "he has had children and he is dead"; *wenijanitaq*, "he has had children who are dead but he is alive."

4. The principal dubitative forms of the first conjugation are as follows: *tluisiptuk*, "I might have been called so"; *tluisiktuk*, "you might have been called so"; *tluisiktuk*, *tluisiktukunik*, "he," "they"; *msɨki'ktnutuknek na'kwek*, "this must have been a great day" (that of the first baptism of Mi'kmaq; speech of Chief Lamorue on the Third Centenary, p. 37); *klu'ltnutuknek*, "it was no doubt beautiful" (a way of saying with doubt); *moqwa'j eskwianutuk?* "was there nothing left?"; *Moqwa'j eskwianuk*, "no."

5. When the verb expresses an agreement with an indirect object in the plural, animate or inanimate, one must add to the singular *-l*, *-ik*, or *-i*, as in the present, but with a euphonic *-n*. If, for example, one wanted to say that it was because of certain things or certain persons that one was so named, one will add for the former: *wjit na't koqoe'l teluisiapnl, teluisi'pnl, teluisisnl* or *teluisipnl, teluisi'kusnl* or *teluisi'kupnl, teluisiyeksɨpnl, teluisiyoqsɨpnl, teluisisnikl, teluisulti'kusnl*, etc.; for the animates: *wjit na't wenik teluisiapnik, teluisi'pnik, teluisisni, teluisi'kusnik* or *si'kupnik, teluisiyeksɨpnik, teluisiyoqsɨpnik, teluisisni* or *teluisisipni, teluisulti'kusnik*, etc., *teluisultiyepsipnik, teluisultiyoqsɨpnik, teluisultisni*; in the negative: *mu teluisiwapnl, mu teluisiwapnik*, etc.

6. If the obviative is the name of something that belongs to the past, according to the rules of Lesson 7 the verb must be made to agree in the following manner: "because of this thing or these things," etc., *wjit na't koqoeyek, koqoeyek teluisiapnek; na't koqoe'kl teluisiapnkl*, etc. If it is the name of a dead or absent person: *wjit na't wenaq teluisiapnaq; na't wenkik teluisiapnaqik* etc.; for the negative: *mu teluisiwapnɨk, mu teluisiwapnkl, mu teluisiwapnik, mu teluisiwapnaqik*, etc.

7. These forms of the past are used also for the imperfect and the other past tenses. If one wishes to make the difference between the preterite and the present perfect, one places *kisi-* before the verb, making the contraction or the elision of the root, if this is appropriate: *kisitluisiap*, "my name was, I was given this name"; for the pluperfect one puts *ki's kisi*: *ki's kisitluisiap*, "already my name was, I had been using this name before another event happened." One can run through the forms of the conjugation, following all the persons or forms given above. But it is better in these cases to employ the conjunct, which is no more than the indicative with **when**, in the present or in the past. Example: *kisipkisinanek, pa'qalaptmep teli-klu'lk ki'k-a*, "ever since my arrival I have admired the beauty of your house"; *ki's kisi-pkisinanek na'tami ta'pu kisna si'st ajietek na tujiw saqmaq naji-mittukwalipnik*, "about two or three hours after my arrival, the chiefs came to see me." To indicate that the action is totally past, especially with *sa'q*, "a long time ago," the present is often used, when one wishes to emphasize the fact that the action is past more than emphasizing the action itself; thus one will say: *pekisinep wlaku, sepey,*

kejikew, "I arrived yesterday," or "this morning," or "just now"; but one will say *ki's sa'q pekisin*, "I got here a long time ago"; moreover, in Mi'kmaw narrations, just like ours, the present constantly replaces the past and very successfully, giving more life to the narration; and it is very useful, when one does not know the conjugations very well.

Future indicative

tluisites, my name will be
tluisitesk (teluisiteks), your name will be
tluisitew, his name will be
tluisitesnu (tluisiteksnu), our (incl.) name will be
tluisitesnen (tluisiteksnen), our (excl.) name will be
tluisitoqsip, your name will be
tluisitaqq, their name will be
tluisultitesnu (tluisultiteksnu), our (incl.) name will be
tluisultitesnen (tluisultiteksnen), our (excl.) name will be
tluisultitoqsip, your name will be
tluisultitaqq, their name will be

Negative Conjugation: *ma' tluisiw*, etc., (as in the present tense), "my name will not be."

Supplementary Forms: 1. Here again we have the third person with **inanimate subject**: *tluisi(kti)tew, tluisi(kti)tal, tluisi(kt)ultital*, "that will be called"; in other verbs this future is in -*titew*, -*tital* such as *kelu'lk*, "it is beautiful or good," *klu'l(k)titew, klu'l(k)tital*; in the negative *ma' tluisinukw, ma' klu'l(k)tnukw*.

2. **Obviative forms**: *tluisilital, tluisilita, tluisultilita*; in the negative: *ma' tluisilikul, ma' tluisilikwi, ma' tluisultilikwi*.

3. Agreements with plural objects only occur in this tense on the third person forms; in the inanimate gender: *tluisi(kti)tal* (dual/plural), *tluisultital* (plural); in the animate gender: *tluisi(li)tal, tluisi(li)ta, tluisulti(li)ta*; negative: *ma' tluisinukul, ma' tluisultinukul; ma' tluisi(li)kul, ma' tluisi(li)kwi, ma' tluisulti(li)kwi*.

Imperative

tluisi, be so named
tluisij, let him be so named
tluisinej, let us be so named
tluisikw, be so named (dual)

tluisi'tij, let them be so named
tluisultinej, let us be so named
tluisultikw, be so named (pl.)
tluisulti'tij, let them be so named

Negative

mu ktluisiw, do not be named so
mu tluisiwij, let him not be named so
mu tluisinej, let us not be named so
mu ktluisipp, do not be named so (dual)
mu tluisiwi'tij, do not let them be named so
mu tluisultinej, let us not be named so
mu ktluisultipp, do not be named so (pl.)
mu tluisulti'tij, do not let them be named so

Supplementary Forms: the third person forms with inanimate subjects are just like the others, but the negative is: *mu tluisinuj, mu tluisultinuj*. When the future is in *-titew*, the imperative is in *-tij, -tnuj*: *klu'ltij, mu klu'ltnuj*.

Remarks: 1. It should be noted that the negation does not change the first person of the dual and the plural, nor ordinarily the third person.

2. The second person imperative is formed from the first person of the present indicative, without any other change except contraction, except for the verbs in *-ei*, which become *-eye'n*; but in the negative, a euphonic *k-* is introduced in the second persons, between *mu* and the verb, and also a *-t-*, when the verb begins with a vowel other than *u*, as in the subordinative. In the second person of the dual and the plural, the negative is obtained by changing final *-k* or *-kw* to *-p*; example: *wlkwija'sultikw, mu kwe'kwata'sultipp, ni'n na*, "be glad, fear nothing, it is me"; *welkwija'si* "to rejoice"; *we'kwata'si*, "to be afraid."

Conjunct or indicative with *When*

teluisiyanl, teluisiyanek, when my name is, was
teluisinl, teluisinek, when your name is, was
teluisijl, teluisitek, when his name is, was
teluisi'kwl, teluisi'kwek, when our (incl.) name is, was
teluisiyekl, teluisiyekek, when our (excl.) name is, was
teluisiyoql, teluisiyoqek, when your name is, was
teluisi'tijl, teluisi'titek, when their name is, was
teluisulti'kwl, teluisulti'kwek, when our (incl.) name is, was
teluisultiyekl, teluisultiyekek, when our (excl.) name is, was

teluisultiyoql, teluisultiyoqek, when your name is, was
teluisulti'tijl, teluisulti'titek, when their name is, was

The **Negative conjunct**: *mu teluisiwanl, mu teluisiwanek*, "since my name is, was not," etc., *-siwnl, -siwnek, -sikwl, -sikwek, -siwkwl, -siwkwek, -siwekl, -siwekek, -siwoqwl, -siwoqwek, -si'tikwl, -si'tikwek, -sultiwkwl, -sultiwkwek, -sultiwekl, -sultiwekek, -sultiwoqwl, -sultiwoqek, -sulti'tikwl, -sulti'tikwek.*

This mood replaces our participle and can mean: "my name being, being named, having been named," or "when, since, seeing that I am named or was named thus." Many forms in the paradigm resemble those of the present indicative with an inanimate plural object agreement.

Supplementary Forms: 1. **Inanimate**: *teluisikl, teluisikek, teluisultikl, teluisultikek; mu teluisinukwl, mu teluisinukwek, mu teluisultinukwl, mu teluisultinukwek.*

2. **Obviatives**: *teluisilijl, teluisilitek, teluisultilijl, teluisultilitek; mu teluisilikwl, mu teluisilikwek, mu teluisultilikwl, mu teluisultilikwek.*

3. **Inaccessible**: For those who are not available, dead or absent, and things far away: *teluisitka, teluisultitka; teluisilitka, teluisultilitka; teluisikeksipnek, teluisikeksipnikl.*

Conjunct or indicative with *If*

tluisiyan, tluisiass, tluisiasn, if my name is, was, had been
tluisin, tluisi'sip, tluisisipn, if your name is, was, had been
tluisij, tluisiss, tluisisn, if his name is, was, had been
tluisi'kw, tluisi'kuss, tluisi'kusn, if our (incl.) name is, was, had been
tluisiyek, tluisiyeksip, tluisiyeksipn, if our (excl.) name is, etc.
tluisiyoq, tluisiyoqsip, tluisiyoqsipn, if your name is, etc.
tluisi'tij, tluisi'tiss, tluisi'tisn, if their name is, etc.
tluisulti'kw, tluisulti'kuss, tluisulti'kusn, if our (incl.) name is, etc.
tluisultiyek, tluisultiyeksip, tluisultiyeksipn, if our (excl.) name etc.
tluisultiyoq, tluisultiyoqsip, tluisultiyoqsipn, if your name, etc.
tluisulti'tij, tluisulti'tiss, tluisulti'tisn, if their name, etc.

Supplementary Forms: 1. **The Negative Conjugation** is like that of the present and past indicatives, adding the syllable *-n* for the pluperfect; but the first person becomes *-wan, -wass, -wasn; mu tluisiwan, mu tluisiwass, mu tluisiwasn; mu tluisiwn, mu tluisiwsip, mu tluisiwsipn; mu tluisiwk, mu tluisiwksip, mu tluisiwksipn; mu tluisiwkw, mu tluisiwkuss, mu tluisiwkusn; mu tluisiwek, mu tluisiweksip, mu tluisiweksipn; mu tluisiwoq, mu tluisiwoqsip,* *mu tluisiwoqsipn*; *mu tluisi'tiwk, mu tluisi'tiwksip, mu tluisi'tiwksipn*; *mu tluisultiwkw, mu tluisultiwkuss, mu tluisultiwkusn*, etc.

2. The **Inanimate forms**: *tluisik, tluisiss, tluisisn*; *mu tluisinuk, mu tluisinuss, mu tluisinusn*; *wle'k, wle'ss, wle'sn*, "if it is good," etc.

3. The **Obviative forms**, but little used, would be: *tluisilij, tluisiliss, tluisilisn* (singular and dual); *tluisultilij, tluisultiliss, tluisultilisn* (plural).

Rand uses the **Subordinative**: *Niskam ankamapni wnmian me' wen wnsitue'lin aqq wkwilualin Kisu'lkwl*, "God looked to see if there were anyone intelligent, who might seek for the Lord" (Ps. 13, 2 and 52, 2). That is very nicely put.

Conditional

tluisikk (ap), my name would be
tluisikk (p), your name would be
tluisiss, his/her name would be
tluisi'kupp, our (incl.) name would be
tluisikekk (p), our (excl.) name would be
tluisikoqq (p), your name would be
tluisi'tiss, their name would be
tluisulti'kupp, our (incl.) name would be
tluisultikekk (p), our (excl.) name would be
tluisultikoqq (p), your name would be
tluisulti'tiss, their name would be

Past conditional

tluisikapn, my name would have been
tluisikpn, your name would have been
tluisisoqq, his/her name would have been
tluisi'kupn, our (incl.) name would have been
tluisikekpn, our (excl.) name would have been
tluisikoqpn, your name would have been
tluisi'tisoqq, their name would have been
tluisulti'kupn, our (incl.) name would have been
tluisultikekpn, our (excl.) name would have been
tluisultikoqpn, your name would have been
tluisulti'tisoqq, their name would have been

Supplementary Forms: 1. **Negative**: *mu tluisiwkapn, mu tluisiwkpn* or *mu tluisikpn, mu tluisisoqq, mu tluisiwkupn, mu tluisiwkekpn, mu tluisiwkoqpn, mu tluisi'tisoqq, mu tluisultiwkupn*, etc.

2. **Inanimate subjects**: *tluisiss, tluisisoqq, klu'ltiss, klu'ltisoqq; mu tluisinuss, mu tluisinusoqq; mu klu'ltnuss, mu klu'ltnusoqq*; also used for the dual and the plural; *mtue'ss, mtue'soqq*, "this would be difficult"; *mu mtue'nuss, mu mtue'nusoqq*.

3. **Obviatives**: *tluisiliss, tluisilisoqq; tluisultiliss, tluisultilisoqq; mu tluisilikuss, mu tluisilikusoqq, mu tluisultilikuss, mu tluisultilikusoqq*.

Remarks: 1. The letters between brackets are only put in here to show how the past is formed; they are not pronounced or written in the present.

2. The conditional is also used to express obligation: *Isak tluisikpn*, "you should have been called Isaac"; *tlimikoqpn* (6th conjugation), you should have told me so (6 words in one).

Subordinative

ntluisin, that my name is
ktluisin, that your name is
wtluisin, that his/her name is
ktlusinenu, that our (incl.) name is
ntluisinen, that our (excl.) name is
ktluisinew, that your name is
wtluisinew, that their name is
ktluisultinenu, that our (incl.) name is
ntluisultinen, that our (excl.) name is
ktluisultinew, that your name is
wtluisultinew, that their name is

Supplementary Forms: 1. **Inanimate**: there are no different forms in this verb, but those verbs which have *-titew* in the future here show *-ten* or *-tnen*. The negative forms are rare in the subordinative; one does however find *-inun, -tenun*.

2. **Obviatives**: *wtluisilin*; the dual and the plural should be: *wtluisilinew, wtluisultilinew*; but everywhere one sees the last syllable suppressed; example: *Se'sus telkimaji wtalismita'lin*, "Jesus commands them to sit down"; *alisma'si*, "to stretch oneself out here and there"; *wnaqapem kisa'laji wtepita'lin aqq wnikani-asoqma'lin*, "he has his apostles, his disciples go on board ship"; *tepa'si*, "to embark"; *asoqma'si*, "to cross over." When the verb is preceded by a prefix, the initial of the pronoun is put in front of this latter; as can be seen in the above example: *nikani*, "ahead, out front"; *telkimaji, kisa'laji*, are in the present, which is often used for expressing the past.

INFINITIVE OR IMPERSONAL (INDEFINITE SUBJECT)

teluisimk, teluisultimk, to be so named, one's name is
teluisimkiss, teluisultimkiss or *kip*, one's name was
tluisiten, tluisultiten, one's name will be
tluisimkij, tluisultimkij, let one be so named
teluisimkl, teluisultimkl, since, when one is so named
teluisimkek, teluisultimkek, when one was so named
tluisimk, tluisultimk, if one is so named
tluisimkiss, tluisultimkiss, if one were so named
tluisimkisn, tluisultimkisn, if one had been so named
tluisiness, tluisultiness, one would be so named
tluisinesoqq, tluisultinesoqq, one would have been so named
tluisin, tluisultin, that one is so named

Negative

mu teluisimmik, mu teluisultimmik, one's name is not
mu teluisimmiksip, mu teluisultimmiksip, one's name was not
ma' tluisimmik, ma' tluisultimmik, one's name will not be
mu teluisimmikl, mu teluisultimmikl, since, when one is not so named
mu teluisimmikek, mu teluisultimmikek, since, when one was not so named
mu tluisimmik, mu tluisultimmik, if one is not so named

For the others there is no change in the negative.

Remarks: 1. It can be seen that this sort of infinitive is conjugated in all tenses and moods, in the affirmative and the negative, in the form of the dual and the plural; the latter is used when one knows or when one supposes that the number, however indeterminate, is considerable.

2. The present and the past take *-ik* or *-l*, when they have an indirect agreement with an object in the plural; for example: *teluisimkik, teluisimkil, teluisultimkik, teluisultimkl*, "one is called thus because of such people or such things"; *teluisimkisnik, teluisimkisnl, tluisultimkisnik, teluisultimkisnl*, "one was called thus," etc.

3. The past can also take *kisi* and *ki's kisi* to exactly translate the perfect and the pluperfect; with negation *mna'q*, "not yet," is used: *mna'q mijisimmiksip ta'n eli-pusimkiss, jel mawi-pusultimkiss ke'sk mna'q mijisultimmiksip*, "one had not yet eaten when someone started to paddle away, and everyone left before eating"; *(k)e'sk mna'q*, "when not yet."

LESSON ELEVEN

EXAMPLES OF THE FIRST CONJUGATION

Like *teluisi* are conjugated:

1. The following verbs in *-i* preceded by a vowel or a consonant, and mentioned in the preceding lessons, namely: *l'nui, elue'wi, wikewi, witui, kisikui, Niskamewit, pestie'wi, (wimk); saqmawi, (witek), sape'wi, Kjisape'wit, tleyawi, ji'nmui; emteski, wesaqmami, kaqmi, puntemi; wejimanit, weptni; papi, epi, waju'pi; nenaqita'si, waqasit, milesi, wekwisi, taluisi, teluisi, usi, kesalkusi, (sit), kelu'si, kelusi, pusi, i'-pusi, wetusi, wikapuksi, puntoqsi, minu'nsi, (sit), watapsi, epsi, eptek, meko'tik; awije'ji, eule'ji, wekwiji, weniskamiji, kewji, kelji, keltik, mujaji, poqji, (jit).*

Here are some others:

Emteski, -kin, -kit, "to be arrogant"; *mteskites* or *mɨteskites, -ki, -kin, mu kmteskiw* or *kmɨteskiw*; these verbs take *-ult* in the plural between *k* and *i,* except in the following:

Netukuli, -lin, -lit, -li'kw, forms its plural *netukuli'ti'kw,* "chase, hunt"; *ntukulites, -li, -lin; mu kntukuliw; neta'tukulit,* "to a be clever hunter"; *mili-altukuli'tijik* (Jo. 290), "they hunt everywhere and in every way."

Etuli, -lit, "to build a canoe"; *etltuli,* "to make it there"; *netutuli,* "to be capable, clever."

Atkitemi, -min, -mit, "to cry"; *pustemit,* "who cries a lot"; *puntemi,* "stop crying"; *mu ktatkitemiw,* "don't cry."

Wenijani and *wen'jani, -nin, -nit,* "to have children"; *wnjanites, nnijanin, wnijani, mu knjaniw.*

Epi, epin, epit (short *e*), "to be seated"; *pites, pi, ntipin* (see conj., gr. p. 59); *Nujjinen wa'so'q epin*, "our Father who art in heaven."

Waju'pi, -pin, -pit, "to be full": *waju'pinl sape'wuti'l*, "you are full of grace, of virtues."

Pisi, -sin, -sit, "to be inside, contained"; *pisites, pisi, npisin, mu kpisiw*; *pisit laplusuniktuk*, "he is in prison"; *wjijaqmijl pisilijl*, "his soul is also there (in the host)"; *ta'sijik puessuaq mun'tiktuk pisijik?* "how many bushels are contained in a barrel?" *ne'sisijik eta*, "three"; *mesta pisiyek elue'wutiktuk*, "we are all immersed in sin" (Par. II, p. 372).

Ankita'si, -sin, -sit (long *a*), "to think, reflect"; there is no contraction; *mu ktankita'siw*.

Awan'ta'si, -sin, -sit, "to forget."

Winpasi (short *a*), *-sin, -sit*, "to try, to make efforts."

Milesi, -sin, -sit, "to be rich"; *milesuti*, "wealth."

Eskipe'si, -sin, -sit, "to wait for"; *skipe'sites, mu ktiskipe'siw*.

Teli'si (long *i*), *-sin, -sit*, "to speak thus"; *tli'sites, tli'si, ntli'sin, mu ktli'siw*; *mili'si*, "to speak different languages."

Mijisi (short *i*), *-sin, -sit*, at Restigouche one says *mijji*, "to eat."

Kelu'si (long *u* as in English *to lose*), *-sin, -sit*, "to be good"; this is the model of this conjugation given by M. Maillard; but the inanimate is *kelu'lk, klu'ltitew, klu'ltij, wklu'ltn* or *-tnen, mu kelu'ltnukw, -tnuj, -tnun*, "that is good, that is not ..."; God is often called *Kelu'sit*, "Good, above all," or *Kji-kelu'sit*, "the Most Beautiful and the Most Good; *kelu'suti*, "beauty."

Kelusi (short *u*, pronounced /u/, as in English *to loose*), *-sin, -sit*, "to speak"; *klusites, klusi, nklusin, mu kklusiw*; from that *klusuaqn*, "word"; *Kji-klusuaqn*, "the Word"; *meltamtuk Kji-klusuaqniksip*, "in the beginning was the Word"; *Kjiklusuaqn ewa'qewa'siss*, "the Word was made flesh"; *ewa'qewa'si, -sin, -sit*, "to be made flesh"; *wa'qewa'sitew*, "he will be made," *wa'qewa'sij*, "let him be made flesh."

Klujjiewtosi, -sin, -sit, "to make the sign of the cross."

Naqati, -tin, -tit, "to shoot arrows"; *nqatites, nqati, ninqatin, mu kinqatiw*; *kis naqatianek*, "I have already shot" (Rem. gr. p. 17); *na wji nqatitaq wtininewaql*, "that is why they will shoot at them" (Par. II, 375).

To these verbs we must add all the passives in *-ta'si, -uksi, -kusi*, the pronominal or reflexive verbs in *-si*, preceded by a vowel or a consonant, especially *l*, as well as the reciprocals in *-ti'kw*, *-tulti'kw*, which do not have a singular. Such are:

Anko'tasi, -sin, -sit, "to be protected, looked after."

Pepso'tasi, -sin, -sit, "to be dominated, vanquished."

Welo'tasi, -sin, -sit, "to be blessed."

Wino'tasi, -sin, -sit, "to be desecrated."

Telamuksi, -sin, -sit, "to appear such."

Kesamuksi, -sin, -sit, "to be glorified, to appear brilliant."

Eulamuksi, -sin, -sit, "to appear miserable."

Kesalkusi, -sin, -sit, "to be loved"; *kesalsi, -sin, -sit,* "to love oneself"; *kesalti'kw, -tulti'kw,* "to love each other."

Eulite'lmkusi, -sin, -sit, "to be an object of pity, of compassion"; *eulite'lsi, -sin, -sit,* "to have pity on oneself"; *eulite'lti'kw, -tulti'kw,* "to have pity on each other."

Nemi'kusi, -sin, -sit, "to be seen"; *nemi'si, -sin, -sit,* "to see oneself"; *nemi'ti'kw, -tulti'kw,* "to see each other."

Keji'kusi, -sin, -sit, "to be known"; *keji'si, -sin, -sit,* "to know oneself"; *keji'ti'kw, -tulti'kw,* "to know each other."

Ankweyasi, -sin, -sit, "to take care of oneself, to protect oneself"; *ankweyati'kw, -tulti'kw,* "to protect one another."

Apoqnma'si, -sin, -sit, "to help oneself"; *apoqnma'ti'kw, -tulti'kw,* "to aid each other."

Ketlamsitasi, -sin, -sit, "to believe (in oneself), to hold as true"; reflexive of *ketlamsitaq,* "to believe someone"; *ketlamsitati'kw, -tatulti'kw,* "to believe each other."

Pekwatasi, -sin, -sit, "to procure, make for oneself"; *pekwatati'kw, -tatulti'kw,* "to procure, make for one another"; *pekwatatimkewey elue'wuti,* "scandal."

A number of other verbs are formed from nouns by the addition of *-i* or *-mi*, the first ending replacing our verb *be* and the second our verb *have*, when joined to nouns, pronouns or adjectives, which are all conjugated like *teluisi*.

See below, Lesson Twenty.

On the other hand, there are many verbs which form nouns by changing *-i* into *-uti* or *-waqn*, with contraction of the first syllable, if the verb is susceptible to it. Thus from:

Wisqisi, *-sin*, *-sit*, "to be sick," one gets *wisqisuti* and *wisqisuaqn*, "contagious disease"; these nouns in their turn become other verbs by the addition of another *-i*, *-in*, *-it*; *-ik* in the third person inanimate signifies: "there are some, there are none": *wisqisuti*, *wisqisutik* or *wisqisuaqnik*, "there is illness"; *mu wisqisutinukw*, *wisqisuaqninukw*, "there is none."

Welita'si, *-sin*, *-sit*, "to be content, happy"; *wlita'suti*, *wlita'suaqn*; *wlita'sutik*, *wlita'suaqnik*, "that is fun, there is rejoicing."

Sape'wi, *-win*, *-wit*, "to be wise, holy, virtuous"; *sape'wuti*, "virtue, wisdom"; *sape'wutik*, "there is virtue, that is wisdom itself"; *mu sape'wutinukw*, "there is none"; *mu sape'wutinukw na'te'l*, "there is no wisdom in that."

Elue'wi, *-win*, *-wit*, "to be bad, a sinner"; *elue'wuti*, *elue'wutik*, "sin, that is a sin"; *l'ue'wites*, *l'ue'wi*, *ntlue'win*, *mu ktlue'wiw*. Hence also *l'ue'winui*, *l'ue'winu'skowi*, "to be a sinner, a sinneress"; *l'ue'winu*, "a sinner"; *sape'winu*, "a saint"; *nu'skw*, *nu'skwe'j*, *nu'j*, *nui*, *nu'skowi*, *nu'skwe'jui*, *nu'jui*; *teltawe'j elue'wutij*, "let his prayer (of the evil-doer) be a sin" (Ps. 108, 7). Dubitative: *l'ue'wiutuk*, *l'ue'ultiutuk*, *-tukunik*, "perhaps they have been bad again" (*Hist. Sainte*, 115, 117).

Weskijinui, *-uin*, *-uit*, "to be born, to live"; *wskijinuuti*, "birth, life, nature"; *wskijinu*, "person"; *wskijinuik*, *l'nuik*, "there are people"; *iapji-wskijinuuti*, "eternal life"; *minui-wskijinuuti*, "new life"; *minui wskijinui*, *-nuin*, *-nuit*, "to be reborn"; *sape'wuti'l mawiaj*, "communion of the saints," lit., "that the holy things should be common"; from *mawieyikw*, imperative form of the inanimate gender; *l'ue'wuti'l mniaj*, from *meniey*, *meniaq*, "to move aside, to withdraw, remission of sins"; *ma'qeyl apijipe'tal*, "flesh (pl.) will be restored to life"; *apijipei*, *pati'kw*, "to come back to life"; these three verbs are of the third conjugation.

We should note that in verbs with *-wi* there is a small modification in the plural: whereas the others insert *-ult* before *-i*, these latter which already have a *-u* add only *-lt*.

Examples: *l'nui*, "I am a man, Indian"; *l'nulti'kw*, "we are"; *ketuapsi*, "I want to profit by it"; *ketuapsulti'kw*, "we want."

Eskwi, *-win*, *-wit*, "to sneeze"; *eskulti'kw*.

Otherwise these verbs and all the preceding ones are regular. But there are three other categories, which offer some important modifications and require a special secondary model. The first is in *-ai*, which takes only *-ulti'kw* in the plural without dropping *i* and makes the third person in *-ik* instead of *-it*; model: *wekai, -in, -ik, -ulti'kw*, "to get angry"; *wkwaites, nukwain, wkwai, mu kukwaiw*. The second is in *-ei*, which on the contrary drops these two letters and makes its plural in *-o'lti'kw*, the third person is in *-e'k*, the imperative in *-eye'n, -eyikw, -o'ltikw*; model: *welei, -ein, -e'k*, "to be well, happy"; *welei'kw, welo'lti'kw, wle'tes, wleye'n, nulein, mu kuleiw*. The third is in *-a'si*, it expresses movement or tendency; it changes *s* to *t* in the dual: *-a'si, -a'ti'kw*, and makes the plural in *-ita'yikw*; model: *ala'si, -sin, -sit*, "to go for a walk, to go here and there, from side to side"; *ala'ti'kw, alita'yikw; ala'sites, ala'titesnu, alita'tesnu; ala'si, ala'ti'kw, alita'q, mu ktala'siw, ktala'tipp, ktalita'pp*. And so we have ...

2. *Wekai*, first secondary model, "to get angry, to be angry, in a rage"; *wekaiep, kai'sip* or *kai'p, kaiss* or *kaip, kai'kuss* or *kai'kup, kaieksip* or *kaiekip, kaioqsip* or *kaioqop, kaiksipnik, kaiulti'kup; wkwaites, wkwai, -ij, -inej, -ikw, -i'tij, -iultinej, nukwain, mu kukwaiw; wekaianl, -nek; wkwaian, -iass, -iasn; wkwaikk, -ikapn; wekaimk, wekaiultimk; puski-wkwaimk*, "anger"; it should be noted in the last case, just as in the forms of the verb where there is contraction, this introduction of *w* after *wk* is a euphonic *w* caused by what precedes; it is not part of the word and should not be introduced into the other forms of the verb.

Aljai, -ain, -aik, "to be painted, stained" (literal and fig.); but this forms *aljo'lti'kw* in the plural; it is the same for *netuai*.

Ewai, -ain, -aik or *-ewait*, "to have, possess"; *ewaiulti'kw; ewaites, ewai, ntewain, mu kuaiw*, "don't take for yourself."

E'tmai, -ain, -aik, "to come after."

Netuai, -ain, -aik, "to be a scout, spy"; *netuo'lti'kw*.

Pa'qlai, -ain, -aik, "to be astonished, surprised, to admire"; *pa'qlaiulti'kw; mimajuinu'k pa'qlaiultijik*, "the people were astounded" (Luke 11, 16); often the present is used for the past, as has already been said; *kiplno'l lo'q weji-pa'qlaik*, "the governor is (for was) very surprised at it" (Matt. 27, 14); the third person is the same in the inanimate gender, except in the negative: *msit wskitqamu weji-pa'qlaik*, "the whole universe is astonished at it" (Apoc. 13, 3); negative *mu pa'qlainukw*.

Sepai, -ain, -aik, "to hunt in the morning."

3. *Welei, -ein, -e'k*, the second secondary model, "to be well, happy, to be in good health"; *welei'kw, lo'lti'kw; weleiep, leisip* or *lei'p, le'ksip* or *le'kip, lei'kuss, leieksip, leioqsip, le'ksipnik* or *le'kipnik, lo'lti'kuss*, etc.; *weleianl, -anek; wleian, -ass, -asn; wleikk, -kapn, wleikpn, wle'soqq; wleie'n, wleij,*

wleinej, wlei'tij, wlo'ltinej; mu kuleiw, -leipp, -lo'ltipp; nulein, weleimk, welo'ltimk.

This verb has two, even three, inanimate forms: *wele'k*, "that is a good thing," *mu wele'nuk; weltek*, "that is well placed," *mu weltenukw*; then *weliaq* (which belongs to the third conjugation in *iei*), "that is all right"; *mu welianukw*. It is the same for several others.

The obviative forms are *wele'lijl, wele'liji, welo'ltiliji; wle'lital, wle'lita, wlo'ltilita; wle'lij, wle'li'tij, wlo'ltilij*.

Telei, -lein, -le'k (-e'k, -tek, -iaq), -lei'kw, -lo'lti'kw, "to be such, in such a state." Notice the possible meaning: "in an interesting state"; do not ever ask the question: *Talein*, "how are you, in what state?" That attracts the prompt reply: *moqwa taleiw*, "I am not in any state." But one says either: *tali-wlein*, or as well: *me' welein*, "are you always well?" Likewise, in the third person: *tale'k*, "how is he?" If something is not quite satisfactory, one would answer: *mu l'nim*, "not too bad"; or else: *moqwa kesi wleiw*, "I am not very well." Moreover:

Talei, -lein, -le'k, "who am I? in what state?" is conjugated exactly as *welei, -lein, -le'k; talo'lti'kupn Ewjit Niskam mu l'nua'siwksipn?* "what would we have become if the Son of God was not made a man?" *Elnua'si*, "to be made a man (Indian)"; *elnua'lasnl*, "he (the Holy Spirit) made him a man." *Msɨt eta pa mn'tua'kik l'ta'qupn*, "we would all certainly have gone to hell"; *mntua'ki*, "hell," *mntu'k eta wikuow*, "that is the residence of demons"; *nujj, alasutmelsewi, ki's pikwelkl kisi-tleianl*, "my father, pray for me, for I am (guilty) of many things"; *tleianl*, contracted because of *kisi*.

Amasikei, -ein, -e'k, "to be miserly, close-fisted"; *amasikeimk*, "avarice."

Espei, -ein, -e'k, "to be elevated, of high rank, pretentious."

Malei, -ein, -e'k, "to be lazy," *maleimk, malo'qn*, "laziness, sloth."

Metuei, -ein, -e'k, "to be hard, troublesome"; *metue'k*, "that is troublesome, sad"; *mtue'tew*, "that will be sad"; *metue'kaq e'pitaq* (past), "a bad woman"; *mtue'nutuk* (dubitative form) *etuk telkimuloq?* "is what I order you then so difficult?" (Ms. 2, 119).

Meskei, -ein, -e'k, "to regret, to be sad"; *msɨke'tes*, "it will be painful for me"; *meskei'p*, "it was painful for you"; *msɨkeie'n*, "repent"; *mu kmsɨkeiw*, "do not regret."

Nutqwei, -ein, -e'k, "to be young, inexperienced"; *nutqwo'ltijik*, "youths."

Pekajei, -ein, -e'k, "to be straight, pure, well preserved"; *meltami-pekaje'k*, "immaculate"; *meltami* from *meltamtuk*, "from the beginning."

Kiskajei, -ein, -e'k, "to be prepared"; *kiskatte'k*, "it is ready"; *msit kaqi-kiskajiaq*, "everything is used up"; from *kiskajiey* (third conjugation), "to be ready, completed, finished."

Waqmei, -ein, -e'k, "to be pure"; *waqmo'ti*, "purity"; *Waqmitkuk*, "Bonaventure, pure, clear river."

Weskewei, -ein, -e'k, "to laugh"; *wsikewe'tes, wsikeweie'n, mu kwsikeweiw*.

The ordinal numerals and other adjectives and substantives in *wey* become verbs if one adds to them an *i* or if the diphthong *ey* is changed to *ei*, and they are conjugated like *welei*, but in the third person of the singular and dual they become *weit* and *wejik*, and the whole plural is in *-weiulti'kw*, like that of *wekai* (see Rand, Dict. xxii).

Examples: *amskwesewey*, "first"; *amskweseweyi, -in, -it*, "to be the first"; *wejik, weyultijik; tapuoweyi, sisteweyi*, etc.

Kespiaqeweyi, poqtamkiaqeweyi, kaqi-kiskaja'tasikeweyi, "I am the (first and the) last, the beginning and the end" (Rev. 22, 13).

4. *Ala'si, -sin, -sit*, the third secondary model, "to go from side to side, to roam, to be a vagabond"; *ala'ti'kw, alita'yikw, ala'siap, -sian, -siass, -siasn, -sik, -sikapn, -sites; ala'si, ala'tinej, alita'nej, alita'q; mu ktalita'pp; ntala'sin, ala'simk, ala'timk, alita'mk*.

Tela'si, -a'ti'kw, -ita'yikw, "to act thus"; *ni'n tela'si*, "that is my fault"; inanimate: *tela'sik, tela'tikl, telitaql: ta'n telite'tkl tela'tikl*, "all that he wants happens."

Epa'si, epa'ti'kw, epita'yikw, "to be seated"; *pa'sites, pa'titesnu; pa'si, pa'tikw, pita'qw, mu ktipa'siw, ktipa'tip, ktipita'p*.

Kina'si, kina'ti'kw, kinita'yikw, "to advance, to continue, to press on."

Emitklpukua'si, kua'ti'kw, kueta'yi'kw, "to kneel down"; notice *e* here in the plural in place of *i*; *mitklpukua'sites, mitklpukueta'qw*, "get on (your) knees"; one also says *emetklpukua'si, metklpukueta'qw*.

Maja'si, -a'ti'kw, -ita'yikw, "to move, stir, to depart"; *maqmikewek maja'siksipnek*, "the earth trembled"; *nqasi-majita'nej*, "let's get out of here."

Poqtamka'si, -ka'ti'kw, -kita'yikw, "to leave (by land)"; *poqtamkiey* or *pusi* (by water); *pqotamka'sites, pqotamka'si, mu kpoqtamka'siw*.

Nisa'si, -sa'ti'kw, -sita'yikw, "to go down."

Wenaqkwija'si, -ja'ti'kw, -jita'yikw, "to raise one's thoughts"; *wnaqkwija'sites; mu kunaqkwija'siw meteskuaqniktuk*, "do not raise him by pride."

Add also the verbs of the preceding lessons: *aqma'si, aja'si, elnua'si, wejuowa'si, ejikla'si, wenaqa'si, kipoqwa'si, mila'si, nama'si, papka'si, pitawa'si, punmila'si, taultna'si*.

5. Finally there are impersonal verbs, and also nouns and verbal adjectives, which are conjugated like the inanimate form of *teluisi, teluisik*. Here are some:

Kesik, "it is winter"; *kesikek, ksitew*; it is better to use *ksin, ksinuk*, and the compounds with *-puk* (see the fifth conjugation); *tekik*, "it is cold"; *tekipuk*, "a cold winter."

Sikw, "the spring"; *sikkwek, siktew*; better *sikun, sikunuk*.

Maqatkwik, "the sea is bad, rough, high"; *maqatkwikek, maqatkwitew*; *tkwik*, "there's a sea running"; *tku*, "wave"; *tku'k*, "waves."

Meski'k, "large"; *msiki'ktitew, msiki'kti-j, mu msiki'ktnuj*.

Winjik, "that is bad"; *winjittew* or *winjiktitew, tal*.

A'qataik, "half."

Kipitaik, "above, on high"; *pejili-pkitaik*, "in the highest."

Elmi'knik, "the future, in the future"; *(i)apjiw elmi'knik*, "world without end."

Temik, "it is deep."

Sipikk, "it is hard, tough."

Tepkik, "night."

Remark: It is very important to practice in turn each tense of *teluisi* while conjugating these verbs, first those which have no variations, then the others. Be careful of the contractions. After each Mi'kmaw form give the English translation.

LESSON TWELVE

SECOND CONJUGATION (INTRANSITIVE) IN AY

Principal model: *Alasutmay*, to pray

Present Indicative

alasutmay, I pray.
    man, you pray.
    mat, he prays.
    mayikw, we pray (incl.).
    mayek, we pray (excl.).
    mayoq, you pray.
    majik, they pray.
    ma'ti'kw, we pray (incl.).
    ma'tiyek, we pray (excl.).
    ma'tiyoq, you pray.
    ma'tijik, they pray.

Negative Conjugation: *mu alasutmaw*, "I do not pray," etc., *-mawn*, *-mawk*, *-mawkw*, *-mawek*, *-mawoq*, *-ma'tiwk*, *-ma'tiwkw*, *-ma'tiwek*, *-ma'tiwoq*, *-ma'ti'tiwk*.

Supplementary Forms: 1. **Inanimate**: *alasutmaq*, *-maql*, *-ma'tikl*; *mu alasutmanukw*, *-manukwl*, *-ma'tinukwl*, "a Christian thing, Catholic, non-Catholic." "The Catholics are the ones who pray," *alasutme'winu'k*, or *ta'nik alasutmajik*.

2. **Obviative subject**: *alasutmalijl*, *-maliji*, *-ma'tiliji*; *mu alasutmalikwl*, *-malikwi*, *-ma'tilikwi*; ex.: "God sees the one who prays," *Kisu'lkw nemiajl alasutmalijl*; he has mercy on the poor," *eulite'lmasnika eule'jultilitka* (absent).

3. **Missing persons, dead or absent**: *alasutmataq, -matkik, -ma'titkik; -malita, -malitka, ma'tilitka; mu alasutmaqwaq, -maqwik, -ma'tikwi'k; mu alasutmalikwa, -malikwika, -ma'tilikwika.*

4. Likewise an inanimate subject in the **past** will require *alasutmaqek, -maqekl; mu alasutmanukwek, -kwekl.*

5. With an indirect object in the plural, animate or inanimate, for example: "because of certain things or persons I pray"; *na't koqoe'l weji-alasutma'nl, na't wenik weji-alasutma'nik*, the following forms are found: *alasutma'nl, -manl, -majl, -mayikwl, -mayekl, -mayoql, -ma'tijl, -ma'ti'kwl, -ma'tiyekl, -ma'tiyoqwl, -ma'ti'tijl; -ma'nik, -manik, -maji, -mayikwik, -mayekik, -mayoqik, -ma'tiji, -ma'ti'kwik, -ma'tiyekik, -ma'tiyoqik, -ma'ti'tiji*; in the negative: *mu alasutmawanl, -mawnl, -ma'qwl, -mawkwl, -mawekl, -mawoql, -ma'tikwl, -ma'tiwkwl, -ma'tiwekl, -ma'tiwoql, -ma'ti'tikwl; -mawanik, -mawnik, -maqwi, -mawkwik, -mawekik, -mawoqik, -ma'tikwi; -ma'tiwkwik, -ma'tiwekik, -ma'tiwoqik, -ma'ti'tikwi.*

Past Indicative

alasutmayep, ma'p, I prayed.
    ma'sip, ma'p, you prayed.
    mass, ma'p, masp, he prayed.
    mayikuss, kup, kusp, we prayed.
    mayeksip, kip, kiss, we prayed.
    mayoqsip, qop, qoss, you prayed.
    masnik, pnik, sipnik, they prayed.
    ma'ti'kus, kup, kusp, we prayed.
    ma'tiyeksip, kip, kiss, we prayed.
    ma'tiyoqsip, qop, qoss, you prayed.
    ma'tisnik, pnik, sipnik, they prayed.

Negative Conjugation: *mu alasutmawep*, "I didn't pray," etc., *-mawsip, -mawksip, -mawkup, -mawekip*, or *-maweksip, -mawoqop* or *-mawoqsip, -mawksipnik, -ma'tiwkup* or *-ma'tiuksip, -ma'tiwekip* or *-ma'tiweksip, -ma'tiwoqop* or *-ma'tiwoqsip, -matiwksipnik.*

Remark: For the different forms *-as, -a'p, -us, -up, -snik, -pnik*, see above, first conjugation. (p. 45).

Supplementary Forms: 1. Third persons with **inanimate subject**: *alasutmaqsip, -maqsipnl, -ma'tiksipnl; mu alasutmanuksip, -manuksipnl, -ma'tinuksipnl.*

2. **Obviative forms**: *alasutmalisnl, -malisni, -ma'tilisni*; negative: *alasutmaliwksipnl, -maliwksipni, -ma'tiliwksipni*.

3. For the **missing, dead or absent**, one can use the forms of the present, which have a true past sense. There are also, however, the following forms of the past: *alasutmasnaq, -masnika, -ma'tisnika*; there are also the following obviatives: *alasutmalisna, -malisnika, -ma'tilisnika*. In the negative: *alasutmaliwksipna, -maliwksipnika, -ma'tiliwksipnika*.

When the verb agrees with an indirect object in the plural, animate or inanimite, it is necessary to add *-ik* or *-l* to the singular, as follows: *alasutma'pnik, -masipnik, -masni, -mayikupnik, -mayeksipnik, -mayoqsipnik, -ma'tisni, -ma'ti'kupnik, -ma'tiyeksipnik, -ma'tiyoqsipnik, -ma'ti'tisni; -ma'pnl, -masipnl, -masnl, -mayikupnl, -mayeksipnl, -mayoqsipnl, -ma'ti'snl, -ma'ti'kupnl, -ma'tiyekiipnl, -ma'tiyoqsipnl, -ma'ti'tisnl*. In the negative: *alasutmawapnik, -mawapnl*, etc.

5. If the obviative is the name of a thing or a person in the **past**, according to the rules of Lesson Seven, No. 3, the verb is made to agree, by changing *-l* to *-ek, -ekl*, and *-ik* to *-aq, -aqik*.

6. **Dubitative** forms: *alasutmatuk*, "he might have prayed"; *-matuss* ("perhaps" *tuksip*), "perhaps he prayed"; *tuknik*, "perhaps they prayed"; *matup*, "I, you prayed"; *alasutmaqeptuk* (conditional), "I would pray." *Tawaqtmatup*, "I would beg," *-tukup*, "we ...," *-tuoqop*, "you ...," *-tuk, -tukupnik*, "he, they ..."; *entuksiktmautup, -tuk, -tukunik*, "I, they, were perhaps laying in provisions."

Future Indicative

Remark: *alasutmay* does not take contraction, but other verbs can take it; take note of the list.

Alasut   *ma's, mates*, I will pray.
        matesk (*teks*), you will pray.
        matew (*tow*), he will pray.
        matesnu (*teksnu*), we will pray.
        matesnen (*teksnen*), we will pray.
        matoqsip, you will pray.
        mataqq, they will pray.
        ma'titesnu, we will pray.
        ma'titesnen, we will pray.
        ma'titoqsip, you will pray.
        ma'titaqq, they will pray.

Negative Conjugation: *ma'alasutmaw*, etc. (as in the present), "I will not pray."

Supplementary Forms: 1. **Inanimate subject**: *alasutmatew, -matal, -ma'tital*; negative: *ma'alasutmanukw, -manukul, -ma'tinukul*, "that concerns prayer, religion; that has nothing to do with it." Other verbs have *-a'qtitew, ma'...-aqtnuk*, such as *wasitpa'q*, "clear night"; *wasitpa'qtitew, ma' wasitpa'qtnukw*.

2. **Obviative forms**: *alasutmalital, -malita, -ma'tilita*; with their negative: *ma' alasutmalikul, -malikwi, -ma'tilikwi*.

3. The relational forms to plural objects also affect only the third persons; the inanimates as in No. 1; the animates, *alasutma(li)tal, -ma(li)ta, -ma'ti(li)ta*.

Imperative

Alasut   *ma*, pray.
        maj, let him pray.
        manej, let us pray.
        maq, pray.
        ma'tij, let them pray.
        ma'tinej, let us pray.
        ma'tikw, pray.
        ma'ti'tij, let them pray.

Negative

Mu   *ktalasutmaw*, do not pray.
     alasutmawij, let him not pray.
     alasutmanej, let us not pray.
     ktalasutmapp, don't pray.
     alasutmawi'tij, let them not pray.
     alasutma'tinej, let us not pray.
     ktalasutma'tipp, do not pray.
     alasutma'ti'tij, let them not pray.

Supplementary Forms: 1. With an **inanimate subject**: it is like the animate, but the negative is *mu alasutmanuj*; and when the future is *-aqtitew*, the imperative is *-aqtij, -aqtnuj*: *newtukuna'q*, "one day"; *nkutukna'qtij*, "let it be one day"; *mu nkutukuna'qtnuj*, "let it not be a (single) day."

2. It can be seen that negation does not alter the first person of the plural and dual, nor the third person plural.

3. The second person singular is formed from the first of the present indicative by dropping *y*; it is the same with the third conjugation; for the second person dual, *-ayikw* is changed to *-aq* and *-eyikw* to *-e'k* or *-e'kw* (without *i*); in the negative *-q* or *-kw* is changed to *-p* and the *-k* and euphonic *-t* are introduced.

Conjunct or Indicative with *When*

Alasut   *ma'nl*, *ma'nek*, praying, having prayed or when I pray, prayed.
         manl, *manek*, when you pray, prayed.
         majl, *matek*, when he prays, prayed.
         mayikwl, *mayikwek*, when we, etc.
         mayekl, *mayekek*, when we.
         mayoqwl, *mayoqwek*, when you.
         ma'tijl, *ma'titek*, when they.
         ma'ti'kwl, *ma'ti'kwek*, when we.
         ma'tiyekl, *ma'tiyekek*, when we.
         ma'tiyoqwl, *ma'tiyoqwek*, when you.
         ma'ti'tijl, *ma'ti'titek*, when they.

Negative Conjugation: *mu alasutmawanl -mawanek*, "not praying, not having prayed, or when I did not pray, have not prayed," *-mawnl -mawnek*, *-maqwl -maqwek*, *-mawkwl -mawkwek*, *-mawekl -mawekek*, *-mawoqwl -mawoqwek*, *-ma'tikwl -ma'tikwek*, *-ma'tiwkwl -ma'tiwkwek*, *-ma'tiwekl -ma'tiwekek*, *-ma'tiwoqwl -ma'tiwoqwek*, *-ma'titikwl -ma'titikwek*.

Supplementary Forms: 1. **Inanimate**: *alasutmaql* (sing. and dual), *-maqek*; *-ma'tikl*, *ma'tikek* (pl.); *mu alasutmanukwl*, *-nukwek*, *-ma'tinukwl*, *-nukwek*.

2. **Obviative Subject**: *alasutmalijl*, *ma'tilijl*, *malitek*, *ma'tilitek*; *mu alasutmalikwl*, *ma'tilikwl*, *malikwek*, *ma'tilikwek*.

3. For the **missing, dead, absent**, or things past or removed: *alasutmatka*, *-ma'titka*, *-malitka*, *ma'tilitka*; *maqsipnek*, *sipnikl*.

4. For *ika'y*, M. Maillard writes *ika'yanl*, *mu ika'wanl* (Published Grammar 49); one can certainly also say: *ika'nl*, *ika'nek*, with long *a*.

Conjunct or Indicative With *If*

Alasut	*ma'n*	*ma'ss*	*ma'sn*	if I pray, prayed, have prayed.
	man	*ma'sip*	*ma'sipn*	if you pray, etc.
	maj	*mass*	*masn*	if he prays, etc.
	mayikw	*mayikuss*	*mayikusn*	if we, etc.
	mayek	*mayeksip*	*mayeksipn*	if we.
	mayoq	*mayoqsip*	*mayoqsipn*	if you.
	ma'tij	*ma'tiss*	*ma'tisn*	if they.
	ma'ti'kw	*ma'ti'kuss*	*ma'ti'kusn*	if we.
	ma'tiyek	*ma'tiyeksip*	*ma'tiyeksipn*	if we.
	ma'tiyoq	*ma'tiyoqsip*	*ma'tioqsipn*	if you.
	ma'ti'tij	*ma'ti'tiss*	*ma'ti'tisn*	if they.

Supplementary Forms: 1. The **negative conjugation** is: *mu alasutmawan, -mawass, -mawasn; -mawn, -mawsip, -mawsipn; -maq, -maqsip, -maqsipn; -mawkw, -mawkuss, -mawkusn; -mawek, -maweksip, -maweksipn; -mawoq, -mawoqsip, -mawoqsipn; -ma'tikw,* etc.

2. The **inanimate forms**, when they are encountered, as in *ika'y*, are: *ika'q, ika'ss, ika'sn*, "if that happens ..."; *mu ika'nuk, -nuss, -nusn*.

3. **Obviative forms**: *alasutmalij, -liss, -lisn; alasutma'tilij; -liss, -lisn*; ex.: *Wujjual mu ksinukwaliwksi-pn, mu mtoqwa'lawisoqq*, "if their father had not been sick, they would not have brought him down (from the woods)."

Conditional

Present

Alasut	*maqq (ap)*, I would pray.
	maqq (p), you would pray.
	mass, he would pray.
	ma'qupp or *mayikupp*, we would pray.
	maqekk (p), we would pray.
	maqoqq (p), you would pray.
	ma'tiss, they would pray
	ma'ti'kupp, we would pray.
	ma'tikekk (p), we would pray.
	ma'tikoqq (p), you would pray.
	ma'ti'tiss, they would pray.

Past

Alasut   *maqapn*, I would have prayed.
       maqpn, you would have prayed.
       masoqq, he would have prayed.
       ma'qupn or *mayikupn*, we would have prayed.
       maqekpn, we would have prayed.
       maqoqpn, you would have prayed.
       ma'tisoqq, they would have prayed.
       ma'ti'kupn, we would have prayed.
       ma'tikekpn, we would have prayed.
       ma'tikoqpn, you would have prayed.
       ma'ti'tisoqq, they would have prayed.

Supplementary Forms: 1. **Negative**, similar to the affirmative. The following are found, however: *mu alasutmawiss, -tiwiss, -wisoqq, -tiwisoqq*; *mu ksika'wiss*, "he would not have been lost" (John 1, 16).

2. **Inanimate**, as above; but in the negative one finds: *mu alasutmanuss, -nusoqq*; *-ma'tinuss, -nusoqq*.

3. **Obviative forms**: *alasutmaliss, -lisoqq*; *-ma'tiliss, -lisoqq*.

4. *Alasutmayikupp o o o!*: public call to prayer which is no longer used since the installation of bells.

See **Remarks**, under the first conj. (p. 51).

Subordinative

Ntalasutman, that I may pray.
Ktalasutman, that you may pray.
Wtalasutman, that he may pray.
Ktalasutmanenu, that we may pray.
Ntalasutmanen, that we may pray.
Ktalasutmanew, that you may pray.
Wtalasutmanew, that they may pray.
Ktalasutma'tinenu, that we may pray.
Ntalasutma'tinen, that we may pray.
Ktalasutma'tinew, that you may pray.
Wtalasutma'tinew, that they may pray.

Supplementary Forms: 1. **Inanimate**: there is no difference for this verb; but those whose future is in *-ti-tew*, here have *-ten* or *-tnen*. There is no negative; but the following are found: *-anun, -atinun, -tnun*.

2. **Obviatives**: *wtalasutmalin, -ma'tilin*; see **Remark** (p. 51).

Infinitive or Impersonal (Indefinite Subject)

Alasut mamk, ma'timk, to pray, one prays.
       mamkiss, ma'timkiss or *kip*, one prayed.
       maten, ma'titen, one will pray.
       mamkij, ma'timkij, let one pray (imperative).
       mamkl, ma'timkl, praying, when one prays.
       mamkek, ma'timkek, having prayed, when one prayed.
       mamk, ma'timk, if one prays.
       mamkiss, ma'timkiss, if one prayed.
       mamkisn, ma'timkisn, if one had prayed.
       maness, ma'tiness, one would pray.
       manesoqq, ma'tinesoqq, one would have prayed.
       man, ma'tin, that one may pray (subordinative).

Negative

Mu alasutmammik, ma'timmik, not to pray, one does not pray.
Mu alasutmammiksip, ma'timmiksip, one did not pray.
Ma' alasutmammik, ma'timmik, one will not pray.
Mu alasutmamkij, ma'timkij, let one not pray (imper.).
       alasutmammikl, ma'timmikl, not praying, when one does not pray.
       alasutmammikek, ma'timmikek, not having prayed.
       alasutmammik, ma'timmik, if one does not pray.
       alasutmammkiss, ma'timkiss, if one did not pray.
       alasutmammkisn, ma'timkisn, if one had not prayed.
       alasutmaness, ma'tiness, one would not pray.
       alsutmanesoqq, ma'tinesoqq, one would not have prayed.
       alasutman, ma'tin, that one not pray (subordinative).

Remarks: 1, 2, 3, as for *teluisi* (p. 52).

4. From the infinitive verbal nouns are formed, as *alasutmamk*, "prayer," or *teli-alasutmamk*, "that is how one prays"; *alasutmamkewey, -kewe'l*, "that which concerns prayer, breviaries, prayer books, missals"; *alasutmamkwamkewe'l*, "ceremonies"; *wejkuiaq meski'k alasutmamk*, "the great solemn celebration is here"; *mawi-alasutmamk*, "public prayer, retreat"; *pejili-klu'lk alasutmamk*, "the most beautiful of prayers." As *alasutmaqn* also

means "religion" and *kji-alasutmaqn*, "sacrament, to make clear that prayer is intended, one says in the Catechism": *alasutmaqn ta'n teli-alasutmamk* (p. 50). *Mu alasutma'timmik ma' wsita'timmik*, "if one does not pray, one will not be saved"; *westay, westamk*, "to escape, to be saved"; verbs which are susceptible to contraction have it in the future of the infinitive, as in that of the indicative, just as in the subordinative and other moods: *nawiaq wsitan*, "it is impossible to be saved, that one can be saved."

LESSON THIRTEEN

EXAMPLES OF THE SECOND CONJUGATION

The verbs of this conjugation, as those of the first, can be divided into several categories, with some more or less important differences.

1. The first is that which keeps the vowel *a* in the ending, in the dual and the plural, as does *alasutmay*, throughout the conjugation; these verbs are absolutely regular; however, the first one takes an *l* in the plural (this is the only one that I know) and the second has no plural; the dual serves as the plural. The future is in *-as*, *-ates*, the imperative in *-a*, *-aq*, *-atikw*, with or without contraction.

Amalkay, *-kan*, *-kat*, "dance"; *-kayikw*, *-kal'ti'kw*; *-ka's*, *-ka*, *-kaq*, *-kal'tikw*, *ntamalkan*; *mu ktamalkaw*, *-kapp*, *-kal'tipp*.

Ika'y, *ika'n*, *ika't*, *ika'q*, "to arrive, bump into, it happens (suddenly); *ika'yep*, *ika's*, *ika'*, *mu ktika'w*, *ntika'n*; *ika'yanl*, *ika'nl*, *ika'jl*, "when ..."; *ika'yan*, *ika'yass*, *ika'yasn*; *ika'n*, *ika'sɨp*, *ika'sɨpn*; *ika'j*, *ika'ss*, *ika'sn*; *ika'qq*, *ika'qapn*, or *ika'ikk*, *ika'ikapn*, "I would arrive, I would have arrived"; *ika'qq*, *ika'qpn*, *ika'ss*, *ika'soqq*, *ika'qupp* or *ika'yikupp*, *-kupn*; *ika'yikekk* *-kekpn*; *ika'yikoqq*, *-qoqpn*; *ika'tiss*, *-tisoqq*.

Ankwiskay, *-kan*, *-kat*, *-kayikwl*, "my, yours, his, our joints."

Epmepikay, *-kan*, *-kat*, "my, your, his side"; these two verbs and a few others are rendered in English by nouns.

Ewi'kay, *-kan*, *-kat*, "to build"; *wi'kates*, *wi'ka*, *ntui'kan*, *mu ktui'kaw*.

Elay, *-lan*, *-lat*, "resemble, to look alike"; it is best to use the reciprocal: *elati'kw*, *elatulti'kw*, "we resemble each other"; *elati'tijl Kisu'lkwl*, "they are similar to God."

Wekwilat, "he barks"; *punkwila*, "stop barking."

Nuta'may, -man, -mat, -maq, "to lack, to not have enough."

Welnmay, -man, -mat, "to be next"; *wlnma's*.

We'kwanmay, -man, -mat, "to be in need, reach the limit."

Awtikmay, -man, -mat, "to guide"; *nutawtikmuet*, "shepherd, guide."

Utqotay, -tan, -tat, -tamk, "to have a funeral, to take part in one."

Westay, -tan, -tat, "to be saved"; *wsita's, mu kusitaw*.

Nuta'y, -ta'n, -ta't, -ta'q, "to lack something; it is missing."

Telitay, -tan, -tat, "to be of such strength"; *ta'n telitay teli-ksaln*, "I love you with all my heart."

Oqwa'y, -qwa'n, -qwa't, -qwa'q, "to arrive by boat, to come ashore, land"; *oqwa'yoq kespitek* (Rem. Gr. 233), "you arrive Saturday"; *oqwa'timk* (55.2).

Elkusua'y, -ua'n, -ua't, -ua'ti'kw, "to leap, to go up by leaps and bounds"; *l'kusuaqn*, "ladder, staircase"; *l'kusuaqnik*, "there is a ladder."

We'kwa'y, -kwa'n, -kwa't, -kwa'q, "to come at the end, that is the end."

Nu'kwa'y, -kwa'n, -kwa't, -kwa'q, "to burn"; *nu'kwa'yekip*, "we have burned"; *niknenek nu'kwa'qek*, "our house was burned" (letter); *newte'jkek wen'ji'kuomek nu'kwa'qek l'pa pekaj kaqoqtek, katu ma wen kaqsiwk*, "a house burned, completely to the ground, but without mishap to anyone" (letter); *nu'kwa'ql mkamlamunl*, "burning hearts."

Peway, -an, -at, "to dream"; *pua's, npuan, mu kpuaw*.

Putmay, -an, -at, "to lack, to omit, to get out of doing."

Note on certain other verbs:

Emel'siktmay, -man, -mat, "to dream, to see, to hear, to imagine strange things, to have bad premonitions"; *mu emel'siktemawn*, "you do not dream" (Leg. 173); *emel'siktmamkewey*, "phantasmagoria"; *emel'siktaq*, "to frighten" (Doc. C.F., I, 17).

Ni'may or *mi'may, -man, -mat*, "to be stocked for a trip"; *mu kni'manew*, "do not carry provisions" (Matt. 10, 9); M. Maillard has *mimai* in his printed grammar (46) changed today to *ni'mai*; *Wli-Ni'mamkewey*, "Extreme Unction."

Nunay, -nan, -nat, "to suckle, to be at the breast"; Rand (122, 2) writes *nuney* and in the Gospel (Matt. 21, 16): *ta'nik nun'tijik*; even M. Maillard (Ms. 9, 108) writes: *nunitijik*, but elsewhere he says that this verb is conjugated like *amalkay* (Ms. 5, 29). In any case it is certain that at Restigouche the plural is *nunatijik*; I have heard these words clearly; *mijua'ji'j moqwa nunawk*, "the infant is not suckling."

2. The second category is that of the less numerous verbs which **change** *a* to *i* in the plural, such as:

Nepay (short *e*), *-pan, -pat,* "to sleep"; *nepayikw, nepiti'kw, npates, npititesnu; npa, npaq, npitikw; mu knpaw, mu knpapp, mu knpitipp; taleyoq nepitiyoq,* "what are you doing, sleeping?"

Elaqamay, -man, -mat, "to braid the middle of the snowshoe"; *elaqamayikw, elaqamiti'kw; laqama's, mu klaqamaw*.

Pimay, -man, -mat, "to hunt birds"; *pimiti'kw*.

3. The third category is that of verbs which make the plural in *-uti'kw, -ulti'kw, -olti'kw,* which are conjugated like that of *teluisi,* such are:

Weskukway, -kwan, -kwat, "to cook"; *weskukwayikw, weskukuti'kw, wskukwas, mu ktuskukwaw*; also *wessukway* and *wissukwey* (third conjugation).

Kesinukway, -kwan, -kwat, "to be sick"; *ksinukwa's, mu ksinukwaw. Kesinukwan ta?* "are you sick?" *kesinukway eta,* "yes"; *kikmenu kesinukwat,* "our neighbor is sick"; *mijua'ji'j kesinukwa'ji'j,* "the child is a little sick." *Tali-ksinukwan?* "what are you sick with?" *nun'ji kesinukuik,* "my head hurts"; *tkey matnik,* "I have a cold"; *wepskuniney* (third conj.), "I am consumptive." *Tali-pkiji-ksinukwan?* "for how long?" *tapusijik tepknusejik,* "for two months"; *tatuji-ksinukwan?* "how seriously?" *mu lnim meski'ktnuk,* "not too bad."

Nusukway, -kwan, -kwat, "to follow"; *nusukuti'kw*.

Metkway, -kwan, -kwat, "to have a bare head"; *metkuti'kw*.

Wesimukway, -kwan, -kwat (or *-kwet*), "to flee"; *wesimukul'ti'kw, wsimukwa's, mu kusimukwaw*.

Nekapikwa'y, -kwa'n, -kwa't (or *-kwek*), "to be blind"; *nekapikwo'lti'kw*.

Nesamuqway, -qwan, -qwat, "to drink"; *nesamuqwo'lti'kw, nsamuqwa's, mu knsamuqwaw; ketu'-samuqway,* "to be thirsty"; *msit newte'telamu'kwek mjijaqmijueyek nesamuqwamkek nesamuqwo'lti'tisnek,* "they all drank from the same spiritual drink"; *mita wet-samuqwo'lti'tisnek kun'teweyek, toqu na pa tele'k Sesukuli*; "for they drew it out from the rock, which was Christ" (1 Cor. 10, 3).

Pitlikay, -kan, -kat; "to have a long stride"; *pitlikolti'kw; pitlika'si, -sin, -sit,* "to take a long stride."

Te'sipuna'y, -na'n, -na't, "to be so old"; *te'sipuno'lti'kw; ta'sipuno'ltiyoq?* "how old are you?" *newtipuna'y, tapui ..., nesi ..., newi ..., nani ..., asukom te'sipuna'y*, "1, 2, 3, 4, 5, 6 years"; *newtiskekipuna'y* or *metla'sipuna'y*, "10"; *tapui ..., nesi ..., newi ..., nani ..., asukom te'siskekipuna'y*, "20, 30, 40, 50, 60"; *kaskmtlnaqnipuna'y, ta'pu k., si'st k.*, "100, 200, 300 years."

Nesay, -san, -sat, "to fear, mistrust, to suspect danger"; *neso'lti'kw, nsa's, mu knesaw*.

Natuay, -an, -at, "to harpoon"; *natuti'kw*; hence *Natuaqnek*, "Eel Ground"; also *nantuay* and *nenatuay*.

4. The fourth category is composed of verbs of movement, which form their dual in *-a'ti'kw* and their plural in *-ita'yikw*, just like the verbs in *-a'si*. Such are:

Piskwa'y, -kwa'n, -kwa't, "to enter"; *piskwa'ti'kw, -kweta'yikw; piskwa's, piskwa', -kwa'tikw, kweta'qw; mu kpiskwa'w, -kwa'tipp kweta'pp*.

Toqjua'y, -jua'n, -jua't, "to go up"; *toqjua'ti'kw, -jueta'yikw; tqojua's,* or *-a'tes; tqojua', -a'tikw, -eta'q; mu kitqojua'w*.

Metma'y, -ma'n, -ma't, "to stroll, take a trip"; *metma'ti'kw, mita'yikw, mtma's, mtma', mu kmtma'w; telkitasit wtli-pmi-mtma'n nekml teli-mtma'lip*, "he (the Christian) should go as He (Jesus)"; *eli-mtma't poqnitpa'q* (1 John 2, 6, 11), "he (the unbeliever) walks in darkness"; *Se'sus pemi-tqojui-mtma't Selu'salemk, elaji: Na pemi-tqojui-mtmita'yikw*, "Jesus went up to Jerusalem, saying (to his disciples): Now we are going up there" (Matt. 20, 17); *napi-mtma'nej*, "let us walk in his footsteps" (Par. I, 119).

5. Finally, the **impersonals** in *aq*, like the third person inanimates, are conjugated as follows:

Pesaq, "it is snowing"; *psatew, psaj, mu psanuj*.

Kikpesaq, "it is raining"; *mu kikpesanuk*, "it is not raining"; *nukwek*, "when it was not raining."

Kaqtukwaq, "it is thundering," or rather, "there is thunder," or, simply "thunder"; *kaqtukowik*, "it thunders"; *mu kaqtukowinuk*.

Metukuna'q, "bad weather"; *mtukuna'qtitew, -tej*; Fr. Maillard writes: *metu'na'q; kaqai'sukuna'q*, "several days"; *mu kaqai'sukuna'qtnukw*, "not many days"; *pikwelukuna'q* or *pukwelukuna'q*, "a good many days"; *tekelukuna'q*, "a few days."

Aqtatpa'q, "midnight"; *aqtatpa'qtitew, ma' aqtatpa'qtnukw; aqtatpa'qtij, mu aqtatpa'qtnuj*. Likewise *wasitpa'q*, "clear night"; *poqonitpa'q* or *piqnitpa'q*, "dark night," and, in general, "darkness, shadows"; *tekitpa'q*, "cold night."

Tlueyan: *poqnitpa'q miamuj anqunaitew*, "if I say: the shadows will cover me"; *toqu tepkik kiwkto'qwi-wasoqwetew ntinink weskewkwija'sianl*, "now the night will shine around me in my pleasures."

Wela'k, more exactly *wela'kw*, "the evening"; *ma'wla'kwnukw*; *teki-wla'kw*, "cold evening."

Toqwa'q, "autumn"; *toqwa'qek*, "it was during the autumn."

Tetpaqa'q, "what it's all about, what happens."

Astaq, "heat (of the sun)."

Nekpa'q, "a flood in the house."

Ketapa'q, "flood"; *mesta ktapa'qek*, "deluge (past)."

Wejkwapa'q, "rising tide"; *jukwapa'qti-tew*.

Note: it is very important to drill successively each tense of these verbs, as with those of the first conjugation, first on those which have no variations, or almost none, then on the others. Say the English translation after each Mi'kmaw form. Then conjugate the verbs, one in one person, another in another, in forward or reverse order.

LESSON FOURTEEN

THIRD CONJUGATION (INTRANSITIVE) IN EY

Principal model: *Ewi'kikei*, to write

Present Indicative

Ewi'ki key, I write.
ken, you write.
ket, he writes.
keyikw, we write (incl.).
keyek, we write (excl.).
keyoq, you write.
kejik, they write.
kiti'kw, we write.
kitiyek, we write.
kitiyoq, you write.
kitijik, they write.

Negative Conjugation: *mu ewi'kikew*, "I do not write," etc., *-kewn*, *-kewk*, *-kewkw*, *-kewek*, *-kewoq*, *-ketiwk*, *-kitiwkw*, *-kitiwek*, *-kitiwoq*, *-kititiwk*.

Supplementary Forms: 1. **Inanimate**: this is in *-ek*, little used, except in the negative: *mu ewi'kikenukw*, "that does not write," *-kekl*, *-kitikl*, *-kenukwl*, *-kitinukwl*; verbs in *-iey* have inanimate forms *-iaq*, *-ianuk*, etc.

2. **Obviative subject**: *ewi'kikelijl*, *-keliji*, *-kitiliji*; *mu ewi'kikelikwl*, *-kelikwi*, *-kitilikwi*.

3. **Missing persons, dead or removed**: *ewi'kiketaq*, *-ketkik*, *-kititkik*; *ewi'kikelita*, *-kelitka*, *-kitilitka*; *mu ewi'kikekwaq*, *-kekwi'k*, *-kitikwi'k*; *mu ewi'kikelikwa*, *-kelikwika*, *-kitilikwika*.

4. Likewise an inanimate subject in the **past** requires *ewi'kikekek*, *-kekkl*.

5. With an indirect **object** in the **plural**, animate or inanimate, one has:

ewi'kikeyanl or *-ka'nl*, *-kenl*, *-kejl*, *-keyikwl*, *-keyekl*, *-keyoql*, *-kitijl*, *-kiti'kwl*, *-kitiyekl*, *-kitiyoqwl*, *-kiti'tijl*; then *ewi'kikeyanik*, or *-ka'nik*, *-kenik*, *-keji*, *-keyikwik*, *-keyekik*, *-keyoqik*, *-ketiji*, *-kiti'kwik*, *-kitiyekik*, *-kitiyoqik*, *-kiti'tiji*. In the negative: *Mu ewi'kikewanl*, *-kewnl*, *-kekwl*, *-kewkwl*, *-kewekl*, *-kewoql*, *-ketikwl*, *-kitiwkwl*, *-kitiwekl*, *-kitiwoql*, *-kiti'tikwl*; then *mu ewi'kikewanik*, *-kewnik*, *-kekwi*, *-kewkwik*, *-kewekik*, *-kewoqwik*, *-ketikwi*, *-kitiwkwik*, *-kitiwekik*, *-kitiwoqik*, *-kiti'tikwi*.

Past Indicative

Ewi'ki keyep, *ka'p*, I wrote.
    ke'sip, *ke'p*, you wrote.
    kess, *kep*, *kesp*, he wrote.
    keyikuss, *kup*, *kusp*, we wrote.
    keyeksip, *kip*, *kiss*, we wrote.
    keyoqsip, *qop*, *qiss*, you wrote.
    kesnik, *pnik*, *sipnik*, they wrote.
    kiti'kuss, etc., we wrote.
    kitiyeksip, etc., we wrote.
    kitiyoqsip, etc., you wrote.
    kitisnik, etc. they wrote.

Negative Conjugation: *mu ewi'kikewep* or *-kewap*, "I did not write," etc., *-kewsip*, *-kewksip*, *-kewkup* or *-kewkuss*, *-kewekip* or *-keweksip*, *-kewoqip* or *-kewoqsip*, *-kewsipnik*, *-kitiukup*, *-kitiweksip*, *-kitiwoqsip*, *-kitiwksipnik*.

See **Remark** 1, for the past of *teluisi* (p. 50).

Supplementary Forms: 1. **Inanimate**: *ewi'kikeksip*, *-keksipnl*, *-kitiksipnl*; *mu ewi'kikenuksip*, *-kenuksipnl*, *-kitinuksipnl*.

2. **Obviative subject**: *ewi'kikelisnl*, *-kelisni*, *-kitilisni*, (or *-pni*); *mu ewi'kikeliwksipnl*, *-keliwksipni*, *-kitiliwksipni*.

3. For the **missing, dead or absent**, one may use the forms of the present, which have a true past sense. There are also, however, the following forms in the past: *ewi'kikesnaq*, *-kesni'ka*, *-kitisni'ka*; then, the obviative forms, *ewi'kikelisna*, *-kelisnika*, *-kitilisnika*; *mu ewi'kikeliwksipna*, *-keliwksipnika*, *-kitiliwksipnika*.

4. When the verb expresses a relation to an **indirect** object in the **plural**, animate or inanimate, it is necessary to add *-ik* or *-l* to the singular, in this manner: *ewi'kika'pnik* (*n* here and elsewhere throughout is only euphonic), *-ke'sipnik* or *-ke'pnik*, *-kesni*, etc., *-keyikupnik*, *-keyeksipnik*, *-keyoqsipnik*,

-ke'tisni, -kiti'kupnik, -kitiyeksi-pnik, -kitiyoqsipnik, -kiti'tisni; -ka'pnl, etc., in changing *-ik* or *-i* or *-l*. Often *-sip* is suppressed; thus one finds: *patataqatiyeknl*, "the things of which we have been guilty" (7 pr. 102), *telmetoqnl*, "his bad behaviour in several things." In the negative: *Mu ewi'kikewapnik, -pnl*, etc.

5. If the obviative is the name of a thing or a person from the **past**, according to the rules of the seventh lesson, No. 3, the verb is made to agree, by changing *-l* to *-ek*, *-ekl* and *-ik* or *-i* to *-aq*, *-aqik*.

6. **Dubitative forms**: *wi'kiketukk, -tukupp, -tukuni'k, -tupp, -tupnik, -tukupnik*.

Future Indicative

Wi'ki ka's, ketes, I will write.
    ketesk, keteks, you will write.
    ketew, ketow, he will write.
    ketesnu, teksnu, we will write.
    ketesnen, teksnen, we will write.
    ketoqsip, you will write.
    ketaqq, they will write.
    kititesnu, we will write.
    kititesnen, we will write.
    kititoqsip, you will write.
    kititaqq, they will write.

Negative Conjugation: *ma'wi'kikew*, etc. (as in the present), "I will not write."

Supplementary Forms: 1. **Inanimate**: *wi'kike(kti)tew, -ke(kti)tal, -kitital; ma' wi'kike(kti)nukw, -kenukul, -kitinukul*. The other verbs form *-titew, -tnukw*.

2. **Obviative subject**: *wi'kikelital, -kelita, -kitilita; ma'wi'kikelikul, -kelikwi, -kitilikwi*.

3. Agreements with **plural** objects are added only to the third persons: *wi'kiketal, -kitital; -ke(li)tal, -ke(li)ta, -kiti(li)ta*.

Imperative

Wi'ki ke, ka, write.
    kej, let him write.
    kenej, let us write.
    kekw, (you dual) write.

ke'tij, let them write.
kitinej, let us write.
kitikw, write.
kiti'tij, let them write.

Mu *kwi'kikew*, do not write.
wi'kikewij, let him not write.
wi'kikenej, let us not write.
kwi'kikepp, do not (you dual) write.
wi'kikewi'tij, let them not write.
wi'kikitinej, let us not write.
kwi'kikitipp, do not write.
wi'kikiti'tij, let them not write.

Supplementary Form: 1. **Inanimate**: it is like the animate, but the negative is *mu wi'kikenuj*; when the future is in *-titew*, the imperative has: *-tej*, *-tnuj*.

2. and 3. Same as *alasutmay* (p. 65). At Restigouche one says *wi'kika* instead of *wi'kike*.

Conjunct or Indicative with *When*

Ewi'kikeyanl (*ka'nl*), *keyanek*, writing, having written, or when I write, wrote.
    kenl, *kenek*, when you, etc.
    kejl, *ketek*, when he.
    keyikwl, *keyikwek*, when we.
    keyekl, *keyekek*, when we.
    keyoqwl, *keyoqwek*, when you.
    ke'tijl, *ke'titek*, when they.
    kiti'kwl, *kiti'kwek*, when we.
    kitiyekl, *kitiyekek*, when we.
    kitiyoqwl, *kitiyoqwek*, when you.
    kiti'tijl, *kiti'titek*, when they.

Negative Conjugation: *mu ewi'kikewanl*, *-wanek*, "me not writing, not having written," or else, "when I do not write, did not write," etc., *-kewnl -wnek*, *-kekwl -kwek*, *-kewkwl -kwek*, *-kewekl -kek*, *-kewoqwl -qwek*, *-ke'tikwl -kwek*, *-kitiwkwl -kwek*, *-kitiwekl -kek*, *-kitiwoqwl -qwek*, *kiti'tikwl -kwek*.

Supplementary Forms: 1. **Inanimate**: *ewi'kikekl*, *-kekek* (s. and dual), *-kitikl*, *-kitikek*; plural: *mu ewi'kikenukwl*, *-nukwek*, *-kitinukwl*, *nukwek*.

2. **Obviative subject**: *ewi'kikelijl, -kitilijl, -kelitek, -kitilitek; mu ewi'kikelikwl, -kitilikwl, -kelikwek, -kitilikwek.*

3. For the **missing, dead or absent**, or things past or removed: *ewi'kiketka, -kititka, -kelitka, -kitilitka; -keksipnek, -keksipnikl.*

Conjunct or Indicative with *If*

Wi'ki keyan   keyass   keyasn, if I write, wrote, have written.
     ken   ke'sip   ke'sipn, if you write, etc.
     kej   kess   kesn, if he writes.
     keyikw   keyikuss   keyikusn, if we write.
     keyek   keyeksip   keyeksipn, if we write.
     keyoq   keyoqsip   keyoqsipn, if you write.
     ke'tij   ke'tiss   ke'tisn, if they write.
     kiti'kw   kiti'kuss   kiti'kusn, if we write.
     kitiyek   kitiyeksip kitiyeksipn, if we write.
     kitiyoq   kitiyoqsip kitiyoqsipn, if you write.
     kiti'tij kiti'tiss   kiti'tisn, if they write.

Supplementary Form: 1. **Negative conjugation**: *mu wi'kikewan, -wass, -wasn; -kewn, -kewsip, -kewsipn; -kewk, -kewksip, -kewksipn; -kewkw, -kewkuss, -kewkusn; -kewek, -keweksip, -keweksipn; -kewoq, -kewoqsip, -kewoqsipn; -ke'tiwk, -ke'tiwksip, -ke'tiwksipn; -ki-tiwkw,* etc.

2. The **inanimate** form is the same as the indicative, with contraction; **negative**: *mu wi'kikenuk, -nuss, -nusn.*

3. The **obviative** is rarely found in this mood; it would be: *wi'kikelij, -liss, -lisn; kitilij, -liss, -lisn.*

Conditional

Wi'ki kekk (ep), I would write.
    kekk (p), you would write.
    kess, he would write.
    ke'kupp, we would write (incl.).
    kekekk (p), we would write (excl.).
    kekoqq (p), you would write.
    ke'tiss, they would write.
    kiti'kupp, we would write (incl.).

kitikekk, we would write (excl.).
kitikoqq, you would write.
kiti'tiss, they would write.

Past

Wi'ki kekapn, I would have written.
    kekpn, you would have written.
    kesoqq, he would have written.
    ke'kupn, we would have written (incl.).
    kekekpn, we would have written (excl.).
    kekoqpn, you would have written.
    ke'tisoqq, they would have written.
    kiti'kupn, we would have written (incl.).
    kitikekpn, we would have written (excl.).
    kitikoqpn, you would have written.
    kiti'tisoqq, they would have written.

Supplementary Forms: 1. **Negative**: *mu wi'kikewkapn*, "I would not write, have written," -*kewkpn*, -*kesoqq*, -*kewikupn*, -*kewikekpn*, -*kewikoqpn*, -*kewi'tisoqq*, -*kewiti'kupn*, -*kewitikekpn*, -*kewitikoqpn*, -*kewiti'tisoqq*. M. Maillard puts the third person negative of the past here: *mu wi'kikewksoqq*, -*keutisoqq*, -*kitiutisoqq*; even the other persons are rather confused, in the dual and plural: *mu wi'kikeyukekpn*, -*keyukoqpn*, -*kiti'kupn*, -*kitikewpn* (no doubt -*kitiukekpn*), -*kitiwkoqpn*. It is not worthwhile to consider them further.

2. **Inanimate negative**: *mu wi'kikenuss*, -*nusoqq*, -*ki-tinuss*, -*nusoqq*.

3. **Obviatives**: *wi'kikeliss*, -*kelisoqq*, -*kitiliss*, -*kitilisoqq*; *mu wi'kikelikuss*, -*kelikusoqq*, -*kitilikuss*, -*kitilikusoqq*.

Subordinative

Nui'kiken, that I write.
Kui'kiken, that you write.
Wui'kiken, that he write.
Kui'kikenenu, that we write.
Nui'kikenen, that we write.
Kui'kikenew, that you write.
Wui'kikenew, that they write.
Kui'kikitinenu, that we write.
Nui'kikitinen, that we write.

Kui'kikitinew, that you write.
Wui'kikitinew, that they write.

Supplementary Forms: 1. **Inanimate**: there is no difference of form in this verb; but those which have the future in *-titew* have here *-tn* or *-tnen*; negative; *-nun* or *-tnun*.

2. **Obviative**: *wui'kikelin, wui'kikitilin* (See **Remark**, p. 52, 2).

Infinitive or Impersonal (Indefinite Subject)

Ewi'kikemk, kitimk, to write, one writes.
Ewi'kikemkiss, kitimkiss, to have written, one wrote, etc.
Wi'kiketen, kititen, to have to write, one will write.
Wi'kikemkij, kitimkij, let it be written (imperative).
Ewi'kikemkl, kitimkl, writing, when one writes.
Ewi'kikemkek, kitimkek, having written, when one wrote, etc.
Wi'kikemk, kitimk, if one writes.
Wi'kikemkiss, kitimkiss, if one wrote.
Wi'kikemkisn, kitimkisn, if one had written.
Wi'kikeness, kitiness, one would write.
Wi'kikenesoqq, kitinesoqq, one would have written.
Wi'kiken, kitin, that one write (subjunctive).

Negative

Mu ewi'kikemmik, kitimmik, not to write, one does not write.
Mu ewi'kikemmiksip, kitimmiksip, not to have written, one has not written.
Ma' wi'kikemmik, kitimmik, not to have to write, one will not write.
Mu ewi'kikemmikl, kitimmikl, not writing, when one does not write.
Mu ewi'kikemmikek, kitimmikek, not having written, when one did not write.
Mu wi'kikemmik, kitimmik, if one does not write.

The others are similar to the affirmative.

See the **Remarks** on the infinitive of *teluisi*, (p. 52).

LESSON FIFTEEN

EXAMPLES OF THE THIRD CONJUGATION

The verbs of this conjugation, as those of the two previous ones, may be divided into several categories, with more or less important differences.

1. The first is that of the verbs which, like *ewi'kikey*, keep the *e* or *i* in the ending in the dual and plural. For the verbs in *-ekey*, there are those in which this syllable (the penultimate) is long. Such are:

Awase'key, -keyikw, -kiti'kw, "to spoil."

E'y, e'n, e't, e'yikw, e'yek, e'yoq, e'jik, e'ti'kw, "to say" (see *teluey*). *E'y,* "to say," and *eym,* "to be somewhere," have many tenses which resemble one another; thus in the future *i'tes,* "I will be there" and *(h)i'tes* (with aspiration), "I will say"; imperative *i'e'n, i'k; ejele'k mu i'n,* "impossible not to say" (indefinite subordinative), and even better: *nawiaq nti'n, msiki'ktitew wlita'suti* (7 pr. 126), "it is impossible for me not to say: there will be a great joy," *mu kte'w, mu kti'pp, mu kte'tipp,* "do not (you s., dual, pl.) say."

Ela'kittekey, -keyikw, -kiti'kw, "to file"; *la'kitteketes, mu kla'kittekew.*

Elutmaqnikey, -keyikw, -kiti'kw, "to tell tales, to spread gossip"; *lutmaqniketes, mu klutmaqnikew*; perhaps, *mu ktlu.*

Kutekey, -keyikw, -kiti'kw, "to pour out, to tip."

Kwetapey, -peyikw, -piti'kw, "to endure, to be punished"; *kutapetes, mu kutapew; kwetapet,* "the ox" (the long-suffering animal); to say to a punished child: *Kwetapen!* is more painful to him than the punishment itself.

Paqekey, -keyikw, -kiti'kw, "to throw everything."

Pewi'key, *-keyikw*, *-kiti'kw*, "to sweep"; *pui'ketes, pui'ke, pui'ka, mu kpui'kew*.

Tewekey, *-keyikw*, *kiti'kw*, "to throw out"; *tueka's, -ketes*.

Pekwatelikey, *-keyikw*, *kiti'kw*, "to buy"; *pkwateliketes*; *mu kipkwatelikew*.

Punekey, *-keyikw*, *-kiti'kw*, "to leave alone, to stop doing something"; *puneketes, puneke, puneka*, "leave that alone"; *mu kpunekew*.

Taqtekey, *-keyikw*, *-kiti'kw*, "to hit"; *tqateketes, mu kitqatekew*.

Tema'kittekey, "to saw"; *tma'kitteketes, mu ktma'kittekew*.

Temte'key, "to work hard"; *tmte'ketes*; *mu ktmte'kew*.

Tepekey, "to put into the collection, to make a gift"; *tpeketes, mu ktipekew*.

Tepi'key, *-ken*, *-ket*, *-keyikw*, *-kiti'kw*, "to divide, to distribute"; *tpi'ketes, mu ktipi'kew*; *nuji-tpi'ket*, "the Indian agent" (the distributor).

Jikitqatekey, "to disturb, to annoy by striking noisily."

Ji'mey, *-meyikw*, *-miti'kw*, "to row, to paddle."

2. The secondary category, more numerous, is that of verbs which **change** *e* to *a* in the plural; these are especially the verbs in *-uey*. Thus:

Aknimuey, *-mueyikw*, *-mua'ti'kw*, "to proclaim, to confess."

Apatnmuey, *-mueyikw*, *-mua'ti'kw*, "to return."

Apoqnmuey, *-mueyikw*, *-mua'ti'kw*, "to aid"; *nuji-apoqnmuet*, "assistant."

Ela'luey, *-lueyikw*, *-lua'ti'kw*, "to lead, to conduct"; *la'lua's, mu ktla'luew*.

Etawalsewey, *-seweyikw*, *-sewa'ti'kw*, "to intercede for someone"; *tawalsewates, mu ktawalsewew*; *Nuji-Kaqama'tawalsewet*, "The Intermediary"; *pekwatawalsewet*, "he redeems"; *Nuji-Pkwatawalsewet*, "the Redeemer."

Iknmuey, *-muen*, *-muet* "to give, to make a gift"; *-mueyikw*, *-mua'ti'kw*; *iknmua's* or *-wetes*, *-mua*, *-mue*; *mu ktiknmuew*; *ntiknmuen, iknmuemk, -mua'timk*. M. Maillard (Rem. gr. p. 67) says that when the Mi'kmaq use *iknmuey*, they always give it the literal meaning of a pure gift; the term which they use for returning or lending is *wejkunm*, "I give such a thing to be used, that one may use it, provided that it is returned to me." Today, they especially use *maqatui*, "lend me," meaning that it is for a long time, of long maturity, and in practice never falling due. There are exceptions.

We'kwa'muey, *-mueyikw*, *-mua'ti'kw*, "to dispute, discuss."

Weska'qelmuey, *-mueyikw*, *-mua'ti'kw*, "to greet (also) to embrace";

wsɨka'qelmua's, -muetes; *wsɨka'qelmua, -mue, -mua'ti'kw*; *mu kwsɨka'qelmuew, -mua'tipp*.

Wejipulkwey, -kweyikw, -kwa'ti'kw, "to have convulsions."

Welapukuey, -kueyikw, -kua'ti'kw, "to speak well"; *wlapukuetes*.

Winapukuey, -kueyikw, -kua'ti'kw, "to speak bad."

Kaqmatawalsewey, -weyikw, -wa'ti'kw, "to be a reconciler, a mediator, a bondsman"; *kaqamatawalseulkw, -sewinamɨt*, "he is our reconciler, our mediator."

Pa'qapukuey, -kueyikw, -kua'ti'kw, "to confess one's sins," there is no contraction; *pa'qapukua's, -kuetes, -kua, -kue*; *mu kpa'qapukuew*.

Telapukuey, -kueyikw, -kua'ti'kw, "to speak thus"; *tlapukua's, -kuetes*; *mu ktlapukuew*.

Teluey, -lueyikw, -lua'ti'kw, "to speak, to talk thus," used more than *e'y*; *tlua's, tluetes, tlua, tlue, tluekw, tlua'tikw*; *mu ktluew, -lua'ti'pp*.

Tettuey, -tueyikw, -tua'ti'kw, "to owe, to be in debt"; *tettuo'qn*, "debt," a French word; debts such as we understand them did not exist or did not have a name among the ancient Mi'kmaq.

Jipaluey, -lueyikw, -lua'ti'kw, "to fear, to be fearful, timorous."

Ney, nen, net, "to die"; *neyikw, na'ti'kw*; *mu netawi-newk*, "it (the soul) is not mortal"; *teli-na'ti'tij elue'wultijik ansma winiaq, mors peccatorum pessima*, "the death of the wicked is very bad"; *iapji-nejik*, "they are dead forever"; (obviative) *iapji-neliji*.

Elue'wiey, -wieyikw, -wia'ti'kw, "to be mad, crazy"; the endings are identical in the following eight verbs, it is unnecessary to repeat them.

Epitkuiey, "to make a genuflection"; *pitkuia'tikw*, "make a genuflection!"

Ipajiey, "to be humiliated."

Welapskiey, "to get tipsy," a gentler way of saying *ketkiey*.

Wipiey, "to be with, accompany"; no contraction.

Ketapekiey, "to sing"; *ktapekia's, kietes*; *mu ktapekiew*.

Ketkiey, "to get intoxicated, to be drunk"; insulting language (even if true).

Koqqwajiey or *kiqqwajiey*, "to be appropriate, in order"; *koqqwajiaq*, "it is appropriate, suitable, as it should be."

Nespiey, "to have with oneself"; *wi'katɨkn nespiet*, "he has a book."

Alispey, -peyikw, -pa'ti'kw, "to be soaked"; similarly for the following.

Amaskwiplney, "to suffer torture."

Eulite'lkey, "to have compassion."

Ekiljey, "to read, count"; *kilja's, -jetes, kilja, kilje, kiljekw, kilja'tikw; mu kkiljew* or *mu ktikiljew*, "do not read."

3. The third category includes the **verbs** in *-ekey*, which change the two *e*'s in the plural to *a*'s; these are the ones with a short penultimate vowel; they are almost all in *-tekey*. Thus:

Alaqtekey, -tekeyikw, -taqati'kw, "to sail"; and so on.

Ankaptekey, "to look"; *mu ktankaptaqatipp*, "do not look."

Elekey, "to throw dice, to vote"; *eleke'wit*, "the chosen, the king"; *laqatimkewey*, "election"; *lekenej*, "let us draw lots."

Ika'tekey, "to set down, to make an offering"; *ika'taqatimk*, offertory."

Wela'tekey, "to do well, to do good"; *wla'teka's, -ketes*.

Kespukwa'tekey, "to deceive"; *ksipukwa'teka's, -ketes*.

Ketantekey, "to pursue, to hate, also, to hunt"; *ktanteka's, -ketes; mu ktantekew*.

Kisitekey, "to make, to create"; *Mesta Kisiteket*, "the Creator."

Mattaqa'tekey, "to ring" (the bell); *mattaqa'taqatikw*, "ring!"

Pata'tekey, "to commit sins"; *li wantaqeye'n, me'app mu kpata'tekew*, "go in peace and sin no more"; *mu kpata'taqatipp*.

Taqtekey, "to hit, to tap, by extension, to telegraph"; *taqtaqatimkewey*, "a telegram, a message."

Tela'tekey, "to do"; *tla'teka's, -ketes; mu ktla'tekew*, "don't do that, don't act like that"; *ki'l tela'teken*, "that is your fault."

Jiko'tekey, "to sulk"; *pun'jiko'teka*, "stop sulking."

4. The fourth category is that of verbs in *-iey* which express movement, and have two duals: the one regular in *-ieyikw*, which express movement on the water; the other in *-a'ti'kw*, which expresses movement on the ground; the plural is in *-ita'yikw*, like that of the verbs of movement in *-a'si*, which conjugation it follows. See *ala'si* in the first conj. (p. 60). It is possible, however, that this second dual and plural might be only the regular development of a form in *-a'si*, seldom or never used in the singular. In this case, the verbs strictly in *-iey* have no plural, which would not be surprising,

since the number of those who go on the water is necessarily limited and ranged into groups, which perfectly suits the dual. Examples:

Eliey, elieyikw, ela'ti'kw, elita'yikw, "to go"; *eliaq*, "that goes." M. Maillard (Rem. gr. p. 61) gives first of all *ela'ti'kw, elita'yikw*, as dual and plural, but in the course of the conjugation he several times gives the other form, with the note: to go by water; in the future he gives: *lia's* or *elietes*; in the imperative: *lia* (sic), then *elienej*; in the conditional, *eliekk, eliekapn*, without making the contraction; today it is certainly made in all these forms; again in the imperative: *la'tik* (sic) and *lita'ik*, "go!" the latter is also certainly *lita'qw*; in the conjunct, which he calls the pluperfect subjunctive or conditional, *lian, eliasn*, etc.

Here, then, is its correct conjugation:

Eliey, -ien, -iet, "I go, you go, he goes"; *elieyikw, -ieyek, -ieyoq, -iejik*; *ela'ti'kw, -tiyek, -tiyoq, -tijik; elita'yikw*, also *el'ta'yikw, -ta'yek, -ta'yoq, -ta'jik*; inanimate: *eliaq*, "that goes," *iaql, a'tikl, ita'ql*.

Elieyap, -ie'sip, -iess, "I went, etc."; *elieyikup, -ieyeksip, -ieyoqsip, -iesnik*; *ela'ti'kup, -tiyeksip, -tiyoqsip, -tisnik; elita'yikup, -ta'yeksip, -ta'yoqsip, -ta'snik*; inanimate: *eliaqsip, -iaqsipnl, -a'tiksipnl, -ita'qsipnl*; also *eliap, -lietep, -liep; eliepnik, -la'tipnik, -lita'pnik*.

L'ia's, l'ietes, l'ietesk, l'ietew, "I will go, etc."; *l'ietesnu, -tesnen, -toqsip, -taqq, l'a'titesnu*, etc.; inanimate: *l'iatew, l'iatal, l'a'tital*.

L'ia, l'ie, "go!" *liej*, "let him go"; *l'ienej, l'iekw, l'ie'tij; l'a'tinej, l'a'tikw, l'a'ti'tij; l'ita'nej, l'ita'qw, l'ita'tij*; inanimate: *l'iaj*, for all numbers.

Elia'nl, -a'nek, -enl, -enek, -ejl, -etek, etc., "when ..."; *l'ia'n, l'ia'ss, l'ia'sn; l'ien, l'ie'sip, l'ie'sipn; l'iej, l'iess, l'iesn*, "if..."; *l'ieyikuss, -kusn, l'ieyeksip, -sipn, l'ieyoqsip, -sipn, l'ie'tiss, -tisn; l'a'ti'kuss, -tiyeksip, -tioqsip, l'a'ti'tiss, -tisn; l'ita'yikuss, -ta'yeksip, -ta'yoqsip, -ta'tiss, -tisn*.

L'iekk (ap), l'iekk (p), l'iess, l'iekapn, l'iekpn, l'iesoqq, "I would go, I would have gone, you, he"; *l'ie'kupp, -kekk, -koqq, -pn, l'ie'tisoqq, l'a'ti'kupp, l'ita'qapp*, etc.

Ntelien, etc., "that I go"; *ntlita'nen*, "that we may go."

Eliemk, ela'timk, elita'mk, "to go."

One says of an absent person: *tami elietaq?* "where has he gone?" *ela'titkik, elita'tkik; elietkik*, "they have gone by water."

Pemiey, -ieyikw, -a'ti'kw, -ita'yikw, "to walk"; *pemiaq*, "that goes, continues, flows" (time).

Elmiey, -ieyikw, -a'ti'kw, -ita'yikw, "to go home (one's own)"; *l'mia's, l'mietes, l'mie, l'mia, l'miekw, l'ma'ti'kw, l'mita'qw; mu ktlmiew, mu ktlmita'pp; elmiaq,* in the future.

Ajiey, -ieyikw, -a'ti'kw, -ita'yikw, "to advance, to progress"; *ta's ajiet,* "what time is it?" *ajiaq suliewey,* "interest."

Wejiey, -ieyikw, -a'ti'kw, -ita'yikw, "to come from, to have been there."

Tewiey, -ieyikw, -a'ti'kw, -ita'ykw, "to go out"; *tuie tuia, tu'a, tua'tikw, tuita'qw,* "go out, get out!"

5. A certain number of verbs in *wey* form their plurals in *-uti'kw, -ulti'kw, -auti'kw*:

Elukwey, -kweyikw, -kuti'kw, "to work"; *ellukwey,* "to go to work."

Se'skwey, -kweyikw, -kuti'kw, "to shout, cry"; *se'skutipnik,* "they have shouted" (Ps. 17, 41; implies disorderly shouts).

Ila'skukwey, -kweyikw, -kuti'kw, "to play cards."

Wissukwey, -kweyikw, -kuti'kw, "to do the cooking."

Etlewo'kwey, -kweyikw, -kuti'kw, "to speak, to chat."

Nepuskwey, -kweyikw, -kuti'kw, "to go look for meat."

Plamue'key or *-mukwey, -muti'kw,* "to fish for salmon"; the first makes *plamuaqati'kw.*

Sesupa'lukwey, -kweyikw, -kuti'kw, "to glide, to slide."

Kwetajikwey, -kweyikw, -kuti'kw, "to have a dreadful appearance"; *kwetejk,* "the Mohawks."

Pesi'kwey or *pesi'kukwey, -kweyikw, -kuti'kw,* "to drive the wood down the river"; perhaps also *pesu'kwey* or *-kway, -kweyikw, -kulti'kw,* "to leap up, to rush headlong."

Saqsikwey, -kweyikw, -kuti'kw, "fish by torch."

Wesimukwey (-kway), -kweyikw, -kulti'kw, "to flee"; *wsimukul'tikw,* "flee!"; abbreviated to *wesimul'tikw*; *msit wnaqapemka wesimultilisnika,* "all his disciples fled" (Passion, likewise Ps. 48, 5).

Etlikwey, "to grow"; *welikwey,* "well"; *eulikwey,* "badly"; *-kweyikw, -kul'ti'kw, -kwekl, -kul'tikl.*

Naskwet, "virgin (to be a)," gives *naskultijik* (see Hier. lit. p. 125); however Rand gives *naskwaq* ... (Matt. 25, 5); *Weli-Naskwet,* "the holy Virgin"; *wenaskomij ntinin,* "I am his servant."

Eli'sewey, -seweyikw, -sauti'kw, "to sew"; *li'sewa's, -wetes*.

Eltaqnewey, -neweyikw, -nauti'kw, "to spin"; *ltaqanewa's, -wetes*.

Ikatne'wey, -ne'weyikw, -nauti'kw, "to race"; *nikatne'wey*, "to win a race"; *mlki-ji'nm ketui-ikatne'wejl*, "the strong man runs his race (Ps. 18, 5).

Kewkunewey, -neweyikw, -nauti'kw, "to hold, to be a godfather or godmother."

Netawey, -taweyikw, -tauti'kw, "to call out, to sell at auction"; *ntawa's, -wetes, -ntaweten*, "there will be an auction"; *mu kntawew, kntautipp*; *Kisu'lkwiktukl l'i mawi-ntautikw*, "lift up your voices together to the Lord" (Par. 1, 540).

Neskawey, -kaweyikw, -kauti'kw, "to sing with gestures and responses"; *nskawaqn*, "this song"; *nskawe, nskautikw*, "sing!" (s., pl.).

Nutnewey, -neweyikw, -nauti'kw, "to be a bearer, by extension, servant, acolyte, candle-holder."

Jinpeknewey, -neweyikw, -neuti'kw, "to milk."

6. Finally here are some impersonal verbs in *-ek* and *-iaq*, which follow the inanimate forms of this conjugation.

Ansue'k, "it is strange."

Wenqaje'k, "it is troublesome, hard, difficult; less used than *metue'k*.

Weju'sik, "it is windy, the wind is blowing"; *mu weju'sitnukw*, "it does not blow"; *wettik*, "the wind comes from"; *tami wettik?* "where does the wind come from?" *oqwatnuk*, "from the north"; *wjipnuk*, "from the east"; *tkesnuk*, "from the west"; *teksik*, "wind from the northwest"; *pketesnuk*, "from the south"; *senusaqtnuk*, "from the southwest"; *teklamsik*, "cold wind"; *teki-kis-kik*, "cold day."

Welikiskik, "it is a fine day."

Miaula'kwek or *meluia'kwek*, "noon."

Ketatkwe'k, "it (death) threatens."

Niwetek, "the tide is out"; *niwe'k*, "dried up."

Pe'sketek, "the gun goes off"; *pe'skewey*, "gun"; *tulkewey*, "cannon."

Te'sipunqik, "each year, every year."

Alukwiaq, "the sky becomes overcast"; *eupniaq*, "it is calm."

A'qatekiaq, "the tide is halfway out"; *elmekiaq, -kiatew*, "the tide goes out, ebbs."

Wapniaq, "daylight appears, it is dawn"; *pettniaq*, "the wind rises."

Kloqoejuiaq, "the stars appear" (Amer. 1, 115).

Nawiaq, "impossible, a thing which one cannot manage, or do."

Musquiaq, "the weather clears."

Naqmasiaq, "that is easy"; *naqmaje'jk*, "an easy thing."

Piskiaq, "late, dark"; *keket piskiaq*, "it is nearly night"; *mna'q piskianukw*, "not yet"; *ki's piskiaq*, "it is already night"; *piskiatew*, "it will be night."

Tepiaq, "that is enough"; *tetpiaq*, "it is time"; *tetapuiaq*, "the time has come." *Teliaq*, "that is true"; *tliaj*, "let it be so."

LESSON SIXTEEN

FOURTH CONJUGATION (ACTIVE INANIMATE) IN M AND OTHER CONSONANTS

Principal model: *Nestm*, to understand

Present Indicative

Nes tm, I understand.
    tmn, you understand.
    tik, he understands.
    tmu'kw, we understand (incl.).
    tmek, we understand (excl.).
    tmoq, you understand.
    tmi'tij, they understand.
    tmu'ti'kw, we understand.
    tmu'tiyek, we understand.
    tmu'tiyok, you understand.
    tmu'tijik, they understand.

Negative Conjugation: *mu nestmu*, "I do not understand," etc., -*mu'n*, -*muk*, -*mukkw*, -*muek*, -*muoq*, -*mi'tiwk*, -*mu'tiwkw*, -*mu'tiwek*, -*mu'tiwoq*, -*mu'ti'tiwk*.

Supplementary Forms: 1. The form of the third person of the dual should be *nestikik*, but it is not in use and it is replaced by the same person of the conjunct, without contraction, *nestmi'tij*.

2. **Inanimate**: the inanimate forms are hardly appropriate to this verb, except in the negative; but they can be encountered in others, as *taqtm*, "to strike"; *taqtik, taqtikl, taqtmu'tikl*, "that hits, etc."; *mu taqtnukw*, -*nukwl*, -*mu'tinukwl*.

3. Verb with **obviative subject**: *nestmlijl, -tmliji, -tmu'tiliji; mu nestmlikwl, -tmlikwi, -tmu'tilikwi.*

4. **Missing persons, dead or absent**: *nestikaq, nestmitkik, mu'titkik; nestmlita, nestmlitka, nestmu'tilitka; mu nestmukwaq, -tmukwi'k, -tmu'tikwi'k; mu nestmlikwa, -tmlikwika, -tmu'tilikwika.*

5. Likewise an **inanimate subject** in the past would require: *nestikek*, as in *taqtikek, -tikekl, -tmu'tikekl; mu taqtnukwek, -kwekl, -tmu'tinulwekl.*

6. When the inanimate object is in the **plural**, or if there is an indirect object which is an animate noun, we would have, for the first: *nestmanl, -mnl, -kl, -mu'kwl, -mekl, -moql, -mi'tijl, -mu'ti'kwl, -mu'tiyekl, -mu'tiyoql, -mu'ti'tijl*; in the negative: *mu nestmuanl, -mu'nl, -mukwl, -mukkwl, -muekl, -muoql, -mi'tikwl, -mu'tiwkwl, -mu'tiwekl, -mu'tiwoql, -mu'ti'tikwl*; for the second: *nestmanik, -mnik, -ki (nestiiki), -mu'kwik, -mekik, -moqik, -mi'tiji, -mu'ti'kwik, -mu'tiyekik, -mu'tiyoqik, -mu'ti'tiji*; in the negative: *mu nestmuanik, -mu'nik, -mukwi, -mukkwik, -muekik, -muoqik, -mi'tikwi, -mu'tiwkwik, -mu'tiwekik, -mu'tiwoqik, -mu'ti'tikwi*. In the latter case there would normally be use of the TA two-goal verb: *nestmaqik, -majik, -muaji*, etc.

Past Indicative

Nes   *tmep, map*, I understood.
      tmu'sip, mu'p, you understood.
      tiksip, tikiss, tikip, he understood.
      tmu'kuss, kup, kusp, we understood.
      tmeksip, kiss, kip, we understood.
      tmoqsip, qoss, qop, you understood.
      tiksipnik, kisnik, kipnik, they understood.

or   *tmi'tisnik, pnik, sipnik*, they understood.
      tmu'ti'kuss, etc. we understood.
      tmu'tiyeksip, etc., we understood.
      tmu'tiyoqsip, etc., you understood.
      tmu'ti'tisnik, etc., they understood.

Negative Conjugation: *mu nestmuep*, "I did not understand," etc., *-muwsip, -muksip, -mukup*, etc., *-muekip, -muoqsip, -mi'tiwksipnik*, etc., *-mu'tiwkup, -mu'tiweksip, -mu'tiwoqsip, -mu'ti'tiwksipnik.*

See **Remark** 1, in the past of *teluisi* (p. 45).

Supplementary Form: 1. **Inanimate**: *-taqtiksip, -tiksipnl, -tmu'tiksipnl; mu -taqtnuksip, -nuksipnl, -mu'tinuksipnl.*

2. **Obviative forms**: *nestmlisnl, -tmlisni, -tmu'tilisni; mu nestmliwksipnl, -tmliwksipni, -mu'tiliwkiipni.*

3. For the **missing, dead or absent**, the forms of the present can be used, which have a true past sense. There are, however, also the following: *nestiksipnaq, nestiksipnika, nestmu'tisipnika*; then, for obviative forms: *nestmlisna, -mlisnika, -mu'tilisnika; mu nestmliwksipna, -mliwksipnika, -mu'tiliwksipnika.*

4. When the object (inanimate) is in the plural, *-nl* must be added in the singular, with or without modification of the vowel, in this manner: *nestmapnl, -mu'sipnl, -tiksipnl, -tmu'kupnl, -tmeksipnl, -tmoqsipnl, -tmi'tisnl, -tmu'ti'kupnl, -mu'tiyeksipnl, -mu'tiyoqsipnl, -mu'ti'tisnl; mu nestmuapnl, -mu'sipnl, -muksipnl, -mukupnl, -mueksipnl, -muoqsipnl, -mi'tiwksipnl, -mu'tiwkupnl, -mu'tiweksipnl, -mu'tiwoqsipnl, -mu'ti'tiwksipnl.*

5. When the verb expresses an indirect agreement to an animate plural, *-l* is changed to *-ik* or *-i* (in the third person): *nestmapnik, -mu'sipnik, -tiksipni,* etc. Ex.: "I understood what is going on among the Indians," *nestmapnik ta'n pemiaq wjit l'nu'k,* or better *l'nuiktuk.*

6. If the **object** is a name of a thing or person in the **past**, according to the rules of the seventh lesson, No. 3, the verb is made to agree by changing *-l* to *-ek, -ekl,* and *-ik* to *-aq, -qik.* Ex.: *Moqwa koqoeyek wesko'tmi'tiwksipnek,* "they did not have anything" (speech of Our Lord, Luke 7, 42).

7. For the perfect and the pluperfect, *kisi-* and *ki's kisi-* are also used, which are placed before the verb in the past. See p. 46.

Future Indicative

Nsittes, I will understand.
    tesk, you will understand.
    tew, he will understand.
    tesnu, we will understand.
    tesnen, we will understand.
    toqsip, you will understand.
    taqq, they will understand.

Nsi tmu'titesnu, we will understand.
    tmu'titesnen, we will understand.

tmu'titoqsip, you will understand.
tmu'titaqq, they will understand.

Negative Conjugation: *ma'nsitmu*, etc. (as in the present), I will not understand.

Supplementary Forms: 1. **Inanimate subject**: *-tqattew, -tqattal, -tqatmu'tital (nsittitew, nsittital, nsitmu'tital); ma' -tqatnukw, -nukul, -mu'tinukul (ma' nsitnukw, nsitnukul. nsitmu'tinukul)*

2. **Obviative subject**: *nsitmlital, -tmlita, -mu'tilita; ma' nsitmlikwl, -tmlikwi, -tmu'tilikwi.*

3. The relationships to **plural objects** in this tense only modify the third persons: *nsittal, nsitmu'tital; nsitta, nsitmu'tita (nsituata, nsitua'tita)*.

Imperative

Nsite'n, understand.
Nsitj, let him understand.
Nsitmenej, let us understand.
Nsitmukw, understand (you dual).
Nsitmi'tij, let them understand.
Nsitmu'tinej, let us understand.
Nsitmu'tikw, understand (you pl.).
Nsitmu'ti'tij, let them understand.

Mu knsitmu, do not understand.
Mu nsitmuij, let him not understand.
Mu nsitmenej, let us not understand.
Mu knsitmupp, do not understand.
Mu nsitmi'tiwij, let them not understand.
Mu nsitmu'tinej, let us not understand
Mu knsitmu'tipp, do not understand.
Mu nsitmu'tiwij, let them not understand.

Supplementary Forms: 1. **Inanimate subject**: similar to the animate; but the negative is *mu nsitnuj* for the three numbers. When the affirmative is in *-tej*, the negative becomes *-tnuj*: *kepijoqtm*, "I block it off," *kpijoqtej, kpijoqtnuj*, "let it close up."

2. and 3. As for *alasutmay* (p. 64); except that *-m* of the indicative is changed to *-n* or *-e'n*, and to the other consonants one adds *-e'n*: *elisin, lisine'n*, "stay down, stay lying down."

Conjunct or Indicative with *When*

Nes tmanl, manek, understanding, having understood, or when I understand, understood.
  tmnl, mnek, when you.
  tikl, tikek, when he.
  tmu'kwl, kwek, when we.
  tmekl, kek, when we.
  tmoqwl, qwek, when you.
  tmi'tijl, titek, when they.
  tmu'ti'kwl, kwek, when we understand.
  tmu'tiyekl, kek, when we understand.
  tmu'tiyoqwl, qwek, when you understand.
  tmu'ti'tijl, titek, when they understand.

Negative Conjugation: *mu nestmuanl muanek*, "my not understanding, not having understood," or better, "when I do not, did not understand," etc., *-mu'nl mu'nek, -mukwl mukwek, -mukkwl mukkwek, -muekl muekek, -muoqwl muoqwek, -mi'tikwl mi'tikwek, -mu'tikkwl mu'tikkwek, -mu'tiwekl mu'tiwekek, -mu'tiwoqwl mu'tiwoqwek, -mu'ti'tikwl mu'ti'tikwek.*

Supplementary Forms: 1. **Inanimate subject**: *-taqtikl, -tikek*; negative: *mu taqtnukwl, -kwek.*

2. **Obviative subject**: *nestmlijl, -litek, -mu'tilijl, -litek; mu nestmlikwl, -likwek, -mu'tilikwl, -likwek.*

3. For the **missing, dead or absent**, or things past or removed: *nestikeka, nestmi'titka, -mu'titka, -tmlitka, -mi'tilitka, -mu'tilitka; -taqtiksipnl, -tiksipnikl.*

Conjunct or Indicative with *If*

Nsɨ	tman	tmass	tmasn	if I understand, understood, have understood.
	tmn	tmu'sip	tmu'sipn	if you understand, etc.
	j (nsɨj)	ss (nsɨss)	sn (nsɨsn)	if he understands, etc.
	tmu'kw	tmu'kuss	tmu'kusn	if we understand, etc.
	tmek	tmeksip	tmeksipn	if we understand, etc.
	tmoq	tmoqsip	tmoqsipn	if you understand, etc.
	tmi'tij	tmi'tiss	tmi'tisn	if they understand, etc.
	tmu'ti'kw	tmu'ti'kuss	tmu'ti'kusn	if we understand, etc.

  tmu'tiyek *tmu'tiyeksip* *tmu'tiyeksipn* if we understand, etc.
  tmu'tioq *tmu'tiyoqsip* *tmu'tiyoqsipn* if you understand, etc.
  tmu'ti'tij *tmu'ti'tiss* *tmu'ti'tisn* if they understand, etc.

Supplementary Forms: 1. **Negative** conjugation: *Mu nsitmuan, -muass, -muasn; -mu'n, -mu'sip, -mu'sipn; -muj, -muss, -musn; -mukw, -mukuss, -mukusn; -muek, -mueksip, -mueksipn; -muoq, -muoqsip, -muoqsipn; -mi'tiwk, -mi'tiwksip, -mi'tiwksipn; -mu'tiukw, -kuss, -kusn; -mu'tiwek, -weksip, -weksipn; -mu'tiwoq, -woqsip, -woqsipn; -mu'ti'tiwk, -tiwksip, -tiwksipn.*

2. **Inanimate**, negative: *mu nsitnuk, -nuss, -nusn.*

3. **Obviative subject**: it is highly unlikely that this paradigm would be encountered; it would be: *nsitmlij, -liss, -lisn; -mu'tilij, -liss, -lisn.*

Remark: It is the third person of the dual of this mood which serves as the indicative in many verbs of this conjugation.

Conditional

Present
Nsi tmukk (*ap*) I would understand.
 tmukk (*p*), you would understand.
 ss (*nsiss*), he would understand.
 tmu'kupp, we would understand.
 tmukekk (*p*), we would understand.
 tmukoqq (*p*), you would understand.
 tmi'tiss, they would understand.
 tmu'ti'kupp, we would understand.
 tmu'tikekk (*p*), we would understand.
 tmu'tikoqq (*p*), you would understand.
 tmu'ti'tiss, they would understand.

Past
Nsi tmukapn, I would have understood.
 tmukpn, you would have understood.
 soqq (*nsisoqq*), he would have understood.
 tmu'kupn, we would have.
 tmukekpn, we would have.
 tmukoqpn, you would have.
 tmi'tisoqq, they would have.
 tmu'tikupn, we would have.
 tmu'tikekpn, we would have.

tmu'tikoqpn, you would have.
tmu'ti'tisoqq, they would have.

Supplementary Forms: 1. The **negative** has hardly any influence on this mood. See however in the following lesson: *mu puamuiss, sqasikwesmuiss*.

2. **Inanimate subject**: not used, except in the negative, as: *mu kisi nsitnuss, -nusoqq (kun'tew)*, "a stone would not be able to understand that."

3. **Obviative subject**: *nsitmliss, -lisoqq, -mu'tiliss, -lisoqq; mu nsitmliwiss, -liwisoqq, -mu'tiliwiss, -liwisoqq*.

Subordinative

Nsitmn, that I may understand.
Knsitmn, that you may understand.
Wnsitmn, that he may understand.
Knsitmnenu, that we may understand.
Nnsitmnen, that we may understand.
Knsitmnew, that you may understand.
Wnsitmnew, that they may understand.
Knsitmu'tinenu, that we may understand.
Nnsitmu'tinen, that we may understand.
Knsitmu'tinew, that you may understand.
Wnsitmu'tinew, that they may understand.

Supplementary Forms: 1. **Obviative subject**: *wnsitmlin, -tmu'tilin*. *Poqtiikimaji newtiskeksiliji jel ta'pu wpestunmlin aqq wntawinsalalin wisqisultiliji aqq mntu' wtijiklalnin*, "he commanded the twelve to preach (that they preach), to cure sicknesses and to cast out devils."

2. **Inanimate subject**: see *telamu'k*, in the fifth conj. *wtlamu'ktn, mu wtlamu'ktnun; wtqatnen, mu wtqatnun*.

Infinitive or Impersonal (Indefinite Subject)

Affirmative
Nestmik, mu'timk, to understand, one understands.
Nestmiksip, mu'timkiss, to have understood, one understood.
Nsitten, nsitmu'titen, to be about to understand, one will understand.
Nsitmkij, nsitmu'timkij, let one understand (imperative).

Nestmikl, mu'timkl, understanding, when one understands.
Nestmikek, mu'timkek, having understood, when one understood.
Nsitmik, mu'timk, if one understands.
Nsitmiksip, mu'timkiss, if one understood.
Nsitmiksipn, mu'timkisn, if one had understood.
Nsitmness, mu'tiness, one would understand.
Nsitmnesoqq, mu'tinesoqq, one would have understood.
Nsitmn, mu'tin, that one understands (subordinative).

Negative
Mu nestmummik, mu'timmik, not to understand, one does not understand.
Mu nestmummiksip, mu'timmiksip, not to have understood, one did not understand.
Ma' nsitmummik, mu'timmik, one will not understand.
Mu nsitmkij, mu'timkij, let one not understand.
Mu nestmummikl, mu'timmikl, not understanding.
Mu nestmummikek, mu'timmikek, not having understood.
Mu nsitmummik, mu'timmik, if one does not understand.
Mu nsitmummiksip, mu'timmiksip, if one did not understand.
Mu nsitmummiksipn, mu'timmiksipn, if one had not understood.

The others are similar to the affirmative. See the **Remark** concerning the infinitive of *teluisi* (p. 52).

LESSON SEVENTEEN

EXAMPLES OF THE FOURTH CONJUGATION

The verbs of this conjugation are divided into several categories, with more or less important differences. There are a large number of them which are absolutely intransitive, as far as meaning is concerned, which changes nothing in the conjugation, even when they have no object, even indirect.

The first is that of **verbs** in -*tm*, which is by far the most numerous; but the third person is often -*tk* instead of -*tik*, as *kesatm, kesatk*, "to like a thing"; this occurs when *t* is preceded by a vowel, except *ewi'tm, te'pm, almakitm*, which make -*ik*, as *nestm, nestik*; moreover, the difference is more apparent than real, for if the verb is preceded by a prefix requiring contraction, for example, *weli-*, "well," it will become *weli-nsitm, weli-nsitk*, "I understand, he understands well," just like *kesatm, kesatk*; it should also be noted that in this case the contraction, even in the simple verb, is made, not by dropping the vowel of the first syllable, but by moving it. The same thing occurs whenever the *e* of the first syllable is followed by two consonants.

Thus we have, first *kesatm, kesatmn, kesatk*, "to like," *ksattes, ksate'n, ksatj, mu ksatmu, -mupp, -mu'tipp*; *ksaj, ksass, ksasn*, "if he loves, loved, had loved"; *ksatmukk, -mukapn* "I would like, I would have liked"; *ksass, ksasoqq*, "he would love, he would have loved"; *kesatmik, -mu'timk*, "to love, one loves."

Toqwatm, -qwatmn, -qwatk, "to put with another"; *tqwattes*.

Pewatm, -watmn, -watk, "to want, to have need of"; *puatj*.

Pitkmatm, -atmn, -atk, "to load (a ship, cart)"; no contraction; *pitkmattes, -maten*.

Ewi'katm, -katmn, -katk, "to build"; *wi'kattes ni'k*, "I will build my house."

Pekitqatm, "to remain for a long time in one spot," *-qatmn, -qatk*; *pkitqattew, pkitqatj*; *mu kpikitqatmu*.

Etlaqatm, tetlaqatm, aptaqatm, "to remain there, always"; hence *tlaqatik,* "Tracadie, where one lives, colony, village, settlement"; *tlaqatike'jk,* "former name of Carleton, little Tracadie, a colony formed from another."

Alqatm, "to remain here and there"; from this Arcadia, Accadia, Acadia. Added to another word, as an ending, it means someone's or something's place or home.

Wetqapatm, "to put something to soak"; *wtaqapattes.*

Wisunkewatm, "to give a name"; *ewi'tm,* "to name"; *wi'tites, wi'te'n; telui'tm,* "to name thus"; *tlui'titen,* "one will name thus."

Musuatm, "to lack, to be bored, to feel the need of something."

Kiwatqatm (*nik*) or *siwatqatm,* "to be bored (in one's house)."

Pa'qapukuatm, "to confess (one's sins)"; *pa'qapukuo'ti,* "confession."

Ketlamsitm, "to believe"; *ktlamsittes; melki-k.,* "to believe strongly."

Welsitm, -sitmn, -sitk, "to listen with pleasure"; *wlsittes.*

Wetmite'tm, -te'tmn, -te'tk, "to desire"; the verbs in *-te'tem, -te'lmɩk, -te'tasi,* denote intention, wish; those in *-ta'si* (long *a*) the heart (according to Maillard), that is to say thought, mental state, kindness: *wtmite'ttes.*

Kesite'tm, "to admire, to covet"; *ksite'ttes. Kepmite'tm,* "to esteem."

Mikwite'tm, "to remember (simply)." *Nenwite'tm,* "to remember (by recalling the thing)."

Pipanuijkatm, "to examine, to scrutinize"; *pipanuijkatkl mkamlamunl,* "he examines hearts."

Wisuiknetm or *kno'tm,* "to conquer, to surpass, to tame."

Ekitm, ekitmn, ekitk, "to read, to count"; *kittes, kite'n, mu kkitmu; mawkitm,* "to add up"; *menkitm,* "to subtract"; *ankwatkitm,* "to multiply"; *nenesatkitm,* "to divide."

Nutm, -tmn, -tk, "to hear, to hear it said"; *nuttes, nute'n.*

Teplutm, -tmn, -tk, "to judge, to rule"; *tpluttes, tplute'n.*

Ilutm, -tmn, -tk, "to correct orally"; *iluttes, ilute'n, mu ktilutmu.*

Kaqmutm, -tmn, -tk, "to endure"; *kqamuttes, mute'n.*

Malqotm, -tmn, -tk, "to eat."

Apankitm, -tmn, -tk, "to pay"; *-kittes, -kite'n, mu ktapankitmu; apankituowey,* "payment, salary, recompense."

Teko'tm, -tmn, -tk, "to attend, to be at (mass, assembly)"; *tko'ttes*.

Wiktm, -tmn, -tik, "to like the taste of"; *wiktites, wikte'n*.

Saqtm, -tmn, -tik, "to obey, to do something in obedience, to respond to an appeal," *sqattes, sqate'n, sqatj*. It is the model of this conjugation that is given by Maillard in his grammar; little used now, except in the texts of the Lord's Prayer and the Commandments; one says *jiksitm, ketlamsitm*. In the conditional, Maillard gives *skets, sketsoq, sketkes, sketkesoq*; but, although it may have been that in his time, one certainly says today *sqass, sqasoq*, as *ksass, ksasoqq* and for *nestm, nsiss, nsisoqq*.

Aniaptm, -tmn, -tik, "to hold in aversion, to repent."

Telte'm, -te'mn, -te'k, "to chop, to hack"; *taqte'm*, "to strike"; *klujjiewkte'm*, "to crucify"; these verbs with long *e* keep it in the imperative, adding -*e'n* to it; it is pronounced as if there were an aspirated *h* between the two: *tlte'he'n, tqate'he'n, klujjiewte'he'n*; we shall also find further on *sa'he'n, tukwi'he'n*, etc.; fut. *tlte'tes, tqate'tes, klujjiewte'tes*.

Here are some other regular verbs which have a consonant other than *t* and even a vowel in the ending.

Pekwatelm, -telmn, -telk, "to buy"; *pkwateltes, pkwatele'n*.

Kwilm, kwilmn, kwilk, "to look for"; *kwiltes, kwile'n; kwiltoqsip eksuo'qn, quaeritis mendacium* (Ps. 4, 2, future in Hebrew).

Meniskm, -kmn, -kik, "to go and get."

Kejipilm, -pilmn, -pilk, "to attach, to bind"; *kjipiltes, kjipile'n*.

Ewi'km, -kmn, -kik, "to write"; *wi'kites, wi'ke'n, mu kwi'kmu*.

Menwi'km, -kmn, -kik, "to copy, to transcribe": *mnwi'kmukek*, "we would copy it (letter)."

Napui'km, -kmn, -kik, "to copy, to paint, to photograph."

Nenm, nenmn, nenk, "to know"; *nentes, nene'n*.

Kelnm, -nmn, -nik, "to hold," *klntes* or *klnites, klne'n; mestanm*, "to have all"; *msitantes; sape'wuti'l mestankl*, "she has all the virtues, graces."

Toqnm, -nmn, -nk, "to have part of something," *tqontes, tqone'n*, "to have with another."

Kewkunm, -nmn, -nk, "to have, to hold in the hand"; *ku'kuntes, ku'kune'n*.

Wejku'nm, -nmn, -nk, "to bring, to pass," *juku'ntes, juku'ne'n*.

Punewenm, -nmn, -nk, "to stop talking, shouting"; *punewene'n*, "shut up."

Peskwesm, -kwesmn, -kwesk, "to mow, to harvest, to scythe"; *psikwestes, psikwese'n, mu kpiskwesmu.*

Te'pm, te'pmn, te'pik, "to deserve"; *mu te'pmu*, "I don't deserve it."

Saqsikwesm, -kwesmn, -kwesk, "to light (by rubbing)"; *sqasikwestes, sqasikwese'n, kwesij; mu ksaqsikwesmu, mu sqasikwesmuij.*

Pewa'm, pewa'mn, pewa'q, "to sweep"; *pua'tes, pua'e'n (pua'he'n), mu kpua'mu, mu pua'muij; wen e'pit ta'n wesko'tkl newtiska'ql pkesiknl sulieweyl, aqq etuk newte'jk entoq, mu ta sqasikwesmuiss wasoqnmaqn aqq pua'muiss wen'ji'kuom, aqq menaqaj al'kwilmuiss mi'soqo ta'n tlisip we'jitoq?* (Luke 15, 8), "what woman who, having ten drachmas (*pkesikn*, "a piece of silver worth about 20 cents"), happens to lose one of them, would not light a lamp, sweep the house and look for it diligently until she had found it?

Esa'm, esa'mn, esa'q, "to expel"; *sa'tes, sa'e'n (sa'he'n), malo'qn sa'mnej*, "let us drive away laziness."

Aptisqa'm or *appusqa'm, -qa'mn, -qa'q*, "to lock"; *qa'mu'kw, qa'mu'ti'kw; qa'tes, qa'e'n, mu ktaptisqa'mu, -mupp, -mu'tipp.*

E'um, e'umn, e'uk, "to take, to use"; *e'utes, e'ue'n, mu kte'umu.*

Keum, keumn, keuk, "to fell trees"; *keumu'kw, -moq, -mek, keumu'ti'kw, keutes, kewe'n.*

Kepijoqm, -qmn, -joqq, "to plug up, to obstruct"; *qmu'kw, qmu'ti'kw; kpijoqtes; joqe'n.*

Also: *Eym, eymn, eyk*, "to be in a place"; *eymu'kw, eymu'ti'kw, i'tes, i'e'n*. See lesson 18.

Nep, nepn, nepk, "to die," also belongs to this conjugation, although it does not have, at least not everywhere, the ending *-m*; *nepu'kw, nepek, nepoq, nepkik; nepu'ti'kw*, etc.; *npites, npe'n, npij, npnej, npukw, npetij, npu'tinej, npu'ti'kw, npu'ti'tij; nepmik, nepu'timk; a'qati-npm*, "half dead"; *ketui-npm*, "I will die"; *moqwa nepu, ma'npu*, "I am not dying, I will not die." *Nsaqmam, i'mu'sipn ula tett wijikitiyekaq mu npuisoqq* (John 11, 21, and 32), "Lord, if you had been here, my brother would not have died."

The second category includes the **verbs** in *-m*, *-n*, and other consonants, whose plural is in *-ulti'kw* or *-o'lti'kw*, and which follow the conjugation of *teluisi* or *welei*; the singular and the dual follow the latter regularly, as:

Pema'm, -ma'mn, -ma'q, -mo'lti'kw, "to swim"; *netawa'm*, "to know how to swim"; *ela'm*, "to swim in one direction"; *ala'm*, "in every direction."

A'su'na'm, -na'mn, -na'q, -no'lti'kw, "to be clothed"; *welqwana'm*, "well clothed"; all pronounced *-a'm, -a'mn, -a'q* (long).

Mkisna'm, *-na'mn*, *-na'q*, *-no'lti'kw*, "to have footwear."

Wapekna'm, *-na'mn*, *-na'q*, *-no'lti'kw*, "to be dressed in white."

Maqtawekna'm, *-na'mn*, *-na'q*, *-no'lti'kw*, "to be dressed in black"; *maqtawekna'qewey kekina'matimk*, "doctrine of the Black Robes."

A'lm ? a'lik, *a'likik*, *a'lultijik*, "to swim around (fish)"; *nme'jik lampo'q ia'lultijik, alt piamkilultijik, alt pejili-apje'jultijik* (7 pr. 60), "the fish swim in the water, some are very large, others very small."

Ketkwi'm, *-kwi'mn*, *-kwi'k*, "to run"; *ketkwi'mu'kw*, *-mek*, *-moq*, *-kwi'kik*, *ketku'lti'kw*, *-tiyek*, *-tiyoq*, *-tijik*, *ketkwi'mep*, etc.; *tukwi'tes*, *-tesk*, *-tew*, *-tesnu*, *-tesnen*, *-toqsip*, *-taqq*, *tuku'ltitesnu*, etc.; *tukwi'e'n*, *tukwi'j*, *tukwi'mnej*, *tukwi'mukw*, *tukwi'tij*, *tuku'ltinej*, *tuku'ltikw*, *tuku'lti'tij*; *ntukwi'men*, etc.; *ketkwi'mk*, *ketku'ltimk*, etc. *Mu ketkwi'mu*, *-mu'n*, *-mukw*, *-mukkw*, *-muek*, *-muoq*, *-mukwik*, *ketku'lti'kw*, etc.

Sesaki'm, *-ki'mn*, *-ki'k*, *-ku'lti'kw*, "to be barefoot"; *sesaki'kewey kekina'matimk*, "doctrine of the Barefooted Ones [i.e., Franciscans, Capuchins].

Pitasuim, *-imn*, *-ik*, *-ulti'kw*, "to walk in the snow."

Al'tukwi'm, *-i'mn*, *-i'k*, *u'lti'kw*, "to run around."

Kiwto'qotukwi'm, "to run around, in a circle"; *kiwkto'qitukwites*, "I will run thus," for example: in baseball.

Aqmi'm, "to go in snowshoes"; *aqma'm*, *aqmo'lti'kw*, "to have snowshoes."

Pemaqmi'm, *-mi'mn*, *-mi'k*, *-multi'kw*, "to walk on snowshoes, move ahead."

No'qm, *-mn*, *-oq*, *-ulti'kw*, "to cough"; *no'qe'n, mu kno'qmu*.

Ekum or *nukum*, "to pulverise."

Jikalukum, *-kumn*, *-kuk*, *-kumu'kw*, *-kumek*, *-kumoq*, *-kumi'tij*, "to go alone in a boat."

Tapukumu'kw (no singular or plural); *-kumek*, *-kumoq*, *-kukwik*, "to go by twos."

Nesukumu'kw, *-kumek*, *-kumoq*, *-kukwik*, "to go by threes."

Asukom te'sukumu'kw, etc., "to go in sixes."

Metla'sukmu'kw, "to go in tens"; *pukweluku'k, mu pukwelukumu'k*, "there are many people on board, or else there are not many."

Nalsi'kum, *-kumn*, *-kuk*, "to scratch, to scrape."

Pekisin, -sinn, -sink, -sinu'kw, -sinek, -sinoq, -sinkik, -sulti'kw, "to come"; *pkisintes, pkisine'n, -sinj, -sinnej, -sinu'kw, -sini'tij; mu kipkisinu, mu pkisinuij, mu pkisinnej, mu kipkisinupp, -sul'tipp, npikisinen, pekisinmk, -sultimk*.

Kewisin, etc., "to be hungry"; *kuisintes; kuisine'n, mu kuisinu*.

Weltesin, "to succeed, to be lucky"; *wltesintes*.

Saqatuetesin, "to fall, to stretch out on the ground"; *sqatuetesintes*.

Elisin, "to be lying down"; *lisintes; lisine'n* (to a dog) "lie down"; for a person that would be an insult, one would use *lisma'si*, "go lie down, stretch out" (slowly).

Ewjisin, "to be stretched out on"; *ewjisintes*.

Naptesin, "to have the same fate."

Alaqsin, "to fly, flap around," *alaqsultijik*, "they fly, flap around."

L'nu'tesin, "to dance in the manner of the Indians," *l'nu'tesulti'kw*.

Kiwto'qotesin, "to leap around, to whirl around."

Elko'jin, "to incline the head to one side, obliquely"; *ela'ko'jin*, "to the front."

Epmeko'jin, "to have the head inclined."

Ketapetesin, "to dive, to plunge under the water"; *ketapa'si*, "to sink" (slowly).

Pematal, -ataln, -atalk, -lu'kw, -lek, -loq, -lkik, -lulti'kw, "to eat" (intransitive); *pmataltes, -atale'n, mu kpmatalu, pematalmik, -lultimk; puskatalmik*, "greediness."

Meskil, -kiln, -kilk, "to be large"; *msikiltes, msikile'n, mu kmsikilu*; inanimate, *meski'k, -ki'kl; meskilnijl, -niji, -lultiliji; mu meski'ktnuk*.

Pejilkil, "larger"; *apjikil, apjikik*, "little" (less large).

Welkil, "of good height"; *-kiln, -kilk, -ki'k, welkilultijik*.

Telkil, -kiln, -kilk, "to be of such height"; *telkili'tij, telkilulti'tij; telki'k, telki'kl* (thing).

Keskul, -kuln, -kulk, "heavy"; *ksukultes; keskulkik, keskulultijik*.

Pukwelu'kw, pikwelu'kw, -lulti'kw, "several, numerous"; no singular, except in the third person: *pukwelk ji'nm*, "many men"; singular collective, as in English, *many a one*, or, in French, *beaucoup de monde; pukwelkl*, "several things"; *mu pukweltnukw, mu pukwelu'kw*, "not many." One says also *pikwelk, pikwelkik, pikwelnijl, pikwelkl*, "several things"; *mu pikwelu'kw, mu pikweltnukw*, "not many."

3. Add certain **impersonal** verbs which are related to the fourth conjugation. First we can put *kelu'lk*, although it serves as the third person inanimate for *kelu'si* (see the first conj.); "to be good"; then:

Welekisk, -kiskl, "it is fine at sea"; *wlekistew, ma' ... tnuk. Welikiskik, -kikl*, "it is fine on land"; *wlikiskittew, ma' ... kitnukw* (third conj.).

Patekisk, -kiskik, "the weather gets bad."

Wapk, "it is daylight"; *waptitew, ma'waptnukw*.

Ewask, "the lightning before the storm."

Kwanask, "driftwood," *senkatikn*, "raft."

Tetapu'tesk, "it happens just right."

Saqntesk, -teskl, "to fall lightly."

Nepewisk, "moonlight."

Ela'qatesk, "the trap falls, closes."

Naqmaje'jk, "that is easy" (see *naqmasiaq*, third conj.).

Peknetk, "it gets dark"; also *poqnitpa'q* (second conj.).

Anesk, "an odd number, a quantity from which something is lacking."

Tepesk, "an even number," *tepeskl* (used in the plural), "equals."

Oqwatk, "the north, wind from the north," *oqwatke'l*, "from the north side" (Gr. Ma. 41; Dict. 125, 1); *oqwatn, -tnuk, -tnukwl*, "same meaning."

Nipk, "the summer"; *tekinipk*, "early summer"; *te'sinipk*, "every summer."

Wine'jkl, "bad things, lewdness"; *ntaqo'qnl*, "shameful."

Wjipisk, -piskl, "root."

Kaqai'sk, -i'skl, -i'stital, "several times."

Finally the verbs expressing the running of water: *pemitk, pempekitk*, "it flows"; *elitk*, "in one direction"; *alitk*, "in different directions"; *esitk*, "it spills"; *se'sitk*, "it flows in all directions"; said also of the mind which wanders; *welpekitk, winpekitk*, "well," "badly"; *pesikitk*, "it forks" (Windsor); *wantaqpekitk*, "calm"; *kesikawamkitk*, "swift" (see *Reading Book*, p. 27). *We'kopekitk* or *we'kwapetkitk*, "the tide rises to there," the name of Truro, formerly Cobequid; *apskwopekitk*, or *apskwapekitk*, "comes back" (Jordan), *-pekitkiss, -pekitnusip*; the first person, if it existed, would be: *-pekitm, -pekitmn, -pekitk, -pekitnep, -pekitnu'sip, -pekitkiss*, just like *nep*.

LESSON EIGHTEEN

FIFTH CONJUGATION (ACTIVE INANIMATE) IN U

Principal model: ***Mena'tu***, to remove, to tear out

Present Indicative

Mena'   *tu*, I remove, I tear out.
        tu'n, you remove.
        toq, he removes.
        tu'kw, we remove (incl.).
        tuek, we remove (excl.).
        tuoq, you remove.
        toqik? tu'tij, they remove.
        tu'ti'kw, we remove.
        tu'tiyek, we remove.
        tu'tiyoq, you remove.
        tu'tijik, they remove.

Remarks: 1. In this conjugation the **negative** does not differ from the affirmative except in the third persons, and also the first and second persons of the plural: *mu mena'tukw, -tu'tiwk, -tu'ti'tiwk, -tu'tiwkw, -tu'tiwek, -tu'tiwoq*. It is the same in the other tenses. This stems from the fact that the *u*, which otherwise would be added for the negation, is already there in the affirmative.

2. Although this conjugation is a transitive conjugation, it includes, as does the preceding one, a large number of intransitive verbs; such a one is *welmitu*, "to behave well," which I had at first chosen as the model, and many others. This does not affect the conjugation, where there may be relational objects typical of intransitive verbs, as well as direct objects typical of transitive verbs.

Supplementary Forms: 1. **Inanimate subject**: *mena'toq, -toql, -tu'tikl*: the negative, if it were encountered in this verb, would be: *mu mena'tnukw, -tnukwl, -tu'tinukwl*. See *telamu'k* below.

2. **Obviative subject**: *mena'tulijl, -tuliji, -tu'tiliji*; *mu mena'tulikwl, -tulikwi, -tu'tilikwi*.

3. **Missing persons (subject), dead or absent**: *mena'toqaq, mena'toqi'k, -tu'titki'k*; (object) *mena'tulita, -tulitka, -tu'tilitka*; *mu mena'tukwaq, -tukwi'k, -tu'tikwi'k, mu mena'tulikwa, -tulikwika, -tu'tilikwika*.

4. Likewise an **inanimate subject** in the past would require: *mena'toqek, -toqekl, -tu'tike'kl*; *mu mena'tnukwek, kwekl*.

5. When the inanimate **object** is in the **plural**, or when the indirect object is an animate plural noun, the former would give: *mena'tuanl, -tu'nl, -toql, -tu'kwl, -tuekl, -tuoql, -tu'tijl, -tu'ti'kwl, -tu'tiyekl, -tu'tiyoql, -tu'ti'tijl; mu mena'tuanl, -tu'nl, -tukwl, -tu'kwl, -tuekl, -tuoql, -tu'tikwl, -tu'tiwkwl, -tu'tiwekl, -tu'tiwoql, -tu'ti'tikwl*; -- for the second: *mena'tuanik, -tu'nik, -toqi, -tu'kwik, -tuekik, -tuoqik, -tu'tiji, -tu'ti'kwik, -tu'tiyekik, -tu'tiyoqik, -tu'ti'tiji; mu mena'tuanik, -tu'nik, -tukwi, -tu'kwik, -tuekik, -tuoqik, -tu'tikwi, -tu'tiwkwik, -tu'tiwekik, -tu'tiwoqik, -tu'ti'tikwi*; these plural forms are little used: the dual is used instead.

Past Indicative

Mena'   *tuep, tuap*, I removed.
    tu'sip, tu'p, you removed
    toqsip, toqiss, toqip, he removed.
    tu'kup, kuss, kusp, we removed.
    tuekip, tuekiss, tueksip, we removed.
    tuoqop, tuoqoss, tuoqsip, you removed.
    toqopnik, toqosnik, toqsipnik, they removed.
    tu'ti'kup, kuss, kusp, we removed.
    tu'tiekip, tu'tiekiss, tu'tieksip, we removed.
    tu'tioqop, tu'tioqoss, tu'tioqsip, you removed.
    tu'tipnik, tu'tisnik, tu'tisipnik, they removed.

Supplementary Forms: 1. **Negative**: *mu mena'tuksip*, etc., *-sipnik*; *mu mena'tu'tiwkup, -tiweksip, -tiwoqsip, -ti'tiwksipnik*.

2. **Inanimate subject**: it can hardly occur in *mena'tu*; see *telamu'k*.

3. **Obviative subject**: *mena'tulisnl (-pnl), -tulisni (-pni), -tu'tilisni (-pni)*; *mu mena'tuliwksipnl, -tuliwksipni, -tu'tiliwksipni*.

4. For the **missing, dead or absent**, the forms of the present, which have a true past sense, can be used. There are also the following, however: *mena'toqsipnaq, -toqsipnika, -tu'tisnika, -tulisna, -tulisnika, -tu'tilisnika*; *mu mena'tuliwksipna, -tuliwksipnika, -tu'tiliwksipnika*.

5. There is also, in the third person of the dual, *telintoqosni'k*, "they sang thus" (Printed grammar. p. 63).

6. When the **object** (inanimate) is in the **plural**, it is necessary to add *-l, -nl* in the singular: *mena'tuapnl, -tu'sipnl* or *-tu'pnl, -toqsipnl, -tu'kupnl, -tueksipnl, -tuoqsipnl, -tu'ti'kupnl*, etc.; as for example: *mena'tuapnl pleku'l*, "I have pulled the nails out"; *mu mena'tuapnl, -tuwsipnl, -tuksipnl, -tukupnl, -tueksipnl, -tuoqsipnl, -tu'tiwksipnl, -tu'tiwkupnl, -tu'tiweksipnl, -tu'tiwoqsipnl, -tu'ti'tiwksipnl*.

7. When the verb expresses an indirect agreement to a **plural** of the **animate** gender, *-l* is changed to *-ik* (to *-i* in the third person): *mena'tuapnik, -tu'sipnik* or *-tu'pnik, -toqsipni*, etc.

8. If the **obviative** is a name of a thing or a person in the **past**, according to the rules of the seventh lesson, No. 3, the verb is made to agree with it, by changing *-l* to *-ek, -ekel*, and *-ik* or *-i* to *-ika*. Ex.: *mena'tuapnika nepu'titkika wtalame'smual-a*, "I have deprived the deceased of their masses"; *mena'tu'tisipnika nepu'tilitka wtalame'smual-a*, "they have deprived them," etc.; and if it refers to masses which should have been said a long time ago (as those which Our Holy Father the Pope has had replaced from November 2), one indicates this by saying *wtalame'smuowekl-a*.

9. For the perfect and the pluperfect, *kisi-* or *ki's-kisi-* is used before the verb in the past without modification of the ending. See p. 39, No. II, and p. 46, No. 7.

Future Indicative

Mna'tu tes (mna'ttes), I will remove.
    tesk, you will remove.
    tew, he will remove.
    tesnu, we will remove.
    tesnen, we will remove.
    toqsip, you will remove.
    taqq, they will remove.

Mna'tu'titesnu, we will remove.
>*titesnen*, we will remove.
>*titoqsip*, you will remove.
>*titaqq*, they will remove.

Remarks: 1. In current usage, *u* is suppressed in pronunciation, in the future affirmative of verbs in *-tu* (*mena'ttes*, etc.).

2. In practice, also, the third person of the plural is replaced by that of the dual.

Supplementary Forms: 1. **Negative**: *ma' mna'tu*, etc., as in the present.

3. For an **inanimate subject**, see *telamu'k*.

4. For an **obviative subject**: *mna'tulital, -tulita, -tu'tilita; ma' mna'tulikul; -tulikwi, -tu'tilikwi*.

5. Agreements with **plural objects** occur only in this tense in the third persons of the affirmative (the negative using the present forms with *ma'*): *mna'tutal, mna'tu'tital; mna'tuta, mna'tu'tita*.

Imperative

Mna'tu, remove it.   *Mu kmna'tu*, do not remove it.
Mna'tuj, let him remove.   *mna'tuij*, let him not remove.
Mna'tunej, let us remove.   *mna'tunej*, let us not remove.
Mna'tukw, remove.   *kmna'tupp*, do not remove.
Mna'tu'tij, let them remove.   *mna'tu'ti'wij*, let them not remove.
Mna'tu'tinej, let us remove.   *mna'tu'tinej*, let us not remove.
Mna'tu'tikw, remove.   *kmna'tu'tipp*, do not remove.
Mna'tu'ti'tij, let them remove.   *mna'tu'tiwi'tij*, let them not remove.

Remarks: 1. With **inanimate subject**, see *telamu'k*.

2. The second person is like the first person of the present indicative, with contraction, just as for *teluisi*, when the verb is susceptible to contraction. Such is *telintu*, the model given by Maillard (Published grammar, p. 64): *tlintu*, "sing"; he gives third person negative forms that are the same as the affirmative: *tlintuj, tlintu'tij*; but I am sure the Indians say: *mu tlintuij, -ntui'tij* and *mna'tuij, -tui'tij*; on the other hand, the third person plural is not used, the dual form is substituted for it, in this verb and in many others.

Conjunct or Indicative with *When*

Mena't uanl, tuanek, my removing, having removed, when I remove, removed.
    tu'nl, tu'nek, when you remove, removed.
    toql, toqek, when he removes, removed.
    tu'kwl, tu'kwek, when we remove, removed.
    tuekl, tuekek, when we remove, removed.
    tuoqwl, tuoqwek, when you remove, removed.
    tu'tijl, tu'titek, when they remove, removed.
    tu'ti'kwl, tu'ti'kwek, when we remove, removed.
    tu'tiyekl, tu'tiyekek, when we remove, removed.

Supplementary Forms: 1. **Negative**, third persons: *mu mena'tukwl, -tu'tikwl*, etc.

2. **Inanimate subject**: see *telamu'k*.

3. **Obviative subject**: *mena'tulijl, -tulitek, -tu'tilijl, -tu'tilitek; mu mena'tulikwl, -tulikwek, -tu'tilikwl, -tu'tilikwek*.

4. For the **missing, dead or absent**: *menatoqeka, -tutitka, -tulitka, -tu'tilitka; mu mena'tukweka, -tu'titkweka, -tulitkwa, -tu'tilitkwa*.

Remark: For the third person M. Maillard gives for *telintu*, "I sing thus," *telintoql* or *-toqwl* (Published grammar, p. 65), "when he sings," and in the past: *telintutek* or *-ntoqwek*; but one may certainly keep to the forms given above.

Conjunct or Indicative with *If*

Mna	*'tuan,*	*tuass,*	*tua'sn*, if I remove, removed, have removed.
	tu'n,	*tusip,*	*tusipn*, if you remove, removed, have removed.
	toq,	*toqsip,*	*toqsipn*, if he removes, removed, has removed.
	tu'kw,	*tu'kuss,*	*tu'kusn*, if we remove, removed, etc.
	tuek,	*tueksip,*	*tueksipn*, if we had removed.
	tuoq,	*tuoqsip,*	*tuoqsipn*, if you had removed.
	tu'tij,	*tu'tiss,*	*tu'tisn*, if they had removed.
	tu'ti'kw,	*tu'ti'kuss,*	*tu'ti'kusn*, if we had removed.
	tu'tiyek,	*tu'tiyeksip,*	*tu'tiyeksipn*, if we had removed.
	tu'tiyoq,	*tu'tiyoqsip*	*tu'tiyoqsipn*, if you had removed.
	tu'ti'tij,	*tu'ti'tiss,*	*tu'ti'tisn*, if they had removed.
	tu'tiyoqwl	*tu'tiyoqwek*, when you remove, removed.	
	tu'ti'tijl,	*tu'ti'titek*, when they remove, removed.	

Supplementary forms: 1. **Negative**, as in the present and past indicative, with contraction, when the verb is susceptible to it; *mna'tu*, "do not take it"; moreover, the negative form differs from the affirmative only in the third persons and in the first and second person plural *mu mena'tukw, -tuksip, -tuksipn; -tu'tiwk, -tu'tiwksip, -tu'tiwksipn; mu menatu'tiwkw, -tu'tiwkkuss, -tu'tiwkkusn; -tu'tiwek, -tu'tiweksip, -tu'tiweksipn; -tu'tiwoq, -woqsip, -woqsipn.*

2. For an **inanimate subject**, see *telamu'k*.

3. The forms for **obviative subject** are met with but infrequently in this mood.

Remark: M. Maillard gives for the third person pluperfect *telintusn* and *tlintoqsipn*, "if he had sung" (Published grammar 66).

Conditional

Mna' tukk (ep), I would remove.
    tukk (p), you would remove.
    tuss, he would remove.
    tu'kupp, we would remove.
    tukekk (p), we would remove.
    tukoqq (p), you would remove.
    tu'tiss, they would remove.
    tu'ti'kupp, we would remove.
    tu'tikekk (p), we would remove.
    tu'tikoqq (p), you would remove.
    tu'ti'tiss, they would remove.

Past

Mna' tukapn, I would have removed.
    tukpn, you would have removed.
    tusoqq, he would have removed.
    tu'kupn, we would have removed.
    tukekpn, we would have removed.
    tukoqpn, you would have removed.
    tu'tisoqq, they would have removed.
    tu'ti'kupn, we would have removed.
    tu'tikekpn, we would have removed.
    tu'tikoqpn, you would have removed.
    tu'ti'tisoqq, they would have removed.

Remark: just as in the conditional of *teluisi* (p. 51).

Supplementary forms: 1. **Negative**: *mu mna'tuiss, -tu'tiwiss, -wisoqq; -tu'ti'wkupp, -pn, -tu'tiwekekk, -pn, -tu'tiukoqq, -pn.*

2. With **inanimate subject**: see *telamu'k*.

3. **Obviative subject**: *mna'tuliss, -tu'tiliss, -tulisoqq, -tu'tilisoqq, mu*

mna'tuliwiss, -tu'tiliwiss, -tuliwisoqq, -tu'tiliwisoqq; difficult to find in this mood.

4. Other forms of the past: *ntui'sketukwa's*, "I would have sold."

Subordinative

Nmna'tun, that I remove.
Kmna'tun, that you remove.
Wmna'tun, that he remove.
Kmna'tunenu, that we remove.
Nmna'tunen, that we remove.
Kmna'tunew, that you remove.
Wmna'tunew, that they remove.
Kmna'tu'tinenu, that we remove.
Nmna'tu'tinen, that we remove.
Kmna'tu'tinew, that you remove.
Wmna'tu'tinew, that they remove.

Supplementary forms: 1. **Negation** does not affect this mood. For the past add *ki's*, "already": "I wish they had removed," *wlite'tmukk ki's wmna'tunew*.

2. **Obviative subject**: *wmna'tulin, -tu'tilin*.

3. **Inanimate subject**: see *telamu'k*: *wtlamu'ktn, -tnen, mu wtlamu'ktnun*.

Infinitive or Impersonal (Indefinite Subject)

Affirmative
   Mena'tmk, tu'timk, to remove, one removes.
   Mena'tmkiss, tu'timkiss, to have removed, one removed.
   Mna'tuten (mena'tten), tu'titen, to be about to remove, one will remove.
   Mna'tmkej, tu'timkej, let one remove (imperative).
   Mena'tmkl, tu'timkl, removing, when one removes.
   Mena'tmkek, tu'timkek, having removed, when one removed.
   Mna'tmk, tu'timk, if one removes.
   Mna'tmkiss, tu'timkiss, if one removed.
   Mna'tmkisn, tu'timkisn, if one had removed.
   Mna'tuness, tu'tiness, one should remove.
   Mna'tunesoqq, tu'tinesoqq, one should have removed.
   Mna'tmkn, tu'timkn, that one removes (subordinative).

Negative

Mu mena'tmmik, tu'timmik, not to remove, one does not remove.
  mena'tmmiksip, tu'timmiksip, not to have removed, one did not remove.
Ma'mna'tmmik, tu'timmik, not to have to remove, one will not remove.
Mu mna'tmkij, tu'timkij, let one not remove (imperative).
  mna'tmmikl, tu'timmikl, not removing, when one does not remove.
  mena'tmmikek, tu'timmikek, not having removed, when one did not remove.
  mna'tmmik, tu'timmik, if one does not remove.

The rest as in the affirmative.

Remarks: 1. The first form is used to represent one person or thing, or a small number; the second, if there is a large number, a crowd.

2. In the negative, M. Bellenger (Ms. Gr. p. 43) gives: *mu mena'tmmuksip*, by confusion with the verbs in *-tm*, inf. *-tmk*, which, in the negative, double this *m*, as we have seen for *nestm*. Those in *-tu*, inf. *-tmk*, have simply *-tmik*, not *-tmuk*, still less *-tmmik*. [Our own information confirms that of Fr. Bellenger, and we have consequently changed the paradigm above from that given by Fr. Pacifique. There appears to be some variation, but the facts are far from clear].

3. With an inanimate plural object, direct or indirect, the following forms take *-l* or *-nl*; these endings change to *-ik* or *-nik*, if it refers to an animate indirect object: *mena'tmkl, -tu'timkl, -tmkisnl, -tu'timkisnl*; *mu, ma' mna'tmmikl, -tu'timmikl, -tmmiksipnl, -tu'timmiksipnl*; *mena'tmkik, -tu'timkik, -tmkisnik, -tu'timkisnik*; *mu, ma' mena'tmmkik, -tu'timmkik, -tmmksipnik, -tu'timmksipnik*. *Ta'nl nemitmkl aqq mu nemitmmikl kisitoqsipnl*, "he made the things which are seen and those which are not seen (visible and invisible)."

TELAMU'K

Here, as a guide, is the complete conjugation of *telamu'k*, "it is similar, of the same nature, of the same kind."

Present Indicative: *telamu'k, -mu'kl*; *mu telamu'ktnukw, -tnukwl*.

Missing things: *telamu'kwek, -mu'kwekl*; *mu ... tnukwek, -tnukwekl*.

With a plural object: *telamu'kwl, -mu'kwi*; *mu ... tnukwl, -tnukwi*.

Past: *telamu'ksip, -mu'kuss, -mu'kup*; all three mean, "it was similar"; for the plural add *nl*: *telamu'ksipnl, -mu'kusnl, -mu'kupnl*; if there is an animate plural object, one puts *-ni*: *telamu'ksipni -mu'kusni, -mu'kupni*; for dead persons, *-na*,

-*nika*; for removed things, -*nek*, -*nikl*; such is the long word in the Lord's Prayer: *telamu'kupnikl*, "in the same way," or word by word, "the things of the same type with which you have nourished us, (let it be with) the same that you nourish us today."

Negative: *mu telamu'ktnuksip, -tnukuss, -tnukup*, with all the same additions.

Future: *tlamu'ktitew, -tital; ma' tlamu'ktnukw, -tnukwl*.

Imperative: *tlamu'ktij, mu tlamu'ktenuj* (singular and plural).

When: *telamu'kwl, -mu'kwek; mu telamu'ktnukwl, -nukwek*.

If: *tlamu'kk, -mu'kuss, -mu'kusn; mu tlamu'ktnukk, -tnuss, -tnusn*.

Conditional: *tlamu'kuss, -mu'kusoqq; mu tlamu'ktnuss, -tnusoqq*.

Subordinative: *wtlamu'ktn; mu wtlamu'ktnun*.

Infinitive: *telamu'ktmk, -tmkiss, -titen, -tmkl, -tmkek, -tlamu'ktmk, -tmkiss, -tmkisn, -tuniss, -tunisoqq, -tmkej, -tmkn*.

LESSON NINETEEN

FAMILIES OF THE FIFTH CONJUGATION

Like *mena'tu* are conjugated:

1. The other **transitive** or **intransitive verbs** in *-tu* which are most numerous, as:

Apkwa'tu, "to loosen, to put back"; *apkwa'tutes* (no contraction).

Ajknewa'tu, "to confuse, harm"; *wiaqa'tu*, "to mix, mingle."

Ela'tu, "to take it"; *la'tutes*, *la'tu*, *mu ktla'tu*; *ila'tu*, "to prepare, to repair"; *ilitu*, "renew, remake"; *il'jo'qwa'tu*, "repair, rectify, to set in order, to ratify"; *elitu*, *el'tu*, "to make."

Elue'wa'tu, "to turn something bad, to make a sin of it"; *l'ue'wa'tutes*.

Enqa'tu, "to stop"; or *nenqa'tu*, contraction *naqa'tu*, "stop that!"

Ejikla'tu, "to move it, to remove"; *jikla'tutes*, "I will move it."

Ika'tu, "to put in place"; *ika'tuewey*, "stake (in a game), wager."

Ilta'tu, "to close"; *kepsaqa'tu*, "to lock"; *sepanqa'tu*, "close a book"; *spanqa'tu*, "close it!"

Wela'tu, "to treat (a thing) well"; *wla'tu*, *wla'tutes*.

Oqnipkwa'tu, "to hide, to cache in the ground, to cover with earth," by extension, "to inter, to bury"; or better *utqotalk*, *utqotatm wtinin*, "to inter him, to inter his body."

O'pla'tu, "to offend, to curse"; *wina'tu*, "to dirty, to spoil, to do wrong."

Kasa'tu, "to obliterate"; *ke'sa'tu*, "to burn, to destroy"; *keska'tu*, "to lose, to demolish": *aniapsimk elue'wuti'l kasa'toql*, "penance erases sins; *sikntatimk keska'toql*, "baptism eliminates them"; *kesispa'tu*, "to wash": *ksispa'tutal alikal*, "she will wash the clothes"; *Ksispa'sue'kati*, "Purgatory"; *nemja'tu*, "to raise."

Kewa'tu, "to knock down, to upset"; *kewiey*, "to collapse."

Kiskaja'tu, "to accomplish (a task, penance, duty)"; *nuku'j to'q nqasi kiskaja'tunej ktiki-wla'kw telapukuati'kupnl*, "now therefore let us accomplish as soon as possible that which we promised the day before yesterday," *naqsi*, "promptly."

Natqa'tu, "to bring out, to deliver"; *tuopitia'tu*, "to frame"; *natqaspeka'tu*, "to withdraw"; *pela'tu*, "to miss"; *alame's pela'tu'sip*, "did you miss mass?"

Ne'a'tu, "to show"; *muskatu*, "to divulge"; *musika'tu*, "to clean, to clear, to strip."

Nepsa'tu, "to raise"; *pesua'tu*, "to dry"; *pewitu*, "to dream about something."

Nisa'tu, "to lower" (trans.); *nisa'si* (intrans.), "to descend."

Panta'tu, "to open" (a door); *pana'tu*, in general; *pansaqa'tu*, "to open with a key, as a chest," *lisqeikn* (Ms. 2, 127-193); *pananqa'tu*, "a book"; *panilja'tu*, "to open another's hand"; *panilja'si*, "to open the hand."

Pema'tu, "to carry"; *elma'tu*, "to carry away"; *sama'tu*, "to touch."

Pekwatu, "to make, to cause, to bring about"; *sespena'q pekwatoq*, "he causes trouble"; *kinu na pekwatu'kw*, "we are the cause of it, it is our fault."

Pesoqwa'tu, "to miss out, to divert"; *pesoqopskatu*, "to fail (one's duty, goal, word of honor), to break (commandments)"; *sewiska'tu*, or *sekwiska'tu*, "to break, to violate."

Piptoqoqwa'tu, also *piptoqwa'tu*, "to make round"; *piptoqopska'tu*, "to form, to shape in the round, to mold."

Piskwa'tu, "to bring in" (a thing); *piskwo'tu*, "to bring in" (a quantity).

Puna'tu, "to cease, to renounce"; *punitu*, "to stop making something."

Tala'tu? "what do I do with it?" *moqwa tala'tu* or *natala'tu*, "nothing" (bad); *na'tala'toq*, "he does something wrong, harmful" (Rem. gr. p. 4).

Tela'tu, "I do that thus"; *tla'tutes*, "I will do it"; *puski-tla'tu*, "I often do it this way and that"; *i'-tla'tu*, "I have that habit."

Tewa'tu, "to get something out"; *tewaqa'tu*, "to take it outdoors."

Tewalqa'tu, "to rip out"; *pitapeka'tu*, "to pass something the length of."

Tepa'tu, "to set down" (an offering); *tepo'tu*, "to set down" (a quantity).

Tetapua'tu, "to do exactly, to satisfy."

Toqwanqa'tu, "to join"; *toqwanqa'toql wpitnl me'su'tekl*, "he puts his bare hands together." (Cat.).

Toqopukua'tu, "to place together, to unite"; *tqopukua'tutes*.

Apu'kwetu, "to send"; *apaja'tu*, "to bring back, to return."

Esmuetu, "to furnish food"; *smuetutes*, "I will furnish it."

Eskipetu, "to wait for" (a thing); *netui'sketu*, "to sell"; *ntui'sketutes*.

Iknmuetu, "to give a thing, to make a gift, to give away."

Welmitu, "to be good, to behave well"; *nekla e'pitkik mu welmitu'tiwksipni'k* (Gr. Ma., p. 42), "these women did not behave well"; *wlmitutuk, -tuknik, -tu'tituknik*, "perhaps he is, they are, they have been good" (dubitative form).

Wetqoluetu, "to forbid a thing"; *wtoqoluetutes*.

Winmitu, "to be bad, to behave badly."

Telmitu, "to behave thus."

Awanitu, "not to know how to"; *koqqwa'tu* or *kiqqwa'tu*, "to seize, to take, to grab hold of"; it is little used except for expeditions of war or the procedures of justice; it signifies properly, "to seize violently from the enemy" (Rem. gr. p. 84); even for an ordinary police officer one says *nuji-wsua'teket*.

Elitu, el'tu, "to make, to shape, also to celebrate" (the mass).

Kejitu, "to know"; it redoubles the *j* when there is contraction: *kjijitutes*, "I will know"; *weli-kjijitmk*, "one know well"; *nuji-kjijiteket*, "a learned man"; *nikani-kjijitekewinu*, "a prophet."

We'jitu, "to find"; *we'jitutes*, "I will find it."

Kisitu, "to make, to create, to carry out"; *kisa'tu*, "to make (with effort), to succeed"; *ma'kisa'tukw*, "he will not be able to make it."

Nemitu, "to see a thing"; *nmituss, -tusoqq*, "he would see, would have seen, it."

Pekisitu, pejo'tu, wejkwa'tu, "to bring, to fetch"; *pkisitutes, pejo'tutes, jukwa'tutes*.

Ajipjutu, "to hope, to wait for."

Esiputu, "to sharpen"; *sipua'tu*, "to change into a river": *sipua'toqsipnek kun'tewek*, "he (God) changed the rock into a river" (Ps. 113, 8).

Ketapo'tu, "to sink, to make sink into the water"; *ktapo'tutes*.

Telewistu, "to speak thus"; *etlewistu*, "to chat, to blab, to gossip."

Telintu, "to sing thus"; it is the model of this conjugation that is given by Fr. Maillard in his grammar (partially printed) p. 64; *welintu, winintu*, "to sing well, badly"; it is better to use *ketapekiey* (third conj.).

Tettu, -tu'n, -toq, "to have, to possess in one's own right, to owe"; *tettoqol sape'wuti'l*, "holy" (in the *Confiteor*), also *sape'wuti'l mestankl*, same meaning, applied to the Blessed Virgin and to Saint Michael.

2. Other verbs in *-u* which have *-uk* in the third person: *ketu, ketu'n, ketuk*, "to cry, to proclaim, to toll, to ring"; *e'sk mna'q ki'kli'kwej ketuk*, "before the cock crows"; *newt ktuj*, "let it ring once"; *ketu'kw, ketu'ti'kw, ketu'tiyek. Ktuan*, "if I howl" (war-whoop). *Ktui-ktuk ktuj*, "if he wants to yell, let him yell." *Ketukwl*, "on the signal" (Dict. 64), "when one rings." *Ketukipnl pipukwaqnl*, "the instruments were playing."

Kesalku, -ku'n, -kuk, "to be likeable"; *pejili-ksalku'n*, "you are the beloved."

Jipalku, -ku'n, -kuk, "to be frightening; passive sense."

Neku, -ku'n, -kuk, -ku'kw, -kuek, -kuoq, -kujik; nkutes, nku, "to bring game."

Sitniku, -ku'n, -kuk, "to blow one's nose"; *-ku'tijik, -kutes: -ku, -kuk*.

Eli'ku, -ku'n, -kuk, "to serve soup, to soak, to drain, to hollow out, to clear away."

Ilpilaqu, -qu'n, -quk, "to undo the strap of a pack."

Nalsi'ku, -ku'n, -kuk, "to scratch, to scrape."

The following three verbs have *-oq* in the third person of the affirmative and thus are regular, but the third is defective.

Ika'taqu, -qu'n, -qoq, -qu'kw, -quek, -quo'q (long), plural *ika'taqu'tijik*, "to be a farmer": *l'nu ika'taqoq aqq melmuapateket, skatu Kisu'lkw pemiteket*, "man cultivates and waters, but it is God who makes things grow" (1 Cor 3, 7); *ika'taqu'tipnik aqq ewi'ka'tipnik*, "they (the contemporaries of Noah) tilled the soil and built" (Luke 18, 28).

Do not confuse this verb with *ika'ta'qw*, "we offer to someone" (seventh conjugation).

Wesamatesiku, -ku'n, -koq, etc., "to be overburdened."

Etoq, etu'tijik, "he makes his nest, they make their nest."

3. **Impersonals** or **inanimates**:

Telamu'k, "of this type"; *welamu'k*, "of a good kind, of good appearance"; *eulamu'k*, "puny"; *kesamu'k*, "brilliant"; see the conjugation above (p. 132), *wtlamu'ktnen*, "that it be so."

Kta'nuk, "towards the open sea."

Newtipuk, "one winter"; *aqtapuk*, "in the middle of winter"; *tekipuk*, "a cold winter"; *welipuk*, "a good winter"; *newtipunqik*, "one year"; *te'sipunqik*, "each year, every year" (third conj.).

Short Sentences

Ki's we'jitu'sip wi'katikn ta'n entu'sip ktiki-wla'kw? ki's eta (kisna) mna'q, "Have you found the book which you lost the other evening? yes, (or), no, not yet." *Ula e'pite'ji'j nekwaspit wen'ju'su'naqsi*, "that little girl is sitting quietly under an apple tree." *Ni'n aqq nekm kesi-wli-tko'tmek kekina'matimk*, "she and I like to go to school"; *wesko'tk wi'katiknji'j, toqu ni'n kun'tew nespiey wi'kikemkewey*, "she has a little notebook and I a slate." *Kjijitu'sipn moqwe maja'siwkpn*, "if you had known it, you would not have left." *Moqwe kejituwkw ta'n tl-tawa'ti'kupp, skatu Weji-wli Niskam apoqnmuet epetoqsutiktuk ta'nl me'si-wi'tmekl* (Rom. 8, 26), "we do not know what we should ask, but the Holy Spirit comes to our aid with unutterable groanings."

[For table of endings of AI and TI verbs, see next page].

Table of Endings of Verbs without Animate Goal

I		II		III	IV		V	
Teluis	i	Alasutm	ay	Ewi'kikey	Nest	m	Mena't	u
	in		an	en		mn		u'n
	it		at	et		ik		oq
	i'kw		ayikw	eyikw		mu'kw		u'kw
	iyek		ayek	eyek		mek		uek
	iyoq		ayoq	eyoq		moq		uoq
	ijik		ajik	ejik		ikik/mi'tij		u'tij
	ulti'kw		a'ti'kw	iti'kw		mu'ti'kw		u'ti'kw
	ultiyek		a'tiyek	itiyek		mu'tiyek		u'tiyek
	ultiyoq		a'tiyoq	itiyoq		mu'tiyoq		u'tiyoq
	ultijik		a'tijik	itijik		mu'tijik		u'tijik

In the **Past** one adds *-ip, -sip, -sp, -ps, -snik, -pnik*, with some modifications of the vowels; in the **Future** one adds uniformly *-tes, -tesk, -tew, -tesnu, -tesnen, -toqsip, -taqq, -titesnu, -titesnen, -titoqsip, -titaqq*.

Here is the Imperative:

Tluis	i	Alasutm	a	Wi'kik	e/a	Nsite'n	Mna't	u
	ij		aj		ej	j		uj
	inej		anej		enej	mnej		unej
	ikw		aq		ekw	mukw		ukw
	i'tij		a'tij		e'tij	mi'tij		u'tij
	ultinej		a'tinej		itinej	mu'tinej		u'tinej
	ultikw		a'tikw		itikw	mu'tikw		u'tikw
	ulti'tij		a'ti'tij		iti'tij	mu'ti'tij		u'ti'tij

Infinitive:

Teluis	imk	Alasutm	amk	Ewi'kik	emk	Nest	mik	Mena't	mk
	imkiss		amkiss		emkiss		miksip		mkiss
Tluis	iten		aten	Wi'kik	eten	Nsitten		Mna't uten	
	imkij		amkij		emkij	Nsitmkij			mkij
	ultimk		a'timk		itimk	Nsitmu'timk			utimk
	etc.		etc.		etc.	etc.			etc.

LESSON TWENTY

TO HAVE AND TO BE

In French the verb "to be" (*être*) used alone is called a substantive verb; followed by a participle, it is an auxiliary; it is the same for the verb "to have" (*avoir*). M. Maillard gives in Mi'kmaw *eymik* and *wesko'tmik*; but he immediately adds that they do not enter into any conjugation as auxiliaries, and that the former does not mean "to be someone or something" (Gr. Ma. 162); it means "to be somewhere": *ula eym*, "I am here," *na'te'l eymn*, "thou art there," *Niskam wa'so'q eyk, maqmikek eyk, msit eta pa ta'n telki'k kisitasik msit pa eyk jel moqwe'j eskwi-i'muk*, "God is in heaven, on earth and in everything which (is made) exists, and there is nothing where he is not" (Cat. p. 9). *Wesko'tmik* means "to possess"; it is conjugated like *nestm* (fourth conjugation); so is *eymik*; but some complications are met with in the latter which render a summary conjugation useful.

I. Conjugation of Eym

Present Indicative: *eym*, "I am," etc., *eymn, eyk* or *eyt, eymu'kw, eymek, eymoq, eykik, eymu'ti'kw, eymu'tiyek, eymu'tiyoq, eymu'tijik*; inanimate: *eyk, eykl, etek, etekl*; obviative: *eymlijl, eymliji, eymu'tiliji*; negation: *mu eymu, -mu'n, -muk, -mu'kw, -muek, -muoq, -mi'tiwk, mu eymu'ti'kw*, etc.; *mu eytnuk, etenuk, eymnuk*, plural *-nukwl*; ex.: *moqwe'j ula eymnuk*, "it's not there," or else, "there is nothing here"; *lamikuomk eymoq*, "you are in the hut"; *ki's l'nu'k nenua'tijl Kisu'lkwl wa'so'q eymlijl*, "the Indians now know the Creator who is in heaven"; *wen ta kisiasni l'nu'maqmikek eymliji?* "Who created the men (the Indians) who are on the earth?" *Kisu'lkw iknmuasni l'nu'wnijanua wskitqamu'k wti'mlin*, "it is God who has put the children of men on the earth (that they might be there)"; *mimajuinu'k eymu'kwik*, "we are with people"; *eymanik*, "I am at their place"; *si'stewey wi'katikn eyk*, "it is in the third book."

Past: *eymep*, "I was," etc., *eymu'sn* or *eymu'p*, *eykuss* or *eykip*, *eteksip*, *eymu'kup* or *-kuss*, *eymeksip*, *eymoqsip*, *eykisnik*, *eymu'ti'kup*, etc.; *eykisnl*, *eykisnikl*.

Future: *i'tes*, "I will be there," etc., *i'tesk*, *i'tew*, inanimate *i'ttew* for *i'titew*, *i'tal*, *i'tesnu*, *i'tesnen*, *i'toqsip*, *i'taqq*, *i'mu'titesnu*, etc.; *ma' i'mu*, *-mu'n*, *-mukw*, as in the present, with contraction or elision of *e*; this elision here and elsewhere is often omitted: *eymu'titesnu*, *ma eymu'tiwoq*.

Imperative: *i'e'n*, "stay!," *i'j*, *i'tij* or *tej*, "let him stay"; *i'mnej*, "let us stay"; *i'k* or *i'mu'kw*, "be!"; *i'mu'tinej*, *i'mu'tikw*, *i'mi'tij*; *mu kti'mu*, *ktipp*, *kti'mupp*, *kti'mu'tipp*.

When Conjunct: *eymanl*, *eymnl*, *eykl*, *eymu'kwl*, *eymekl*, *eymoqwl*, *eymi'tijl*; *eymanek*, etc., "being there, having been there, when I am, was there."

If Conjunct: *i'man*, "if I am there," etc., *i'mn*, *i'j*, *i'mu'kw*, *i'mek*, *i'moq*, *i'mass*, *i'mu'sip*, *i'ss*, *i'mu'kuss*, *i'meksip*, *i'tiss* or *i'mi'tiss*, *i'masn*, etc.; *mu i'muasn*, *i'muwsipn*, *i'musn*, *i'mu'kusn*, *i'mueksipn*, *i'muoqsipn*, *i'mi'tiwksipn*, (see Pub. Gr. p. 37); but here M. Maillard gives all the way through *eym*, without elision. Inanimate: *I'k*, *i'ss*, *i'sn*, or *tek*, *tes*, *tesn*, "if it was there"; *tej*, *i'ttij*, "let it be there."

Conditional: *i'mukk*, *i'mukapn*, "I would be, I would have been," etc., *i'mukpn*, *i'ss*, *i'soqq*, *i'mu'kupp*, *-pn*, *i'mukekk*, *-pn*, *i'mukoqq*, *-pn*, *i'tiss*, *i'tisoqq*, *mu i'musoqq*, "he would not have been."

Subordinative: *nti'mn*, "that I may be there," *kti'mn*, *wti'mn*, *wti'mlin*, *wti'mitnen*, *kti'mnenu*, *nti'mnen*, *kti'mnew*, *wti'mnew*, *kti'mu'tinenu*, etc.; *Kesaltimkewey wti'mitnen wtininewaq aqq ni'n nti'mn wtininewaq* (John 17, 26), "that charity might be in them and that I myself might be in them."

Infinitive: *eymik*, *eymiksip*, *i'mitn*, "to be, to have been, to be going to be," or better, "one is," etc., *i'mtej*, "let one be"; *eymikl*, *i'mik*, *i'miksip*, *i'miksipn*, *i'mness*, *i'mnesoqq*, *i'mn*; also *eymu'timk*, etc., as *nestmu'timk*.

II. Meaning

In the catechism, to the question: When, during what time has God existed, *ta'n Niskam eykiss*? one answers: *Sa'q eta me'j eykiss, nike'j eyk aqq me'j i'tew*, "for a long time, he has always existed, he exists now and he will always"; it seems that his being or his existence was intended, a meaning which is not in the Mi'kmaw expression; so, the question which comes immediately after more or less puts everything straight: *Ke'sk mna'q koqoeyinukwek tami eykiss?* "where then was he before anything else existed?" *Moqwe'j eta tami eymuksip, wniskameutiktuk eta sik eykiss*, "truly, he was in no place, it was in his divinity alone that he existed." M. Maillard, to whom we owe the catechism, has also written somewhere: *mijua'ji'j eymn*, to indicate: "you are a child"; but really this means: "you have a child"; for *eym* means also "to have, to have in one's possession or at one's disposition," as we shall see. Mr. Rand likewise tries to use it in the sense of "to be," "to exist," without succeeding any better; thus he makes Saint John the Baptist say: *Eykip e'sk mu eymuanek*, "Jesus existed before I did" (John 1, 27); likewise he translates the beginning of the Gospel by: *Kji-klusuaqn eykip*, "there was the Word"; the proper term, still a poor translation, would have been: *Kji-klusuaqniksip*.

But *eym* quite often has the meaning "to have." Thus M. Maillard writes, in his questionnaire on confession, this question, which can be put to the penitent: *Pa'qapukuo'tiktuk wi'katikn eymn*? "do you have a note of confession (from the preceding confession)?" and he gives the answer: *Mu eymu* or *mu kewkunmu*, "I do not have it"; one can in fact use the latter expression, as in *wesko'tm, mu wesko'tmu*; it is often simpler. Elsewhere (Rem. gr. 73), he writes: *suliewey eym*, "I have money"; then he adds that this verb should, in this case, be followed by an object of the inanimate gender, that with an object of the animate gender one uses *eyaq, eyat, eyuajl*; but this is not correct today, for one also says: *te'sipow eym*, "I have a horse." As for *eyaq*, it is hardly used at all except to mean to have children, and furthermore, says Mr. Maillard, in the spirit of the language this would mean to be pregnant: *mijua'ji'jl eyuajl*, "she is pregnant"; *alasutmelsewin mijua'ji'j nteyuan*, "pray for me that I may become a mother"; *pikwelniji mijua'ji'j eyua'tiji*, "they have several children." He says again: *Tlia'j moqwe'j eymu'n mijipjewey kweltamultimkewey* (Ms. 3, 186), "even when you do not have the appropriate foods for abstinence."

III. General Rule

But the real way to express in Mi'kmaw "to be someone or something" and also "to have" is to add *-i (-wi)* and *-mi* to the noun, pronoun and adjective, with or without modification of the stem; the first ending itself will have the meaning "to have" in words expressing relationship, the parts of the body and others in which "to be" would be nonsense. This will become clear from examples. Moreover, when one wants to express the actual usage of the item in question, the use made of it, or the occupation, *-mi* is changed to *-a'm*. "The syllable *a'm* suffixed to any noun changes it into a verb and denotes occupation, present tense; thus *tmi'kn*, 'an axe'; *tmi'kna'm*, 'I have an axe in my possession'; *wen'ji'kuom*, 'a house'; *wen'ji'kuoma'm*, 'I occupy a house', though it may not be my own" (Rand, Dict. E.-M. 183). The forms in *-i* and *-mi* are conjugated like *teluisi*, *-a'm* like *nestm*, but with the plural in *-o'lti'kw*, which also follows the first conjugation, on the model of *welei, welo'lti'kw*.

The third person inanimate in *-ik*, with its negative *mu...inukw*, means: "there is, there is not such-and-such," and serves for the two genders, as *awti*, "road," *awtiik*, "there is a road," *mu awtiinukw*, "there is no road"; *elnuik*, "there's a crowd"; *mu elnuinukw*, "there's no one." If the noun ends in *-i* (as *awti* itself), this vowel is doubled in the first person, or else prolonged. If it ends in the diphthongs *-ay* or *-ey*, these diphthongs are changed into two syllables, *-a-i*, *-e-i*, but the third persons are in *-it*, *-ijik*, *-ultijik*, keeping *-i* in the plural, as *pa'qla-i*; ex.: *apijipmkewey*, "resurrection"; *apijipmkeweyi, -weit, -weijik, -weio'ltijik*, "I am the resurrection, he is ..."

IV. Note on Negation

It is appropriate to insert here a general note on negation, which has already been discussed several times.

We have seen that it plays such an important role in the conjugations that it in fact doubles them.

It consists first of all, as in other languages, of placing negative particles before the verb: *mu*, in the future *ma'*, "not"; *matew*, "never"; *mna'q*, "not yet"; *e'sk mna'q*, "before"; *moqwa, moqwa'j, moqwe, moqwe'j*, "no, not"; *ma'wen*, "nobody." Then it becomes necessary to change each ending of the verb itself. It is only indirectly that negation affects also the nouns, adjectives and pronouns, always used in this case in the verbal form. The sound *u* or *a* is introduced in the ending for the verbs without animate goal, and *nu*, when the subject itself of those verbs is of the inanimate gender.

1. **Examples**: *pipnaqn*, "bread"; *pipnaqnik*, "there is some bread"; *mu pipnaqninukw*, "there is none"; with an animate subject one would say: *pipnaqni, -nin, -nit*, "I am, you are, he is bread"; *mu pipnaqniw, -niwn, -niwk*, "I am not bread," etc.; *kun'tew*, "stone"; *kun'tewin*, "you are a stone"; *kun'tewit*, "he is a stone"; *kun'tewik*, "it is stony, there is stone"; *mu kun'tewinukw*, "there is none." *Nu* is often preceded by *t* or *te*, as in *meski'k, kelu'lk, telamu'k*, "it is large, beautiful, similar," *mu meski'ktnukw, kelu'ltnukw, telamu'ktnukw*, "that is not big," etc. Nouns of the animate gender, preceded by negation, take in the verbal form the same ending to signify that there is not any: *elnuit*, "he is a man, an Indian," *mu elnuiwk*, "he is not one"; *elnuik*, "there are people," *mu elnuinukw*, "there are none"; the plural *mu elnuinukwl* would indicate that it has to do with several places; *wela'sik*, "it is going well," *mu wela'sinukw*, "it is not going well," *mu wela'sitnukw*, "that is not well placed." The persons ending in *-t* change this letter to *-k* after *-w*; those in *-jik* become *-tiwk*, which is pronounced nearly like *-tikw* (voiceless *w*), so that it is difficult to distinguish the third person singular negative from the

first person affirmative dual or even negative: *moqwe teluisiwk*, "his name is not"; *teluisi'kw*, "our (two) name is"; *moqwe teluisiwkw*, "our name is not."

2. The **transitive** verbs, in their agreements with third persons, take *-a*, *-aw* before *-k*: *westawi'k*, "I save him"; *mu westawiaq*; *alasutmelsewk*, "I pray for him," *mu alasutmelsewaq*; those in *-aq*, *-uajl*, take *-u* before *-aq*: *iknmaq*, "I give it to him," *mu iknmuaq*; these in *-aq*, *-ajl*, change not at all or little: *esa'q*, "I chase him," *mu esa'q*, *esa'wt*, *esa'qwl*; those in *-ik* change *-i* to *-a*: *wela'lik*, "I do him a good turn," *mu wela'laq*, *ewi'tik*, "I name him," *mu ewi'taq*. The future is like the present, with *ma'* and contraction: *ma'wi'taq*, *ma'wla'laq*, *ma'sa'q*, *ma'wsitawiaq*.

3. The **imperative** is in *-aw*, *-awij*; but in the plural *-k* or *-kw* is changed to *-p*; moreover, in the second persons one adds, after *mu*, *k* or *kt*, the latter only in those verbs which take *-t* in the subordinative: *tlimukw*, "tell them"; *mu ktlimapp*; *anko'tmu*, "keep that for him," *mu ktanko'tmuapp*.

4. In the **infinitive**, the negative of the inanimate verbs is formed by placing *i* between *m* and *k*: *mu teluisimik, alasutmamik, ewi'kikemik, mena'tmik*; in verbs in *-m*, *-mk*, which already have the *i*, the *m* is doubled: *mu nestmmik*; *ma' nsitmmik*; *pa'kewimk*, "Easter, past," *pa'kewimkek*: *tapukuna'qek ke'sk mna'q pa'kewimikek tlisip klujjiewto'ss*, "he was crucified two days before Easter." [See also note on p. 115, Section 2]

For the TA verbs, in their agreements with third persons, *-ut*, *-ot*, *-uss*, *-oss* are changed to *-at* or *-amik*, *-amiksip*, and *-iat*, *-uat* for those which have these vowels in the indicative: *mu nemiat*, or *nemiamik*, *alasutmelsewat*, *iknmuat*, etc. In agreements with the other persons, they resemble those of the other paradigms: *mu, ma'nmi'imik, nmu'lmik*, "one does not, will not see me, you."

5. Here are some more **Examples**:

Alasutmaq, or *alasutmaqnik*, "that is Christian," alluding to prayer or religion; *moqwa alasutmanukw, alasutmaqninukw*, "that is not"; *alasutmo'kuom moqwa alasutmanuk*, "Protestant church"; *aklasie'wey etli-kina'matimk*, "place for the English, Protestant sermon"; for the Mi'kmaq they are synonymous.

Wasitpa'q, "clear night," *welitpa'q*, "beautiful night"; *mu weli, wasitpa'qtnukw*, "that is not"; *welikiskik*, "beautiful day"; *mu welikiskiktnukw*, "that is not one."

Wasoqotesk, "lightning"; *mu wasoqotestnukw*, "there is none"; *nemi'kip mntu wji-wisqi-nisien wa'so'q isteke wasoqoteskel* (Luke 10, 18), "I have seen Satan fall from the Heaven like lightning."

Kaqtukwaq, "thunder"; *mu kaqtukwanuk*, "there is none"; *kaqtukowik*, "it thunders"; *mu kaqtukowinukw*, "it does not thunder." *Kelu'lk*, "beautiful," *welikisk*, "beautiful weather," *naqamje'jk*, "easy"; *tetapu'tesk*, it arrives on time; *mu tetapu'testnukw*, "it is not in time"; *welikistnukw, naqmaje'jtnukw*.

Moqopa'q or *mekopa'q*, "wine"; *moqopa'qek*, "that is wine," or else, "there is some"; *mu moqopa'qtnukw*, "there is none, there is no more" (after the consecration).

Samuqwan, "water," *samuqwanik*, "there is water"; *mu samuqwaninuk*, "there is none"; *samuqwaniksip, mu samuqwaninuksip; samuqwanikek, mu samuqwaninukwek; samuqwanikl, mu samuqwaninukwl, ... ninukwekl*.

Wetewipnemk, "to complain"; *mu wetewipnemik*, "one does not complain."

Kisu'lkwl moqwe'j me'si'kuk (Ms. 3, 176), "nothing is impossible for God"; *ma' koqoey me'su'luoq*, "nothing will be impossible for you"; *mu weji-tualqa'siwk* (Matt. 17, 20), "he (the devil) is not driven out."

Kisiku Nuelewimkewa'j

(Father Christmas)

Teli-napui'kasit meski'k mun'ti pema'toq kisna topaqn wajuiaq papitaqnl, ke'j apsute'kan, tu'aqn, wa'kn, lipkmutaqn, jikjawiknej, mimi'l aqq kaqai'si-milamu'kwl koqoe'l wjit ta'n te'siliji weni. Teluemk wejiet wastewe'katik lo'q amasek. Tipituk moqwe nekm weniwk, aqq mna'q wenl nemi'kukwl pasɨk eta wi'katikniktuk. Meluij ta'n te'sit kelu'sit mimajuinu, ta'n ketui-wleiwaji mijua'ji'jl wjit Niskam Mijua'ji'jl tlisip weskijinuilitek nipi-alasutmamkek, na nekm tlite'lmuj Nuelewimkewa'j ketlewey.

LESSON TWENTY-ONE

ANIMATE VERBS

We call **animate** verbs those which are conjugated with persons or things of the animate gender as objects. This object causes changes in each person or form of the verb throughout the conjugation. There are however three fundamental forms in the singular with a third person object also in the singular: "I (see) him, you him, he him"; four in the plural, because of the different endings for *kinu* and *ninen*: "we him (2), you him, they him"; then seven others, if the object is in the plural: "I them, you them, he them, we them (2), you them, they them." There will be eight when the direct object is the second person: "I you, he you, we you, they you, I you (pl.), he you, we you, they you." Finally ten forms can be counted for first person objects: "you (s.) me, he me, you (pl.) me, they me, you (s.) us, he us (2), you (pl.) us, they us (2)." That makes thirty-two forms, except in the imperative and in the infinitive. On the other hand, there is no difference between dual and plural in these verbs.

Here is the **table** of these forms, according to the order of the conjugation:

I	him	I	them
you (s.)	him	you (s.)	them
he	him	he	them
we	him (2)	we	them (2)
you (pl.)	him	you (pl.)	them
they	him	they	them
I	you (s.)	I	you (pl.)
he	you	he	you
we	you	we	you
they	you	they	you
you (s.)	me	you (s.)	us

he	me	he	us (2)
you (pl.)	me	you (pl.)	us
they	me	they	us (2)

In the Imperative

(see)	him	(see)	them
let him	him	let him	them
(let us see)	him	(let us see)	them
(you pl. see)	him	(you pl. see)	them
let them	him	let them	them
let him	let them (see)	(you s.)	you (pl.)
(you s. see)	(you pl. see)	me	us
let him	let them	me	us

In the Infinitive

one	him	one	them
one	you (s.)	one	you (pl.)
one	me	one	us (2)

N.B.: In the infinitive these forms are developed in all tenses and moods; for "one me," "one us," each form is double.

Remarks: 1. We do not give here: "I myself," "you yourself," "he himself," etc., because these pronominal forms, as they are in French and English, constitute in Mi'kmaw another whole class of verbs (reflexive and reciprocal) which follow the model of the first conjugation (intransitive). For the **mixed** (i.e. double goal) verbs, in place of "I him," "I them," etc., we have to say in English "I to him," "I to them," etc.

2. Since the animate verb may have in the third person a subject of the **inanimate** gender, the latter, especially when it is in the plural, modifies some of the persons that it governs. Likewise, if the animate verb in the third person is the **object** of another of the same person, it takes, like the others, the syllable -*li*-: thus *nemiajl*, "he sees him," gives *nemialijl*, "the one who sees him." There is, furthermore, a **passive** form in the third person; it is formed by dropping the *a* of the active or by changing it to *i*: thus, from the same person *nemiajl*, "he sees him," is formed *nemi'jl*, "he is seen by him" [inverse form]. The peculiarities of certain verbs and of certain tenses will be found indicated in their respective places. Moreover the verbs take, in each case, endings which agree with the **missing, dead or absent**, persons or things, just as those of the **plural**, when there is another indirect object of the persons or things. Finally there is the whole **negative** conjugation. We generally give it in full;

other supplementary forms are indicated for each tense; but one should not try to learn them all before mastering the basic conjugation, affirmative and negative.

All the animate verbs end in -*k* or -*q*; this consonant is preceded by the vowels *a e i u i*: -*aq*, -*ek*, -*ik*, -*uk*, -*ik*, -*oq*, or the other consonants, -*lk*, -*mk*, -*nk*, -*pk*, -*sk*, -*tk*, *i* then being elided.

Conjugations

We could identify six animate conjugations; but by taking *nemi'k* as the principal model it will be easy to relate the other verbs to it, by pointing out the differences, in four secondary models. We will moreover give the complete conjugation of a mixed verb (or two-goal), which will also serve as the model for a whole class of active verbs in -*aq*; each conjugation will occupy two lessons, followed by a list of examples. Almost all these verbs have a corresponding transitive inanimate, which serves as a base for the mixed verbs, as we call those transitive verbs which have a second object, animate or inanimate. They are all formed in -*maq* or -*taq*, based on inanimate transitives in -*m* or -*tu*: -*aq* is added to the first, and for the second *u* is changed to -*aq*; thus *nestm*, "to understand something," gives *nestmaq*, "to understand a thing which belongs to someone" (or to pay attention to it), such as his words, for example, or his gestures; *mena'tu*, "to remove something," *mena'taq*, "to remove it from someone"; this does not prevent these verbs from having their simple transitive animate form, *nestaq* and *mena'lik*, "to understand someone," "to remove him, to send him back"; likewise a thing of the animate gender: *pitu'kun mena'lik*, "I remove the humeral veil," *mena'taq*, "I take it away from him" (from the priest). These mixed verbs are conjugated exactly like *nestaq* and the other actives in -*aq*. The model given further on is *kisitaq*, "to make something (as a product) for someone." These verbs in -*aq* differ from *nemi'k* in that they take *u* in the forms "he him, them; you me, us," of the present and past, throughout the future, etc.

(M. Maillard also gives only these two conjugations; but he bemoans the fact that he is not able to state more clearly his theory of the agreements between the persons (subjects and objects) of these verbs. It is indeed somewhat confusing, as also his treatment of the reflexive verbs, which he tried, unsuccessfully, to derive from inanimate intransitives, whereas they are easily derived from transitive animates, as we shall see in the paradigms. It is the same with the mixture of verbs of every class and conjugation, of which M. Bellenger complained (Gr. p. 80), in the Remarks of M. Maillard, which are otherwise so valuable, and which he calls a masterpiece for the elegance, precision and purity of the Mi'kmaw language. If one carefully and slowly follows our conjugations and the list of different verbs in each, this puzzlement will be avoided. There will be no lack of gaps; but when one succeeds in finding forms for some of them, it will be immediately obvious how to use them; that is no small advantage, intellectual as well as literary.)

There is a small number of other verbs in -a'q (long a), which do not take this u, and which, furthermore, have their "I you (s.)" forms in -o'l, "you (s.) me" in -a'in, throughout the conjugation; they follow the first secondary model: esa'q, "to drive out"; the infinitive is in -o't, -o'lk, -a'imk: eso't, eso'lk, esa'imk, "one expels me, you, him"; the imperative: sa', sa'j, so'q, sa'i, sa'ik, so'lij, so'loqj.

The verbs in -e'k (long e) are conjugated in the same manner and hardly require the alternate secondary model: eskipe'k, "to wait for"; eskipo'l, pe'in, po't, pe'imk, po'lk, pe', pa', po'q, pe'i, po'lij, po'loqj.

The verbs in -ik follow the principal conjugation, except that in the imperative they drop i as well as k: ewi'tik, "I name someone," wi't, "name him!"; ewi'kik, "I describe him, I paint him," wi'k, "describe him!" Those in -uk are still more regular, if possible; but the presence of the u throughout makes them resemble the verbs in -aq, -wajl.

The verbs in -lmik are difficult to distinguish from those in -lmk, but this has hardly any importance for the animate conjugation; we will return to this for the formation of the passive, reflexive and reciprocal verbs, which are all of the first conjugation. The other verbs in -mk and those in -nk, -pk, -sk, -tk should be conjugated like those in -mik, -nik, -pik, -sik -tik.

But those in -lik, -lk follow two other secondary models: elue'wa'lik and kesalk, "I make wicked" and "I love" (which is not the same thing); we even have ika'lik (long a), which means "to place," and ikalk (short a) which means "to protect"; their transitive inanimate forms are ika'tu and ikatm; those of the others elue'wa'tu and kesatm. The principal difference is found in the forms "I you (s.), I you (pl.)" which are in -ln, -lnoq, -lnan, -lnin, -lnites, because of the two l's, which would otherwise occur together.

LESSON TWENTY TWO

SIXTH CONJUGATION (ANIMATE)

Principal model: *Nemi'k*, to see someone

Present Indicative

Ne mi'k, mi'kik, I see him, them.
    mi't, mi'jik, you see him, them.
    miajl, miaji, he sees him, them.
    mi'kw, mi'kwik, we see him, them.
    mi'kit, mi'kijik, we see him, them.
    mioq, mio'q, you see him, them.
    mia'tijl, mia'tiji, they see him, them.

Ne mu'l, mu'loq, I see you (s., pl.).
    mi'sk, mu'loq, he sees you (s., pl.).
    mu'lek, we see you (s., pl.).
    mi'skik, mu'loq, they see you (s., pl.).

Ne mi'n, miek, you see me, us.
    mi't, mu'lk, mi'namɨt (excl.), he sees me, us.
    mioq, miek, you (pl.) see me, us.
    mi'jik, mu'lkwik, mi'namijik (excl.), they see me, us.

Negative

Mu ne miaq, miaqik, I do not see him, them.
    miawt, miawjik, you do not see him, them.
    miaqwl, miaqwi, he does not see him, them.
    miawkw, miawkwik, we do not see him, them.
    miaqat, miaqajik, we do not see him, them.

   miawoq (*qik*), you do not see him, them.
   mia'tikwl, mia'tikwi, they do not see him, them.

Mu ne *mu'lu, mu'luoq*, I do not see you (s., pl.).
   mu'lukw, mu'luoq, he does not see you (s., pl.).
   mu'luek, we do not see you (s., pl.).
   mu'lu'kw, mu'luo'q, they do not see you (s., pl.).

Mu ne miun, miwek*, you do not see me, us.
   miwk, mu'lukw, mi'namewk, he does not see me, us.
   miwoq, miwek, you (pl.) do not see me, us.
   mi'tiwk, mu'lukwik, mi'namewkwik, they do not see me, us.

Remarks: 1. For "you (pl.) see them," theoretically, there should be *nemioqik*, but in practice one often simply lengthens -*oq* to -*o'q*.

2. It can be seen that *nemu'loq* is used for saying: "I see you (pl.), he sees you (pl.)," it is the same in the negative, *mu nemu'luoq*, and for the other tenses.

Supplementary Forms: 1. **Inanimate subject**: it affects only the following forms; for the others nothing is changed; *nemi'k* is better presented under the interrogative form: "does this, do these things see me, you, him?" *etuk nemi'k, -mi'kl, -mi'sk, -mi'skl, -mu'lk, -mu'lkwl, -mi'namik, -mi'namikl*? "no," *moqwe* or *moqwa, mu nemi'nukw, -mi'nukwl, -mu'lukw, -mu'lukwl, -mi'naminukw, -mi'naminukwl*; *meski'k ta'n teli-wla'linamikl wekla wi'katiknl*, "it is a great service that these books render us (letter)"; in the negative third persons, it would be: *mu nemianukwl, nemia'tinukwl*. For **missing things, past or removed**, one uses *nemi'kek, -kekl, mu neminukwek, -kwekl*. Another example: *na keseulik*, "that pleases me"; *etuk elp keseulisk*, "to you too?" "no, not to me, not you, not him," *moqwa (qwe) keseulinuk, keseulnuk, keseulkuk; me'j etuk mu tami kisi-wja'lat e'pit ta'n mu keseulkuk wpuske'wistu'n*? "couldn't one find somewhere a woman who was not too talkative?" (Rem. gr. 99).

2. **Plural object** (indirect) of the **inanimate** gender; one adds -*l, -al, -ol, -ul*, with or without modification of the preceding consonant: *nemi'kl, -mi'jl*, without change in the third persons which already have *l*; *nemi'kwl, -mi'kijl, -moql, mu nemiaql, -miawjl, -miawkwl, -miaqajl, -miawoql; nemu'lanl, -mi'skl, -mu'lekl, -mu'loql; mu nemu'luanl, -mu'lukwl, -mu'luekl, -mu'luoql; nemi'nl, -mi'jl, -mioql, -mi'jikl, -mu'lkwl, -mi'namijl, -miekl, -mu'lkwikl, -mi'namijikl; mu nemiunl, -miwekl, -miukwl, -mu'lukwl, -mi'naniwkwl, -miwoql, -mi'tiwkwl, -mu'lukwikl, -minamiwkwikl*.

3. For the **plural object** of the **animate** gender, -*l* is changed to -*ik* or -*i'*; furthermore, when this form is "we them, we to them," the two endings are alike, and the thing is adequately expressed by other words; for example: "I see these better than those," *wekla me'weli-nmi'kik mu nkutey waqla*, without

changing anything in the verb. Here is an example of the inanimate plural with "you him, I him": *kaqai'skl pipnu'jaqmati'l tetli-nemi'jl*, "you see him in several mirrors"; *msit koqoe'l pajiji-ksalnanl*, "I love you above all things"; *msit wenik pajiji-ksalnanik*, "above all people"; *kesalnanl* is better pronounced *kesalnann*.

4. The **verb** with **obviative subject** has *nemialijl, -liji, -mia'tilijl, -tiliji*; *mu nemialikwl, -likwi, -mia'tilikwl, -tilikwi*; example: *Kisu'lkw welamaji apoqnmua'tiliji wikmawa*, "God looks with satisfaction on those who help their neighbours."

5. **Passive** form: *nemi'jl, -mi'ji, -mi'kwi'tijl, -mi'kwi'tiji*, "he is seen, they are seen"; *mu nemi'kukwl*, "he is not seen by him"; this repetition of -*ku*- is certain, but I do not know how to account for it; it does not exist in the plural, nor with an inanimate subject: *mu nemi'kukw, nemi'kwi*, then *mu nemi'kwi'tikwl, -kwi'tikwi*, "they are not seen by him, them"; this form seems to be taken from the verbs in -*ku* of the fifth conjugation; for obviative forms, one says *nemi'lijl, -mi'liji, -mi'kwilijl, -mi'kwiliji; mu nemi'likwl, -mi'likwi, -mi'kwilikwl, -mi'kwilikwi*.

6. If the verb has for object the name of a **missing person, dead or absent** (which can of course only be met with in third person forms), it becomes: *nemi'kaq, -mi'taq, -miaja, -mi'kwaq, -mi'kitaq, -mioqwaq, -mia'tija, -nemi'kwika, -mi'kijika* or -*mikitka, -mioqika, -mia'titka*.

Past Indicative

Ne mi'kip, pnik, I saw him, them.
    mi'sip or *mi'tip, pnik*, you (s.) saw him, them.
    miasnl, sni or *pni*, he saw him, them.
    mi'kup, pnik, we saw him, them.
    mi'kitsip, pnik, we saw him, them.
    mioqsip or *nemioqop, pnik*, you saw him, them.
    mia'tisnl, sni, they saw him, them.

Ne mu'lep, mu'loqsip, I saw you (s., pl.).
    mi'skiss, mu'loqsip, he saw you (s., pl.).
    mu'leksip, we saw you (s., pl.).
    mi'skisnik, mu'loqsipnik, they saw you (s., pl.).

Ne mi'sip or *mi'p, mieksip*, you (s.) saw me, us.
    mi'ss or *mi'p, mu'lkuss, mi'namitsip*, he saw me, us.
    mioqsip, mieksip, you saw me, us.
    mi'snik or *mi'pnik, mu'lkusnik, mi'namitsipnik*, they saw me, us.

Negative Conjugation: III. *Mu nemiaqap, -miawsip, -miaqsipnl, -miakup, -miaqatsip, -miawoqsip, -mia'tiwksipnl*, "I not him," etc.; for "I not them," etc. add *-pnik* or change *-pnl* to *-pni*.

II. *Mu nemu'luep, -luoqsip, -luksip, -lueksip, -luksipnik, -luoqsipnik*.

I. *Mu nemiusip, -miweksip, -miwoqsip, -miwsip, -mu'luksip, -minamiwksip, -sipnik*.

Remarks: 1. This tense represents the past in general, especially the imperfect; to express more clearly the definite or indefinite past, one uses *kisi*, "already," after, or another particle, which is put before each person without modifying the ending: for the pluperfect or past anterior, one adds *ki's kisi*, "previously"; in the negative, *mna'q, me'mna'q*, "not yet," with the negative form of the verb.

2. There are in this tense, for almost all persons, three forms, which have not all been added to the paradigm, to avoid confusion; they unquestionably express nuances in meaning. Here they are in the order of the conjugation: "you him," *nemi'tip* and *nemi'p*; the first seems more affirmative than *nemi'sip*; the same is true for the negative: *mu nemiawtip*; *nemi'p* is a shortened form; "he him," *nemiapnl* and *nemiasipnl*; *mu nemiaqsipnl*; likewise *mu keske'lmaqsipnl*, "he did not spare him," *katu kise'lmasnl wjit ta'n te'si'kw*, "but he delivered him for us all" (Rom. 8, 32); "we him," *nemi'kuss, -kusnik, -kusipnik*; *nemi'kitip* shortened to *nemi'ktip*, and even *nemi'kkit* (Rem. gr. 69), *nemi'kitkiss, -snik, -kitkip, -pnik*; moreover, in verbs in *-ik*, what follows it is elided, and this person ends in *-ktip*; thus *kesalk* forms *kesalkitip*, "we loved him"; *klujjiewte'k* (long *e*), *klujjiewte'kitip*, "we crucified him"; but *ewi'tik*, "I name him," becomes *ewi'tiktip*; *elue'wa'lik*, "I make him wicked," *elue'wa'liktip, elue'wa'likitsip*, however is found; *mesnk*, "I welcome him," *mesniktip*, "we acquired him"; *nuji-kina'muet mesniktip*, "we acquired a teacher" (of singing – letter); "you pl. him," *nemioqoss, -snik, -qop, -pnik*; "they him, they them," *nemia'tipnl, -tisipnl, -pni*; "we you s., we you pl.," *nemu'lektip, -lekiss, mu nemu'luektip, -luekiss*; *nemu'loqoss, -loqop; mu nemu'lukuss, -lukwip, -luoqoss, -luoqop*; "he, they you s.," *nemi'skip, -pnik*; "you s. me, you pl. me," *nemi'tip, -mi'p; mu nemi'wtip, -wektip; nemiwoqoss, -oqop, -ekiss, -ekip*; Our Lord said to the Pharisee: *Mu weska'qelmiwtip, mu iknmuiwtip samuqwan*, "you did not embrace me, you did not give me water" (to wash my feet); "he, they me, us," *nemi'p, -pnik, -mi'sipnik; nemu'lkup, -mi'namittip, -pnik*; by abbreviation *nemi'naminik; mu nemi'wtip, -mu'luktip, -pnik*.

Supplementary Forms: 1. For the **missing, dead or absent**, *-naq* is added to the first two persons, and in the third *-nl* is changed to *-na, -nika*; example; *ula ji'nm nemi'kip*, "I (already) saw this man (present here)"; *ula'aq ji'nmaq nemi'kipnaq*, "I saw that man," who is spoken of, who is dead or removed. M.

Maillard gives: *nemi'kaq*; indeed this form of the present in *-aq* serves very well for the past: *wskitqamu mu kejiaqapna* (John 1, 10), "people did not know him," or as well *mu kejiaqwa*. For past, missing, or removed thing, see the following section.

2. An **Inanimate subject** gives the following forms: *etuk nemi'ksip, nemi'ksipnl, -mu'lkuss, -mu'lkusnl, -mi'namiksip, -mi'namiksipnl,* "did that see me, did those things see me, etc.?" *moqwa* or *moqwe,* "no," *mu nemi'nuksip, -sipnl, -mu'luksip, -sipnl, -mu'lukup, -kupnl, -mu'lukuss, -kusnl, -mi'naminuksip, -sipnl.* For past things, *nemi'ksipnek, -pnikl*.

3. To express a second object in the **inanimate plural**, *-l* or *-nl* is added to the persons which do not have it; for a plural of the **animate** gender, *-ik* or *-nik* is added, in other words *-sip* is changed to *-sipnik*, except in the third person, where *-nl* is changed to *-ni*.

4. **Obviative subject**: *nemialisnl, -lisni, nemia'tilisnl, -tilisni; mu nemialiwksipnl, -tiliwksipnl, -pni*.

5. **Passive forms**: *nemi'snl, -mi'sni, -mi'kwi'tisnl, -kwi'tisni; nemi'lisnl, -sni, -mi'kwi'lisnl, -sni; mu nemi'kuksipnl, -sipni, -mi'ti'kuksipnl, -sipni; mu nemi'li'kuksipnl, -mi'li'tikuksipnl, -sipni*.

6. **Dubitative forms**: *nmiatuk, -tuknik; nmu'lkutuk, -tuknik; nemi'namittuk, -tuknik*; likewise *apoqnmuinutuk, -tuknik*, "perhaps that helped me, I do not know for sure."

Future Indicative

N *mia's, miates,* I will see him, them
   miatesk (teks), you (s.) will see him, them.
   miatal, miata, he will see him, them.
   miatesnu, we will see him, them.
   miatesnen, we will see him, them.
   miatoqsip, you will see him, them.
   mia'tital, mia'tita, they will see him, them.

N *mu'ltes, mu'ltoqsip,* I will see you (s., pl.).
   mu'ltew, mu'loqtew, he will see you (s., pl.).
   mu'ltesnen, we will see you (s., pl.).
   mu'ltaqq, mu'loqtaqq, they will see you (s., pl.).

N *mi'tesk, mi'tesnen,* you will see me, us.
   mi'tew, mu'lkutew, mi'namitew, he will see me, us
   mi'toqsip, mitesnen, you (pl.) will see me, us.
   mi'taqq, mu'lkutaqq, mi'namitaqq, they will see me, us.

Remark: There are two forms for "I him, I them"; the second is not used at Restigouche. In place of *nemu'ltew*, in the prayers and in Maillard's grammar is found: *nemu'litew*, which seems to indicate a progressive action, done little by little. Likewise he writes *nemi'teks* (midex), *nemi'teksnu*; it is still pronounced that way in Cape Breton, and that seems to be the original form.

Supplementary Forms: 1. **Negative**, as in the present, with *ma'* in the place of *mu*: *ma'nmiaq, nmu'lu, nmiun,* etc.

2. When the verb expresses an indirect relationship to things of the **inanimate** gender in the **plural**, all the persons in *-tew* and *-taq* change this ending to *-tal*: "he will love you above all things," *msit koqoe'l pajiji-ksalnital*; *ksalnitew*, "he will love you." Likewise, if there is an inanimate subject in the plural, *-tal* is put in place of *-taq*: *kiqqwattekl awti'l knekk l'a'lnital*, "the upright ways will take you far"; *ma'tli-la'lnukul*, "they will not lead you thus." Finally, if an animate object of the third person is encountered with an inanimate plural subject, the verb becomes *-tal* for a double reason, if the object is in the singular, and *-ta* if it is in the plural; there is a curious combination of this kind in the following translation from St. Paul: *Omnis lingua confitebitur Deo–* O.L.C.D. (Rom. 14, 11), "every tongue shall give glory to God," *ta'n te'sikl milnu'l wlima'tital Kisu'lkwl*.

3. **Passive** form: *nmi'kutal, -kuta,* "he will be seen by him, them"; *nmi'kwi'tital, -kwi'tita,* "they will be seen by him, them." If the object is inanimate, one puts *nmi'kutew, -kutal*: *etuk wsitawi'kutew ta'n teli-ktlamsitk?* "will he be saved by his faith?" (7 Pr. 121). *Mu pa ma wsitawi'kuk, mu kiskaja'tuk ta'n telkimut,* "certainly not, if he does not do as he is told."

Imperative

Nmi (short *i*), see him, them.
Nmiaj, let him see him, them.
Nmianej, let us see him, them.
Nmikw, (you pl.) see him, them.
Nmia'tij, let them see him, them.
Nmu'lij, nmu'li'tij, let him, them see you.
Nmu'loqj, let him, them see you (pl.).
Nmi' (long *i*), (you s.) see me.
Nmi'j, let him see me.
Nmi'kw, (you pl.) see me.
Nmi'tij, let them see me.
Nmi'n, (you s., pl.) see us.
Nmu'lkuj, nmi'namij, mitij, let him, them see us.

Negative

Mu knmiaw, do not see him, them.
　　nmiawij, let him not see him, them.
　　nmianej, let us not see him, them.
　　knmiapp, do not (you pl.) see him, them.
　　nmiawi'tij, let them not see him, them.

Mu knmu'liwij, luoqj, let him, them not see you (s., pl.).

Mu knmi'w, mi'wipp, do not (you s., pl.) see me.
　　knmi'win, do not (you s., pl.) see us.
　　nmi'wij, wi'tij, let him, them not see me.
　　nmu'lukuj, mi'namiwij, wi'tij, let him, them not see me.

Remark: 1. In general the imperative is formed from the present of the indicative by dropping *k* and making whatever contraction the verb is susceptible to; thus *nemi'k* makes *nmi*; *kesalk*, "I love him," *ksal*, "love him!" *telimk*, "I tell him," *tlim*, "tell him!" The exceptions will be seen in the lists of lessons XXVI and XXVII (p. 158) and **Remarks** (p. 150). *Nmi'*, "see me," resembles "see him," but in appearance only, because the lengthened *i* is equivalent to two *i*'s; the same holds for *nemikw* and *nemi'kw*, "(you pl.) see him! see me!"

2. For: "do not (you pl.) see me, us," one can just as well say: *mu knmip, knemin*; example: *Kji-saqmaw, nmja'si, mu ktapji-jikla'lin*, "Lord, arise, cast us not off forever" (Ps. 43, 24); *ejikla'lik*, "to dismiss, to reject"; when there is a prefix before the verb, *k* and euphonic *t* of the second person are placed before the prefix: *apjiw, apji*, "always," *mu ktapji*, "do not forever."

3. With an **inanimate subject** the affirmative is the same; here is the negative for *askaiwaj, askaiwlij, askaiwij*, "let that trouble him, you, me": *mu askaiwanuj, askaiwinuj, askaiwlnukuj, askaiwinamnuj, mu ktaskaiwlinuj, mu ktaskaiwlnuoqj*.

LESSON TWENTY THREE

SIXTH CONJUGATION (CONTINUED)

Conjunct or Indicative with *When*

Ne mi'kl, mi'kek, my seeing, having seen, or when I see, saw him, them.
    mi'jl, mi'tek, when you see, saw him, them.
    miajl, miatek, when he sees, saw him, them.
    mi'kwl, mi'kwek, when we see, saw him, them.
    mi'kijl, mi'kitek, when we see, saw him, them.
    mioqwl, mioqwek, when you (pl.) see, saw him, them.
    mia'tijl, mia'titek, when they see, saw him, them.

Ne mu'lanl, lanek, when I see, saw you (s.).
    mi'skl, mi'skek, when he, they see, saw you (s.).
    mu'lekl, lekek, when we see, saw you (s., pl.).
    mu'loqwl, mu'loqwek, when I, he, they see, saw you (pl.).

Ne mi'nl, mi'nek, when you (s.) see, saw me.
    mi'jl, mi'tek, when he sees, saw me.
    mioqwl, qwek, when you (pl.) see, saw me.
    miekl, miekek, when you (s., pl.) see, saw us.
    mu'lkwl, kwek, when he, they see, saw us.
    mi'namijl, mitek, when he, they see, saw us.

Supplementary Forms: 1. **Negative**: *mu nemiaql, -qek, -miawjl, -tek, -miaqwl, -qwek, -miawkwl, -kwek, -miaqajl, -tek, -miawoqwl, -qwek, -mia'tikwl, -kwek*; --*mu nemu'luanl, -nek, -mu'lukwl, -kwek, -mu'luekl, -kek, -mu'luoqwl, -qwek*; --*mu nemiunl, -nek, -mi'kwl, -kwek, -miwoqwl, -qwek, -miwekl, -kek, -mu'lukwl, -minamikwl, -kwek*.

2. With a subject of the **inanimate** gender, add to the corresponding form of the indicative *-al, -l, -ul, -wl* for the present, *-ek, -uek* for the past.

3. **Passive**: *nemi'jl, -tek; -mi'kwi'tijl, -tek.*

4. **Obviative subject**: *nemialijl, -litek; -mia'tilijl, -litek.*

5. This mood in the present very much resembles the present indicative with an inanimate plural complement; if one of them is found here, it will change nothing in the present, but in the past it will still be necessary to add *l*, eliding the first *e*: *milamu'kwl teli-wleyulankl*, "my having favoured you in various ways"; likewise *nemu'lankl, nemi'nkl*, even *nemi'kkl*.

Conjunct or Indicative with *If*

Remark: This mood has three tenses; present, past, pluperfect; the present differs from the indicative only in a few persons; but it takes contraction throughout, if the verb is susceptible to it; the pluperfect is formed from the past by adding *-en* in all persons of this tense.

N   *mi'k, mi'kik, mi'kiss, sn*, if I see, saw, had seen him, them.
     mi'j, mi'sip, pn, if you (s.) see, saw, had seen him, them.
     miaj, miass, sn, if he sees, saw, had seen him, them.
     mi'kw, mi'kuss, sn, if we see, saw, had seen him, them.
     mi'kij, mi'kitsip, pn, if we see, saw, had seen him, them.
     mioq, mioqsip or *oqoss, pn* or *sn*, if you (pl.) see, etc. him, them.
     mia'tij, mia'tiss, sn, if they see him, them.

N   *mu'lan, mu'loq, mu'lass, mu'loqs, sn, sipn*, if I see you (s., pl.).
     mi'sk, mu'loq, mi'skiss, mu'loqs, sn, sipn, if he sees you (s., pl.).
     mu'lek, mu'leksip, pn, if we see you (s., pl.).
     mi'skik, mu'loq, mi'skiss, mu'loqs, sn, if they see you (s., pl.).

N   *mi'n, mi'ek, mi'sip, mi'eksip, pn*, if you (s.) see, etc. me, us.
     mi'j, mu'lkw, mi'ss, mu'lkuss, sn, if he sees me, us.
     mi'namij, mi'namitsip, pn, if he sees, saw, had seen us.
     mioq, mi'ek, mioqsip, mi'eksip, pn, if you (pl.) see me, us.
     mi'tij, mu'lkwik, mi'tiss, mu'lkuss, sn, if they see me, us.
     mi'namitij, mi'namitiss, sn, if they see us.

Remark: This mood also has an optative sense, of hope or hesitation, as *nmu'lan*, "that I might see you (s.)," *kjiju'lan*, "that I might know you" (Rem. gr. 233); *teli-ksalin tli-ksalnan*, "that I might love you as you love me" (prayer).

Supplementary Forms: 1. The **negative** form differs little from that of the indicative; here is that of the past, which will serve as a guide for the two others: *mu nmiaqass, -miawsip, -miaqsip, -miawkuss, -miaqatsip, -miawoqsip, -mia'tiwksip*; *mu nmu'luass, -luoqs, -mu'loqsip, -mu'lueksip*; *mu nmi'wsip, -mi'weksip, -mi'woqsip, -mu'lukuss, -mi'namiksip, -mi'woqsip, -mi'weksip, -mi'tiwksip, -mu'lukuss, -mi'namitiwksip*.

2. The **inanimate** form in the negative gives *-anuj, -enuj, -inuj, -nuss, -nusn*: *mu nemi'nuj, -nuss, -nusn*, "if that does not see me," *nmi'namnuss*, etc.

3. **Passive**: *nmi'j, -mi'ss, -mi'sn*, "if he is seen by him," etc.: *wnaqapem nemi'j* (when Conjunct), "Jesus having been seen by his disciples" (Matt. 14, 26).

4. **Obviative subject**: *nmialij, -mi'lij, -liss, -lisn*.

5. Some other variants are found, besides *nmioqoss, -oqosn*: *nmi'kitkiss, -kitkisn*, "if we should see them"; *nmi'namitkiss, -mitkisn*, "if he saw, had seen us"; *nmi'namijik*, "if they see us"; but this latter is certainly incorrect.

Conditional

N *mi'ekk* (*op*), *mi'ekapn*, I would see, have seen him, them.
   miaqq (*p*), *miaqpn*, you would see, have seen him, them.
   miass, miasoqq, he would see, have seen him, them.
   mia'qupp, miaqupn, we would see, have seen him, them.
   miaqekk, miaqekpn, we would see, have seen him, them.
   miaqoqq, miaqoqpn, you (pl.) would see, have seen him, them.
   mia'tiss, mia'tisoqq, they would see, have seen him, them.

N *mu'likk, likapn, likoqq, likoqpn*, I would see, have seen you (s., pl.).
   mu'liss, lisoqq, loqs, loqsoqq, he would see, have seen you (s., pl.).
   mu'likek, kekpn, we would see, have seen you (s., pl.).
   mu'liss, lisoqq, loqs, loqsoqq, they would see, have seen you (s., pl.).

N *mi'kk, mi'kpn, mi'kekk, mi'kekpn*, you (s.) would see, have seen me, us.
   mi'ss, mi'soqq, mu'lkuss, mu'lkusoqq, he would see, have seen me, us.
   mi'namits, mi'namitsoqq, he would see, have seen us.
   mi'koqq, koqpn, kekk, kekpn, you (pl.) would see, have seen me, us.
   mi'tiss, soqq, mu'lkuss, soqq, they would see, have seen me, us.
   mi'namitiss, mi'namitisoqq, they would see, have seen us.

Remark: It is very useful to note that in all the transitive animate verbs, however different they may be from each other, the first form "I him, I them" of this mood is similar to "you us" of the present indicative, except for the contraction; thus *kesaliek*, "you love us," makes *ksaliekk*, "I would love him";

iknmuiekk, "I would give him"; *apu'iek*, "you send us," *apu'iekk*, "I would send him or to him."

Supplementary Forms: 1. **Negation** influences this mood but little; nevertheless one says: *mu nmiawiss, -wisoqq; mu nemia'tiwiss, -wisoqq,* "he, they would not ... him, them"; *mu nmi'wiss, -tiwiss, -wisoqq,* "he, they do not ... me."

2. **Obviatives**: *nmialiss, -lisoqq;* **passive**: *nmi'ss, -mi'tiss, -soqq.*

Subordinative

Nnmian, that I may see him, them.
Knmian, that you may see him, them.
Wnmian, wnmi'kun, that he may see him, them.
Knmianew, nnmianen, that we may see him, them.
Knmianew, that you (pl.) may see him, them.
Wnmianew, wnmikunew, that they may see him, them.

Knmu'lin, knmu'linew, that I, he may see you (s., pl.).
Knmi'kun, mi'kunew (passive form), that he may see you (s., pl.).
Knmu'linen, that we see you (s., pl.).
Knmu'linew, knmi'kunew, that they may see you (s., pl.).

Knmi'n, knmi'nen, that you (s.) may see me, us.
Nnmi'n, nnmi'nen, knmu'lkunenu, that he may see me, us.
Nnmi'kun, nnmi'kunen, knmi'kunenu, that he may see me, us.
Knmi'new, knmi'nen, that you (pl.) may see me, us.
Nnmi'new, nnmi'nen, knmu'lkunenu, that they may see me, us.
Nnmi'kunew, nnmi'kunen, knmi'kunenu, that they may see me, us.

Remark: 1. With "he, they" as subject, the subordinative has two forms: when the object is "me, you (s.), us, you (pl.)," M. Maillard uses constantly the second in *-kun, -kunenu, -kunen, -kunew*, whereas with "him, them," he uses both. I do not know the reason for this difference; moreover the Indians generally say, for example, *knmu'lkunenu;* Mr. Rand also uses it sometimes; thus, *kuji-apattelu'lkunenu* (Tit. 2, 14), "that he might redeem us." I think that the two forms are regular: the second has a passive sense. With "he, they, to him, to them," M. Maillard often uses the first: *wtiknmuan mtuanew*, "that he, they may give to him, to them" (Rem. gr. 64); even in his grammar (p. 72) there is *wi'kmuan; u* was printed instead of *n.*

2. It is quite remarkable that in this mood the first letter should be *k* (from *ki'l, kilew*, "you" (s., pl.)) every time that mention is made of the second person, as

subject or object: *n* (from *ni'n, ninen*, "I, we") only when the other person is third; finally *w* (from *ula, wekla*, "he, they") when there are only third persons; intentional or instinctive, it is a very delicate courtesy towards those to whom one speaks. Here is a striking example of it: *wjiaj telki'k kpekwate'tmuinen, santewit Naskwet Ma'li teltamkijl npekwatawalsewkunen*, "that **you** may grant us what (she) the B.V.M. acquires for us by her prayer which we ask of her" (Ms. 9, 316); *pewatm ktlimkun*, "I want you to tell me" [him-you?] (letter); *ntlimkun*, "that he may tell me," *wtlimkun*, "that he may tell him."

Supplementary Forms: 1. **Negation** changes nothing in the subordinative, except in the inanimate forms: *mu wtaskaiwanun, -ulinun, -winun* or *-wiktnun, -ulukun, -winamnun* or *-winamiktnun*.

2. **Obviative forms**: *wnmialin*, which serves for all numbers; example: *ika'tuajl Se'susl wklujjiewtalin*, "he delivers Jesus to them to be crucified" (John 19, 16).

Infinitive or Impersonal (Indefinite Subject)

Nemu't, mu'jik, to see him, one sees him, them.
Nemu'ss, mu'snik, to have seen him, one saw him, them.

Nmiaten, miatiten, to be about to see him, one will see him, them.
Nmu'j, mu'tij, let one see him, them (imperative).

Nemu'jl, mu'tijl, seeing him, them, when one sees him, them.
Nemu'tek, mu'titek, having seen him, them, when one saw him, them.

Nmu'j, mu'tij, if one sees him, them.
Nmu'ss, mu'tiss, if one saw him, them.
Nmu'sn, mu'tisn, if one had seen him, them.
Nmianess, mia'tiness, one would see him, them.
Nmianesoqq, mia'tinesoqq, one would have seen him, them.
Nmian, mia'tin, wnmi'ken, mi'kenew, that one may see him, them.
Nemu'lk, to see you (s., pl.), one sees you (s., pl.).
Nemu'lkiss, to have seen you (s., pl.), one saw you (s., pl.).

Nmu'lten, mu'loqten, to be about to see you, one will see you (s., pl.).
Nmu'lkij, let one see you (s., pl.) (imperative).
Nemu'lkl, mu'lkek, seeing, having seen, when one sees, saw you (s., pl.).
Nmu'lk, mu'lkiss, mu'lkisn, if one sees, saw, had seen you (s., pl.).
Nmu'liness, mu'linesoqq, one would see, would have seen you (s., pl.).
Nmu'lkn, mu'lknew, knmi'kn, mi'knew, that one may see you (s., pl.).

Nemi'mk, mi'timk, mu'lk, mi'namit, to see me, us, one sees me, us.
Nemi'mkiss, mi'timkiss, mu'lkiss, mi'namitsip, one saw me, us.
Nmi'ten, mi'titen, mu'lkuten, mi'namiten, one will see me, us.
Nmi'mkij, mi'timkij, mu'lkij, mi'namitij, let one see me, us.
Nemi'mkl, mi'timkl mu'lkl, mi'namijl, seeing, when one sees me, us.
Nemi'mkek, mi'timkek, mu'lkwek, mi'namitek, having seen, when one saw me, us.

Nmi'mk, mi'timk, mu'lk, mi'namij, if one sees me, us.
Nmi'mkiss, mi'timkiss, mu'lkwiss, mi'namitsip, if one saw me, us.
Nmi'mkisn, mi'timkisn, mu'lkwisn, minamitsipn, if one had seen me, us.
Nmi'ness, mi'tiness, mu'lkuness, mi'namitness, one would see me, us.
Nmi'nesoqq, mi'tinesoqq, mu'lkunesoqq, mi'namitnesoqq, one would have seen me, us.
Nmi'n, mi'tin, mu'lkn, mi'namitnen, nnmi'kn, knen, knmi'knenu, that one may see me, us.

Remark: The infinitive is only the impersonal conjugated with indefinite subject in all tenses and moods. It is nevertheless a genuine infinitive, but one which includes modifications expressed in English by auxiliaries, and at the same time those which are required in Mi'kmaw by the relations to personal objects: "to see, to have seen, to be going to see, etc. me, you (s.), him, us, you (pl.), them." If one wishes to express obligation by itself, the adverb *amuj* or *miamuj* is added to it.

Supplementary Forms: 1. Here first of all are the **negative** forms, with the translation of the first of each group only:

Mu nemiat, -miajik or *-miammikik, -miammikik*, "not to see him, them, one does not see him, them"; *mu nemiass, -miammiksip, -sipnik; ma' nmiat*, etc.; *-miaj, -miatij; -miass, -mia'tiss; -miasn, -mia'tisn; -mianess, -mianesoqq, -mia'tiness, -mia'tinesoqq*; for the others there is no difference.

Mu nemu'lummik, "not to see you (s., pl.), one does not see you (s., pl.)"; *-mu'lummiksip, -mu'lummkij, -mu'lummikl, -kek, -mu'lummikiss, -kisn, -mu'liness, -nesoqq, -mu'lummkn, -knew* and *mu knmi'kn, -knew*, without change.

Mu ma'nemi'mmik, -mi'timmik, -mu'luk, -mi'namik, "not to see me, us; one does not, will not see me, us"; *-mi'miksip, -mi'timiksip, -mu'luksip, -mi'namiksip; -mi'mikl, -mi'timikl, -mu'lukwel, -mi'namikwl, -kwek*; no other change.

2. To express the indirect relationship to objects in the **plural**, we have *nemu'jl, -mu'snl, -mu'ji, -mu'sni; nemu'lkl, -mu'lkisnl, mu nemu'lmmikl, -mu'lmmiksipnl*.

3. For the **missing, dead or absent**, one uses *nemu'taq, -mu'snaq, -mu'tkaq, -mu'tka, -mu'tkik, -mu'tkika, -mu'titkika*, also *nemu'tnaq, -mu'tnik*.

LESSON TWENTY FOUR

SEVENTH CONJUGATION (MIXED)

Kisitaq, *-tul*, *-tuin*, to make something for someone.

Present Indicative

Kisi   taq, taqik, I make for him, them.
        tat, tajik, you make for him, them.
        tuajl, tuaji, he makes for him, them.
        taqw, taqwik, we make for him, them.
        taqat, taqajik, we make for him, them.
        tuoq, tuo'q, you (pl.) make for him, them.
        tua'tijl, tua'tiji, they make for him, them.

Kisi   tul, tuloq, I make for you (s., pl.).
        task, tuloq, he makes for you (s., pl.).
        tulek, we make for you (s., pl.).
        taskik, tuloq, they make for you (s., pl.).

Kisi   tuin, tuiek, you make for me, us.
        tuit, tulkw, tuinamit, he makes for me, us.
        tuioq, tuiek, you (pl.) make for me, us.
        tuijik, tulkwik, tuinamijik, they make for me, us.

Negative

Mu kisi   tuaq, tuaqik, I do not make for him, them.
           tuawt, tuawjik, you do not make for him, them.
           tuaqwl, tuaqwi, he does not make for him, them.
           tuawkw, tuawkwik, we do not make for him, them.

tuaqat, tuaqajik, we do not make for him, them.
tuawoq (qik), you (pl.) do not make for him, them.
tua'tikwl, tua'tikwi, they do not make for him, them.

Mu kisi *tulu, tuluoq*, I do not make for you (s., pl.).
tuluk, tuluoq, he does not make for you (s., pl.).
tuluek, we do not make for you (s., pl.).
tulu'k, tuluoq, they do not make for you (s., pl.).

Mu kisi *tuiun, tuiwek*, you do not make for me, us.
tuiwkw, tulukw, tuinamɨk, he does not make for me, us.
tuiwoq, tuiwek, you (pl.) do not make for me, us.
tui'tiwk, tulukwik, tuinamɨkwik, they do not make for me, us.

Remarks: 1. Here we see that, as for *nemi'k*, *kisituloq* is used for: "I, he, they make for you"; likewise, in practical terms, *kisituoq*, is used for: "you make for him, them," but *-o'q* (lengthened) is used in the plural, because in theory, this should be *kisituoqik*. In the Manuscript Grammar (second p.p. 1) we find *weleiwoq* for both singular and plural.

2. It is a very practical and interesting exercise to conjugate with *kisitaq* another verb of the same conjugation in *-maq*, as follows: *kisitaq ta'n pewatmuit*, "I make for him what he wants from me"; *kisituloq ta'n pewatmuioq*, "I make for you (pl.) what you want me to"; *kisituinamijik ta'n mu pewatmuaqajik*, "they make for us what we do not want from them," etc.

3. The Indians often make the form "we him" in *-u'kw* instead of *-aqw*, without weighing the difference; the mixed form, in fact, corresponds to a transitive inanimate, as *kisitu*, "I make a thing," and *kisitaq*, "I make it for someone, or with regard to him, or because of him"; the first gives *kisitu'kw*, "we make it," the second *kisitaqw*, "we make it for him"; the difference is considerable. In the **Catechism** of M. Painchaud, certainly written with the aid of an interpreter, it is said of sin: *Kniskaminu alsutkl elistmaqwl*, "we disobey the commands of the Lord."

Supplementary Forms: 1. For the **missing, dead or absent**, the appropriate form is *kisitaqaq, -tataq, -tuata*; but it is little used and not very euphonic in this conjugation; if necessary one could borrow this form from the past tense: *kisitaqapnaq*, etc.

2. With **inanimate subject**: *koqoey ta kisituik, -tuikl, -tulk, -tulkwl, -tuinamɨk, -tuinamikl, -task, -taskl*? "what does that make for me, us, you (s.)?" *Moqwa koqoey kisituinukw, -nukwl, -tuluk, -tulukl, -tuinamnuk, -nukwl*, "no, nothing." For past things, missing or removed, one says *kisituikek, -ke'kl*, etc.

3. When a verb is the **object** of another, the two being in the third person, the obviative marker *-li-* is introduced into the second, as in other verbs; example:

kisituajl ta'n pewatmuajl, "he makes for him what he (the subject) wants from him"; *kisituajl ta'n pewatmualijl*, "he makes for him what he (the object) wants from someone else. If the second verb refers to the subject of the first, it is necessary to turn to the passive as below.

4. **Passive form**: *kisitajl* or *kisitaj*, "what is made for him"; *kisitaji, -takwi'tijl, -takwi'tiji; mu kisitakukwl, -takukwi, -takwi'tikwl, -takwi'tikwi; kisitalijl, -taliji, -takwilijl, -takwiliji; mu kisitalikukwl, -talikukwi, -takwilikwl, -takwilikwi*; thus, in the preceding example, if we suppose that it refers to a mother, who makes for her husband what he wants her to, one would say: *kisituajl ta'n pewatmajl*; but if she makes for him what he wants from their child, one will say: *kisituajl ta'n pewatmualijl wnijanual*.

5. When the direct **object** is in the **inanimate plural**, *l* is added: *kisitaql*, "I make several things for him," *-tajl, -tuajl, -taqwl, -taqajl, -tuoql, -tua'tijl, kisitaqikl*, etc., little used; preference is given to the noun or the pronoun: *wekla koqoe'l*, "these things." With an **animate** plural second object, *-ik* or *-i* is added to the persons which do not already have them; for example: "I make him a rosary (an. pl.)," *kisitaqi sunmink, kisitulanik, -taski, -tuaji*; with the last of these we should be put *sunmin*, according to the rule of the seventh lesson; *etuk mu kisi-iknmuiunik sunminji'jk*? (genuine request): "can you not give me a little rosary?"

Past Indicative

Kisitaqap, pnik, I made, have made for (to) him, them.
tasip, tatip, tap, pnik, you made, have made for him, them.
tuasnl, pnl, sni, pni, he made for him, them.
taqup, quss, pnik, snik, we made for him, them.
taqatsip or *kiss, kip, snik, pnik*, we made for him, them.
tuoqsip or *qoss, qop, snik, pnik*, you (pl.) made for him, them.
tua'tisnl or *pnl, sni, pni*, they made for him, them.

Kisitulip, kisitoqsip, I made for you (s., pl.).
taskiss, or *kip, tuloqsip* or *loqoss, qop*, he made for you (s., pl.).
tuleksip or *lekiss, kip*, we made for you (s., pl.).
taskisnik, tuloqsipnik, they made for you (s., pl.).

Kisitui'sip or *ui'tip, ui'p, tuieksip*, you (s.) made for me, us.
tuiss, tulkuss, tuinamitsip, he made for me, us.
tuioqsip, tuieksip, or *qoss, qop, kiss, kip*, you (pl.) made for me, us.
tuisnik, tulkusnik, tuinamitsipnik, they made for me, us.

Remark: As for *nemi'k* (p. 134).

Supplementary Forms: 1. **Negative**: *mu kisituaqap, -tuawsip, -tuaqsipnl, -tuaqop, -tuaqatsip, -tuawoqsip, -tua'tiwksipnl,* "I did not make for him, them," etc.; for "I not them," etc., put *-pnik* or change *-pnl* to *-pni. Mu kisituluip, -luoqsip, -luksip, -lueksip, -luksipnik, -luoqsipnik. Mu kisituiusip, -tuiweksip, -tuiwsip, -tuluksip, -tuinamiksip, -sipnik, -tuiwoqsip.*

2. There are in this tense some **other forms**, which it is useful to know in order to understand what is heard or read rather than to use, at first; shortened form for "we them, you (pl.) them" *kisitaqatnik, -tuoqotnik*; "he, they us," *kisitulkup, -kunik, -kupnik; kisituinamittip, -tnik, -tipnik*; "you (pl.) us" *kisituiektip*; "you not him, you not them" *mu kisituawtip* or *-tuakusip*.

3. For the **missing, dead or absent**, add *-naq* to all forms of the singular with their variants, and *-a* or *-ka* in the plural; in the third person of the singular *-nl* is changed to *-na*: *An'tleo'q kisitasipnaq kelu'lkek lisqeiknek*, "you made a beautiful casket for the deceased André."

4. With an **inanimate subject**: *etuk suliewey kisituiksip, -sipnl, -taskiss, -kisnl, -tass, -tulkuss, -kusnl (-kupnl, -kusipnl), -tuinamiksip, -sipnl wlo'ti?* "has money brought good luck to me, you, him, us, etc.?" *mu pa kisituinuksip, -tuluksip, -tasip, -tulukuss, -tuinamnuksip, -sipnl,* "not really." For past or missing things one puts *-sipnl, -sipnikl.*

5. **Obviative forms**: *kisitualisnl*, etc.

6. **Passive forms**: *kisitasnl, -sni, -takwi'tisnl, -sni*; see *nemi'k.*

7. To express a secondary relation to an **inanimate plural**, *-l* or *-nl* is added to those persons which do not have it: *kisitaqapnl, -tulapnl, -tui'pnl nekla koqoe'l*, "I for him, I for you, you for me made these things"; for missing things *-pnek* will be added to the singular and *-pnikl* to the plural; likewise *-l-* or *-nl*, plural *-ni*, is added when there is a secondary relation to an **animate** object of the third person, if the subject is also of this person; *-ik* or *-nik*, if the subject is of the first or second; ex.: *iknmuloqopnl Weji-wli Niskaml ktininewaq* (I Thess. 4, 8), "he gave you the spirit of God in yourselves"; *kekinua'taqapnik kkuisunm*, "I informed them of your name"; *iknmaqapnikl wi'katiknkl*, "I gave them the papers"; *koqoey wjit mu emqatuawsipnek nsulieweymek nuji-maqatui'kiti'tij?* "why did you not lend my silver to the bankers?" (Luke 19, 23).

Future Indicative

Kisi tua's, tuates, I will do to him, them.
       tuatesk, you will do to him, them.

Kisi *tuatal, tuata*, he will do to him, them.
tuatesnu, tuatesnen, we will do to him, them.
tuatoqsip, you (pl.) will do to him, them.
tua'tital, tua'tita, they will do to him, them.

Kisi *tultes, tultoqsip*, I will do to you (s., pl.).
tultew, tuloqtew, he will do to you (s., pl.).
tultesnen, we will do to you (s., pl.).
tultaqq, tuloqtaqq, they will do to you (s., pl.).

Kisi *tuitesk, tuitesnen*, you will do to me, us.
tuitew, tulkutew, tuinamitew, he will do to me, us.
tuitoqsip, tuitesnen, you (pl.) will do to me, us.
tuitaqq, tulkutaqq, tuinamitaqq, they will do to me, us.

Remarks: 1. The negative is like that of the present with *ma'* in place of *mu*: *ma' kisituaq, -tulu, -tuiun*, "I will not do it to him, I not to you, you not to me.

2. There are two forms for "I to him, I to them"; the second is not used at Restigouche; for "you to him, you to them" the original form was *kisituateks* (M. Maillard writes *dex*); it is still used in Cape Breton and elsewhere; likewise in the old days they said and wrote: *kisituitex, -dexnu, -dexnen*; *kisitulitew, -tulitaqq* are also found, as for *nemi'k*.

Supplementary Forms: They are rarer in the future.

1. If there is a subject of the **inanimate** gender in the third person plural, *-tew* and *-taq* are changed to *-tal*; let us take as an example *askaiaq*, "to disturb someone": *askaiwik, -wikl*, "that, these things disturb me, do me wrong"; in the future this becomes: *askaiwital, -iulkutal, -iwinamital, -iultal, -iuloqtal, -iwatal, -iwa'tital*. The same change occurs in the case of an inanimate plural object; ex.: *likpenikn kisituitew*, "he will make me a basket"; *likpeniknl (-knn) kisituital*, "he will make me baskets"; *kisitulkutal, -tuinamital*, "he, they will make for us."

2. **Passive forms**: *kisitakutal, -kuta, -kwi'tital, -kwi'tita*, "some will be made for him, them"; *koqoey ta iknmakwi'tital pa'tlia'sl?* "what will be given to them by the priest?" *alame's eta*, "it is (it will be) the mass." But if the object is of the inanimate gender and in the singular, *-tew* will be left unchanged: *koqoey ta pkwatakutew alasutmaqn?* "what will be obtained for him (the child at baptism) by religion?" *iapji-wskijinuuti eta*, "it will be eternal life."

Imperative

Kisi *tu*, make for him, them.
tuaj, let him make for him, them.

tuanej, let us make it for him, them.
tuk, (you pl.) make it for him, them.
tua'tij, let them make it for him, them.
tu'lij, tu'loqj, let him, them, make it for you (s., pl.).
tui, tuin, do it for me, make it for us.
tui'kw, tuin, (you pl.) make it for me, make it for us.
tuij, tui'tij, let him, them make it for me.
tu'lkuj, tuinamij, tuinamitij, let him, them make it for us.

Negative

Mu kkisituaw, tuap, do not (you s., pl.) make it for him, them.
kisituawij, wi'tij, let him, them not make it for him, them.
kisituanej, let us not make it for him, them.
kkisitu'liwij, tu'loqj, let him them not make it for you (s., pl.).
kkisituiw, tuip, tuin, do not (you s., pl.) make it for me, us.
kisituiwij, ui'tiwij, let him, them not make it for me.
kisitu'lukuj, tuinamiwij, wi'tij, let him, them not make it for us.

Supplementary Forms: 1. **Obviatives**: in theory one has *kisitualij, -tuilij*; but in practice they are hardly used.

2. **Inanimate subject**: it produces no change in the affirmative; for example: *pkwatuaj, -tulij, -tuij*, "may it earn him, you, me, something, obtain something, get something done"; but in the negative the forms are: *mu pkwatuanuj, -tulinuj, -tuinuj*; likewise in the plural: *mu pkwatulnukuj, -tuinamnuj, -tulnuoqj*.

3. **Passive form**: *kisitaj, -takwi'tij*, as *pkwataj, -takwi'tij*, "let it be done for him, procured by another."

Remark: The verbs in *-aq* (*-uajl*) make their imperative in *-u, -uk*: *kisitu, -tuk, -wleyu, -yuk, iknmu, -muk*; *wsua'tuk ula nkatikn aqq iknmuk ta'n ki's newtiska'ql kewkunkl*, "take his talent away from him and give it to him who already has ten" (Luke 19, 24).

LESSON TWENTY FIVE

SEVENTH CONJUGATION (MIXED): KISITAQ (CONTINUED)

Conjunct or Indicative with *When*

Kisi *taql, taqek,* my making, having made for him, them, or when I make, made for him, them.
tajl, tatek, when you make, made for him, them.
tuajl, tuatek, when he makes, made for him, them.
taqwl, taqwek, when we make, made for him, them.
taqajl, taqatek, when we make, made for him, them.
tuoqwl, tuoqwek, when you make, made for him, them.
tua'tijl, tua'titek, when they make, made to him, them.

Kisi *tulanl, tulanek,* my making, having made, or when I make, made for you (s.).
taskl, taskek, when he, they make, made for you (s.).
tulekl, tulekek, when we make, made for you (s., pl.).
tuloqwl, tuloqwek, when I, he, they make, made for you (pl.).

Kisi *tuinl, tuinek,* you making, having made for me, or when you (s.) make, made for me.
tuijl, tuitek, when he makes, made for me.
tuioqwl, tuioqwek, when you make, made for me.
tuiekl, tuiekek, when you (s., pl.) make, made for us.
tu'lkwl, kwek, when he, they make, made for me.
tuinamijl, mitek, when he, they make, made for us.

Supplementary Forms: 1. **Negative**: *mu kisituaqal, -qek, -tuawjl, -tek, -tuaqwl, -qwek, -tuawkwl, -kwek, -tuaqajl, -tek, -tuawoqwl, -qwek, -tua'tikwl, -kwek; -mu kisituluanl, -nek, -tulukwl, -kwek, -tuluekl, -kek, -tuluoqwl, -qwek; -mu kisituiunl, -nek, -tuikwl, -kwek, -tui'tikwl, -kwek, -tuiwoqwl, -qwek, -tuiwekl, -kek, -tulukwl, -kwek, -tuinamikwl, -kwek.*

2. This mood in the present is very similar to the present indicative with an inanimate plural object. With an **object** of this gender in the **past**, another *l* is added to *-ek*: *pukwelkl koqoe'l iknmaqekl*, "my having given him, them several things."

3. With a **subject** of the **inanimate** gender, the endings *-al, -l, -ul, -uel* and *-ek, -uek* are added to the corresponding form of the indicative.

4. **Passive**: *kisitajl, -tatek, -takwi'tijl, -takwi'titek*.

5. **Obviative subject**: *kisitualijl, -litek, -tua'tilijl, -litek*.

6. For the **missing**: *kisitatka, -tatkika; Se'sus telimasnika nekla naji-ankistatka*, "Jesus said to those who came to listen to him" lit., "that he might be listened to by them" (Ms. 4, 236).

Conjunct or Indicative with *If*

Kisi *taq* (*taqik*), *taqass, sn*, if I make, made, had made for him, them.
      taj, tasip, pn, if you make, made, had made for him, them.
      tuaj, tuass, sn, if he makes, made, had made for him, them.
      taqw, taquss, sn, if we make, etc. for him, them.
      taqaj, taqatsip, pn, if we make for him, them.
      tuoq, tuoqsip or *tuoqoss, pn* or *sn*, if you (pl.) make for him, them.
      tua'tij, tua'tiss, sn, if they make for him, them.

Kisi *tulan, tulass, tulasn*, if I make, made, had made for you (s.).
      task, taskiss, taskisn, if he, they make for you (s.).
      tuloq, tuloqoss, tuloqsipn, if I, he, they make for you (pl.).
      tulek, tuleksip, tuleksipn, if we make for you (s., pl.).

Kisi *tuin, tui'sip, tui'sipn*, if you (s.) make, made, had made for me.
      tuioq, tuioqsip, tuioqsipn, if you (pl.) make, made, had made for me.
      tuij, tuiss, tuisn, if he makes, made, had made for me.
      tui'tij, tui'tiss, tui'tisn, if they make, made, etc. for me.
      tuiek, tuieksip, tuieksipn, if you (s.) make for us.
      tulkw, tulkuss, tulkusn, if he, they make for us.
      tuinamij, mitsip, mitsipn, if he makes, made, had made for us.
      tuinamitij, mitiss, mitisn, if they make, etc. for us.

Remark: See *nemi'k* (p. 140). Here are some variants: *kisitaqsip*, "if I made for him"; *kisitaqatkiss, -kisn*, "if we for him"; *kisituinamitkiss, -kisn*, "if he for us." *Awanite 'tmaqsipn Kniskaminu wwisunm aqq alsipiskitaikusn piluey niskamewiktukwe'l, mu ta Niskam kjijituisoqq?* (Ps. 43, 26), "if we had forgotten the name of our God and extended our hands toward a strange god, would not God have known it?"

Supplementary Forms: 1. **Negative** (past): *mu kisituaqass, -tua'wsip, -tuaqsip, -tuaquss, -tuaqatsip, -tuawoqsip, -tua'tiwksip; mu kisituluass, -tuluksip, -tuluoqoss, -tulueksip; mu kisituiwsip, -tuiwksip, -tuiweksip, -tuiwoqsip, -tulukuss, -tuinamitiwksip*.

2. With **inanimate subject** in the negative, as *nemi'k* (p. 140).

3. **Passive**: *kisitaj, -tass, -tasn; kisitakwi'tij, -tiss, -tisn*: *wen wkwisl kwilutmaj pipnaqn, etuk iknmuass kun'tew?* "will someone whose son asks for bread give him a stone?" (Luke 11, 11).

4. **Obviative forms**: *kisitualij, -liss, -lisn*; of rare usage here.

Conditional

Kisi *tuiekk* (*ap*), *tuiekapn*, I would make, have made for him, them.
tuaqq (*p*), *tuaqpn*, you would make, have made for him, them.
tuass, tuasoqq, he would make, have made for him, them.
tua'qapp, tua'qapn, we would make, have made for him, them.
tuaqekk, tuaqekpn, we would make, have made for him, them.
tuaqoqq, tuaqoqpn, you would make, have made for him, them.
tua'tiss, tua'tisoqq, they would make, have made for him, them.

Kisi *tulikk, tulikapn*, I would make, have made for you (s.).
tuliss, tulisoqq, he, they would make, have made for you (s.).
tulikoqq, tulikoqpn, I would make, have made for you (pl.).
tulikekk, tulikekpn, we would make, have made for you (s., pl.).
tuloqs, tuloqsoq, he, they would make, have made for you (pl.).

Kisi *tuikk, tuikpn*, you (s.) would make, have made for me.
tuiss, tuisoqq, he would make, have made for me.
tuikoqq, tuikoqpn, you (pl.) would make, have made for me.
tui'tiss, tui'tisoqq, they would make, have made for me.
tuikekk, tuikekpn, you (s., pl.) would make, have made for us.
tulkuss, tulkusoqq, he, they would make, have made for us.
tuinamits, tuinamitsoqq, he would make, have made for us.
tuinamitiss, mitisoqq, they would make, have made for us.

Supplementary Forms: 1. **Obviative**: *kisitualiss, -lisoqq*.

2. For **negation** one says: *mu kisituawiss, -wisoqq, -tuawi'tiss, -wi'tisoqq*, "he, they would not make, have made for him, them." Elsewhere there is no difference from the affirmative, which itself has a negative appearance. That is perhaps why they so often confuse the one with the other.

Remark: M. Maillard, in the conjugation of *ewi'kmaq*, here gives *wi'kmaqapp, -maqapn* (Gram. p. 76), "I would write to him, I would have written him"; *wi'kmaqpin*, "you would have written to him." But the form given here is certainly correct. Rand gives, in Psalm 80, 15: *wisuiknetmuiekapn* for Latin *humiliassem*, "I would have confounded them," and *kwilutmuaqpn*, "you would have asked of him" (John 4, 10); M. Maillard also gives *wsitawiekapn*, "I would have saved them" (Rem. gr. 106); but in the second person we have *wsitawikpn*, which means: "you would have saved me," whereas elsewhere he wrote, for example, *nmiekapn* and *nmiaqpn* (p. 67), "I, you (s.) would have seen him"; then *emtoqwaliekapn, -laqpn*, "I, you (s.) would have praised him (p. 102); *alasutmelsewiekapn, -sewaqpn*, "I, you would have prayed for him" (p. 156); *ku'kuniekapn, ku'kunaqpn*, "I, you (s.) would have held him" (p. 154), etc. Finally I recall having received a letter from a chief in which he said: If I had known the author of these statements, I do not know "how I would deal with him," *ta'n kisa'liekk*; and, in a recent conversation on the subject of the wake of a dead person, someone said: *Jipaliekk ni'n*, I'd be afraid of them, I would"; *jipalk*, "I fear someone," and indeed *jipaliek* [single -k] means: "you (s.) fear us, you (pl.) fear us" (see Rem. p. 38). This form of the conditional is therefore certainly correct. See also *wji-we'jia'qupp* (Amer. I, 110), "we would find him because of that.

Subordinative

Nkisituan, that I may make for him, them.
Kkisituan, that you (s.) may make for him, them.
Wkisituan, wkisitakun, that he may make for him, them.
Kkisituanenu, that we may make for him, them.
Nkisituanen, that we may make for him, them.
Kkisituanew, that you (pl.) may make for him, them.
Wkisituanew, wkisitakunew, that they may make for him, them.

Kkisitulin, tulinew, that I, he may make for you (s., pl.).
Kkisitakun, takunew, that he may make for you (s., pl.) (passive form).
Kkisitulinen, that we may make for you (s., pl.).
Kkisitulinew, takunew, that they may make for you (s., pl.).

Kkisituin, tuinen, that you (s.) may make for me, us.
Nkisituin, tuinen, kkisitu'lkunenu, that he may make for me, us.
Nkisitakun, takunen, kkisitakunenu, that he may make for me, us.
Kkisituinew, kkisituinen, that you (pl.) may make for me, us.
Nkisituinew, tuinen, kkisitu'lkunenu, that they may make for me, us.
Nkisitakunew, takunen, kkisitakunenu, that they may make for me, us.

Remark: See *nemi'k* (p. 142).

Supplementary Forms: 1. **Negation** changes nothing in the subordinative, except in the inanimate form: *nesutm mu nula'tuinun, -tuiktnun,* "I fear it may not do me any good"; likewise *kula'tulinun, wula'tuanun, -tulukun, -tuinamnun,* you (s.), him, us, you (pl.).

2. **Obviative**: *wkisitualin,* for all members.

Infinitive

Kisi *tut, tujik,* to make it for him, them, one makes it for him, them.
tuss, tusnik, to have made it for him, them, one made it for him, them.
tuaten, tua'titen, to be about to make it for him, them, one will make it for him, them.
tuj, tutij, let one make it for him, them.
tujl, tutijl, making it for him, them, when one makes it for him, them.
tutek, tu'titek, having made it for him, them, when one made it for him, them.
tuj, tuss, tusn, if one does, did, had made it for him, them.
tuaness, tuanesoqq, one should make, should have made it for him, them.
tuan, tuatin, wkisitakun, takunew, that one may make it for him, them.

Kisitulk, to make it for you (s., pl.), one makes it for you (s., pl.).
tulkiss, tulkip, to have made it for you (s., pl.), one made it for you (s., pl.).
lten, tuloqten, to be about to do it for you (s., pl.), one will make it for you (s., pl.).
tulkij, let one make it for you (s., pl.).
tulkl, tulkek, doing, having made, when one makes it for you (s., pl.).
tulk, tulkiss, tulkisn, if one makes, made, had made for you (s., pl.).
tuliness, tulinesoqq, one would make, would have made it for you (s., pl.).
tulkn, knew, kkisitakn, knew, that one may make it for you (s., pl.).

Kisituimk, tuitimk, tulkw, tuinamit, to make for me, us, one makes it for me, us.
tuimkiss, tuitimkiss, tulkiss, tuinamitsip, one made it for me, us.
tuiten, tuititen, tulkuten, tuinamiten, one will make it for me, us.

tuimkij, tuitimkij, tulkij, tuinamitij, let one make it for me, us.

tuimkl, tulkwl, tuinamijl, making it for me, us, when one makes it for me, us.

tuimkek, tulkwek, tuinamitek, having made it for me, us, when one made it for me, us.

tuimk, tulkw, tuinamij, if one makes it for me, us.

tuimkiss, tulkwiss, tuinamitsip, if one made it for me, us.

tuimkisn, tulkwisn, tuinamitsipn, if one had made it for me, us.

tuiness, tulkuness, tuinamitness, one would make it for me, us.

tuinesoqq, tulkwunesoqq, tuinamitnesoqq, one would have made it for me, us.

tuin, tulkwn, tuinamitnen, that one may make it for me, us.

nkisitakun, takunen, kkisitakunenu, that one may make it for us.

Remark: As for *nemi'k* (p. 143).

Supplementary Forms: 1. **Negation**: *mu kisituat, -tuajik, -tuammik, -tuammikik; -tuass, -snik, -tuammiksip, -pnik; ma' kisituat*, etc.; *mu kisituaj, -a'tij; -tuaqwl, -qwek; -tuaj, -tuass, -tuasn; -tuaness, -nesoqq; -tuan, -tua'tin, -takun, -takunew; --mu, ma' kisitulummik, -mmiksip; tulmkij, -tulmkl, -tulmkek; -tulmmek, -tulmkiss, -tulmkisn; -tuliness, -nesoqq; -tulmkn, -kunew, -takun, -kunew; --mu, ma' kisituimmik, -mmiksip; -tuimkij, -tuimmikl, -mmikek; -tuimmik, -tuimkiss, -tuimkisn; -tuiness, -tuinesoqq; -tuin, -uitin, -takun; -tulukw, -tuinamik, -tuluksip, -tuinamiksip; -tulukwl, -tuinamikwl, -kwek*; the rest as in the affirmative.

2. M. Maillard (Rem. gr. p. 65) gives in detail the following forms for: "that one may give to me, you (s.), him, us, you (pl.), them": *ntiknmaken, ktiknmaken, wtiknmaken, ktiknmakenenu, ntiknmakenen, ktiknmakenew, wtiknmakenew*; the Indians confuse it with the personal subordinative: *ntiknemakun*, etc.

3. One also finds: *iknmutnik, ewi'kmutnik*, "one gave, wrote to them," *apattelutnik*, "they have been redeemed" (Rev. 14, 4).

4. For the **missing, dead or absent**, one uses *iknmutaq, -musnaq, -mutka, -mutkik, -mutkika; -kisitutaq, -tusnaq*, etc.

Table of Endings of Animate Verbs

Present Indicative

I	him them–to him to them	k	kik
you (s.) him them–to him to them		t	jik
he	" "	jl	ji
we (incl.)	" "	kw	kwik
we (excl.)	" "	kit (kt)	kijik (kjik)
you (pl.)	" "	oq	o'q (oqik)
they	" "	ji	tiji

I	you (s.)	ul (ln)	
I	you (pl.)–he they you (pl.)	loq (lnoq)	
he	you (s.)–they you (s.)	sk	skik
we	you (s.)–we you (pl.)	lek (lnek)	

you (s.) me–you (pl.) me		in	ioq
he me–they me		it	ijik
you (s.) us–you (pl.) us		iek	
he they us (incl.)		ulkw	ulkwik
he they us (excl.)		inamit	inamijik

For the **Past**, add to the present -p, -pnik, -pnl, -pni or -snl, -sni.

For the **Future**, change -k etc. to -as or -ates, -tesk, -tew, -tesnu, -tesnen, -toqsip, -taqq, -ultes, -itesk, etc.

Imperative

(you s.)	him, them	(i u)	
let him, them	" "	j	tij
(let us)	" "	nej	
(you pl.)	" "	kw (ukw)	
let him, them	you (s.)	lij (lnij)	
let him, them	you (pl.)	loqj (lnoqj)	
(you s., pl.)	me	i	ikw
(you s., pl.)	us	in	in
let him, them	me	ij	i'tij
"	us (incl.)	ilkuj	
"	us (excl.)	inamij	inamitij

Infinitive

One him, them: *-ut, -uss, -aten; -uj, -ujl, -utek; -usn, -aness, -an.*
One you (s., pl.): *-ulk, -ulkiss, -ulten; -ulkij, -ulkl, -ulkek; -ulkisn, -uliniss, -ulken.*
One me: *-imk, -imkiss, -iten; -imkij, -imkl, -imkek; -imkisn, -iness, -in.*
One us: *-ulk, -ulkiss, -ulkuten; -ulkij, -ulkl, -ulkek; -ulkisn, -ulkuness, -ulkn.*
One us (excl.): *-inamit, -inamitsip, -inamiten; -inamij, -inamijl, -inamitek; -inamitsipn, -inamitniss, -inamitnen.*

LESSON TWENTY SIX

EXAMPLES OF THE SIXTH AND SEVENTH CONJUGATIONS

On the model of *nemi'k* and *kisitaq* are conjugated all the verbs with **animate** and **mixed** objects. They all have, as we have already said (p. 150), a *-k* or *-q* in the first person singular (I-him), preceded by one of the vowels or another consonant: *-aq*, *-e'k*, *-i'k*, *-uk* or else *-lk*, *-mk*, *-nk*, *-pk*, *-sk*, *-tk*; but the latter all relate to verbs in *-ik* whose *i* is suppressed by the arrangement of the preceding letters; thus the verb *kelnik*, "I hold him," becomes in compounds *melknk*, "I hold him strongly." It is the same for the others in *-lik*, *-mik*, *-nik*, *-pik*, *-svk*, *-tik*, all except *-kik*.

1. We will begin with the verbs in *-i'k*, the most regular, which are conjugated exactly like *nemi'k*. They almost all have their corresponding inanimate and mixed [i.e. two goal] paradigms in *-itu*, *-itaq*, as *nemitu*, "I see a thing"; *nemitaq*, "I see a thing which belongs to someone or concerns him": *nemitaqatnl wkloqowejueml wjipnuk*, "we have seen his star in the east" (Matt. 2, 2).

Apji'k, *-u'l*, *-i'n*, *-itu*, *-itaq*, "to do good (to)," with the idea of deserving gratitude; *kesi-apju'lkuss Kniskaminu*, "Deo gratias!" *apju'lkwik*, *apji'namijik*, "they do us good"; *apji'n*, "you do good to me, render me a service, you please me by that" (Rem. gr. 143). M. Maillard adds that the Indians say: *apji'n*, as we say: "thanks, thank you"; today, in the current language, they say: *wela'lin* or *ke'n wela'lin*; Mr. J. Hamel writes: *kaine*. *Apji'timk*, "to do good to each other"; *pejili- apji'timkewey*, "the highest benefit, the Eucharist."

Emqatui'k, *-tu'l*, *-tui'n*, *-tuitu*, *-tuitaq*, "to lend to someone"; *maqatuia's* (*-tu'a's*), *-tu'ates*, "I will lend to him" (note this type of contraction); *maqatui'*, (long i), "lend me!"; *maqatui* (short i), "lend him"; *mu kmaqatui'w*, "do not lend me"; *mu kmaqatuiaw* (almost *-tu'aw*), "do not lend to him"; *ketui-maqatui'k*, "I want to lend him"; *emqatui'ketu*, "to lend"; *koqoey wjit mu* *emqatu'awsi-pnek nsulieweymek ta'nik nuji-maqatui'ketu'tij?* "why have you not lent my money to the bankers?" (Luke 19, 23). Intransitive *emqatui'key.*

Westawi'k, -u'l, -wi'n, -witu, -witaq, "to save"; *wsitawi'tew,* "he will save me"; *wsitawiatal,* "he will save him"; *Westau'lkw,* "the Saviour" (he saves us); *Kwestau'lkuminu,* "our Saviour"; *westawi'wet,* "he saves" (in general); *nuji-wsitawi'wet,* "he is the one who saves, the Saviour"; *westay, -tan, -tat,* "to be saved."

Keji'k, -ju'l, -ji'n, -jitu, -jitaq, "to know, to be acquainted with"; double *-ji-* with contraction: *kjijia's,* "I will know him"; *mu kjijiawij,* "let him not know him"; *tlia' ki's wtininiktuk keji'kitip Se'sukli, mu nuku'na teli-kjijiaqat,* "if we knew Christ according to the flesh, now we would no longer know him in this way" (2 Cor. 5, 17); *kjiji'sipn kwilutmuaqpn samuqwan mimajik,* "if you had known him, you would have asked him for the living water"; *aqq iknmulisoqq,* "and he would have given it to you" (John 4, 10).

Kisi'k, -su'l, -si'n, -situ, -sitaq, "to make, to create, to manufacture" (easily); *Kisu'lkw,* "God, the Creator"; *kisiteket,* "he creates"; *Mesta Kisiteket,* "the Author of all things"; *kisitua'tita,* "they will make, manufacture for them."

Pewi'k, pewu'l, pewi'n, "to dream about someone," *pewitu,* "about something," *pewitaq,* "which concerns him"; *ma'pui'namiwk,* "he will not dream about us."

Tepi'k, -pu'l, -pi'n, -pitu, -pitaq, "to make a division, distribution"; intransitive *tepi'key, -ken, -ket,* "to distribute"; *nuji-tpi'ket,* "the agent, the distributor"; *tepi'k ta'n tepe'k, tepiajl ta'n tepme'lijl,* "I, he gives him what he deserves."

2. The verbs in *-uk* are also regular; but the presence of this *u* creates a resemblance, in several persons, with the verbs in *-aq* (*-uajl*).

Apu'k, apu't, apu'ajl, apu'l, apu'in, "to send, to make an envoy of someone"; *apu'a's, apu', peji-apu'ipnikl sulnalji'jkl,* "you sent the *Messengers* to me." To say: "to send someone, to give him a mission," *elkimk* or *elulk* is used; *apu'kwetu, -taq,* "to send things."

Ataluk, -lut, -luajl, "to feed"; *kisataluk,* "to satisfy"; *weji-kisataluajl mjijaqmijl kewisilnijl kelu'sutiktuk,* "he satisfied the hungry soul with good things" (Ps. 106, 9); *welataluksisnik,* "well nourished" (Ms. 2, 115).

Ewi'kikewk, -wt, -wajl, "to write for someone"; *-kewl, -kewin.*

Wisunkewk, -kewatm, -tmaq, "to give a name"; *wisunkewate'n, tlui'taten Se'sus,* "he will be named, he will be called Jesus."

Alasutmewk, -wul, -win, "to make to pray, to lead in prayer" (Rem. 156).

Alasutmelsewk, -wul, -win, "to pray for someone"; *sewatm,* "to get something."

Apankitawalsewk, -wul, -win, "to pay for, to be a server, surety."

Kaqmatawalsewk, -sewul, -sewin, "to come between, to be a mediator"; this is the characteristic word which is used only for Our Saviour"; *nekla kaqmatawalsewulkwek aqq apankitawalsewulkwek,* "when he made himself our mediator and our surety by paying for us.

Nestmalsewk, -sewatm, -tmaq, "to interpret."

3. The verbs in *-aq* are of two types: the first becomes in the third person *-uajl, -uaji,* and takes this *u* throughout the future, the subordinative and elsewhere. These verbs are regular and are conjugated exactly like *kisitaq*; they are in Mi'kmaw the simple transitive verbs, even those which have in English a second object, as *iknmaq,* "I give to him"; it is this latter which I had at first chosen as the model of the mixed conjugation; but in fact this word does not have, as do the others of this class, corresponding transitive inanimate in *-m,* from which is formed the true mixed conjugation in *-maq; iknmuetu, -taq,* means "to give away." Thus the difference between these transitive animate verbs and the mixed forms is not in the conjugation, which is the same, but in the meaning: in the transitives the direct object is the person, in the mixed it is the thing or another person relating to the former, and the original person then becomes an indirect object.

Let us begin with the verbs in *-ayak* and *-eyak*; the latter are very numerous; the inanimate is in *-o'tm,* the mixed in *-o'tmaq.*

Askayaq or *askeyaq, askaiwajl, -iwul, -iwin,* "to disturb, to do injury"; *asko'tm,* "to disturb a thing"; *-tmaq,* "belonging or relating to someone."

Wekayaq, -iwul, -iwin, "to displease, to offend, to provoke, to bring down someone's wrath, to make angry at oneself" (Rem. gr. 76); *ntlue'wuti'l wekayaskl,* "my sins displease you" (act of contrition); *apiksiktaqajik wekaiwinamitipnik,* or *mitnik,* "we pardon those who have offended us"; *wkwaiwa's, mu kwkwaiwaw.*

Munsayaq or *munseyaq, -so'tm, -tmaq,* "to beset, to flatter, cajole, coax, to strive, to persist."

Netayaq, "to frighten"; *kwetayaq,* "to scare" (children, animals).

Weleyaq, -lo'tm, -tmaq, "to treat well, to bless"; *weleyat, weleiwajl, -eyaqik, -eyajik, -eiwaji, -eyakw, -eyaqat, -eiwoq, -eiwa'tijl, -eyakwik, -eyaqajik, -eiwo'q (-oqik), -eiwa'tiji; weleyul, -yuloq, -yask, -yaskik; weleiwin, -wit, -wiek, -ulkw, -winami-t, -wioq, -wijik, -ulkwik, -winami-jik; weleyaqap, wleiwa's, -wates, wleiw, iuk; nuleiwan; wleiaqasn; wleiwiekapn; weleyut, -yulk, iwimk;* -- in the subordinative *kuleiwinew, -nen,* "that you me, us" (sic *k*); *nuleiakunen, kuleiakunew,* "that he us, that he you (pl.)"; *nuleiakunew,* "that they me."

Kweseyaq, -iwul, -iwin; *kweso'tm, -tmaq*, "to protect, to look after, to take care"; *wli-wso'tmuk Kisu'lkw wtiplutaqanml*, "observe faithfully God's commandments"; intransitive sense *kweso'tm*, "to be fasting for communion."

Ankweyaq or *aqneyaq, -iwul, -iwin*, "to look after someone"; *anko'tm*, "something"; *anko'tmaq*, "of something belonging to someone or for him."

Tekweyaq, -iwul, -iwin; *teko'tm, -tmaq*, "to be with, to assist"; *tkweiwa's, tko'ttes, tko'tmua's*; *Ksaqmaminu tekweyask*, "Our Lord is with you"; *Kji-saqmaw tkweyuloqj*, Latin *Dominus vobiscum*, "the Lord be with you"; *aqq ktalita'suaqn elp tko'tj*, "and also with your spirit" (your thought); *mu ktikweiwaw ta'nik mu welo'lti'wk*, "do not be with those who are not good" (Rem. gr. 97).

We give now some examples of the same regular verbs in *-aq* preceded by another consonant. The inanimate is ordinarily in *-m* and the mixed in *-maq*.

Meniskaq (-kuajl), -kul, -kuin; *meniskm, -kmaq*, "to go to look for."

Napkaq, -kul, -kuin, "to replace, to keep a place, to be curate"; *napkuajl Se'susl*, "he (the Pope) is Vicar of Jesus Christ"; *napkm*, "to reproduce, to copy."

Kwilaq, kwilm, -lmaq, "to look for, to inquire into"; *elkwilaq*, "to go and look for"; *al'kwilaq*, "to look around for"; *kwilua's, kwiltes, kwilmua's*, "I will search"; *kwiluk Kji-saqmaw aqq wmlkikno'tim, mu kpuni-kwilutmuapp wsiskw*, "seek the Lord and his might, do not cease to search for his face" (Ps. 14, 4).

Pekwatelaq, -lm, -lmaq, "to buy"; *apattelaq*, "to redeem."

Apoqnmaq, -matm, -matmaq, "to help"; *nuji-apoqnmuiek*, "you are our succour"; *se'skutipnik, skatu ma'wenl apoqnmakwi'tiwksipnl, jel oqoj Kji-saqmawiktuk, skatu mu asitemakwi'tiwksipnl* (Ps. 17, 41), "they cried out but were helped by no one, even to the Lord, but he did not respond to them"; *apoqnmakutal Mesta Kisitekelijl*, "he will be helped by the Creator."

Iknmaq, -mul, -muin, "to give"; *iknmulanl, -lanik, -lekl, -lekik*, "I give you these things, these persons, we give them"; *mestanmaq*, "to give all"; *mawnmaq*, "all together"; *kesmnmaq*, "to offer"; *kesmnmulekik sunmink*, "we offer you this rosary"; *kesmnmatimkewey*, "sacrifice"; *pneknmaq*, "to give from on high"; *pneknmuin nilu'nen*, "give us (from heaven) our nourishment"; *iknmuinamitip*, "he gave it to us" (the well of Jacob). *Na nekm pa'tlia's iknmasip (masnl) Kisu'lkwl wntawi-kasa'tuan wtlue'wutiwal ta'ni weli-pa'qapukua'tiliji*, "it is the priest to whom it has been given by God to pardon the sins of those who confess well" (Ms. 3, 110).

Nenaq, nenat, nenuajl, nenul, nenuin, nenm, nenmaq, "to know" (by sight); *keji'k,* "to know that he is"; *netna iapji-wskijinuuti knnaken,* "it is eternal life to know you" (John 17, 3); *nenustaq,* "to know by the voice"; *moqwe nenulukup wskitqamu,* "the world did not know you."

Nestaq, nestm, -tmaq, "to understand."

Nutaq, -tm, -tmaq, "to hear."

4. The second class of verbs in *-aq* includes those which do not take *u* in the third person, and show *-el* and *-ein* where the others have *-ul, -uin*; they follow, because of this, a secondary model of conjugation, as do those with long *-e'k*, which have the same irregularities.

Here first is the summary conjugation of *esa'q,* "to pursue someone, banish them"; inan., *esa'm,* "to pursue something."

Esa'q, esa't, esa'jl, esa'qw, esa'qat, eso'q, esa'ji, esa'qik, etc.; *eso'l, eso'lek, eso'loq, esa'sk, esa'skik*; *esa'in, esa'iek, esa'ioq, esa'it, eso'lkw, esa'inamit, esa'ijik,* etc. The negative forms are rare: *mu esa'wt, esa'qwl, esa'woq; eso'lu, -luk, -luoq, -luek; esa'iun, -iwoq, -iwek, -o'lukkw, -inamik.*

In the past add the endings of *kisitaqap,* etc.

Future: *sa's, sa'tesk, sa'tal, so'ltes, sa'itesk,* etc.

Imper.: *sa, sa'j, sa'nej, so'q; so'lij, so'loqj; sa'i, sa'in, sa'ij, sa'ik, so'lkuj, sa'inami-j.*

Others: *sa'qq, sa'ss, sa'sn; sa'j, sa'sip, sa'sipn; sa'j, sa'ss, sa'sn; so'lan, so'lass, so'lasn; sa'in, sa'isip, sa'isipn; sa'iek, sa'iekapn, sa'qq, sa'qpin, sa'ss, sa'soqq; so'likapn, so'likoqpn; sa'ik, sa'ikpn, sa'iss, sa'isoqq, so'lkuss, so'lkusoqq, sa'inamits, sa'inamitsoqq; ntisa'n, ktso'lin, ktisa'in; eso't, eso'ss, sa'ten, so'j; eso'lk, eso'lkiss, so'lten, so'lkij; esa'imk, esa'imkiss, sa'iten, sa'imkej. Wetsa'q* or *weji-sa'q,* "to hunt because of that": *mu kuji-sa'iw newt kisna ta'pu a'qati-ksipukua'likik sulnalji'jl nujikitmi'tijl, teli-kipoqwa'si na,* "do not reject me, even if I once or twice deceive the readers of the *Micmac Messenger* a little, that is my temperament" (letter of a correspondent, whose pen name was *Kluskap; keluskapewit,* "he is a deceiver, liar"); *nan'temi-wtiso'lip nkamlamuniktuk,* "I have constantly chased you from my heart" (Par. 1, 86).

Aptisqa'q, -qo'l, -qa'in, -qa'm, -qa'maq, "to lock up"; *aptisqo'q, -qo'qwik* (sic), "you lock him, them up"; *aptisqa', -qa'e'n,* "close it, that" (a thing).

Ne'paq, -po'l, -pa'in, "to kill"; *ne'po't, -po'ss, -pa'ten,* "one kills him," or better "he is killed, has been killed, will be killed"; *kisi-pkwatuan ne'pa'iekk ta'n te'sit u'j aqq wo'kejit*, "if I could, I would kill all the flies and spiders" (2d Rea. 11); *msit maqamikewek ketapa'qsipnek l'nu'k ne'pa'kwi'tiss*, "all men were killed by the universal deluge"; *se'k weji-mulqatmi'tiss maqmikew nne'pa'kuna* (Ps. 35, 7), "it is in vain that they dug a ditch to make me perish"; *jukwa'lukw nikamu'tasit wen'jutia'mu'j aqq ne'po'q*, "bring the fatted calf and kill it"; *ula ne'pma'ik l'ue'wuti*, "this sin, this vice is killing me"; *npisun, puktewijk*, "this medicine, fire-water." The inan. *ne'patu* means also, and how justly, "to get for oneself, to make one's living"; the mixed *ne'pataq*, "to kill, to destroy a thing or even an animal of another": *ne'patajl nikamu'tasilijl wen'jutia'mu'jl*, "you killed the fatted calf for him" (Luke 15, 23).

Nepa'q (short *e*) means "to put to sleep," and follows the same conjugation; thus *ula npisun ne(')pa'ik* can mean, according to its pronunciation, "this cure makes me sleep or kills me."

Netui'ska'q, -ko'l, -ka'in, "to sell for someone"; *ntui'sko'ltes*, "I will sell it for you"; imperative *ntui'ska'*, as for *sa'*; the verbs in *-aq, -uajl*, change *a* to *u*: *weleyaq, wleiw*. Inan.: *ntui'sketu, -ketaq*, "to sell a thing, of one's own."

5. The verbs in *-e'k* (long *e*) are conjugated like those of the preceding class, having *-o'l, -ein* where the others have *-o'l, -a'in*: moreover, there are even some of them in *-ain*; as for example the first two.

Ankune'k, -no'l, -ne'in or *-na'in*, "to cover"; it seems that "you me, he me covers," ought to be *ankune'in*, as *klujjiewte'in*; but Rand clearly gives *poqnitpa'q ankuna'itew*, "the darkness will cover me" (Ps. 133, 11) and *ankuna'in*, "cover us" (Luke 23, 30); likewise M. Maillard gives for the next verb: *atkna'ip* (Ms. 3 p. 162); *ankuna'ji wpitnl e'wkl*, "he (the bishop) covers them with his hands" (at the confirmation). Inan.: *ankuno'tu, -taq*, "to cover a thing."

Atkne'k, -no'l, -ne'in or *-na'in*, "to do his share, to make participate"; *atkne'waqn*, "share"; *atkno't, -no'sit*, "he has his share, he takes his share."

Eskipe'k, -po'l, -pe'in, "to wait for"; second secondary model; *eskipetu*, "to wait for a thing"; *-taq*, "of his, from him, or that concerns him."

Klujjiewte'k, -to'l, -te'in, "to crucify"; *-te'm* "a thing," also "to consecrate it"; *-te'maq, -te'muit*, "I bless that for him, he blesses it for me"; *klujjiewte, -ta, -to'k*, "(you s., pl.) crucify him!"; *klujjiewta'jl, -te'jl*, "he crucifies him, he is crucified." The third person passive is formed by changing *a* to *e*: likewise *eskipe'jl, matte'jl*, "he is beaten by him"; in the verbs in *-a'q, -a'jl*, all one has to do is to shorten this vowel: *ne'pa'jl*, "he kills him," *ne'pajl*, "he is killed by him"; this gives us a vastly different action for a very small difference of sound. *Apj klujjiewta'tijl Niskam Wkwisl wtininewaq aqq ika'la'tijl me'su'tuk* *ntaqo'qniktuk*, "they crucify again the Son of God in themselves and deliver him to ignominy" (Heb. 6, 6); *ta'n te's meski'kl elue'wuti'l kiskaja'tu'nl, te's Westau'lkw minui-klujjiewte't aqq ne'pa't kkamlamuniktuk*, "each time that you commit great sins, you crucify him anew and make the Saviour die in your heart" (Rem. gr. 48); *mu ika'nuj ntininkl nuji-pilui-mtoqwalsin sik eta Nse'susem wklujjieweymiktuk, weji-klujjiewte'mikl wskitqamu'kewe'l wjit ni'n, toqu elp ni'n weji-klujjiewte'imk wjit wekla*, "God keep me from boasting save in the cross of Jesus, for whom the world is crucified for me, as I am for the world"; *msit pa'qi-kjijitu'tij Niskam wkwisian nekla Se'susl, ta'nl kilew klujjiewto'qopnl, wkji-saqmawilin aqq wklistewilin*, "that the whole world might know that this Jesus whom you have crucified is the Son of God, the Sovereign Lord and the Christ" (Acts. 2, 36); *iknmuaten wmalikimanew, wnipisoqnta'new aqq wklujjiewta'new*, "they will be allowed to jeer at him, to whip him and to crucify him" (Matt. 20, 19); *kjijitua'tisn mu klujjiewta'tisoqq kesamuksutie'l Kji-eleke'wilijl*, "if they had known him, they would never have crucified the great King of glory"; *klujjiewte'mi'tijl wa'qeiwal*, "they crucify their flesh" (Gal. 5, 24). *Kelatkwete'k*, "to nail"; *oqotkwete'k*, "to attach."

Nipisoqnte'k, -to'l, -te'in, "to whip"; *nipisoqnto'q!* "whip him!" (Par. II 608).

LESSON TWENTY SEVEN

EXAMPLES OF THE SIXTH AND SEVENTH CONJUGATIONS (CONTINUED)

6. The verbs in *-ik*: *-kik, -lik, -mik, -nik, -pik, -sik, -tik*, are regular; but the ordering of the letters which precede this ending can lead to the suppression of the *i* and provide the long series of verbs in *-lk, -mk, -nk, -pk, -sk*; this does not change the conjugation in any way, but has a great effect on the passive, reflexive and reciprocal verbs, as we shall see in the following lesson. The only peculiarity they bring to the conjugation is the dropping of *i* with *k* in the imperative, and only in the forms where another vowel occurs in the ending. Moreover, the verbs in *-lik, -lk* constitute a separate class and require a secondary model of conjugation. Finally those in *-lmik*, which are very numerous, are difficult to distinguish from those in *-limk*, whether in pronunciation or in writing; but this does not change the conjugation in any way.

I. We give first examples of those in *-kik, -pik, -sik, -tik* and *-pk, -sk*, which make up a class by far the least numerous.

Ewi'kik, -kit, -kajl, -kul, -kin, "to write, to mark, to photograph"; for the latter it is better to use *napui'kik*, "to copy"; inanimate and mixed *ewi'km, -kmn, -kik*, "to write a thing"; the latter (third person) is pronounced exactly as the first animate; it is the same for many other verbs; *ewi'kmaq*, "to write to someone"; *wskittukwi'kmui*, "write me the address"; *wi'kmuiekapn*, "I would have written to him"; *ewi'kut, -kutek, -kutipnik* (heard in conversation); *wi'k naniskeksijik*, "write fifty" (bushels).

Pe'skik, pe'skm, -kmaq, "to fire a gun at someone, something"; *pe'sk, -kuk, pe'ske'n, -kmuk*, "(you s., pl.) fire!"; *koqoey pe'skmoq?* (Jo. 360); *pe'skul, pe'skin, pe'skulkuten*, "we will be fired at"; *pe'skewey*, "gun"; *pe'skitek*, "it goes off."

Elu'pik, -pm, -pmaq, "to carry on one's back"; *elu'put, elu'pul, elu'pin*.

Wikpik, wiktm, -tmaq, "to like" (the taste); *kata wikpaji*, "he likes eels"; *wiktmuajl teli-wisku'pijl*, "he likes what is cooked for him"; *wenik wikpijik?* "what animals (meat) do you like?" *moqwe wikpaq wowkwis, moqwe malqomaq*, "I do not like fox, I do not eat it" (Rea. 22); *wikpikik plawej, kwimu, ples, sinumkw, kopit, tia'm, muin, aqq kiunaqaj kulkwi's*, "I like partridge, loon, pigeon, bustard, beaver, moose, bear, and especially pork."

Wisku'pik, -pm, -pmaq, "to cook for someone"; *wisku'pit, -pajl, -pijl*.

Apkwepk, apkwetm, -tmaq, "to untie with the teeth."

Eskipk, eskitm, -tmaq, "to eat raw"; *eskipt, -pajl, -pul, -pin, -put; eskip, -puk*, "(you s., pl.) eat!"; *eske'k*, "raw"; *Eskmaw, -maq*, "Eskimos."

Ketupk, ketutm, -tmaq, "to want to eat, to feel a craving for some food."

Kaqsik, -sm, -smaq, "to burn"; *kaqsit, -sajl, -sul, -sin, -sut; kaqsit, kaqtek*, "burnt"; *kaqoqtek*, "consumed"; *kaqsitaq epsaqtejkaq*, "the stove burned."

Ketmesik, -sm, -smaq, "to burn completely"; *ketmesmkl pekitnmatimkewe'l*, "burnt offerings."

Pese'k, pesetu, -taq, "to smell, to scent"; *telima't, -ma'q*, "smell."

Temsik, -sm, -smaq, "to cut" (with knife, sickle, etc.); *ki's temsasikl kulumkl aqq te'sipo'man*, "the wheat and oats have been cut"; *mu kusamtmsaw kqosi'k*, "do not cut your nails too close."

Epa'qask, -qasm, -smaq, "to warm" (a stone, iron, stove); *epa'qast, -qasajl, -qasul, -qasin, -qasut; epa'qasikn* and *epsaqtej*, "stove."

Epa'kwesk, -kwesm, -smaq, "to put away, to put aside"; *epa'kwesajl eptaqnl*, "she put the plates away."

Paqtisk, -tism, -smaq, "to fill with smoke"; *paqtisit*, "he is sick of it"; *paqtist, -tisajl, -tisjl; paqtisul, -tisin*, "I you, you me."

Peskwesk, -kwesm, -smaq, "to shear, to reap, to harvest"; *pskwesa's, pskwe's, -suk; peskwesul, -sin; mu kipskwesapp*, "do not clip them."

Awiupqo'qosk, -sm, -smaq, "to cense"; *awiupqo'qosut*, "he has incense burned before him."

Ewi'tik, -tm, -tmaq, "to name"; *telui'tik*, "to name him thus"; *ewi'tit, -tajl, -tul, -tin*; *wi'ta's, wi't, wi'tuk*; *ke'sik wi't ta'n taqmisk*, "name, therefore, him who strikes you"; *ewi'tikijik*, "we call them by name"; *msit ta'n ewi'tajl Ksaqmaminal wji-jikla'lisij pata'sutiktuk*, "let whoever speaks the name of the Lord remove himself from iniquity" (2 Tim. 2, 19).

II. Verbs in *-mek* and *-amk, -emk, -imk, -omk, -umk*.

Taqmk, taqtm, -tmaq, "to strike"; *koqoey wjit taqmin?* "why do you hit me?" (Gr. Ma. 61); *tqama's*, "I will hit him"; *tqam*, "hit him!"

Ankamk, -kaptm, -tmaq, "to look at"; *Niskam tapu'kl weji-nenuite'lmujl: msit koqoe'l kisitoqsipnl ankaptmikl, aqq msit koqoe'l e'snl ketlamsitmikl*, "one knows God in two ways: by seeing all that He has made and by believing all that He has said: *ankam, ankapte'n, ankaptmu*.

Greetings to the Sun. *Ke'sik ankam na'ku'set teli-amqusqa'wit* (*how round it is*); *wsika'qlem to'q: Pusu'l ki'l kesalkusin Na'ku'setewin, teli-wlkwija'si nemu'lanl, teli-ksamuksin aqq paqtasin, wji-wla'litisk kiskuk; paqtapatek* (*the light of the sun*) *welkwija'lik; jel ni'n suel kisi-pkwatukk* (*I could do*) *paqtapatek: ke'j eta wsikewikwa'sian, wlewistuan, elelmian, wla'lueyan; na oquj ketl pa welkwija'luek.*

Wekamk, wekaptm, -tmaq, "to irritate (*torvis oculis*) [with fierce eyes], to glare at."

Weska'qelmik, -qeltm, -tmaq, "to kiss, to greet with a kiss, to embrace"; *weska'qelmik ta'n weska'qelmit*, "I greet who greets me"; *wska'qelm, -muk*, "(you s., pl.) greet him!"

Meselmik, -seltm -tmaq, "to call upon someone, to ask for something, to ask it from him"; *i'paji-mseltmul*, "I humbly ask you for that."

Esmik, -muetu, -taq, "to feed"; *esmit, -majl, -mul, -min; sma's, sm, smuk*, "(you s., pl.) feed him!" *wetsmik*, "to feed with"; *wa'qey wetsmulkw*, "he gives us his flesh to eat"; *telamu'kupnikl esmie'kl tlamu'ktij pneknmuin nilu'nen* [give us this day our daily bread]; *smutukk, -tukunik* (dub.), "I should perhaps feed him, them."

Eulite'lmik, -te'tm, -te'tmaq, "to have pity, compassion"; *eulite'lma's, -te'lm, -te'lmuk* (without contraction); *eulite'lmtupp, -tukk, -tukunik*, "perhaps ...." The verbs in *-te'lmik, -te'tm, -te'tmaq* and *-ita'si* express thought, desire.

Nenuite'lmik, -te'tm, -te'tmaq, "to know it in the mind."

Mikwite'lmik, -te'tm, -te'tmaq, "to remember" (willingly).

Wijikmk, -kmkik, "to have as brothers, sisters, near kin"; *wijikmuloq*, "you are my brothers"; *ta'n te'si'tij wijikmo'q*, or even *wijikitioq, -kitultioq*, "all your brothers."

Ekimk, ekitm, -tmaq, "to read, to count, to recite"; *kim, kite'n, kitmu, kitmuk*; *kaqkimujik sunmink*, "one recites the whole rosary."

Almimk, -mitm, -tmaq, "to insult, to curse"; *almikitm, almakitm*, "to swear."

Pilsimk, -simul, -simin, "to bear false witness"; *ma'wen kpilsimaw*, "do not bear false witness against anyone."

Telimk, -mul, -min, "to say to someone"; *tlim, tlimuk; tlimiekapn, tlimaqpn*, "I, you, should have said it to him."

Malqomk, -otm, -tmaq, "to eat, to devour" (lit. and fig.); *pku malqomkit, kataq, malqomkijik*, "we eat toffee (gum), eels."

Alsumk, -utm, -tmaq, "to dominate, to be the master"; *alsusit, ntalsusitem*.

Alasumk or *elasumk, -utm, -tmaq*, "to worship, to honour, to pray": *teli-alasmulekl* or *alasumulekl eulistmuin*, Latin *suscipe deprecationem nostram*, "hear our prayers."

III. Verbs in *-nik* and *-ank, -enk, -onk, -unk*.

E'nik, entu, entaq, "to lose"; *e'nit, e'najl, e'nul, e'nin; na's, e'n, naj; tali-wlapesiss wen wsko'ss ta'n tetutki'k wskitqamu, toqu naj wjijaqmijl?* "what use would it be for a man to win the whole world, if he lost his soul?" *naj, nass, nasn*, "if he loses, lost, had lost"; *e'nikipnaq pessmkeweyaq*, "I have lost my medal"; *e'nusit*, "he is lost"; *e'nu'kw, e'nikit, e'noq, e'najl, e'naji; e'nut, e'nulk, e'nimk*.

Kelnik, -nm, -nmaq, "to hold"; *kln, klne'n, klnmu*; intransitive *kelnekey, -ken, -ket*, "to be a godfather or godmother"; *kilew kelnekeyoq tlnuk ula mijua'ji'j*, "you godparents hold that infant thus"; *telnik, -nm, -nmaq*, "to hold thus"; *nklnikn, nklniknen*, "my, our godchild."

Amaskwiplnik, -nm, -nmaq, "to torment"; *amaskwiplnutaq*, "he suffered"; *teli-amaskwiplnuss Sesukuli Ksaqmaminu*, "the Passion of Our Lord Jesus Christ."

Mesnik, -nm, -nmaq, "to take, to receive"; *msna's, msn, msne'n, msnmu; mesnikup mjijaqmij*, "we have received a soul."

Napnik, -nm, -nmaq, "to return"; *napnit, -najl, -nul, -nin*.

Matnik, -nm, -nmaq, "to wrestle against"; not to be confused with *matte'k,* "to beat"; *matn ta'nik matnijik,* "fight with those who fight against me" (Ps. 34, 1).

Awank, awanitu, -taq, "to be unfamiliar with, unsure of."

Wantaqnk, -qnul, -qnin, "to keep quiet"; *wantaqa'lik,* "to pacify."

Ketank, ketantu, -taq, "to detest, to pursue, to hunt"; *ketuank,* "to want to kill"; *ketanaji tutupia,* "he gathers spruce roots" (Am. I, 121).

Mestank, mestanm, -nmaq, "to have all"; *sape'wuti'l mestankl,* "all holy."

Pekwank, pekwanm, -nmaq, "to help, to nurse (a patient), to move"; *pekwansit* (reflexive verb), *me'si-pkwansit,* "he can, cannot help himself, cannot move."

Nutnik, -nm, -nmaq, -nawey, "to carry, to hold (candlesticks), to be an acolyte."

A'maqnk, -qntm, -tmaq, "to paint, to stain"; *mim'kwnk,* "to anoint"; *mu mim'kwniwtip, katu u't e'pit weji-a'maqntikl nkatl a'maqnsutiktuk,* "you did not give me oil for my head, whereas this woman anointed my feet."

Melknk, -nm, -nmaq, "to hold strongly"; *melknt, -knajl, -knu'kw, -knkit, -knoq, -kna'tijl, -knisk, -knik, -knit; mlkn, -knuk, -kni, -knin: mlknin me'j winsuti'l mu ktika'linen,* "fortify us against temptations" [lead us not into temptation].

Sepiljenk, -jenm, -nmaq, "to hold in the hand" (closed).

Kewkunk, -kunm, -nmaq, "to hold in the hands, to carry in the arms"; *ku'kuna's, ku'kun; kewkunit, kewkusk* (for *kewkunisk*), when substantives, mean godfather and godmother; one even says *nkewkuskm, nkewkunitm* indifferently for both; *u't mijua'ji'j kewkunoq?* "are you godfather and godmother of this infant?" *kewkunkit eta,* "yes, we are"; *ku'kuniekapn, -naqpn, -nasoqq, -naqekpn, -naqoqpn, -na'tisoqq,* "I, you, etc. would have held him"; *kewkunkitip, -kitipnik* or *-kitnik,* "we held him, them."

Mimaju'nk, -ju'nm, -nmaq, "to endue with life, to give and maintain life"; *wele'k, nikmatut, mimaju'nuj ta'n mu neskwaq kisi-koqqwa'luj,* "it is good, my brothers, to give life to those who do not seek revenge, having laid down their arms" (Man. Gr. II, 27, note), more exactly, "to him who does not resist after having been captured."

Nan'tunk, -tunm, -tunmaq, -tunewey, "to seek (with the hand), to feel, to grope about."

Newtunk, -tunm, -nmaq, "to have (to hold) one of them"; *nkutun, nkutuna's; tapunaji, nesunaji, neunaji,* "he has two, three, four of them."

Ninasunk, -sunm, -nmaq, also *meknk,* "to choose."

Toqnk, -qnm, -qnmaq, "to hold between, to hold with another," also "to receive from another": *elue'wuti Ataek weji-tqonkip*, "he (the infant) has inherited the sin of Adam"; *toqnasijik*, "they live together"; *tepqatkik*, "they are married."

Jitunk, -tunm, -nmaq, "to protect."

IV. The verbs in *-lik* and *-alk, -elk, -ilk, -olk, -ulk* show the peculiarity of taking *-n* instead of *-ul* with second person objects, although in practice *-ul* is often used, in spite of the proximity of the two *l*'s, which is what caused this modification; thus *elue'wa'lik*, "render wicked," and *kesalk*, "to love," which will be the two secondary models of this class, instead of giving *elue'wa'lul* and *kesalul*, as *nemu'l*, give *elue'wa'lin* and *kesaln, -salnoq, ksalnites*, etc. The corresponding transitive inanimate of those in *-a'lik* is in *-a'tu*, of those in *-alk* in *-atm*. The vowel which precedes *-lik* is long, that which precedes *-lk* is short; *i* remains in the third person passive in the first: *elue'wa'lijl*; wheras *kesalajl* gives *kesaljl*; "we him, them ..." give respectively: *elue'wa'lukw, -lukwik, kesalkw, -lkwik, elue'wa'likit, -likijik, kesalkit, -kijik*. It is the same in the remainder of the conjugation.

Here are the principal endings of *elue'wa'lik*, with those of *kesalk* in parentheses, where they are different.

Pres.: *elue'wa'lik, -a'lit (-alk, -alt), -a'lajl, -a'lukw, -a'likit (-alkw, -alkit), -a'loq, -a'la'tijl*; in the plural add *-ik* or *-i*; *-a'ln (-aln), -a'lnoq, -a'lnek, -a'lisk (-alsk); -a'lin, -a'lit, -a'lik, -a'liek, -a'lioq, -a'lnukw, -a'linamit; -mijik*.

Past: *elue'wa'likip (-alkip)*, etc.; *-a'lneksip, -a'lnoqsip, -a'lnu'kup*, etc.

Fut.: *lue'wa'la's, ksala's* or *-lates*, etc. *-a'lnites, -a'lnitew, -a'lnitoqsip, -a'lnoqtew; -a'litisk, -a'litoqsip, -a'litesnen, -a'lnukutew, -a'linamitew*.

Imp.: *lue'wa'l, ksal, -a'luk, -a'laj, -a'lanej, -a'lnij, -a'lnoqj, -a'li, -a'likw, -a'lin, -a'lij*.

When: *elue'wa'likl, -kek*, etc. *-a'lnanl, -a'lnekl, -a'lnoqwl, -ek, -uek; -a'linl, -a'linek*, etc.; *-a'lnukwl, -a'lnukwek*.

If: *lue'wa'lik, -a'liksip, -a'liksipn (-alk, -alkiss, -alkisn), -a'lij (-alj), -a'lisip, -a'lisipn, -a'laj, -a'lass, -a'lasn, -a'lukw (-lkw), -kuss, -kusn, -a'likij (-alkij), -kitsip, -kitsipn*, etc. *-a'lnan, -a'lnass, -a'lnasn, -a'lisk (-alsk), -kiss, -kisn; -a'lnoq, -a'lnoqos, -a'lnoqsipn, -a'lnek, -a'lneksip, -a'lneksipn; -a'lin, -a'lij*, etc.; *-a'lnu'kw, -a'lnu'kuss, -a'lnu'kusn*.

Cond.: *-a'liekapn, -a'laqsipn*, etc.; *-a'lnik, -kapn, -a'lnikoqq, -a'lnikekk, -koqpn, -kekpn; -a'lniss, -a'lnoqs, -soqq; -a'lik, -a'likapn, -a'likpin, -a'lisoqq, -a'lnukuss, -usoqq, -a'linamitsoqq*.

Sub.: *ntelue'wa'lan, -wa'lnin, -wa'lnukunenu, -wa'lnukunen.*

Inf.: *-a'lut*, etc.; *-a'lnukk, -a'lnuksip, -a'lnuten, -nukej, -kunesn, -kunesoqq.*

Examples

Elue'wa'lik, -a'tu, -a'taq, "to pervert, to make wicked, harmful."

Apkwa'lik, -a'tu, -a'taq, "to untie, to deliver"; *apkwa'l'timkewey,* "absolution."

Elapalk, -atu, -ataq, "to sprinkle with water, to baptise privately"; *kesispa'lik,* "to wash, to purify"; *Ksispa'sue'kati,* "Purgatory"; *lapalitesk isop e'umnl, ksispa'litesk, na wji-pjili-wape'tes aqq wastew,* "Asperges me, you will sprinkle me with hyssop, you will wash me, and I shall be whiter than snow; *wapei, -pein, -pe'k,* "to be white"; *lapaltinewey,* "holy water."

Ika'lik, -a'tu, -a'taq, "to put, to place," also "to wager, to bet, to vote for"; *kejitoqsip Wujjl wtika'takun msit koqoe'l wpitniktuk,* "he knew that his Father had placed everything into his hands."

Wela'lik, -a'tu, -a'taq, "to do good, to please, to render a service."

Ke'sa'lik, -a'tu, -a'taq, "to burn"; not to be confused with *kesalk,* "to love."

Kisa'lik, -a'tu, -a'taq, "to do, to succeed"; implies effort: see *kisitu.*

Kiskaja'lik, -a'tu, -a'taq, "to accomplish, to establish; *kiskaja'linamikek,* "he has established us" (2 Cor. 3, 6); *apustale'wijik kiskaja'la'tisnika ktikika pa'tlia'sewa'lan,* "the apostles established others as priests."

Mesa'lik, -a'tu, -a'taq, "to swallow."

Mesua'lik, -a'tu, -a'taq, "to show."

Pekwalk, -atu, -ataq, "to procure, to acquire, to make, to cause to do, to be the cause"; *pekwatu tasi,* "it is my fault"; *kinu na pekwatu'kw,* "it is we who are the cause of it"; *koqoe'l kiskuk pekwatu'pnl?* "what have you earned today?" *moqwe'j l'n pa pekwatuep,* "nothing at all"; *pekwatatimk* (reciprocal), "to get it for each other"; *pekwatatimkewey l'ue'wuti,* "scandal."

Apkwalk (short *a*), *-atm, -atmaq,* "to deliver"; *apkwalatn,* "he will be delivered."

Emtoqwalk, -atm, -atmaq, "to praise"; *mawi-mtoqwalanej,* "let us all adore him."

Eskmalk, -atm, -atmaq, "to wait for"; *weji-skmalkw,* "we await him from there"; also "to watch over"; *skmnaqn,* "observation post"; *Nsaqmam, skmali,* "Master, wait for me."

Ikalk, *-atm*, *-atmaq*, "to protect."

Utqotalk, *-atm*, *-atmaq*, "to inter, bury"; *utqotatmaq wtinin*, "I inter his body."

Kemutnalk, *-atm*, *-atmaq*, "to steal"; *kemutmk*, "to steal from someone."

Kesalk, *-atm*, *-atmaq*, "to love"; *kesalkit*, *-kijik*, *-kitsip*, *-kitsipnik*, *-kitnik*, *-kitsip*, *-kitsipn*; *-ksalass*, *-ksalasoqq*.

Mui'walk, at Restigouche *mi'walk*, *-atm*, *-atmaq*, "to thank"; *mui'walukw*, "thank him!"

Pewalk, *-atm*, *-atmaq*, "to wish, to desire, to need."

Pestie'walk, *-atm*, *-atmaq*, "to celebrate, to keep as a holiday" (an Old French word, *fester*).

Jipalk, *-atm*, *-atmaq*, "to fear"; *mntu jipatk klujjiewey*, "the devil fears the cross"; *jipalku*, *-kun*, *-kuk*, "to be formidable."

Elk (defective), *elajl*, *elaji*, *eln*, *elnoq*, "to say to someone"; *Kisu'lkul latal*, "he will say to God"; *ketl pa elnoq*, "in truth I say to you."

Eselk, *selm*, *-lmaq*, "to give as food"; *esmik*, "to nourish"; *eselt*, *eselajl*, *-laji*, *eselkw*, *eselkit*, *eseloq*; *eseln*, *-lnoq*, *-lisk*, *-liskik*; *eselin*, *eselnukw*; *netawselk*, "to give willingly"; intrans.: *eselekey*, *-ken*, *-ket*; *mijisotelk*, "to take care of, to feed, to pasture" (cattle); *-telulk* (Dict. 108).

Aptukopiso'tlk, *-tlm*, *-tlmaq*, "to crown"; *-tln*, *-tlin*.

Sepiljo'tlk, "to put in the hand"; *sepiljo'tlut wasoqnmaqn*, "a wax candle is put in his hand."

Kelpilk or *kejipilk*, *-pilm*, *-pilmaq*, "to bind, to attach"; *melkipilk*, "to attach strongly"; *-piln*, *-pilin*, *klpila's*, *klpil*; *kjipila's*, *-lates*.

Nepilk, *-pitm*, *-pitmaq*, "to take care of, to give remedies to"; *nepiln* (*-lul*), *-lin*; *ejeliaq wen wnpitmuan wla'qnml*, "it is impossible to take care of his wounds."

Elo'lik, *-o'tu*, *-o'taq*, "to throw down, to make a heap"; *elo'luj*, *elo'tasit* (child).

Wetqolk, *-otm*, *-otmaq*, "to forbid, to prevent"; *tali wtoqlnu'kw?* "what prohibition is made for us?" *wetqol'timkeweyek minijkek*, "the forbidden fruit"; *wetqolinamittip*, "he prohibited us"; *wtoqle'n kilnu*, "hold your tongue" (7 Pr. 142).

Ketapo'lik, *-o'tu*, *-o'taq*, "to push into the water, to drag under."

Meno'lik, *-o'tm*, *-o'tmaq*, "to dig up (potatoes), to take out of the ground"; *mena'lik*, *-a'tu*, *-a'taq*, "to remove"; *meno'teket*, *-taqatijik*, "those who harvest."

Ajipjulk, -utu, -utaq, "to hope in, to count on."

Elulk, -utu, -utaq, "to send, to command"; *koqoey elulimk naqaji,* "If I am asked to do something, I neglect it" (heard in conversation).

Elu'lik, -u'tu, -u'taq, "to carry by water"; *elu'lit, elu'ljl, elu'lsit, -lu'l,* "transport it!"

Wesimukulk, -utu, -utaq, "to carry away while fleeing"; *wesimukulut* (S.F. 110).

Kelulk, -utm, -utmaq, "to speak to someone"; *kelu'lk* (long *u*) means "a good thing," inan. of *kelu'sit*: *ketui-alasutman mlkite'te'n teli-klult ta'n kisi'skiss,* "when you want to pray think seriously that you are talking to your Creator"; *klul ta'n jiksitask Kji-kelu'sit,* "speak to the Most Good, who hears you"; *jel ki'l jiksitu ta'n wen ma' peli-klulnukw jijikwaqa,* "listen yourself to Him who will not fail to speak to you occasionally"; *lo'q wejuow kimewistutew,* "from close by he will speak softly."

Keseulk, -ult, -ulajl, "to please"; *keseulik, -likl,* "that pleases me"; *kejin, Niskam, matew keseulinuksip ntekweiwan puski-papultipnik,* "you know, Lord, that I have never cared for the company of gamblers" (Rem. gr. 97); *keseuljl,* "he takes pleasure in it."

Netulk, -ult, -ulajl, "to be missed by someone"; *netulijl, -tuljl, -tulisk,* "he is missed by me, him, you"; *netulik, -tulikl, -tulkwl, -tulinamikl,* "that, these things are missed by me, us"; *nusetoqniktuk,* "for my salvation."

Nijkulk, -ult, -ulajl, "to cure"; *Se'sus weji-nisimjuatek kmtniktuk wejkielijl mu netaq nijkilikul naji-alasumjl telimjl: Nsaqmam, puatmn kisi-nijkulikip,* "Jesus having descended from the mountain, a leper who had not been able to be cured came to worship him and to say to him: Lord, if you so wish, you could cure me; then Jesus, extending his hand, touched him and said to him: I so wish; be cured" (Matt. 8, 1; Ms. 2, 112); *na pa Se'sus eli-nsqa'sijl sama'lajl ntelajl: pewatm, nijki.*

Pekisulk, -situ and *-sutu, -taq,* "bring to, lead to"; *pekisult, -sulajl, -suln, -sulin; pkisula's, pkisul, mu kipkisulaw, kipkisulapp; apune'k pekisulsit,* "he humbles himself, degrades himself"; *pekisutajl newte'jilijl tettejl,* "they bring him someone who owes him money."

Reading

Act of Charity. Ta'n telki'k nkamlamun aqq njijaqmij aqq ta'n telitay (*as much as I am able*) na, Niskam, teli-ksaln, msɨt eta pa koqoe'l pajiji-ksalnanl, ki'l oquj kji-sape'win aqq kji-kelu'sin, aqq elp nikmaq teli-ksalkik ni'n ntinin teli-ksatm, wjit ki'l, Niskam telkimin oquj.

Flags. Kmtaweknminu weli-ankamkuk aqq kesalkuk (*is liked*); wiaqiw wape'k, mekwe'k aqq musqunamu'k; wape'k teluek: waqmeye'n (*be pure*), musqunamu'k: ketleweye'n (*be faithful*), mekwe'k: mlkiknewa'si (*be strong*). Aklasie'wey mtawekn weli-nujo'tk (*protects*) kinuowey, isteke pitoqsit mimkwanmusi, melke'k wipoqm (*trunk*), jitunaji snawe'l kmu'jl aqq nipi': teli-wli-ankamkusijik (*are so beautiful*) nipi'k kiwto'qiw kaqapijinkik (*they hang all around*); atu'tuej (*squirrel*) etli-papit psetkuniktuk (*plays in the branches*), aqq we'kow eli-malqotkl mimkwaqnl (*he goes as far as eating the acorns*). Mimkwanmusi etli-saqmawit nipuktuk (*the oak is the king of the forest*). Toqu snawey welamuksit aqq sismoqnit, e'mk, amuj saqma'skowit. Kisu'lkw wleiwaj kteleke'minal, aqq snaweyey nipi teli-kekinukwataqnit me'j wlo'tmulkuj.

LESSON TWENTY EIGHT

CLASSIFICATION OF VERBS

Verbs are divided into three large categories according to meaning: whether they express **state**, **action** or **thought**. In Mi'kmaw each can be developed into at least 15 classes; this amounts to up to 45 verbs, when the structure and the meaning of the root are suitable.

Here, first of all, are the listing, the description and the formation of these verbs. Next we give a schematic of three model categories, with numbers to which the figures in parenthesis refer. The first and third of these categories have the same endings in every verb; but the second one offers a great variety, according to the different kinds of activities, and according to the multiple endings of the transitive animate verbs.

1. We must first introduce the true intransitive verbs, those which Fr. Maillard calls absolutes; they express being or state, even action or thought, but without any relation to an object, such as *elnui*, "I am a man" (Indian), from *l'nu*, "man"; *telei*, *welei*, *eulei*, "I am such, well, miserable"; *teluisi*, "my name is." *Telei*, from the root *teli*, "thus," really expresses what is most fundamental in the state, if one recalls that the verb *to be* exists in Mi'kmaw only in the form of *-i* added to words which, in our languages, serve as attributes. These are the substantive verbs; but since they follow the same paradigm as the others, according to their varying relationships, one can say, consequently, that they express attitude. *Telei*, meaning therefore "state" or "attitude," becomes *tela'si*, "to express action" *per se* or "activity," and *telita'si* for thought, "I act thus, I think thus," or simply "I think": *telita'si amuj mimaji*, "I think, therefore I am" (I live); for: "to be a thinking, reflecting being," there is yet another substantive verb, *telita'suinui* or *ankita'suinui*.

To this first form in *-i* there is often added another in *-iey*, *-iaq*, which means the beginning, the development, and certain movements: *telita'suinuiey*, "I begin to think, I become a reflective person"; *kisikui*, "I am old"; *kisikuiey*,

"I grow old"; *kelu'si, -siey*, "I am, I become good"; *sape'wi, -wiey*, "wise or holy"; *wapei, -piey*, "to be white, to whiten"; *elue'wi, -wiey*, "to be wicked, to become wicked"; the latter has the very special meaning of "insane," as if these unfortunate creatures were always in the state of becoming so, their wickedness being unconscious; *teliaq, weliaq*, "that is true, that is good."

2. Next come the verbs which can be called **intransitive actives**, which also express state or rather attitude, and also action and thought, in relation to a being of the animate or inanimate gender, without otherwise expressing it, such as *kesaluey*, from *kesalk*, "to love"; *nemi'wey*, from *nemi'k*, "to see"; the latter is formed from the transitive animate (No. 3 on the list), by changing the *-k* of the ending to *-wey* or even by adding *-ey* after the *-k*, as *tepik*, "to give his share to someone"; *tepi'key*, "to make the distribution"; *nuji-tpi'ket*, "the agent" (the distributor); the verbs in *-aq* and in *-ek* change these endings to *-uey*: *iknmaq*, "to give to someone"; *iknmuey*, "to make a gift"; *weleyaq*, "to do good to him"; *weleiwey*, "to be beneficent"; the mental verbs suppress the *m* with or without the vowels and form *-te'lkey*; however, *-te'lmuey* is also found. These verbs in *-uey* or *-key* are little used except with *nuji-* or other prefixes, which draw the attention to the subject and make a noun of it; otherwise these words almost always express an explicit goal, and then they are true transitive animate verbs.

When the indefinite object of the others is thought to be of the inanimate gender, this animate intransitive is then formed from the transitive inanimate (9), by changing *-tm* or *-tu* to *-tekey* or another slightly different ending; for *welei* we have *welo'tekey*, from *welo'm*, "to treat well"; *wela'tekey*, from *wela'tu*, "to do well, to behave well, to do good"; *welite'tekey*, from *welite'm*, "to be willing"; *telo'tekey, tela'tekey, telite'tekey*, "that is our attitude, our manner of being, doing, thinking" (8).

3. The **transitive** verbs, animates, inanimates and mixed, are those which have a direct object, of the animate or inanimate gender, or two objects, of which at least one is animate. These verbs are the key to the language; it is on them that one must rely to form all the others. One has only to list each according to its root to obtain the whole class without difficulty. For *telei, welei, eulei*, one has *teleyaq, weleyaq, euleyaq*, "to treat someone thus, well, badly, to have such an attitude, good, wicked towards them"; *telo'm*, the same for a thing; *welo'm* is the word used for: "to bless a thing"; *wino'm*, "to profane"; *tela'tu*, "to make, to treat thus," also "to render thus." We must relate this class, which is very numerous, to another which resembles it in the transitive animate conjugation, and is equally numerous; these are the verbs in *-alk, -atm* (short *a*), such as *kesalk, kesatm*, "to love," *kesaluey, kesatekey. Telite'lmik, telite'm*, "to think him, it, to believe, to judge thus"; *welite'lmik, -te'm*, "to wish him, it, to desire him, it, to consent to him, it." *Naqmaje'jk ta telo'tmn?* "do you find that easy?"

telite'm, "I think so, I suppose so"; someone who had already tried it out or wished to boast, would say: *amuj eta*, "certainly"; or even: *telo'm amuj-a*.

4. The **reflexive** (4) and **reciprocal** (5) verbs, called pronominal in French, because they are conjugated with two pronouns of the same person, are those whose action or thought, even attitude, is produced and received by the same person, or by others of the same group; as *nemi'si, mi'ti'kw*, "I see myself, we see each other, one another." They are formed from transitive animate verbs by changing *-k* to *-si*, as *nemi'k, nemi'si; weleyaq, weleyasi*. Those in *-e'k* (long) make *-o'si: nipisoqnte'k, -to'si*, "to whip oneself"; those in *te'lmɨk* suppress *m*, as for the active intransitives: *welite'lsi, te'l'ti'kw*; the reciprocals, which do not have a singular, take *t* instead of *s* in the dual and plural: *nemi'si, -si'kw, -sulti'kw*, "I see myself, we see ourselves" (each himself); *nemi'ti'kw, -tulti'kw*, "we see each other, one another"; the verbs in *-emɨk, -emk, -mɨk*, form their reciprocal in the same manner, when this ending is preceded by a consonant other than *l*; ex.: *wijikmk*, "to have as a brother"; *wijikɨti'kw, -tulti'kw*, "we are brothers"; *wipemk*, "to sleep with a companion," *wipeti'kw*, "we sleep together." It is the same with some others, which express rather a common action than a reciprocal influence, as *wiputi'kw*, from *wipumk*, "to eat together"; *teko'ti'kw, -tiyek, -tiyoq, -tijik, -tulti'kw*, "to be present together," from *teko'tm*; *wije'ti'kw*, from *wije'wɨk*, "to go together, in a group."

M. Maillard says that these verbs are taken from the single intransitives (Gr. 163). From his examples we can see that he means the transitive inanimate with indefinite object: *nemi'si*, he says, comes from *nemitekey*; *ankamsi* from *ankaptekey*, "to look at oneself"; *minua'lsi* from *minua'tekey*, "to be renewed"; *wenmajeyasi* from *wenmajo'tekey*, "to torment oneself"; *kisi'si* from *kisitekey*, "to develop, to be created oneself," etc. This is a bit far-fetched, for a root which is immediately accessible. In place of the intransitive put the transitive animate and compare; one only has to change *-k* to *-si*; *nemi'k, ankamk, minua'lik, wenmajeyaq, kisi'k*. He is no more successful when he tries to derive them from the animate intransitives: *kesalsi* from *kesaluey* (that is from *kesalk*), to love oneself"; *ela'lsi* from *ela'luey, el-a'lik*, "to transport oneself"; *wela'lsi* from *wela'luey, wela'lik*, "to get a good deal for oneself, to look after one's own interest"; *kekina'masi* from *kekina'muey, kekina'maq*, "to educate oneself"; *iknmasi* from *iknmuey, iknmaq*, "to give to oneself, to attribute to oneself, to appropriate for oneself"; *weska'qelmsi* or *-qelsi* from *weska'qelmuey, weska'qelmɨk*; *malikmsi* from *malikmuey, malikmk*, "to poke fun at"; *nestuimsi* from *nestuimuey, nestuimk*, "to check on oneself, to correct oneself"; *mimaju'nsi* from *mimaju'nuey, mimaju'nk*, "to give oneself life," etc.

5. The **passive** (6, 7) verbs: these are the ones that express an attitude, action or thought received or suffered by the subject, but without saying from whom it comes, although the ending indicates in general if it is an animate

or inanimate being, as *kesalkusi* and *kesatasi*, "to be loved"; *nemi'kusi* and *nemitasi*, "to be seen." The first is formed by adding *-usi* to the animate verb, as *nemi'kusi* and *kesalkusi*; but if the final *k* is preceded by *i* or *a*, it makes *-uksi*, as in *elue'wa'lik, elue'wa'luksi*, "I am perverted, rendered wicked"; *iknmaq, iknmuksi*, "I am favoured by a present"; the verbs in *-aq* (*-ajl*) and *-e'k* (long) give *-o'ksi*, as *-eso'ksi*, "to be dismissed"; *matto'ksi*, "to be beaten"; those in *-uk* add only *-si*: *wisunkeuksi*, "I receive a name"; those in *-te'lmik* have both endings: *eulite'lmuksi* and *eulite'lmkusi*, "I am pitied"; it is the same for verbs in *-mk*, but with a subtle difference of meaning: *welamuksi*, "to look good," *welamkusi*, "to be well considered." The second passive is formed from the transitive inanimate by changing *-tu* or *-tm* into *-tasi*, or better *-u, -m* to *-asi*: *telo'tm, telo'tasi; tela'tu, kesatm, telata'si, kesatasi; telite'tm, kesite'tm, telite'tasi, kesite'tasi; ewi'km, ewi'kasi*, "to be written, described, painted"; *telui'kasik*, "it is written"; *kwilm, kwilasi, kwilasik*, "to be followed." In the verbs in *-tu*, the passive *-tasi* is no different from the inanimate reflexive or mixed: *tela'tasi* means: "I am treated thus in my affairs," or else "to treat myself thus"; but both exist; it is more apparent in the following example: *kisitasi likpenikn*, "I make myself a basket" (one could moreover say more simply: *kisitu likpenikn wjit ni'n ntinin*); *kisitasi nsuiska'tun saqatuetesinan*, "a fall made me break it (lit.), I am rendered the destroyer of it by a fall"; here as elsewhere it can be expressed by the active: "my fall made me break it," *kisituik nsuiska'tun saqatuetesinan*. There is a third passive which signifies rather state or quality; it is formed by adding *-u, -un, -uk* to the animate active, as *kesalku, -kun, -kuk*, "to be loved, to be a person or thing loved"; *jipalku, -kun, -kuk*, "dreaded, formidable, object of fear": *Ki'l sape'win aqq pejili-ksalkun Se'sus wkamlamun*, "thou holy and well-beloved Heart of Jesus" (Par. I, 97); this form is conjugated like *mena'tu*. Along with this form there is also another, at least for the verbs in *-aq*: *iknmakwey, -kwen, -kwet*, "to be favoured by a gift"; *welo'tmakwey*, "to be blessed in one's affairs, object of benediction, of favours."

If one wishes to say whence the action comes, the transitive forms are required: "I am seen by you, by him, by people" (indefinite subject), not by a cart; change to, "you see me, he, they, one ...," *nemi'n, nemi't, nemi'jik, nemi'mk, nemu'lk, nemu't, topaqan moqwa nemi'nuk*. There would only be confusion in the third person, as, indeed, there is in French as well; if, for example, one wanted to change the last element of the following sentence into the active voice: "the thief runs away from the policeman until he is caught by him" (he catches him), *kmutnes wesimuktuajl nuji-wsua'tekelijl mi'soqo koqqwa'lajl*. But precisely in this person there is in Mi'kmaw a passive, which was presented in the supplementary forms throughout the animate conjugation. Thus in this sentence the passive of *koqqwa'lajl*, "he takes him," is *koqqwa'lijl*, "he is taken," just like *kesaljl*, "he is loved"; *nemi'jl*, "he is seen"; *weleyajl, wela'lijl, welite'lmjl*, "he is well thought of, well treated, an object of benevolence."

6. The **mixed** (or two goal) (10) verbs: these are those which have two objects: the principal (indirect) animate, and the other (direct) inanimate or even animate. They are formed from the transitive inanimate forms, by adding *-aq* to those in *-m*, and by changing *-u* to *-aq* for those in *-tu*; for example: *westawi'k, westawitu*, "I save a person, a thing"; *westawitaq*, "I save what belongs to a person (thing or another person); *Kji-saqmaw, wsitawituin nteleke'minen*, "Lord, save our king for us"; *westawituloq ksulieweimuow*, "I save your silver" (for you); *wi'kmuatal wtui'katikn*, "he will write him his letter." For *welei* one will have *welo'tmaq, wela'taq, welite'tmaq*, "to consider something good, to bless what belongs to him or concerns him, to treat it well, to be happy for him."

These verbs can also take other active forms:

An **intransitive** form (11, 12), when the action is as if contained in oneself, without relation to another person or definite thing: *welo'temay* and *welo'tmuey*, "to bless, to do a favour."

A passive form (13), when the subject receives the action, is favoured or blessed in his affairs: *welo'tmuksi, wela'tuksi, welite'tmuksi*.

Finally a **reflexive** (14) or **reciprocal** (15) form, when it has to do with things concerning the subject: *welo'tmasi, wela'tasi, welite'tmasi, -ati'kw*, "to develop, to be wished good by oneself, by one another." Example: *telo'tm melkiknaq asukomikaqn*, "I find the bridge solid"; *nkwis telo'tmaq wkisitaqn*, "I attribute that to the work of my son"; *moqwa, telo'tmasi ni'n ntla'taqn*, "no, I attribute it to my own work"; *pe'l qaskew, meluij mawi-tlite'tmasultinej, tlite'tmatultinej*, "stop! wait a minute! let us rather attribute it to the work of all of us," or else "each to the work of the others"; *toqu tla'tatinej, tla'tatultinej*, "then let us shake on it, both, all," lit.: "let us do this reciprocally"; the gesture supplements the words.

Table of Model Categories
Taken from the root weli-, "well," adverbial prefix

I. State or Attitude
1. *Wel*   *ei, iey, iaq*, to be well, happy; to become happy, that is good.
2.   *eiwey*, to be well-disposed toward others, to be a benefactor.
3.   *eyaq*, to be that towards someone, to consider him good, to treat him well.
4.   *eyasi*, to consider oneself good, to treat oneself well.
5.   *eyati'kw*, to act thus towards one another, each other.

6. *eyuksi, eyaku, eiakuey*, to be well treated, blessed, in one's person.
7. *o'tasi*, to be that in one's property, in one's affairs.
8. *o'tekey*, to do well, to profit, to make progress.
9. *o'tm*, to treat a thing well, to bless it, to arrange it well.
10. *o'tmaq*, to treat or use well what belongs to someone.
11. *o'tmay*, to bless (in general), to do favours.
12. *o'tmuey*, to do them for neighbours in general.
13. *o'tmuksi, o'tmaku, o'tmakwey*, to receive favours, to be blessed in one's affairs.
14. *o'tmasi*, to treat one's own affairs well, to look after one's own interests.
15. *o'tmati'kw*, to do it for each other.

II. Action or Activity

1. *Wel a'si*, to be well, to act well.
2. *a'luey*, to do good, to do a favour, to render a service.
3. *a'lik*, to do it for a specified person.
4. *a'lsi*, to do it for oneself, to flatter oneself.
5. *a'liti'kw*, to do good reciprocally, to each other.
6. *a'luksi, a'liku*, to be favoured (in a specific thing), to be a beneficiary.
7. *a'tasi*, to be helped in one's affairs.
8. *a'tekey*, to do good, to do well, to act good.
9. *a'tu*, to do something good, also, to do a thing well.
10. *a'taq*, to favour the interests of another.
11. *a'tay*, to favour
12. *a'tuey*, to favour others, in general.
13. *a'tuksi*, to be favoured in one's affairs.
14. *a'tasi*, to do good to oneself.
15. *a'tati'kw*, to do it mutually.

III. Thought or Wish

1. *Weli ta'si*, to be content, to have good thoughts.
2. *te'lkey*, to be merry, to have a pleasant meeting, also, to be tipsy.
3. *te'lmik*, to think well of someone, to wish them well.
4. *te'lisi*, to think well of oneself, to be pleased with oneself.
5. *te'liti'kw*, to wish each other well reciprocally, to be happy with each other, one another.
6. *te'lmuksi, te'lmkusi*, to be the object of good thoughts.
7. *te'tasi*, one wishes me well.
8. *te'tekey*, to agree, to be of that opinion.
9. *te'tm*, to agree to something.
10. *te'tmaq*, to be happy for someone, to approve of their doings.
11. *te'tmay*, to agree.

12. *te'tmuey*, to wish well on behalf of others.
13. *te'tmuksi, te'tmaku, te'tmakuey*, I am wished well.
14. *te'tmasi*, to wish oneself well.
15. *te'tmati'kw*, to wish each other well.

Remarks

Mr. Rand, citing a small treatise prepared by Fr. Sigogne, and which can only have come from Fr. Maillard, adds the following to the names of verbs already mentioned:

1. The transsubstantive verbs, indicating the transformation of one substance into another, as *wastew samuqwana'tu*, "to change snow into water" (which is moreover only a change of state), *pipnaqn ewa'qewa'tu*, "to change bread into flesh"; *pipnaqn ewa'qewa'taq*, "I change the bread into his flesh"; it would be more appropriate to say: *pipnaqn ewa'qewa'tasit, moqopa'q wmal'tema'tasit*, "he changes bread into his body, the wine into his blood"; it is the liturgical expression. I suppose that for Mr. Rand there was not a great difference between the former and the latter changes; but we have to be thankful to him for having transmitted this expression to us, due probably to Fr. Sigogne himself; I have not found it in any of the writings of Fr. Maillard, although all these expressions are found there, with others, such as these: *Kji-klusuaqn ewa'qewa'lisiss*, "the Word became flesh"; *mijua'ji'jewa'lisiss*, "became a child"; *apje'ji'jewa'lisiss*, "quite small"; *pipnaqnewa'lisiss*, "bread." Rand furthermore gives *eleke'wa'lul*, "I make you king"; *elnua'lul*, "I make you a man"; but in sum these verbs and the following ones express an action, just as the others do, and are conjugated in the same manner as those of the second category: *-a'lik, -a'tu, -a'lisit, -a'tasit*, etc.

2. The middle verbs or verbs of **mediation** (interlocutory), which express the interposition of the subject as mediator between two other persons. They are formed from the intransitive form of transitive animate or mixed verbs, by changing *-tay* or *-tawey* to *-tawalsewk*, or *-may* to *-melsewk* or *malsewk*. Examples: from *etamk, etawey*, "to ask for, to beg, to seek," is formed *etawalsewk*, "to ask on behalf of another"; *pekwataq, -tay*, "to cause to have, to procure, to be the cause," *pekwatawalsewk*, "to do that for someone, to procure it for him by intervening"; *apankitaq, -tay*, "to pay someone," *apankitawalsewk*, "to pay for him, in place of him"; *kaqmutay*, "to be patient, agreeable, prepared to render service," *kaqmutawalsewk*, "to take the place of another, to serve as a security, guarantee, as an answerable mediator"; *telki'k teli-wla'lnuksip nekla kaqmutawalseulkwek aqq apankitawalseulkwek*, "he favoured us very much when he put himself in our place and paid for us" (Par. II, 575); *kelulk*, "to speak to someone," *kelutmaq*, "to speak to him

about something, to ask of him," *kelutmay*, "to make a request," *kelutmelsewk*, "to make a request for someone else, to intercede"; *alasutmay*, "to pray," *alasutmelsewk*, "to pray for him, them"; *alasutmelsewi, -sewitesnen*, "pray for us, you will pray" (*Ave Maria*); *nestmay*, "to understand," *nestmalsewk*, "to explain, to interpret for someone," ... *-sewatm*, "a thing"; *nsitmalseuti*, "interpretation"; *nestmalseuksi*, "to be interpreted," ... *-sewsi*, "to interpret oneself," ... *-sewti'kw*, "each other." This calls to mind the amazement that Mr. Rand caused his own interpreter when, in studying the verb to cook, he asked him for the translation of: "to cook oneself, to cook one another"; "that is a thing," says he, "the first of which one cannot do, and the second of which one would prefer not to"; one can nevertheless say, without doing it: *wissukwalsi, -kwal'ti'kw*, from *wissukwey*, "to cook, to do the cooking"; he would undoubtedly prefer to say: *wissukwo'l, -kwo'si*, "I cook for you, for myself"; *Alun wijikitioq wsku'tmalseultew mimajuinuiktuk*, "your brother Aaron will speak for you to the people" (Ex. 16). *Wikutm, -tmaq, -tmay*, "to ask for, to claim something"; *wikutmalsewk*, "to ask for it for someone": *alasutmaqn wikutmalsewkit*, "we ask for prayer, religion, faith for him" (at baptism; Ms. 4, 152).

3. The **impersonals** or unipersonals, which can be seen in the different conjugations.

4. Rand also speaks of **inquisitive** verbs, which indicate that one is looking for what is indicated by the root; as *pipnaqne'key*, "to go to look for, to procure bread"; *tia'mue'key*, "for meat"; *sulieweye'key*, "for money"; but this goes back to the verbs expressing action in general (AI verbs with indefinite objects). He calls meditatives and also **mental**, as does Fr. Maillard, those which express thought. Finally, he calls **diminutives** those to which one should be able, insofar as possible, to add intensives and frequentatives; these two last are formed by means of the prefixes *i'-* and *kesi-*, without changing the ending; *ketapekiey*, "I sing," *i'-ktapekiey*, "I often sing"; *ala'si*, "I walk," *i'-ala'si*, "I often go for a walk, I roam around"; *kesinukway*, "I am sick," *kesi-ksinukway*, "I am very sick." The diminutives are formed by adding *-ji* or even *-ji'ji, -jin, -jit*: *kesinukwa'ji, -ji'ji*, "I am a little sick, I am indisposed, a bit off colour"; the meaning of *eule'ji*, "to be poor, is notable"; it is the diminutive of *euley*, which means "to be miserable, worthy of pity"; there is also *euljewe'jit*, only in colloquial usage, "poor little, puny little wretch."

LESSON TWENTY NINE

NUMBERS

I. Cardinal Numbers

The cardinal numbers have three principal forms in Mi'kmaw:

1. The **root** number, which means simply "one, two, three," or else "once, twice, three times." It answers to *ta's*? "how many times?" Each "time" is translated by *te's*, "so many times" by *ta'n te's*; the latter also means, "each time that."

2. The number of the **animate** gender, which is equivalent to "one person, two persons," etc. It answers to *ta'sijik*? "How many persons?" "So many persons" is translated by *te'sijik*; a verbal form in the dual, which can be conjugated, like *teluisi*, in every mood, every tense, every person, even the first and second, in the form of *te'si'kw, te'siyek, te'siyoq*, "we are, you are such a number." It is not used in the plural. There is *te'sit* in the singular, which means "each."

3. The number of the **inanimate** gender, which is equivalent to "one thing, two things," etc. It answers the question *ta'sikl*? "how many things?" *te'sikl*, "so many things"; *ta'n te'sikl*, "all things" (distributively); *msit te'sikl*, "all things" (collectively).

These last two types of number are formed from the root, by adding to it -*ijik*, -*ikl*, slightly modified in the first, for euphony, and *te'sijik, te'sikl*, from *asukom*, "six," onwards; for the tens -*iskeksijik*, -*iska'q*, -*iska'ql*, and *te'siskeksijik, te'siska'q, te'siska'ql*. One says also *te'sinskeksijik, te'sinska'q*. We must also note: 1. that in all its derivations, *si'st*, "three," is changed to *ne's* and takes -*isijik* or -*e'sijik*, -*iskl*: *ne'sijik, ne'siskl*; 2. that *ta'pu*, "two," takes -*sijik*, and -*kl*: *tapusijik, tapu'kl*; 3. that *mtln*, "ten," is used also with -*te'sijik*,

-te'sikl; there are therefore two expressions for saying "ten," and even "three," because the root *metla's*, which is used only in composition, is used as well.

Between the tens, the numbers from ten to one hundred are formed by adding *jel newt, jel ta'pu*, etc. to the ten; in careful speech this second member is also put in the animate or inanimate form; ex.: *ta'sipnik apustale'witkik?* "how many apostles were there?" *newtiskeksipnik jel ta'pu*, or else *tapusipnik*, "there were twelve of them." Used in the third person as the object of another verb of the same person, the numbers take the syllable *-li-*, as do all verbs, and give *newte'jilijl, tapusiliji, ne'siliji, te'siliji, newtiskeksiliji, tapuiskeksiliji jel na'n* or *naniliji*; in the past *newtiskeksilipni*, in the future *nkutiskeksilita*; in the Passion one reads: *telimasnika newtiskeksilisnika jel tapusilisnika wnaqapemka*, "he said to his twelve apostles."

Here now is the **table** of the cardinal numbers, with Arabic and Roman numerals:

1	I	*Newt*, one, once; *newte'jit*, one person, one thing.	*amskwes, tmk*, first	*newte'jk, newte'*,
2	II	*Ta'pu*, two, twice,	*tapusijik*,	*tapu'kl.*
3	III	*Si'st (ne's),*	*ne'sijik,*	*ne'siskl.*
4	IV	*Ne'w,*	*newijik,*	*newkl.*
5	V	*Na'n,*	*nanijik,*	*nankl.*
6	VI	*Asukom,*	*a. te'sijik,*	*a. te'sikl.*
7	VII	*L'uiknek,*	*l'. "*	*l'. "*
8	VIII	*Ukumuljin,*	*u. "*	*u. "*
9	IX	*Pesqunatek,*	*p. "*	*p. "*
10	X	*Mtln (metla's),*	*m. "*	*m. "*
		Newtiska'q,	*newtiskeksijik,*	*newtiska'ql.*
11 to 19		*N. jel newt, ta'pu, si'st,*	*ne'w, na'n, asukom, l'., uk., pesq.*	
20	XX	*Tapuiska'q,*	*tapuiskeksijik,*	*tapuiska'ql.*
21, 22, etc.		*Tjel newt, ta'pu,* etc.		
30	XXX	*Nesiska'q,*	*nesiskeksijik,*	*nesiska'ql.*
40	XL	*Newiska'q,*	*newiskeksijik,*	*newiska'ql.*
50	L	*Naniska'q,*	*naniskeksijik,*	*naniska'ql.*
60	LX	*Asukom te'siska'q*	*a. te'siskeksijik,*	*a. te'siska'ql.*
70	LXX	*L'uiknek "*	*l'. "*	*l'. "*
80	LXXX	*Ukumuljin " u.*	*"*	*u. "*
90	XC	*Pesqunatek " p.*	*"*	*p. "*
100	XC	*Kaskmtlnaqn "*	*k. qnijik,*	*k. qnl.*
1,000	M	*Pitui-mtlnaqn*	*p. "*	*p. "*
1,000,000		*Kji-pitui-mtlnaqn,*	*k. "*	*k. "*

In order to say 200, 300, etc., *ta'pu, si'st*, etc. are placed before one or another form of *kaskmtlnaqn*, likewise for *pitui-mtlnaqn* and *kji-pitui-mtlnaqn*. For 201,

202, 1001, 1002, etc., one does as for the tens, adding *jel* with the root number, even when there is already one or more *jel*'s in the latter; ex.: "in what year are we?" *ta'sipunqik eymu'kw*? "in 1921" (the year in which I wrote this lesson for the first time), or "in 1939" (this year now), *newt pitui-mtlnaqn jel pesqunatek kaskmtlnaqn jel tapuiska'q jel newt te'sipunqik*; implied, "after the coming of Our Lord," *weja'tekemk weskijinuitek Westau'lkw*; *kisna newt pitui-mtlnaqn jel pesqunatek kaskmtlnaqn jel ne'siska'q jel peskunatek te'sipunqik*. For the thousand millions and million millions, one converts by a thousand times one million, two million, etc., *pitui-mtlnaqn te's kji-pitui-mtlnaqn, ta'pu kji-pitui-mtlnaqn*, etc. Ex.: "the troops of horsemen, of which St. John learned the number, counted two myriads of myriads," *vices millies dena millia* (Rev. 9, 16), *telkitasipnik te'sipowo'ltijik ntepluk tapuiska'q pitui-mtlnaqn te's newtiska'q pitui-mtlnaqnipnik, toqu ni'n nutmip ta'n te'sipnik*; lit. "20,000 times 10,000" or just "200 millions," *ta'pu kaskmtlnaqn te's kji-pitui-mtlnaqnipnik*. Today it is generally found easier and shorter to count in English.

II. Ordinal Numbers

In general, the ordinal numbers are formed from the cardinal by adding to the root -*awey*, -*ewey*, or -*owey*, according to the preceding vowel; they give -*we'k* in the animate plural, -*we'l* in the inanimate plural, like other adjectives. The singular also means "firstly," "secondly," etc. "First" is taken, not from *newt*, which means "once," but from *amskwes* or *amkwes*, "firstly," or from *tmk*, "first of all": *amskwesewey* or *tmkewey*, "the first"; *ta'puowey, si'stewey, ne'wowey, na'newey*; and they continue likewise, *asukomewey, l'uiknekewey, ukumuljinewey, pesqunatekewey*; then *mtlnewey* or *newtiska'qawey* for "tenth," to which is added, for "11th, 12th, 13th," etc. *jel newt, jel ta'pu, jel si'st*, as for the cardinals; "20th, 30th," etc. *tapuiska'qawey, nesiska'qawey, newiska'qawey, naniska'qawey*, and then *asukom te'siska'qawey, l'uiknek, ukumuljin, pesqunatek te'siska'qawey*; finally *kaskmtlnaqnewey, pitui-mtlnaqnewey, kji-pitui-mtlnaqnewey*, "100th, 1,000th, 1,000,000th."

One says *tmkewa'j* or *amskwesewa'j, ta'puowa'j, si'stewa'j*, etc., when it is as the name of an individual, his designation, his number in order, his grade, his situation; also the winners in a contest. These ordinals answer the question *ta'sewey, ta'sewa'j*? "what is his rank?" They can be put in the past, as the other adjectives: *ta'seweyaq*? (inanimate) *ta'seweyek*? *asukomeweyaq, l'uiknekeweyek*, "6th, 7th" (thing). They are also used in the future, but then they properly become verbs, which are conjugated in all the persons: *ta'sewe'tes, ta'sewe'tesk, ta'sewe'tew*? "what will be my, you (s.), his rank?"

tapuiska'qawe'tes, tesk jel newt, tew jel ta'pu, "I will be the 20th, you the 21st, he the 22nd," etc.

All the ordinal adjectives can become verbs, by changing the ending *-ey* (diphthong) to *-eyi*; *amskwesewey* or *tmkewey*, "first," *amskweseweyi, -weyin, -weyit,* "I am, you are, he is the first" (to have arrived); *tmkeweyi,* "I am in first place"; this difference of meaning, given by Rand (M.-E. Dict. p. XX), is not absolute; it adds *e'tasewey* to mark rank; but this word means "each, each one." These verbs are not conjugated exactly like *welei*; the third persons become *-weyit, -weyijik, -weyiultijik*; they answer *ta'seweyi? -weyin? -weyit? -weyijik? -weyiultijik?* "what rank?"

III. Combinations

In addition to the principal forms in the table, there are many others, according to the objects to which the numbers refer, as well as combinations with adjectives and verbs.

1. For long and round objects, such as bottles, glasses, barrels, blocks of wood, candles, corn cobs, even for persons and for the word *tepknuset*, "month," which signifies moon (when one wishes to dwell on the length of lunation, a whole moon, a series of its phases) one says, in the animate gender, *newtoqsit, tapuoqsijik, nesoqsijik, nanoqsijik,* then *asukom, l'uiknek, ukumuljin, pesqunatek, mtln, te'soqsijik* or *metla'soqsijik*; for the inanimate *newta'q, tapua'ql, nesa'ql, newa'ql, nana'ql, asukom te'sa'ql,* etc.; they answer the question *ta'soqsijik? ta'sa'ql?* "how many of these things?" *newta'q pie'skmin*, "one ear of corn" (E.-M. Dict. 69); *newa'ql wipitl*, "four teeth" (heard in conversation); *asukom te'sa'ql wasoqnmaqnl,* "six candles"; *ne'soqsijik pu'tayk*, "three bottles"; *metla'soqsijik jel ukumuljin muinaq,* "18 big bears." When one speaks of an object of the inanimate gender expressing contents, we use *newtoqtek, tapuoqtekl, nesoqtekl*, "1, 2, 3," etc., as below (p. 186).

2. For round objects: potatoes, balls, apples, almonds, fruit pits, pebbles, sugar-coated pills, also tobacco pouches, one says: *newtapskisit, tapuapskisijik, nesapskisijik, newapskisijik, nanapskisijik,* then *asukom te'sapskisijik,* etc.; *metla'sapskisijik,* and *newtapskek, tapuapskekl, nesapskekl, newapskekl, nanapskekl, asukom te'sapskekl* (also *te'sapskikl*), *metla'sapskekl kun'tal, tomawe'l, te'sapskisijik* (so many of) *tu'aqnk, tapatank* or *tapatatk*. From this comes one of the roots of the name of Causapscal (*kwesawey telapskek*), *kwesapskiaq,* "the point with the pebbled bottom."

3. For money one says *newtaqik* or *newtaik,* "one dollar"; *telakik* means "a flat round piece of such circumference," here "of such worth"; *tapuaikl,*

nesaikl, newaikl, nanaikl, asukom te'saikl, etc.; *metla'saikl* or *newtiskekaikl, tapuiskekaikl, nesiskekaikl, newiskekaikl, naniskekaikl, asukom te'siskekaikl,* etc.; *kaskmtlnaqnaikl, pitui-mtlnaqnaikl*. They answer the question *ta'saikl*? "how many dollars?"

For cent one says *sumalki*, lit. "piece of copper"; but now the English word cent is used, *sent, sentl* or *sensl*; *newte'* (for *newte'jk*) *sent, tapu'kl sentl, ne'siskl, newkl, nankl, asukom te'sikl, newtiska'ql, tapuiska'ql jel na'n*, "25 cents"; for the latter the Old French word *tlantsu* is currently still used; *tapu'kl tlantsu'l* or *tmipias*, "50 cts."; *kisna a'qataik newtaik, kisna elp naniska'ql sentl; ne'siskl tlantsu'l, kisna l'uiknek te'siska'ql sentl jel na'n*, "75 cts."; even *sansu* (little used today), *newtaik*, "one dollar." Ex.: *talawtikl si'st pitui-mtlnaqsnl wen'ju'su'nl, ke'sk newte' latusan te'sa'ql tlantsu telawtikl? Asukom te'siskekaikl jel ta'pu jel a'qataik*; "what is the price of 3,000 apples, if one dozen is worth 25 cents? $62.50." We add, for the memory, *newtapskutik* (*sumalki*), "the great French *sou*, the English penny," *tapuapskutik, nesapskutik, newapskutik, nanapskutik, asukom te'sapskutik*, etc.; *nesiska'qutik*, "the thirty pieces" (of Judas); *tapuiska'qutik*, "the twenty" (of Joseph).

4. With *na'kwek*, "day," one forms *newtukuna'q*, "one day"; *tapukuna'q, nesukuna'q, nanukuna'q, asukom, l'uiknek, ukumuljin, pesqunatek te'sukuna'q, metla'sukuna'q kisna newtiskeukuna'q, tapuiskeukuna'q*, etc.: *tapuiskeukuna'qek jel nanukuna'qek si'ko'ku's wtitan*, "it was 25 days since the month of spring (March) had begun"; *titat*, "new moon, beginning of the month." With a noun of the animate gender, and with the word *tepknuset*, "month," the number signifies the age or the day of the month: *newtukunit*, "this is the first of the month"; *tapukunit, nesukunit, neukunit, nanukunit, asukom te'sukunit*, etc.; *metla'sukunit, tapuiskeukunit, nesiskeukunit, newiskeukunit, naniskeukunit, asukom te'siskeukunit, kaskmtlnaqnukunit*, if one wanted to count as far as that; but there is also the combination of months and years. *Ta'sukunit? ta'sukuna'q?* "how many days?" Likewise for the night: *Ta'sitpa'q* or *ta'sikl tepkikl?* "how many nights?" *newtitpa'q, tapuitpa'q*, "one night, two nights," etc. I know of no form for the animate gender. The days of the week, *aqntieuti*, are: *aqntie'wimk* or *kekntie'wimk*, "Sunday"; *amskwes elukutimkl*, "Monday" (first day of work); *ta'puowey, si'stewey, ne'wowey, elukutimkl*, "Tuesday, Wednesday, Thursday"; *kweltamultimk*, "Friday" (day of penitence); *kespitek* or *ketu'-aqntie'wimk*, "Saturday." *Newtikiskik*, "a whole day"; *te'sikiskik*, "each day."

5. Years, months, etc.: *ta'sipunqik* or *ta'sikl newtipunqikl?* "how many years?" *Ta'sipuna'n?* "how old are you?, how many years do you count?" *newtipunqik, newtipuna'y; tapuipunqik, tapuipuna'y; nesipunqik, nesipuna'y; newipunqik, newipuna'y; nanipunqik, nanipuna'y; asukom te'sipunqik, te'sipuna'y, -na'n, -na't, -na'ykw, -no'lti'kw; metla'sipunqik, metla'sipuna'y; tapuiskekipunqik, tapuiskekipuna'y*, etc.

Month, *tepknuset*, is expressed in composition by *uiku's*: *ta'suiku's? te'suiku's*, "how many months? so many months"; one can always say: *ta'sijik, te'sijik tepknusejik*. *Te'sukusa'lay, -lan, -lat*, "to spend so many months"; *newtukusa'lay, tapukusa'lay, nesukusa'lay, neukusa'lay, nanukusa'lay, asukom te'sukusa'lay, metla'sukusa'lay*, etc.: *pesqunatek te'sukusa'lasip*, "you passed nine months" (in the womb of your mother); *nesiskekipuna'nek sikntasi'sip aqq newiskeukuna'qek kweltami'sip*, "at 30 years you were baptised and you fasted 40 days" (Hier. 1. 14).

Hour, *ajiet*, lit. "it (the sun) advances": *ta's ajiet?* "what time is it? to how many degrees has it advanced?" *newt ajiet, ta'pu, si'st*, etc.; *mu ta mtln te's ajiewk jel ta'pu newtikiskik?* "are there not twelve hours in a day?" (John 11, 9); one says likewise *newtiska'q ajiet jel a'qataik*, "ten hours and a half"; *jel kal* or *newtiska'ql apje'jkl* or *minitl jel na'n*, "and a quarter or fifteen minutes"; one hears *kamlamimkl*, "respirations, breaths," said for the latter, but this is better used for seconds." *Ajiet* is of the animate gender, but to say "how many hours, so many hours," it is put in the inanimate plural: *ta'sikl, te'sikl ajiejl* or *ajietl*.

6. Classes, groups, pairs, families, types of things: *ta'sunemi'k? -mi'kl? -mi'ksit? -mi'ksi'kw? -mi'ksiyek? -mi'ksiyoq? -mi'ksijik? te'sunemi'k*, etc., "how many? so many"; *newtunemi'ksijik, tapun-, nesun-, newn-, nanun-, asukom te'sunemi'ksijik, metla'sunemi'ksijik*; *kjiwksuk* (pl.), "one family"; *nkutunemi'ksuk*, "one single family of that sort." *Newtikit*, "a single progeny, an only son"; *newtupistay, -tan, -tat*, "my, your, his only (son)," and by extension, "privileged one, cherished one"; *newtupistan Isa'k ta'n kesalt*, "your only Isaac, so dear" (Gen. 22, 2); *newtupistalijl wkwijl*, "the only son of his mother" (Luke 5, 7, 12). *Newtewistoq*, "he speaks alone, soliloquy"; *tapuewistoqq* or *tapuewistu'tij*, "dialogue"; *newtukwa'lukwet*, "to be alone, a bachelor." *Jikalukum, -kumn, -kuk*, "to go alone in one's boat"; *tapukumu'kw, -mek, -moq, -mi'tij*, "to go as two"; *nesu-, neu-, nanu-, asukom te'sukumu'kw, metla'sukumu'kw*, "to go 3, 4, 5, 6, 10 in a boat"; *tapuleyikw, nesuleyikw*, etc., "we are in two, three boats." *I'-nkuj* or *ankuj* means "one by one": *i'nkuj majita'q* or *i'-nkutukweta'q*, "to go one by one, in a line, single file"; *i'-tapusi'kw*, "two by two, two abreast, in couples"; *i'-nesi'kw, i'-newi'kw*, "3 by 3, 4 by 4," etc.; *i'-newijik*, "they are four abreast," used by Rand for pairs, concerning the animals of Noah's ark: *i'-tapusitaqq, l'uiknek i'-te'sitaqq*, "they will be two or seven pairs" (Gen. 7, 3). "For the multiplication of the loaves, Jesus made people sit by groups of 100 and 50": *i'-tepkisi semita'tij i'-kaskmtlnaqnijik aqq i'-naniskeksijik* (Mark 6 and 8). *Wli-Nkuti-Ne'susuti*, "the Holy Trinity"; *nkutiskeksuti*, "a group of ten"; *tapuiskeksuti*, "a score"; *asukom te'siskeksuti*, "a group of sixty." *Newte'k, -te't, -tajl*, "to kill one (in fishing or hunting) by striking, knocking senseless"; *tapute'kik, nesute'kik, neute'kik, nanute'kik, asukom te'sute'kik, -te'jik, -ta'ji*, "2, 3, 4, 5, 6";

when they are taken otherwise, one uses *ketank, ketant, ketanajl*: *newtank, taputanjik, nesutanaji*, "I take one, you take two, he takes three."

7. Dimensions, weights and measures: *tal'pita'q? tal'pitoqsit? tal'-pesuk? tali-amasek?* "of what length? to what distance?" Several words which correspond to them are or seem to be invariable, and the numbers take a *-k*, which is perhaps euphonic, or else an attempt at a singular in words which always express the plural, except for *newt*; whatever the case, here they are: *ta'puk, ne'sisk, ne'wk, na'nk, asukom* (etc.) *te'sik*, "2, 3, 4, 5, 6"; to these numbers are added: *mtijin*, "thumb" [i.e. inch]; *mpitn*, "hand, palm"; *muskunikn*, "cubit"; *empie* (French word), "foot"; *atleka'timk*, "pace, step": *ne'w atleka'timk weja'tekemk ka'qnek*, "four paces from the door" (Amer. 1. 122); *lape'lis*, "yard," of the anim. gender, (pl.) *lape'lisk*; *mail*, "mile," English noun, of universal usage today; *mil, milal* was tried, but is not used; 1760 *te'sijik lape'lisk*, counts the number of yards, 1623 meters; *we'kwaptmik*, "league," lit. "as far as the eye can see"; *ne'sisk mail*, 5280 *te'sijik lape'lisk*. *Nemiaji jujija assma we'kwaptmik; elkusualaji mi'soqo piskwa'q sapteskuaji*, "he sees reptiles as far as the eye can see, he climbs over them until he has leapt over them" (ibid. 104). *Ta'sunasik?* "what depth?" *newtunasik, tapunasik, nesunasik, neunasik, nanunasik, asukom te'sunasik*, "one fathom or span of the arms, 2, 3, 4, 5, 6"; one fathom, equivalent to two yards.

Tali-ksukk? -ksulk? "how heavy?" *n'katikn*, "pound," added to each number; *tuaqjikn*, "ounce"; *mawnmek*, "whole"; *pukwey*, "half"; *a'qataik*, "half," also *tmi-* or *tm-* with certain words: *tmipias*, "half-dollar"; *tmia*, "half pint"; *tmpuessu*, "half bushel" (Fr. *demi-piastre, demiard, demi boisseau*); *amuiw*, "almost"; *na'tami*, "nearly"; *kal*, "a fourth"; *kaltie*, "one quarter" (Fr. *quartier*). For one fourth, one third, what is divided into three, four, is multiplied by one, two, three parts: *newtunmi'k, tapunmi'k, nesunmi'k – nesunmi'katmk, neunmi'katmk* (anim. gen.) *ne'su, neunmi'kaluj; matawiaq newtipunqik*, "a whole year"; *matawiejik sunmink*, "a whole rosary"; said all at one go. "Twofold, threefold," etc., "a hundred times," *ta'pu, si'st, kaskmtlnaqn eli atelk*.

Talki'k? talkilk? ta'soqsit? ta'sa'q? "how big, what capacity?" *malike'w, -ke'wk*, "quarter, barrel"; *malike'wji'j, -ji'jk*, "barrel"; *puessu, -ssuaq*, "bushel"; *n'kalaw, -laq*, "gallon"; *pu'tay, -tayk*, "bottle"; *suppin, -pink*, "cup," [Fr. *chopine* = pint], a little less than a litre; the numbers are placed before these words: *newtoqsit, tapuoqsit*, etc., for *n'kalaw newte'jit*; for *mun'ti, -ti'l*, "bag," (sack); *newtoqtek, tapuoqtekl*, etc.; *kataq nesoqtekl mun'ti'l, katu mu kejitummik ta'n teli-ksukk*, "we had three sacks of eels, but the weight was unknown" (letter).

LESSON THIRTY

PRONOUNS AND ADJECTIVES (DETERMINATIVES)

I. Personal Pronouns

The personal pronouns are: for the first person *ni'n*, "I, me"; *kinu* or *ninen*; for the second, *ki'l*, "you, to you"; *kilew* or *kilow* (very short), "you"; for the third, *nekm*, "he, she, him, that"; *nekmow*, "they."

Remarks: 1. *Nekm* is the only one which is also used for the inanimate gender: *etuk na ki'k? na pa nekm*, "is that your house? Indeed it is."

2. In Mi'kmaw *ki'l*, "you (s.)," is always used for the second person singular, never *kilew*, "you (pl.)." One should not be astonished, therefore, if those who know a little French address us by *tu* or *toi*; it is in the genius of their language. They change when practice leads them to think in our language.

3. There is a great difference between *kinu* and *ninen*, "we." The first is used when speaking to one or several persons included in the reference; this is the first person inclusive (you and I); the second, when those to whom one is speaking are not included in the reference; this is the first person exclusive (he or they and I, not you).

M. Maillard wrote (Gram. Ma. p. 37): *kinu* is used, when speaking only to each other, without addressing anyone in particular; *ninen* is used for addressing a person distinguished from those who are speaking by themselves, or by one who does it in the name of all. This is not terribly clear; but the examples are.

Thus, in speaking to the Whites, the Indians would say: *ninen elnuiyek* or *mi'kmawiek*, "we Indians or Mi'kmaq"; in speaking among themselves: *kinu elnui'kw*. It can be seen that the verb changes; it is the same for the noun which expresses possession, even when the pronoun is understood: in speaking of God they say: *Kujjinu wa'so'q epit*, "our Father (of all) who is in heaven"; in addressing him in prayer, they say (thereby excluding Him): *Nujjinen wa'so'q epin*, "our Father who art in heaven." Likewise, in speaking of the priest among themselves, they say *kujjinu pa'tlia's*; to him, *nujjinen*. Here are some other examples where the pronoun is expressed; they are almost all from Maillard; *kinu na pekwatu'kw*, "it is us who are the cause of it"; *ninen elnuiyek mu kilew wen'juiyoq teli-ntawi-ntupliwek*, "we Indians do not know how to make war the way you French do"; *ninen wen me'wlo'nuk nassamuloqtew*, "one of us will go to see you this evening"; here the rule is not applied, because it is *wen* which is the subject and not *ninen*; with the latter expressed or understood one would have *nassamulti-snen*, "we will go to see you." It is necessary, similarly, to take account of it, when they are the object, expressed or understood: *eyk ta'n kinu ankamulkw*, "one of them is looking at us"; *sapo'nuk nmi'tesnen*, "you (s.) will see us tomorrow." These pronouns are only rarely utilized, for emphasis; they are included in the forms of the verb, as subject or as object; this is what makes the conjugations so extensive; even when expressing and using a pronoun, just as with a noun, you are still required to give the verbs their proper forms.

4. *Ni'n* or *ni'newi* also means, "it is me"; likewise *ki'l*, *ki'lewin*; *nekm*, *nekmewit*. *Ni'n ntinin*, "my self," *ki'l ktinin*, *nekm wtinin*, *kinu ktininenu*, *ninen ntininen*, *kilew ktininewow*, *nekmow wtininewow*; *ntinin* often means "my body, my person"; to effectively express in Mi'kmaw the words of consecration, "This is my body," we have to say: *Ula ntinin*.

II. Demonstrative Pronouns

These pronouns, which are also adjectives, as well as adverbs of place and of time, are as follows:

1. *U't*, *ula*, *net*, *na*, – "this one, that one"; as adjectives, "this, that"; they are also adverbs of place, "here"; *tett* is ordinarily added to them: *ula tett*, "in this very place"; *net ula*, "here it is, behold"; *netna*, "that's it, all right." *U't* designates a person or a thing which is before the eyes, which can be pointed at; *ula* is more distant; but neither one can be added to nouns in the past. *U't* seems to pertain to the first person, *ula* to the second and *ala* to a more distant third.

2. *A't? ala*, also *na*, *na't*, – "that one, that, that person or thing." Rand here gives *a't*; it would seem to correspond well to *u't*, but I have never heard it; he gives as an example: *koqoey a't* (28, 1); now one certainly says quite

clearly: *koqoey na't?* "what is that?" then he adds *ta'n*; but the latter is not demonstrative; it means: "that which."

3. *Wat* (pl. of *u't*), *weket, wekla, neket* (pl. of *net*), *nekla*, – "these things or persons." *Wat, weket, neket* are only adjectives.

4. *Wala, waqat, waqla, nala, naqat, naqla*, – "those things or persons." Rand adds, or rather spells these three words thus: *ekula, wekula, nekula* (E.-M. Dict. 364). M. Maillard gives *ula* for "this one," *na* for "that one"; then *wekla* for "these," *nekla* for "those" (Gr. Ma. 42); and he notes that these two words are used for the singular in the past. In other words this list is not very precise. See the examples.

We should add that *na* is often used only to attract attention, as the expression *c'est* in French: *na nekm*, "that's him"; *ni'n na*, "it's me, myself." *Net* more or less corresponds to the French particles *ci, là* (Rem. Gr. 161): *Net telawtik*, "that is the price, this price, that price."

Interrogative *na?* means: "isn't that so?" *na tlisip*, "then"; *nekla tlisip*, "at that time." *Na* becomes *na't* before *wen* and *koqoey*, to mean "someone or something," but then it is more demonstrative. All these words are invariable in their class.

Other Examples: *ula pataluti, na tmi'kn*, "this table, that axe," or else, "this is the table, that is the axe"; *wala kwitnl, nala pleku'l*, "these canoes, those nails"; *wekla tapu'kl newte'jk kelu'lk, ktik mu nkutey*, "of those two things, one is good, the other not"; *wala tapu'kl wi'katiknl newte'jk ta'n pejili-wl-wi'kasik*, "of these two books one is much better written"; *waqla tapusijik wen pejili-mnaqnat?* "which of those two is the weaker?"

Nekla tepkatisoqq ktla'taqatinew aqq wekla mu kpiplite'tmnew, "you should have done those things and not neglected these" (Matt. 23, 23). *Wekla kisatalulti'titek mui'wala'tisnl Kisu'lkwl*, "these, after their meal, gave thanks to God." *Nekla e'pitkik mu welmi-tu'tiwksi-pnik*, "those women did not behave well." *Sa'q keji'kaq nekla wenujaq*, "I have known that Frenchman for a long time." *Wekla l'nuaq talimi-ski-snaq*, "what did this man tell you?"

There is in these phrases a manner of speaking peculiar to the Mi'kmaq; to say: "this thing is better than that," they will say: *na kelu'lk, katu ktik mu kelu'ltnukw*, or *mu nkutey*, lit. "this thing is good, but the other is not," or else, "the other is not the same"; "all these people go faster than we," that is to say, "all these go fast and we don't," *waqla msɨt kesikawita'jik, kinu moqwa*; "we go more slowly than they," *ninen qaskew pemita'yek, nekmow moqwa*, "we go slowly and they don't."

III. Relative, Interrogative and Indefinite Pronouns

These pronouns, which are also adjectives, are the following:

I. *Ta'n*, "who, which, what, of which," is in Mi'kmaw the only **relative** or **conjunctive** pronoun. It is used in all genders and all persons, except in the third plural, *ta'nik, ta'nl*; in the past, *ta'naq, ta'nek, ta'nkik, ta'nkl*; in the obviative, *ta'nl, tani*. The following verb is put in the person of the antecedent, when the relative is subject of its clause.

Ta'n also means, with or without the corresponding demonstrative, "that which, of which, those things of which, which, of whom, that of which things"; also "where, from where," in the sense of: "in, toward which, from which," etc. Moreover, this little word, which recurs so often in the language, is also an adverb of time and of place.

Examples: *ta'n kiwnaqaj pewatk wsitan*, "he who seriously wishes to be saved"; *ta'naq nekla kji-pa'tlia'sewitaq*, "he who in that time was a great priest"; *ta'nik sikntasultijik naqla telui'tujik alasutmewinu'k*, "those who are baptised are called Christians"; *sik pa westa'tisni'k ta'nkik Naweyo'q wtulk teppultisni'k*, "only those who were aboard Noah's ark were saved" (Gr. Ma. 57).

Ni'n eta ta'n elkomiktuimkiss, "it is I who was invited"; *ki'l ta'n alsumkusin aqq nekm ta'n alsusit*, "it is you who obey and he who commands"; *kinu ta'n mimajulti'kw* (1 Thess. 4, 15), *ninen ta'n mimajultiyek* (2 Cor. 4, 11); "we who live"; *kilew ta'n jipaloq Kji-saqmaw likasultikw wtinin*, "you who fear the Lord put your confidence in him" (Ps. 113, 18); *te'sit kilew ta'n jipalajl ta'nl kisi'pnl wle'tew*, "each one of you who fears him by whom he has been created will be happy"; *na ula ji'nm ta'n weskumsipnl aijl*, "this is (here is) the man of whom so-and-so spoke"; *u't ta'n nemioq mu na nekm ta'naq ni'n nemi'kipnaq kti-ki-wlaku*, "he whom you see is not he whom I saw the day before yesterday."

Ta'n telita'si'sip, ta'nl e'sipnl, "that which you thought, the things that you said"; *klapis kisitu'sipnek ta'nek metue'kek*, "you however made that which was difficult"; *ta'n wape'k*, "that which is white," or "who is white"; "the white race," *wape'kl, wape'kik, wapo'ltijik*; *ki'l ta'n wapein mu kpnoqite'lmaw kikmaj ta'n l'nuit*, "you who are white do not scorn your neighbour, who is Indian" (by race or by nation); *ta'nik wapo'ltijik telui'tusijik jijuaqa pepsite'lma'tiji ta'ni l'nuultiliji, kisna etuk sa'q kisna tami se'k ta'nkik wapo'ltitkik penoqite'lma'tisnika ta'nkika l'nuultilitka*, "sometimes those who are called whites scorn those who are Indian, or perhaps in the past or elsewhere they have done it. The Mi'kmaq have their way of paying them back, by not calling them whites among themselves, nor palefaces, as the other Indians do, but white flesh," *wape'k wa'qey*; those who wish to be polite give the whites the name of each nation, French, English, Irish, Italians, and they prefer that the same be done with respect to them, calling them Mi'kmaq rather than Indians.

Eliey ta'n wejien, "I am going where you've come from, to the place where ..."; *piskwa'n wen'ji'kuomk ta'n weji-tuiey*, "you are entering the house which I am leaving"; *welaptm ta'n tetlaqatmn*, "I like the place where you live." It should be noted that very often, as here, nouns are replaced by *ta'n* with the verb: *ta'n teluisi, -sin, -sit*, "my, your (s.), his name," lit. "that which I, you, he is called"; *ta'ni ketanji, kesalji*, "his enemies, his friends"; *ta'n ewjit, wekwijit, wekwisit, wetusit, wenijanit ktinin*, "your son, daughter, your father, your mother," lit. "he, she who has you for father, mother, son, daughter, child."

When we say that *ta'n* is used for the singular and the two first persons of the plural, this is just like our French expressions: *c'est nous, c'est vous, ce sont eux*.

II. The interrogative pronouns and adjectives are:

Wen, wenik, wenaq, wenkik, wenl, weni, "who, what, of whom, of which, of what": *wen ta nemi't?* "who sees me?"; *ta* is an interrogative particle, like *ne* in Latin, and which is also put after a word; *wenaq tmk nutantekesnaq?* "who was the first murderer?" *Kaino'q eta*, "that was Cain"; *wenik mntua'kik l'ita'taqq?* "who or what are those who will go to hell?" *ta'nik ki'kat-lue'ultijik*, "those who persist in committing sins"; *wenkik tmk kisu'snik?* "who were the first created?" *Atao'q eta aqq tapusi'tisna E'po'q teluisisnaq*, "Adam and his wife named Eve." *Wen* is only used for the animate gender: *wenl, weni* are the obviative forms.

Koqoey, koqoe'l, koqoeyek, koqoeyekl, "what, which thing, which things?" *Koqoey* means "thing"; *na't koqoey*, "that thing"; *winjikl koqoe'l*, "bad things"; but used alone it serves as the interrogative pronoun: *koqoey ta na? koqoe'l wekla?* "what is that? what are these things?" *Koqoey wjit?* "why? because of what?" *na wjit*, "that is why, it is because of that." The word *wjit* before or after a noun or a pronoun means "because of, for the sake of, in consideration of": *ki'l wjit* or *wjit ki'l*, "for you, because of you, in your consideration"; *kinu wjit l'nuulti'kw Sesukuli weji-klujjiewto'ss*, "it is for us that Jesus Christ was crucified"; before the verb *wjit* returns to its adverbial form *weji*; here we have both, which is in this case not at all a pleonasm; *ni'n ta wjit ketui-wi'kupalijik waqla?* "is it for my sake that you want to give a feast to those people?" (Gr. Ma. 62); *Na wjit*, "it is for that reason"; *kejitu kesalin, na wjit ksalultes*, or better *na wji*, with contraction for the future, "I know that you love me, that is why I will love you"; *eulite 'lmi 'p eule 'jianek, na wjit matew awanite 'lmulu*, "you had pity on me in my misery, that is why I will never forget you."

Teken? tekenl? tekenik? tekeni? "what, who, whom, which?" *Teken me' kisikuit?* "which (of the divine persons) is the oldest?" *Teken awti na 'te 'l eltek?* "which is the road which leads there?" *Tekenik tapusijik kisna tekenl tapu 'kl?* "which of the two (persons or things)?"

III. The indefinite pronouns and adjectives are:

Wen, ta 'n wen, na 't wen, "someone, a certain, such"; *na 't wenik,* "some of them, some"; *ta 'n pa wen,* "whoever, anyone who, no matter who"; *na 't wen elelmit kweltamultimk ta 'n aqntie 'wimk atkitemitew,* "laugh on Friday, cry on Sunday"; *ta 'n pasik tapusijik,* "one or the other." "One or someone from among us, you, them," *kinu wen,* or *ninen, kilew, nekmow;* also, *newkte 'jit.*

I '-nkuj or *ankuj,* "one of, a part of, someone, certain ones"; *te 'sit, te 'sit wen,* "each one"; *i '-nkuji,* "in his turn, one by one, one after another"; *ankuj pekisitoq,* "each one brings in his turn, one by one" (Acts. 52); *ankuj majita 'q,* "leave one by one"; *ankuj eymu 'tijik,* "there are so many of them, so many"; *koqoey ne 'patu 'n?* "have you killed something?" *e 'e me' ankuj,* "yes some, a scattered one"; *ankujiw eykik e 'pijik mu l 'nim kisi-ptikima 'tikwi wnijanua,* "there are some women who are hardly able to correct their children" (Jo. II, 94); *newte 'jit kilew apkwa 'litew,* "one of you will betray me"; *poqji-i '-nkuji-klula 'tijl: Nsaqmam, ni 'n ta net?* "they began to say one after another: Lord, is it me?" *ta 'n tetpi-li-nsqatiyekl eptaqniktuk,* "it is he who carries his hand to the plate with me" (Matt. 26).

E 'tas, e 'tas wen, "each one, each one in his turn"; can govern the plural: *e 'tas wen ika 'taqutijik,* "each one cultivates"; *e 'tasit, e 'tasik,* "next one"; *e 'tasewey na 'kwek,* "each day" (of the week); *mu e 'tasiw wen kisi-nmiaqwl,* "it is not just anyone at all who can see him" (Amer. I. 120); *e 'tasaq,* "each one" (in the past); *e 'tekatiyoq,* "you follow one after another"; *e 'tasua 'ti 'kw,* "walk two by two."

There is no special word for an indefinite subject: it is expressed by the infinitives of verbs, which are conjugated impersonally in all moods and in all tenses: *emk* or *teluemk,* "one says"; *tlimiten,* "one will tell me, I shall be told."

Kitk (invariant), "both, both kinds"; *alt ... alt,* "one ... the other, some ... others"; also *alt* or *na 't wenik,* "some people"; *na 't wen ... toqu ktik, na 't wenik ... toqu ktikik,* "someone ... then another, some ... then others"; *wijey, piluey,* "the same, another"; one can add *wen: wijey, piluey wen; wije 'k, pilue 'k wenik.*

Msit, "all"; *msit wen*, "each and every one"; *msit wenik*, "all"; *msit ta'nik* and *msit ta'nik wenik*, "all those who"; *na msit* or *na na msit*, "that is all, that is finished, the end"; *msit wenik telimijik*: *Nsaqmam, Nsaqmam, ma' na wji-piskweta'qwik wa'so'q ta'n tetli-eleke'wa'kik*, "all those who say to me: Lord, Lord, will not just because of that enter into the kingdom of heaven"; *wen nala tela'sit mu kisi-maja'lat iapjiw*, "one who acts thus can never be shaken," lit., "one can not shake him."

Ma'wen, "no one, not one"; formed from *mu, ma'*, "not at all, not, no," and *wen*, "someone"; *moqwe'j, moqwa'j*, or *moqwe, moqwa*, "no, nothing"; formed likewise from *mu*, "not," and from *koqoey*, "something"; today it is used simply for "no, not"; and for "nothing" one says *moqwa koqoey, moqwa koqoe'nuk*, "there is nothing"; one also says *se'kewey*, "it's nothing, a trifle"; *wenik*, "there is someone"; *moqwa weninuk*, "there is no one"; *moqwa weniwk*, "he is a man of no account, a nonentity."

LESSON THIRTY ONE

POSSESSION

In Mi'kmaw there are no **possessive** pronouns or adjectives, properly speaking. Possession is expressed thus:

First Rule. "Mine, yours, his," etc. are expressed by the personal pronouns, to which are added the endings *-ewey, -owey, -uwey*, in the plural *-ewe'k, -owe'k, -uwe'k, -ewe'l, -owe'l, -uwe'l*; in the past *-aq, -aqik, -ek, -ekl* are added to *-ey*. Thus *ni'newey, ki'lewey, nekmewey*, "mine, yours, his"; *kinuowey, ninenewey, kilewowey, nekmowewey*, "ours, yours, theirs"; *ni'newe'k, ni'newe'l*, "mine," etc., as for the other adjectives. "To belong to someone" is expressed by changing *-ey* to *-eyi, -eyin, -eyit, -e'k*: *ni'neweyin*, "you belong to me," *ki'leweyi*, "I belong to you," *nekmewe'jik*, "they belong to him," *nekmoweyit*, "he belongs to them," *nineneweyultioq*, "you all belong to us."

Second Rule. "My, your, his," etc. are expressed by the name of the person or thing possessed, before which one puts the first letter of the pronouns *ni'n, ki'l, ula, kinu, ninen, kilew, wekla*, with an ending more or less in agreement with these pronouns.

In the singular, the ending of the word is left as it is, or else *m* is added to it with or without modification of the final vowel or diphthong. In the first two persons of the plural, the endings of the corresponding pronouns are used; in the third it is that of *nekmow*, although the initial is that of *wekla*; but in the animate gender the third person of the singular and plural takes the obviative form in *l* and *a*, because this word is in the position of object to another noun or pronoun also in the third person; the other persons also use these endings, when they are in the same case, but this happens more rarely.

When the noun begins with a vowel or syllabic sound, a euphonic *t* is placed between the initial letter and this vowel; ex.: *l'ue'wuti*, "sin," *ntl'ue'wuti*, "my sin"; *ika'taqn*, "field," *ntika'taqnm*, "my field"; *ansale'wit*, "angel," *ktansale'm*, "your angel." There is an exception for the nouns in *-u*, in general: *wisun*, "name," *n'uisunm*, "my name" [also *ntuisunm*]; *wa'so'q*, "heaven," *kua'so'qm* [also *ktua'so'qm*], "your heaven"; *wen'ju'sun*, "apple," *nuen'ju'su'nm* [also *ntuen'ju'su'nm*], "my apple"; nevertheless, for *wi'katikn*, *ntui'katikn*, "my book"; for *utan*, "village," there are two: *nutan*, *nutanm*, *nutanji'j*, and *ntutanm* (Leg. p. 21, 376), "my village, my dear little home town." See *ntalikam*, "my property," in the table below.

The words which begin with *n* double it, with or without a schwa between the two, as *Niskam*, "God," *Niniskam*, "my God"; those in *k* do the same in the second person, but without schwa; only a very faint one or else an *i* is introduced before the first *k*; thus *nkij*, "my mother," makes *kkij* (*ikkij* or *ikkij*), "your mother"; in this word and in several others in *ki* or *ka*, in the third person, which begins with *w*, another *w* is added after the *k*, by assimilation: *wkwijl*, "his mother"; *nkamlamun*, "my heart," *kkamlamun*, "your heart," *wkwamlamun*, "his heart"; *nkat*, *kkat*, *wkwat*, "my, your, his foot." In other third person words, a glottal catch is heard after *w*, as a sort of aspiration; it is not necessary to make it felt much; it is often omitted, especially in those forms which already begin with *w*; then it is sufficient to lengthen this vowel: *wlo'ti*, "good fortune," *nwlo'tim*, *kwlo'tim*, "your good fortune," *wwlo'tim*, "his good fortune," with a small aspiration between the two *w*'s.

There is furthermore a modification in the initial syllable of some other words: *tmi'kn*, "axe," gives *nutmi'kn*, *kutmi'kn*, *wutmi'kn*, from which the English have taken their word "tomahawk"; *tomaqn* or *tmaqn*, "pipe": *nutmaqn*, *kutmaqn*, *wutmaqnn* [obviative]; *nmuksnk*, *kmuksnk*, *wmuksn* [obviative plural], "shoes"; *mkikn*, "fish-hook," *nmikkn*, *kmikkn*, *wmikkn*, etc.

The ending of the obviative singular is ordinarily in *-l*, but it can be in *-al*, *-il*, *-ul*, according to the last vowel of the word; it resembles the plural of nouns of the inanimate gender: *nmis*, "my sister" (older than me), *wmisl*, "his sister"; *nitap*, *witapal*, "my, his comrade"; *nti'*, *wti'l*, "my, his dog"; *ntlu'suk*, *wtlu'sukul*, "my, his son-in-law." In the plural, when this person, the *k* truncated, ends in *m*, there is often a rather surprising combination made in the terminative case: this *m* is doubled, and a euphonic *p* is introduced between the two; ex.: *nnaqapemk*, "my servants, my disciples," *knaqapemk*, *wnaqapem* (obv. pl.), *wnaqapempma*; *nmimajuinu'm'k*, "my people," *kmimajuinu'm'k*, "your people"; *emittukwalaji wmimajuinu'm'pma*, "he visits his people" (Luke 1, 70); *wtansale'mpma*, "his angels"; *wninasunutempma*, "his chosen ones." There is no doubt about this form: besides these written examples, I have often heard it from the mouth of the famous interpreter Polycarpe Martin; however I have never found it in the manuscripts of Fr. Maillard: he always gives, for example, in the pattern of *nnaqapemk*, *wnaqapemka*, "his disciples."

Third Rule. There is a special form for "my," when the person himself is addressed, in the case which we have called vocative. Thus *nujj*, "my father," becomes *nu*, "oh father, dad," a term of familiarity and tenderness, which is not ordinarily used for the priest: one uses *nujj*, or better *nujjinen*, "our father"; *nkij*, "my mother," *kiju'*, "oh mother, mom"; *nkwis*, "my son," *kwi's*, "oh son," *kwi'sji'j*, "dear son"; *ntus*, "my daughter," *tu's, tu'sji'j*; *niskami'* or *nijkami'*, "grandfather"; *nukumi'*, "grandmother." Several do not have this form in the singular and have one in the plural; as *nitaptut*, "my friends, comrades" (you whom I address); *nikmatut*, "my friends, my brothers, my neighbours"; *saqmatut*, "gentlemen." See p. 34.

Remark: There are in Mi'kmaw many words which are only used in the possessive form, principally those which express relationship. Thus there are no words for saying "father, mother, son, daughter"; one says *ewjimk* or *wjimk*, "to have a father, to be a son"; *Ewjit Niskam*, "God who has a father, therefore God the Son"; *wekwisimk*, "to have a son"; *Wekwisit Niskam*, "God who has a son, that is to say, God the Father"; *wekwijimk*, "to have a mother"; *wetusimk*, "to have a daughter"; from that *ntus, ktus, wtusl; nkij, kkij, wkwijl; nkwis, kkwis, wkwisl; nujj, kujj, wujjl*. In the words which exist by themselves, there is often an *m*, as *mjijaqmij*, "soul, a soul"; *mtun*, "mouth"; *mpitn*, "hand."

Models

1. *Saqmaw*, master, lord, chief. Voc. *Saqmaw, Sawmatut*.

nsaqmam, my master.	(past) *nsaqmamaq*.
ksaqmam, your master.	*ksaqmamaq*.
wsaqmaml, his master.	*wsaqmama*.
ksaqmaminu, our master, Our Lord.	*ksaqmaminuaq*.
nsaqmaminen, our master.	*nsaqmaminenaq*.
ksaqmamuow, your master.	*ksaqmamuowaq*.
wsaqmamual, their master.	*wsaqmamuowa*.
nsaqmamk, my masters.	*nsaqmamkik*.
ksaqmamk, your masters.	*ksaqmamkik*.
wsaqmam (mamka, mampma), his masters.	*wsaqmamkika*.
ksaqmaminaq, our masters.	*ksaqmaminaqik*.
nsaqmaminaq, our masters, *nsaqmaminatut*.	*nsaqmaminaqik*.
ksaqmamuaq, your masters.	*ksaqmamuaqik*.
wsaqmamua, muaqa, their masters.	*wsaqmamuaqika*.

2. *Ewjimk*, to have a father: *nu, nujtut, nujjinenatut*.

    nujj, my father.   *nujjaq*.
    kujj, your father.   *kujjaq*.
    wujjl, his father.   *wujja*.
    kujjinu, our father.   *kujjinuaq*.
    nujjinen, our father.   *nujjinenaq*.
    kujjuow, your father.   *kujjuowaq*.
    wujjual, their father.   *wujjuowa*.

    nujjk, (not used), my fathers.   *nujjkik*.
    kujjk, your fathers.   *kujjkik*.
    wujj (*wujjka*), his fathers.   *wujjkika*.
    kujjinaq, our fathers.   *kujjinaqik*.
    nujjinaq, our fathers.   *nujjinaqik*.
    kujjuaq, your fathers.   *kujjuaqik*.
    wujjua (*wujjuaqa*), their fathers.   *wujjuaqika*.

3. (inanimate gender) *Alikaw* or *alikew*, goods, linen.

    ntalikam or *ntalikem*, my possession.   *ntalikamek*.
    ktalikam, your possession.   *ktalikamek*.
    wtalikam, his possession.   *wtalikamek*.
    ktalikaminu, our possession.   *ktalikaminuek*.
    ntalikaminen, our possession.   *ntalikaminenek*.
    ktalikamuow, your possession.   *ktalikamuowek*.
    wtalikamuow, their possession.   *wktalikamuowek*.

    ntalikaml, my possessions, goods.   *ntalikamkl*.
    ktalikaml, your goods.   *ktalikamkl*.
    wtalikaml, his goods.   *wtalikamkl*.
    ktalikaminal, our goods.   *ktalikaminuekl*.
    ntalikaminal, our goods.   *ntalikaminenekl*.
    ktalikamual, your goods.   *ktalikamuowekl*.
    wtalikamual, their goods.   *wtalikamuowekl*.

4. *Wikwom*, hut.

    ni'k, my hut, at my place.   (past) *ni'kek*.
    ki'k, your hut.   *ki'kek*.
    wi'k, his hut.   *wi'kek*.
    kiknu, our hut.   *kiknuek*.
    niknen, our hut.   *niknenek*.
    kikuow, your hut.   *kikuowek*.
    wikuow, their hut.   *wikuowek*.

ni'kl, my huts.   *ni'kikl* or *ni'kkl*.
ki'kl, your huts.   *ki'kikl* or *ki'kkl*.
wi'kl, his huts.   *wi'kikl* or *wi'kkl*.
kiknal, our huts.   *kiknu'kl*.
niknal, our huts.   *niknenkl*.
kikual, your huts.   *kikuowkl*.
wikual, their huts.   *wikuowkl*.

Examples: *ksaqmaminu kinu kisu'lkuss jukwita'q alasumanej*, "Our Lord, who created us, come let us adore him" (7 Pr. 254); "for they should worship him," *Kniskaminal alasuma'tij*; *ksaqpiku'ninal l'i-kuta'tij*, "let our tears run" (259); *kujjuaqik mu nenmi'tikupnikl ntawtikl*, "your fathers did not know my ways" (ib.), or *ntawtikkl*.

Ni'n kujj Wniskaml, Apla'm, Isa'k aqq Sa'kop Wniskamual, "I am the God of your father, the God of Abraham, Isaac and Jacob" (Ex. 37, 6).

Wla'qnml nemitu'tij wsaqmamual minuilitek, "they saw (see) the wounds of their risen Lord"; (then) *nemia'tij Wsaqmamuow-a*, "they see their Lord" (Par. II, 651). *Ankaptmuk npitnl, epmepikay aqq nkatl*, "look at my hands, my side, and my feet"; *epmepikay nasaptmui* (to Thomas), "come see my side"; there are some possessives translated by verbs, such as the following: *epmepikay, -kan, -kat*, "my, your, his side"; *ankwiskay, -kan, -kat*, "my, your, his joint"; *maqatpay, apsatpay, -pan, -pat*, "my, your, his large, small head"; *epmepikaj sa'puss* (S. F. 130), "his side was pierced."

Ni'k, "my house," can also mean, "in my house" [ni'kk]. The *k* [or *q*] of the locative case can, when it is not already there, be added to all the possessives: *kiknu*, "our hut," *kiknaq*, "in our hut"; *ktul*, "your canoe," *ktulk* or *ktuliktuk*, "in your canoe," *ktuluow*, "your (pl.) canoe," *ktuluaq*, "in your canoe"; *wmitki*, "his country," *wmitkik*, "in his country," *wmitkiwaq*, "in their country." *Ntinin*, "myself," *ntinink*, "in me," *ktininenal*, "us," i.e., "our bodies, our persons," *ktininenaq*, "in us."

Wsua'tu aptu'n kpitnk, "take the rod in your hand" (Ex. 17, 5), *wtawtiwaq*, "in their paths"; see the seventh lesson, case (p. 33-4). *Wkutputiwaq*, "on their seats." *Kniskaminaq*, "in Our Lord."

LESSON THIRTY TWO

ADVERBS

Adverbs are added to other words, even to nouns and pronouns, in Mi'kmaw, to modify their meaning and sometimes their spelling. They often serve as roots for a great number of verbs and other words. Some are only used in composition; M. Maillard calls them prepositions; the real name should be adverbial prefixes. They are very numerous; we have seen several in the preceding lessons. There is a long list of them below. We present examples and usage rather than grammatical rules, since they are by themselves invariable. In the following list those which form a complete word will be put first; next will be given examples of words which they form, or with which they combine. If they simply precede words which are already complete, as modifiers, I leave a space between the prefix and the word, and even between prefixes, when there are several of them. In French we would put a hyphen; in Mi'kmaw it will be understood, and there will be no words that are too long, whose analysis is difficult.

Adverbs express manner or quality, quantity, time, place and intention (affirmation, negation, doubt, interrogation).

I. Manner (Quality or Lack)

Awani, awan, prefix meaning "ignorance, forgetfulness": *awank, awanitu*, "I do not know someone or something"; *awan'ta'si* for *awanita'si*, "I forget." [Today *awanita'si* means, "I am a muddled thinker"].

Awiw, awi, "around, in a circle": *awiw pqoqsikn*, "censer."

Aunaqaj, auna, "exception, to the contrary" (see *meluij*).

Amali, "variety": *amalika'taqn*, "flower-bed"; *amaloqwan*, "embroidery"; *amali-ntmkewe'l*, "various songs"; *amalkewaqn*, "dance, prancing."

Ani, ana, "abhorrence": *anate'lmik, -te'tm*, "to hate, to detest someone, something"; *aniamk, aniaptm*, "to look unfavourably upon, to detest, to regret"; *aniapsit*, "he does penance"; *aniapsimk, aniapsimkewey*, "penance" (virtue, sacrament, act of contrition).

Apaji, "mental return" (also adverb of place): *apajiey, -ja'si, -ja'lik, -ja'tu*, "to come back, to bring back"; *apajita'si*, "to change one's mind, to be converted"; *apajipey* or *apijipey*, "to come back to life"; *ma'qeil apijipetal*, "the dead shall be raised"; *apijipemk, apijipewey*, "resurrection."

Apuski, apukji, "disorder": *apuskapukuet*, "he speaks badly, coarsely."

Apkw, "deliverance, (also) treachery," according as the ending is long or short: *apkwa'lik*, "I untie him"; *apkwalk*, "I surrender him"; *apkwalaten*, "he will be betrayed": *apkwa'l'timkewey*, "absolution," from the reciprocal form, *apkwa'l'ti'kw*.

Asite, "reply, permission": *asite'tmulk*, "you are allowed to"; *asiteklusit, asitapukuet*, "he answers"; *asitemtimkewey*, "response," from *asitemti'kw*.

Euli, "misery, pity": *eule'ji*, "to be poor"; *eulite'tekey*, "to be merciful"; *euley*, "to lie"; *euleyaq*, "to treat badly."

Eunasi, "mental disorder" (Pub. Gr. 92), *eunasiet*, "non compos mentis, troubled"; *eunasita'si*, "I think I am mentally disturbed"; *eunasite'lmik*, "I think he is."

Eskwi, "left over, remaining": *eskwiey, eskwiaq*, "to be left," etc.; *eskwi-pa'qapukuey*, "to make an incomplete confession, fail to mention sins."

Ejeli, "impotence": *ejelei, ejelo'ltijik*, "to be feeble, unable"; *ejeleyaq, ejelo'tm*, "to be incapable of helping someone or something, or to harm them"; *pewatm mntu ntejeleyakun*, "I want the devil to have no hold on me."

I' (long) at the beginning of words indicates state, habit, frequency: *teluet*, "he says," *i'-tluet*, "he often says, he repeats, he has the habit of saying"; this *i'* is quite different from the one which is found in certain words beginning with *a*, with which it forms a diphthong: *iali, iapjiw, iamuj* (see below). Here we see them both: *i'-al'kwiluk Ksaqmaminu ke'sk i'-we'juj* (7 Pr. 93), "seek the Lord while he may be found"; *ke'sk wejuowa'sij l'i-mselmuk*, "invoke him while he is near."

Wantaqi, "tranquillity": *wantaqei*, "I am peaceful"; *wantaqeye'n, wantaqo'ltikw*, "keep quiet (s., pl.)"; *wantaqi skipe'si*, "wait quietly, patiently."

Wa'qaj, "hardly, almost impossible" (see quantity).

Weli, "well"; *welei*, "I am well, happy"; *weli-pmiey*, "I move, walk well."

Wenmaji, "painful movement"; *wenmajei, wenmajo'ltijik*, "I, they suffer."

Wetmi, "occupation": *wetmei, wetmo'tm, wetmiaq*, "to be busy, to be occupied with something, someone, to disturb"; *wetmite'tm*, "to desire."

Weji, "point of departure, from where, whence": *tami wejiaq?* "whence comes it, how come?" *koqoey weji-tlo'ltiyoq?* "why are you behaving like this?"

Wi'kui, "selfishness, lack of consideration for others": *wi'kue'k*, "that's strange," from *wi'kuei*, "I couldn't care less."

Wikwi, "extinction," from *wikwiey*, "to die"; *wikwia'tiyek*, "at the hour of our death."

Wini, "bad, wicked, dirty": *winiey*, "to be corrupted"; *winiaq*, "it is wicked": *teli nati'tij elue'wultijik ansma pa winiaq*, "the death of sinners is truly evil"; *ketkio'ti*, "drunkenness"; *wini-ktikio'ti*, "disgusting drunkenness."

Wisqwi, "surprisingly" (see *wisqew, wisqi* -- time).

Wiji, "with": *wije'ul*, "I'm going with you"; *wiji-tkweyuloq*, "I am with you"; *witlukuti'kw*, "work together"; *wiji-tkweiwajl wkwijl*, "he stays with his mother"; *witpitaq*, "I am seated with someone"; *mu witpituaqik keluskapeultijik aqq mu wije'waqik ta'nik kespukwa'taqatijik*, "I do not sit with liars and I do not associate with those who are dishonest" (Ps. 25, 4).

Kepmi, prefix meaning "honour, respect"; *kepmi-mui'walkusij*, "let him be respectfully thanked" (in good measure); *kepmite'lmulek*, "we honour you"; *welimulek*, "we bless you."

Kesi, ksi, "very much," indicates the superlative: *kesi-ksaluet*, "he is very loving"; *kesinukwat*, "he is sick," even *kesi-ksinukwat*, "he is very sick"; *kesei, keseyaq*, "to be careful"; *kesiey*, "to be honoured": *msit wskitqamu'k kesieyek* (Par. II, 500).

Kesmi, "to push on, progress" (see adv. of place).

Ketui, "to precede, to wish": *ketui-liey*, "I want to go"; *ketui-piskiaq*, "it will be dark, before dark"; *ketuksi*, "to want to, need to sleep."

Keji, kji, "great, very" (see quantity).

Kia'skiw, "exactly": *kia'skiwowey*, "exactitude."

Kiwnaqaj, kiwnaqa, "especially, principally": *knpim kiwnaqaj puna'tu*, "above all, give up your drinking."

Ki'kajiw, ki'kaji, ki'kat, "in resisting, in spite of all, with all one's might"; *ki'katlue'wultijik*, "obstinate sinners" (Gr. Ma. 56); *ki'katmitoq*, "insubordinate conduct."

Kimi, "secretely": *kimu'tuk*, or *kimtuk*, "in secret"; *kimi-pqa'luet*, "he bites secretly"; *kimewistu*, "to speak in a whisper."

Kisi, "to be able, after" (see time): *kisitu, kisita'si*, "I make up my mind."

Koqqwaji or *kiqqwaji*, "correctly": *kiqqwajiw, kiqqwajiey, kiqqwajiaq*.

Maqaj, "severely, hard" (P. Met.).

Matawi, "to join up": *matawe'k*, "confluent"; *matawiejik sunmink*, "the whole rosary"; *matawiaq newtipunqik*, "the whole year, the whole year round."

Meluij, "rather"; contrary to *auna*.

Melki, "strongly": *melkei*, "to be hard"; *melki-ketlamsitm*, "to believe strongly."

Menaqaj, menaqa, "with care."

Me'si (long e), "to be unable": *me'si'wen*, "you are unshakable" (see *mesi*, quantity, and *mesui*, place).

Metui, "difficult": *metui-nsɨtasik*, "arduous, difficult to understand."

Minui, "again": *minu'nsi*, "I revive"; *minua'tekey* (active).

Munsa, "very remarkable, extraordinary"; also *mujka* or *mujkaj*, "excellently": *munsa kisikui'skwo'q*, "venerable old lady"; *munsayaq, munso'tm*, "to put pressure on, to flatter, to strive to do"; *munsaptmuiekl ntlue'wutiminal*, "you see our sins too clearly"; *mujka maqmikew*, "a very ancient land"; *mujkajewey*, "excellent, useful, pleasant."

Naji, "to come for the purpose of, to be just about to": *nattamultɨs*, "I will come to ask of you"; *nassamultɨs*, "I will come to see you."

Netawi or *natawi, nata'*, indicates "capacity, ability"; contrary to *me'si*: *ne'tata'suti*, "intelligence, wisdom"; *netawei, -we'k, -wo'ltijik*, "scouts." [*ne't* = "quick, sharp"].

Nulmiw, nulmi, "by heart, from memory": *knulmite'tmnew*, "that you should know by heart, rehearse, ponder" (Ms. 1, 160).

Nuji, "of the nature of": *kekina'muet*, "he teaches"; *nuji-kina'muet*, "a master, a teacher"; *nuji-kina'mueti'skw*, "a woman teacher"; *ankapteket*, "he looks"; *nutapteket*, "an inspector, an overseer."

Nqani, "old, worn out, useless": *nqanuisun*, "family name"; *nqani'kuom*, "old hut"; that is almost the proper name of the grotto of Bethlehem, in Mi'kmaw; also *nqani-wen'ji'kuom*, "an old house."

Nkutey, nkuti, "likewise, the same, uniquely."

Pa'qi, "completely"; like *kaqi*, but stronger; *kaqi* pertains rather to quantity, *pa'qi* to quality: *pa'qapukuo'ti*, "confession, complete admission."

Pajijiw, "above": *pajijiaq*, "that which surpasses"; *pajijiw wa'so'q*, "in the highest heavens"; *pajiji-l'ue'wit*, "excess of malice."

Pekaj, pekajiw, "entirely, from top to bottom": *l'pa pekaj kaqoqtek*, "completely burnt"; *pekat*, "last quarter, just finishing."

Pemi, root of *pemiey*, "to walk, to advance": *pemwi'kikey, pemlukwey*, "to continue to write, work"; *pemi'pit*, "to trot"; *pemi'k*, "to last"; *pemiaq*, "actual (sin)"; *pemapeksit*, "to come by generation"; *pemape'k*, "hereditary."

Pejiliw, pjiliw, pejili, pjili, "more, further, superior, by comparison": *pejili-milesin aqq ni'n*, "you are richer than I"; *kinu ta'n pejili* or *pajiji-mlkita't*, "the bravest among us" (Gr. Ma. 27); *pejila'si*, "I go ahead"; *pjila'si*, "advance"; *pjiliw*, "specially."

Pili, from *piley*, "new"; *pilui* from *piluey*, "other"; *piltui* from *piltuey, piltue'k*, "strange, new, unusual": *piltu'-kmnie'uti*, "first communion"; *piltua'teket*, "strange behaviour"; *piltuk*, "new rope."

Pitui, "extreme, beyond, at bottom": *pitui laplusn* or *laplisun*, "the interior of the prison"; *pitui waqlusan*, "the inner tower, or inside the tower"; *pitui-mtlnaqn*, "a thousand"; *pitui-niskamij*, "great-grandfather"; *pitui-kniskamijinaq*, "our ancestors"; *pitui-wuji'ji*, "great grandson."

Puski [or *puksi*], "inclined to, habit, often bad"; "ceaselessly, endlessly, without measure"; also an adv. of time: *awan'ta'si*, "I forget"; *puski-awan'ta'si*, "I am very forgetful"; *atalmɨk*, "to eat"; *puskatalmɨk*, "greediness."

Se'k, "in vain": *se'kewe'l*, "useless things."

Sespi, from *sespei, sespe'k*, "dissipated, restless": *sespeta'si*, "to be restless"; *sespapukuey*, "to talk stupidly."

Tali, "how?" *na taliaq*, "something happens"; *na tala'lik, tala'lit, tala'tu, na tala'lijl*, "to treat in an unpleasant manner"; one does not ask "How are you?" by using *talein*, but by using *tali-wlein*?

Teli, "thus": *telei*, "I am thus"; *teliaq*, "that is true"; *tliaj*, "amen"; *tellukwey*, "I work thus"; *moqwe tallukwew*, "I am idle." *Ta'n pa teli*, "in whatever way"; *ta'n pa kinu telmɨtu'ti'kw*, "whatever we might do"; *ta'n pa ki'l*, "as you wish."

Teki, "cold," from *teke'k*: *tekitpaq*, "cold night"; *tekipuk*, "cold winter"; *teki-eskitpu'k*, "cold morning"; *teki-kiskɨk*, "cold day."

Tetapu, "exactly": *tetapua'teket*, "he behaves properly"; also for time; *tetapuiaq*, "it happened just right."

Jaqali, "with zeal, energetically, quickly, suddenly": *jaqali-npikaq*, "soon dead" (Jo. 380); *jaqali-kiskaja'tu*, "get on with it" (Par. II, 597).

Jajiki, "accurately, completely": *jajiki-sqatmaqwl ta'n telkimulkwl*, "if we accomplish exactly what he prescribes for us" (Par. I, 387); *jajikei, -ke'k*, "to be in good health, to be well"; *jajika'si*, "to follow the shore."

II. Quantity

Awsamiw, awsami, wasamiw, wasami, ewsami, "too much."

A'qataik, a'qati, "half, halfway"; *a'qati-nsitue'k*, "half sensible."

Amiw, "partly, mediocre": *amiamkusi, amiamkuk*, "passable appearance"; *ami-ksikai*, "almost lost" (going into the wrong house).

Api's, "especially, still more"; also adv. of time.

Apj, app, "again, once more."

Aji, "more": *ajiaq suliewey*, "interest"; *atawtik*, "that is more expensive"; *atawtukwey*, "to raise the price."

Elp, elk, "also, still."

Eskwi, "left over, incompletely."

Iaj, "still more": *iaj-pejili-ksaluen*, "still more because you are very loving" (Par. 1, 51).

Wa'qaj, "hardly" (see adv. of manner).

Kijka', kijka'j, "a little": *kijka'ji'jk*, "a touch, a dash."

Kaqi, kaq, "completely": *kaqiey*, "I am finished, at the end, that's all I know of it"; *kaqiaq* or *kaqaiaq*, "it is finished"; *kaqkitmik*, "to read, recite, count it all"; *kaqi-nenkl*, from *kaqi* and *nenkl*, "he knows everything"; *kaqaptikl*, from *kaqi* and *ankaptikl*, "he sees all"; *kaqkikl* or *kaqqakl*, from *kaqi* and *kelkikl*, "he supports all"; *me'si-kaqi-ankwatuanl*, "I cannot sell everything"; *kaqkisitasik*, "it is finished"; *kaqlukwey*, "my work is finished."

Kesi, ksi, keji, kji, "very, many, large."

Lo'q, "much, very."

L'nim, "too much": *mu l'nim*, "not too much"; *l'nim ta na*, "far too much, as without hope, without remedy"; also used as interjection.

Maw, "together," *mawi*, "all together": *mawa'tmk*, "all assembled, all counted"; *mawkitmɨk, kitasik*, "additional"; *mawio'mi*, "society, band, assembly"; *Sante'* or *Santewi Ma'wiomi kkijinu*, "Holy Mother Church."

Me'j, me', "more, still, yet": *ap me'*, etc., "*et cetera*, and so forth."

Mesi (short *e*), "entirely"; from this *misɨt, msɨt*, "all": *na msɨt*, "that is all"; *msɨt wen*, "each one"; *msɨt te'sijik, te'sikl*, "all the individuals, all the objects"; *msɨt-a*, "all together" (final sentence, Rand).

Mili, "number, quantity, variety": *milesit*, "he is rich"; *milesuti*, "riches"; *milita'si*, "to have various kinds of thoughts, to daydream"; *mila'si*, "to play, to do various things, to amuse oneself, to waste time"; *milamu'kl*, "various things"; *milkutat*, "variously dressed"; *miltawemkewe'l*, "various requests, invocations"; *milwikasit*, "mottled"; name for the parrot, which also carries the name *pilokwet*; this name could just as well be French as Mi'kmaw, because *m* is changed to *p* and vice versa: *miloqwet*, "the chatterbox."

Newti, nkuti, nkutey, "the same, only, the same thing": *u't kelu'lk, ula mu nkutey*, "this is better than that"; *newtite'lmk*, "I think only of him."

Pe'ikwi, "throughout, entirely": *pe'ikwi-alsusit*, "universal master."

Pikweli, pukweli, from *pukwelk*, "numerous, many": *pikweli-eulite'teket*, "rich in mercy"; *me' pukwelkɨsn newte' tli-nqasi-ntui'sketukwa's*, "if there had been more of them, I would have sold them just as fast" (letter).

Puktaqi, "uniquely": *puktaqita'simk*, "fixed idea"; *puktaqaptekemk*, "to look at only one object"; *mu ta'n te's welteskuj jijklue'wjik mawo'lti'tij puktaqi-wapo'lti'wk, apjiw pa nkute'jitew kisna me' ateltaqq maqtewo'ltijik*, "when one meets a flock of sheep, there are not only white ones, there are always one or several black ones" (Chs. B.).

Sik, pasik, "only": *ta'n pasik*, "as you wish, anything at all."

Ta's? "how many times?" *ta'sit, ta'sijik, ta'siyek, ta'sikl?* "how many persons, things?" *ta'sukuna'q, ta'sipunqik?* "how many days, years?"

Te's, "each time, so many times"; *te'si*, in comp.: *te'sikiskik, te'sipunqik*, "each day, each year"; *te'si'kw, te'siyek, te'siyoq, te'sijik, te'sikl*, "so many persons, things"; if one wishes to say expressly that there are so many, *-si-* is redoubled: *te'sisi'kw* ... except for *te'sikl*.

Tepi, which gives *tepiaq*, "that is enough": *tepite'm*, "I find that it is enough, that it is just right."

Tetpi, "equally": *tetpikilultijik*, "they are of the same size."

Tatuji, tetuji, "what extent, what age?" etc., "such."

Jel mu, "not even so many": *jel me'*, "still more."

III. Time

Awisiw, awisi, "rarely": *awije'jk, awije'jit*, "it is rare."

Amskwes, amskwesewey, "firstly" (see *tmk, tmkewey*).

Api's, "especially, until": *api's wikwia'tiyek*, "especially until our death."

Apskwi, "repetition, return": *apskwi-pa'qapukuey*, "I return to confession."

Apjiw, iapjiw, apji, iapji, "that lasts forever, eternal": *iapji-wskijinuuti*, "eternal life"; *iapji-nmkewey*, "eternal death"; *me'j iapjiw elmi'knik*, "world without end," lit.: "forever more in the hereafter"; *elmi'knik*, "in the future" (see Rem. gr. 141).

Apj, app, "again, yet again, next": *koqoey apj?* "what next?"

Atel, "about to (v. *keket*), from that moment": *atel poqjikitek*, "from his conception"; *atel elukwet, pemiet, pusit*, "he begins to work, he leaving right away on foot, in a canoe" (Rem. gr. 10); *atel poqji-alame'sik*, "the mass is just beginning"; *atelj oqo*, same meaning, more expressive: *atelj oqo wlaku*, "since yesterday" (awaited with impatience).

Atiew, atiu (French word), "adieu, goodbye": *atiewi*, "to say goodbye"; *atiewimkewey, kewe'l*, "valedictory" (speeches, songs, presents); *atiewiktaq*, "to say goodbye to someone"; *atiewiktatimk, -tatimkl, -tatimkewe'l*.

Ekel, "from time to time," shortened from *jiptueke'l*.

E'sk, ke'sk, "when, while, although"; is also a conjunction.

E'sk mna'q or *e'sku mna'q, ke'sk* ..., "before, i.e., when not yet."

Eskitpu'k, "morning": *eskitpu'nuk* or *eksitpu'nuk*, "tomorrow morning."

Nqasaiw, "immediately": *ta'n teli nqasaiw* or *ta'n pa nqasik*, "as soon as possible"; Rand: "straightaway, at once."

We'kaw or *we'kow*, "then, at once, (also) even, for, until": *i'tes kikuaq we'kaw apajita'yoq*, "I will stay at your home until you return"; *moqwe menuekew we'kow eskitpu'nuk*, "I do not need it before tomorrow morning"; *kina'masul-titoqsip we'kow kespitek*, "you will hear before Saturday"; *we'kaw paniaq-a nsipitew*, "he will remain the whole Spring" (Chs. B.); *we'kow almi'ketek*, "he immediately swears"; *we'kow ni'n*, "then it is me."

Wekla, nekla, "formerly, these past days, in that time": *nekla mimajiasn,* "if I had lived at that time."

Wela'kw, "the evening": *wela'kwek,* "yesterday evening"; *wela'kowey,* "supper."

Wikupj, wikupjik, wipukjik, upukjik, "before long, soon."

Wisqiw, wisqi, "promptly, suddenly, unexpectedly": *wisqi-wkwaik,* "he quickly gets angry"; *wisqi-tmasik,* "it splits easily"; *wisqoq,* "the ash-tree"; *wisqi-npik, jile'k,* "sudden death, by accident" (Jo. 281).

Wtejk, "the last time": *nanipunqik wtejk-a; nute'k, kpaqminaq,* "ago, five years ago."

Wlaku, "yesterday": *ktiki-wlaku,* "the day before yesterday."

Wlo'nuk, "tonight": *wlo'nukwe'l,* "towards the evening."

Kaqai'sk, "several times"; also adj. pl. *kaqai'sijik, kaqai'skl.*

Qaskew (*ko*), "an instant"; Rand includes it among the adverbs, but in practice, it is an interjection: *pe'l qaskew,* "wait a little."

Keket, "before long, about to, already."

Keskmi, "promptly, before time": *keskmi net* or *npik,* "premature death."

Kespi, "the end," from *kespiaq,* "that is the end": *kespi-a'tuksit,* "the end of the story"; this will be also the last word of this work, which is in a way the story of the genius of the Mi'kmaw language. *Mikmawi'simkewa'j; kespi-mima'ltimk,* "Extreme Unction."

Kejikew, -kaw, -ko, "lately, not long ago": *kejikawike'l,* "quite recently"; *kejikewji'jk,* "a brief moment ago."

Ki's, "already"; used also as an affirmative, when it has been used in the question: *ki's telue'sip?* "have you already said it?" *ki's,* "yes"; the opposite is *mna'q,* "not yet."

Kisi, "after"; also means "ability": *kisi-miawla'kwek,* "afternoon"; *kisi-atalultimk,* "after the meal."

Kiskuk, "today."

Kispn, "as soon as, immediately when"; if it happens, happened, by means of; *kispn oqomti'tijl kjijaqmijinaq ktininenal,* "as soon as our souls are separated from our bodies" (Gr. Ma. 39).

Kul'piw, "immediately": *mu kul'piw,* "not right away"; *wisqi,* "promptly"; *wisqwi,* "astonishingly"; *kul'piw kisi-npu'ti'kw,* "immediately after our death."

Klapis, "thus far, finally": *klapis amskwes elukutimkl*, "until Monday"; *klapis ika'n*, "you finally arrived"; is used also for place and manner.

Ketukwl, "at the signal of the bell": *ketuk*, "it rings."

Matew, "never": *me'jeke'l*, "at times, sometimes."

Me' tujiw, "still at present."

Meluia'kwek or *miawla'kwek*, "noon."

Meltamtuk, meltami, "in the beginning, at first": *meltami-pekaje'k*, "pure, straight from the beginning"; *meltamikitamk*, "first-born."

Mi'soqo, mi'soquj, "as far as, until"; also used for place and manner.

Mejijk, "more, still more": *mejijk newt*, "one more time."

Na, "so, now then, now, therefore."

Na'qaji'jk, -ji'jke'l, -ji'jke'le'l, with *me'*, "a little later, just now."

Naqaji, "delay, negligence": *naqajikey, -kemkl*, "to neglect, to delay."

Na'qek, me' na'qek, na'qeke'le'l, "late, later, tendency to be late": *na'qapukuey*, "to speak slowly"; *me' kijka' na'qapukua'tikw*, "speak a little more slowly."

Na'kowi, "by day light": *na'kowi-ntukuli*, "to hunt in the daytime"; *na'ku'set*, "the sun, day-star"; *na'kowiey, na'kowiaq*, "there is daylight"; *na'koqteskm*, "to arrive by day."

Naqsi, "fast": *naqsa'si*, "I hurry"; *naqsi-mijji (si)*, "I eat fast."

Nalaiw, "soon"; *nutaiw*, "late"; also (place) "near, far"; *nutaiw* is the root of *nuta'q*, "lack, incomplete."

Nankmiw, nankmi, "immediately, right away."

Nan'tem, nan'temi, "always, endlessly": *nan'temi wtisolip*, "I kept after you endlessly" (out of love); *esa'q*, "to banish"; *wetsa'q*, "from."

Newt, ta'pu, si'st, "once, twice, three times" (see num. adj.): *newtikiskik*, "one day, a whole day"; *newtitpa'q*, "one night"; *nkutey, nkuti*, "the same." *Nipi*, "at night."

Ne'kaw, "in continuing (time and place), at full length, and so on": *knaqapemk wnijanua ne'kaw wmitkiwaq eymlita* (Ps. 101, 29), "the children of thy servants shall continue to inhabit their land."

Nenaqiw, nenaqi, "fast": *ta'n teli-nenaqiw*, "as fast as possible"; *nenaqi-kjijitoq*, "he learns fast"; *nenaqita'q*, "hurry up."

Nekla, wekla, "formerly, these past days, at that time": *nekla mimajiasn,* "if I had lived at that time" (Gr. Ma. 43).

Nikaniw, nikani, nikantuk, "before, in front of, in advance": *nikani-ntoq,* "song master"; *nikani-kjijitekewinu'k,* "the prophets."

Nike', nike'j, "now": *nike'jewey, -we'l, -we'k,* "of the present."

Nuku', nuku'j, "henceforth, from now on": *nuku'jewij,* "let that be enough for now, stop"; word of the angel to Abraham (Sacred Hist., 119).

Nqasaiw, nqasi, "immediately."

Nkutiw, "at once."

Ntoqo, "then, next" (see *toqu* conj.).

Nspitk, "at the same time."

Pekije'k, pekiji, "long, a long time": *pekitpit,* "seated for a long time."

Pawi, "slowly": *pawei, pawo'ltijik,* "to be slow, lazy."

Poqji, poqt, "beginning": *poqtlukwey,* "I begin to work"; *poqtamka'sit,* "he leaves"; *poqjit,* "he flees."

Puni, "to stop": *punewistu,* "to stop speaking"; *puniey, puniaq,* "it is finished"; *ma' punianuk,* "endless"; *punewene'n!* "stop shouting, shut up!"; *punapei, -pe'k,* "to lack"; *ma' punape'nuk,* "it is ceaseless, cannot fail"; *ma' kaqape'nuk* (Hier. 2, 30).

Pusu'l, "good day": *pusu'l puna'ne,* "happy New Year"; *pusue'l,* "good evening," is no longer used; but the name *Pusue'lk* has been given to a place on the Richibuctou river, where a Frenchman had thus greeted his friends, after a brawl.

Puski, "frequently, subject to": *puski-we'kwata'sit,* "he is a real coward"; *puski-alita'si,* "I am subject to distractions" (Pub. Gr. 92).

Sa'q, "long ago": *ki's sa'q,* "formerly"; *sa'qawe'jk,* "the ancients."

Sapo'nuk, "tomorrow": *ktiki-sapo'nuk,* "the day after tomorrow."

Sepey or *sepay,* "this morning": *sepai, -in, -ik,* "to hunt in the morning."

Siawiw, siawi, "often, continually."

Sipeliw, sipeli, "in rank, in series": *sipelpukua'tuann, -kua'likik, pukuo'tuann, pukuo'likik,* "to arrange them thus" (persons, things).

Siniw, "suddenly, all together": *newt siniw-a,* "one last time."

Skimtuk or *simtuk*, (*skmttuk*, *smttuk*), "next, then, moreover," conj.; "immediately after, all of a sudden, at once," adv. (Rem. gr. 11).

Ta'n, ta'nik, ta'nuk, "when? and when, at the time when," conj. (Gr. Ma. 58).

Tmk, "at first": *tmkewey,* "first of all"; then *ta'puowey, si'stewey,* etc., which mean: "first, firstly, and first time"; for the latter we have *amskwes* or *amkwes*: *amkwes elukutimkl,* "Monday" (the first time that one works); then *ta'puowey, si'stewey, ne'wowey,* "Tuesday, Wednesday, Thursday"; for Friday one says *kweltamultimk,* "day of abstinence"; "Saturday," *kespitek,* "the last," or *ketui-aqntie'wimkl,* "before Sunday"; *aqntie'wimkl,* "Sunday"; one also says and writes *kekntie'wimkl, l'uiknekewey na'kwek,* "the seventh day," and *atlasmutikiskik,* "the day of rest."

Tipituk, "however, only": *l'n tipituk,* same meaning; *l'n,* for (conj.).

Tetapu, "exactly": *tetapuiaq,* "it happens just in time."

Toqu, "then" (conj. particle); *toqu tujiw,* "after."

Tujiw, "then": *me' tujiw,* "at present"; *ta'n pa tujiw,* "whenever, anytime."

Tlisip, "then"; *toqu tlisip,* "then"; *nekla tlisip,* "at that time."

Jiptuk, "perhaps": *jiptueke'l,* "at times, sometimes."

Jijikuaqaj, jijuaqa, "sometimes, at times, soon after" (Cat. pers. 103).

IV. Place

Ala, "there, over yonder"; *alae'l,* "over there, in that direction, there, in that place." Many pronouns and adjectives are, as this one, adverbs of place.

Ali, iali, from *aliey, ala'si, alita'si,* "to go here and there, to walk around, to wander, to roam"; we have to distinguish *iali* from *i'ali,* which indicates frequency: "easily distracted, the habitual prowler"; as *ial'kwilm, ial'kwiluasi* (Pub. Gr. 27), "to seek on all sides," and *i'-al'kwiluasi,* "to seek endlessly, to be a researcher."

Amasek, "far": *aji amasek,* "farther; *amase'ji'jk,* "a bit far."

Anapow, "on one side": *anapowey l'utaqn,* "fence on one side."

Apaqtuk, "at sea, on the high seas": *apaqtu'jk,* "near the shore"; *apaqtu'jke'l,* "some distance off"; *apaqtukewaq,* "the Europeans."

Apune'k, epune'k, "below": *apune'k pekisulsit,* "he's deteriorating."

Apskwi, "return, retreat": *apskwa'si*, "to retrace one's steps, before reaching one's goal"; *apskwapekitk* or *apskwopekitk*, "flow back, ebb"; *apskulapa'si*, "to look back"; *apskwi-pa'qapukuey*, "to return to confess."

Apaji, "anew": *apaja'si*, "to return, after having attained the goal"; *apajita'si, apatkwija'si*, "to feel differently, to convert."

A'se'k, "on the other side" (wall, mountain, woods); also *a'sikuk*; *a'sikm, a'sikaq*, "to meet" (Jo. II, 53); *ta'n ta nekla a'sikatioqsipnik?* (Gr. Ma. 59) "when did you meet them?" *a'sik*, "overleaf, reverse" (of a sheet of paper).

A'sise, a'sisiw, "over": *a'sisepuku'ey, -ku'a'si, -ku'eta'taqq*, "to pass over, step over."

Asite, "response": *asitapukuemkewey*, "a reply."

Asme'k, "on this side, this way": *tett asme'k*, same meaning.

Aji, "movement": *aja'sit, ajiaq, ajiet*, "to advance, to make room."

Eli, li, from *eliey*, "to go": *elukwey*, "I work"; *ellukwey*, "I go to work"; means also: "as, in so far as": *eli niskamewit aqq eli l'nuit*, "as God and as Man"; *elui'tmasi*, "to swear"; *elekey*, "to draw lots"; *eleke'wit*, "king, he who is elected."

Elqamkuk, "on this side, of a sound, estuary"; *ktaqmkuk*, "on the other side" (Newfoundland): *elqam'sipuk, ktaqmsipuk, ..." of a river."

Pkewe'k, "below": *pkewe'ke'l*, "down below"; *pkewiey*, "I go down"; *wa'so'q weji-pkewiess*, "he came down from heaven."

Pqitaik or *kpitaik*, "on high"; also, *kepetaq*, "on high": *pejili-pqitaik*, "in the highest."

Epmetuk, "to the side": *epmetuk awti*, "sidewalk."

E'tmaiw, "next, next in line": *e'tmatek, e'tmasik, e'tmapit*, "who comes next, the second"; *e'taqatiyoq kikmaj kkwe'ji'j* (Ms. 3, 174), "you come next to each other, your younger sister and you"; *e'tmaik*, "she comes after."

Etuiw, etui, "on both sides": *etui-panue'k* or *etu'panue'k*, "open on both sides" (Waverly Lake, Halifax. Co.); *etuiw sipuk*, "both sides of a river" (Rev. 22, 2); *etu'wi'kasik* (5, 1), "written inside and outside."

Etli, "there": *etlaqatk*, "he makes his residence there"; *aptaqatk*, "permanent."

Ejikli, signifies "to sweep aside, to reject": *ejiklekey*, "to reject"; *jikla'si!* "go away!"; *jiklita'q maskelmuksultiyoq!* "draw back, you evil ones!"

Wala, "here," like *ula*, but further away: *walae'l*, "on this side" (Gr. Ma. 43); *waqelaik*, same meaning (Jo. 49).

We'kwi, "the end, the completion," also, "the cessation": *we'kwi-klu'lk*, "the most beautiful possible."

We'kow, "up until": *we'kwa'q*, "that is the end"; *we'kopekitk* or *we'kwapekitk*, "the stream runs right to the end" (Truro, former Cobequid).

Wenaqi, "elevation": *wenaqa'sit, wenaqiet*, "to rise."

Weskiji, wskiji, wskit, "on the outside": *wskittuk*, "over, outside of"; *wskittukewe'l*, "the exterior things"; *weskijinui*, "to be born, to appear"; *wksitqamu'k* or *wskitqamu'k*, "on earth"; *wskitqamu'kewaq*, "people."

Weji, "from": *wejiey, wejiaq*, "I come from, I went there, that comes, results from": *tami wejien?* "where do you come from?" *na' tami* or *na'tami*, "from somewhere"; also expresses cause: *weji-jikli-ksispa'tulkwl ktlue'wutinal wmal'temiktuk* or *wmal'temek* (Rev. 1, 5), "it is by his blood that he took away our sins and purified us"; *weji-tuiet* or *-tu'et*, "he comes out."

Wejuow, "near": *wejuowa'sit*, "he is approaching"; *wejuowe'l*, "nearby."

Ula, "here": *ula tett*, "right here, in this place"; *ulae'l*, "in this direction"; *ula tett eym ma' maja'siw*, "I am here, I'm not moving" (I will not budge); *ktiki-nipn ula tetli-wikepalnoqsip* (Gr. Ma. 43), "I gave you a feast here last summer"; *ula tetli-mawieyikw*, "we meet here."

U't, "here, before our eyes": *u't ta ketui-ktukunin?* "do you want to spend the night here?"

Wuskaluaq, wplaqnek, wpaqmk (see the possessives), "before, behind him."

Qame'k, "on the other side" (river, valley, plain); *qamawtik*, "on the other side of the road or street"; *qamso'q*, "rocks on the other side," Canso.

Qasqe'k, "on the shore": *kjikmuk*.

Ke'kwe'k, ke'kwi, "on high, above": *ke'kwe'ke'l*, "from above"; *ke'kwakuk*, "on the top of a hill"; *ke'kwakw*, "the top of a hill."

Knekk, "far": *knekji'jk*, "a bit far"; *kne'ji'jk*, adv. of time.

Kipitaq, "up": *kipitaqe'l*, "upwards, towards the heights."

Kesmi, "thrust, progress, advance": *kesmi-pukua'sit*, "he is sent on ahead, he advances"; *l'i-ksmienej Kisu'lkwiktuk*, "let us advance towards God"; *kesmi-maunmul*, "I give you my offering with all my heart"; *ksma'tu*, "push" (the bell).

Ketaqamu'k, "in the rear part of the hut, place of honour."

Kiwtaw, kiwto'qwiw, kiwto'qwi, kikto'qwi, "around": *kiwto'qwi-alasutmamk*, "Way of the Cross"; *kikto'qwa'tekey*, "to turn" (the millstone).

Kikjiw, "near": *kikja'simk*, "to approach."

Qwaijk, qwaik, qwaikl, "in the middle, among, close to."

Kujmuk, "outside"; also interj. "out!"

Klapis, "as far as": *na'te'l*, "there."

Kta'nuk, "the edge of the sea": *kta'nuke'l*, "at the edge of the ocean."

Lame'k, lami, lamu, "inside"; *lame'ke'l*, "below": *lami-klujjiewey-iktuk*, "under the cross"; *lamikuomk* or *lamukuomk*, "inside the hut"; *lamua'w*, "the inside of the egg"; *lamqamu'k*, "under the earth, in limbo"; *lamalqik*, "interior of a cave, sepulchre"; *lamlutaqn*, "court, enclosure"; *lamqwan*, "undergarment"; *lamso'q*, "under a rock"; *lampo'q*, "water from the depths, pure water."

Mawi, "together."

Mala, "there, yonder": *malae'l*, "that way, in that direction."

Mekwaik, "among, amidst."

Mesue'k, mesui (short *e*) "openly": *me'su'tek*, "uncovered"; *me'su'tuk*, "publicly."

Miaw, miawe'k, "amidst, among": *miawe'k awtik*, "in the middle of the road."

Mi'soqo, mi'soquj, "up to, until, as far as."

Na'qeke'l, "further, later": *naqaji'jke'le'l*, "a little further on."

Nalaiw, "far"; *nutaiw*, "near": *na'tami*, "somewhere"; *na'tamutuk* (dub.).

Na'te'l, "there": *na'te'l lia's*, "I will go there"; *na'te'l wa'so'q eykik*, "those who are there in heaven"; *kikjiw* or *wejuow na'te'l*, "near there."

Naji, "to come for, to intend"; *na's* and *na't* are also used: *nasaptekey*, *nattawaqtmay*, "I've come to see, to ask for, to seek"; *nattamkipnaq pa'tlia'saq*, "I have been to ask the priest for it" (Ms. 3, 184).

Ne'kaw, "in continuing, and so on."

Nisiw, "descending, downwards."

Nute'k, kute'k, wute'k, "behind me, you, him": *se'skwet kutnaq*, "she cries out behind us" (Matt. 15, 23).

Papke'k, "downstream": *papka'sit*, "he goes down."

Pe'ikwiw, pe'ikwi, "everywhere": *pe'ikwi-eleke'wit*, "universal king."

Pi'taw, "upstream": *pi'tawa'sit*, "he goes up"; *Pi'taupo'q*, "Bradore Lake."

Tal'pesuk? tel'pesuk, "how far? so far."

Tali-amasek? teli-amasek, "how far? so far": *moqwe amasenukw; amasenutuk*, "it is perhaps far."

Tatuji? tetuji, "what extent? such an extent," also "such an age": *tetuje'k, tetujo'ltijik*, "he is, they are, so old."

Tami, "where?" *na'tami*, "somewhere, around" (literal and figurative): *na'tamutuk*, "somewhere or other"; *msit tami*, "everywhere"; *tami se'k*, "elsewhere"; *ta'n tami*, "in those places where"; *tamie'l*, "towards where?" *tamieke'l ela'tiyoq*, "where are you going?" (Jo. 302).

Ta'n, "where? where" (Gr. Ma. 59): *ta'n pa tami*, "anywhere"; *lo'q ketui-nasaptmap ta'n tetlaqatmu'tiyoq* (Gr. Ma. 59), "I very much wanted to see where you live"; *eliey ta'n wejien*, "I am going to the place where you came from"; *kinua'tui ta'n tetli-kiskattek l'nui wi'kupaltimk*, "tell me where the Indian feast was prepared" (ib.).

Te'ksek, "north-west": *te'kseke'l*, "from the north-west side."

Tepaw, "near": *tepawe'l*, "close enough"; also (time) "soon."

Teptek, kettek, "inside a vessel, within."

Tett, ula tett, "here": *tette'l*, "this way, in this direction."

Tetli, "in this place": *tetlaqatm*, "I live there"; *etlaqatm*, "it's my home"; *aptaqatm*, "I live there all the time"; *tetleyawi*, "I am from there"; *tetlaqatm*, "I live there, without being from there"; whence, *tlaqatik*, "Tracadie, our home."

V. Expression of Thought

1. **Affirmation**: *e'e* (ehe), "yes": *e'e pa*, "yes certainly"; *e'e pa'a* (baha), "yes, that is finished, that is all."

Amuj, iamuj, miamuj, "certainly, quite certain"; also expresses commands: *amuj elien*, "it is necessary that you go there."

Asite, "response": *nenaqiw asite wi'kmui*, "answer me quickly in writing."

Ansma or *assma*, "certainly, assuredly": *ansma pa*, more affirmative.

L'pa, "truly."

L'npa, "indeed," *l'napa*, "sure thing": *l'n ta na*, "in fact"; *l'n tepituk*, "however, only."

Eta, affirmative particle, which cannot be translated, but the clause in which it occurs may sometimes have *so* (Rem. gr. 158); it corresponds to the interrogative particle *ta*, "is that so?" *Koqoey ta pewatmn*? "what do you want?" *pa'qapukuo'ti eta*, "confession (is what I want)"; *ki'l ta teley-i'sip*, "was it you who did that?" [was like that?]; *ni'n eta*, "yes it was me, it was so."

Ketl, "truly": *ketl pa*, "yes truly, in truth": *ketl pa, ketl pa e'lnoq*, "verily, verily I say to you"; *ketl pa moqwe*, "certainly not"; *ketl oqu, ketl oquj*, "yes indeed, truly, indeed, is it possible, is it so?"

Ketui, "I want, wanted, would like"; the following verb in Mi'kmaw has the tenses, moods, and persons of wishing in French or English: *ketui-npm*, "I want to die," also "I will die."

Ke'j, ke'sik, "for example, here, try, it's your turn."

Ki's, "yes," when this word is found in a question.

Koqoey ta wjit? "how come? of course, why not?"

Meluij, "rather": *meluij oqu*, "especially."

Me' ta katu, "but of course."

Na, "and so, now, you see": *netna*, "that's it, precisely"; *na taa*, "no doubt"; *na pa jela, na ta jela*, "sure thing."

Pa, "certainly, sure"; used appropriately and ironically.

To'q, "therefore": *jiksitukw to'q*, "now listen"; *nike'j to'q*, "now then" (conj.).

Jel oquj elp me', "and even more, still more" (Ps. 17, 41).

Lo'q etuk pa moqwe, "God forbid, far from it," *absit*.

2. **Doubt**: *etuk*, "perhaps"; Rand says: *etuk* means "indeed," that is, "no doubt," but this really means that it is not sure: *etuk jel*, "probably, it should be"; *etuk suel*, "almost, maybe so"; *ketl etuk*, "no doubt, in truth"; curiously written in Hamel's list, *Catledo*.

Kenuk, kenukuj, kenukej, kenukwej, kunukwej, "although, no doubt."

Suel, "almost, nearly."

Jiptuk, "perhaps, that" (in the Lord's prayer, *utinam*).

3. **Negation**: *mu, ma'*, "not": *matew*, "never, no more."

Ma'wen, "no one" (indef. pron.); *ma'wenl, ma'wenik, ma'weni*.

Mna'q, "no (opposed to *ki's*), not yet."

Moqwe'j, moqwa'j, moqwe, moqwa, "no, not": composed of *mu koqoey*, "nothing"; today the pleonasm *moqwe* or *moqwa koqoey* is in current usage; but it is better to say *moqwa koqoe'nuk*, "there is nothing, it's nothing"; *moqoe'j etuk-a, motua katu*, "not exactly, perhaps not"; *moqoe'j eta*, "certainly not well, no"; *mu ansma*, "not exactly."

4. **Interrogation**: *koqoey*, "what?"

Ta, "is that so?" (second word, like *ne* in Latin); *koqoey ta*? "what is it, what then?" *apj koqoey*? *koqoey ap*? "what else?" *koqoey wjit*, "why?"

A large number of other adverbs are used in an interrogative manner, as *ta'n, ta's, tali, tatuji, talsip, tami, etuk*, etc.

LESSON THIRTY THREE

PREPOSITIONS, CONJUNCTIONS, INTERJECTIONS

I. Prepositions

There are few **prepositions** in Mi'kmaw because they are included in the nouns, pronouns or verbs.

The main one is *iktuk*, which is put at the end of words, like *vobiscum* in Latin; it means "in, with, by means of, at the home of, on"; it is often shortened to *tuk*, or even to the simple locative *k*: *maqmikewiktuk* or *maqmikek*, "on earth"; *nipuktuk*, "in the woods"; *sulieweyiktuk* or *suliewe'ktuk*, "with money"; *l'ikuta'tutew ktininenaq wlo'ti* (Rem. gr. 134), "he will pour out good fortune on us"; *ktininenawiktuk* could be put here; one relies on the ear when joining *iktuk* to its object; *apaqtuk*, "on the sea"; *wskitpaqtuk*, "on the waves" (Matt. 14, 25); *Westau'lkwiktuk*, "in, for the Saviour"; *Kwestau'lkwminuiktuk*, ..." our Saviour"; *Kmnie'utiktuk kina'matimk*, "instruction on communion."

Wjit, "for"; is put before or after the word: *wjit ki'l* or *ki'l wjit*, "for you, because of you"; *wa'so'q wejipkewiess kinu pa wjit l'nuulti'kw*, "truly, he came down from heaven for us, men."

Ke'l, "towards," is also put after the word; it is even added to *iktuk*: *Kisu'lkw*, "God"; *Kisu'lkwiktuk*, "in God, with God"; *Kisu'lkwiktuke'l*, "towards God"; *Kisu'lkwiktuke'l kipoqwa'tu kkamlamun*, "turn your heart towards God"; *ntininke'l*, "towards me"; *wtininewaqe'l*, "towards them"; *inaqneke'l, patatujke'l*, "on the right, left side."

Kuluk means "also, with": *kuluk sape'wultijik*, "with the saints"; root of *kulua'tu, kulua'tmk*, "to join, to mix"; *epmepikaj sa'puss Se'sus samuqwan kuta'siksip kuluk wmal'tem*, "from the pierced side of Jesus water and blood came out" (Par. II, 654); but "with" is better rendered by *wiji, wij, wi* combined with the verb, which becomes reciprocal; thus, "I go with him," is translated by: "we go together," *wije'tiyek*; likewise "from" is translated by *weji*; when it expresses possession, it is included in the possessive. See pp. 33 and 196.

Ke', ke'sik, na, "here is, there is"; Mr. Rand translates these words by *ankapte'n*; that is the literal meaning of the English "behold," but not that of the Mi'kmaw, which is rather an exclamation: *ankapte'n, ankam,* "you (s., pl.) see, do you see?" one also says *nemitu'n*; there is no invitation to look in these.

Klapis, "up until"; *e'sk mna'q,* "before," and many other words are adverbs and prepositions, almost without changing their meaning, most nouns being verbal, or able to become so.

Lukwe'k, "between": *ketantimkewey ika'tutes lukwe'k ki'l aqq e'pit,* "I will make hostility between you and the woman" (Gen. 3, 15).

Mekwaik, miawe'k, "in the middle," also "among": *mimukwasijik mekwaik kmu'jiktuk ika'taqnk tle'l,* "they hid in the midst of some trees in the garden" (ib. 8); *mekwaik tetuje'k,* "he is middle aged"; *miawio'kuom,* "nave"; *etuiw qami'kuoml,* "sideaisle" (of a church); *miawikan,* "the middle of the hut."

Nplaqnek, kplaqnek, wplaqnek, "before me, you, him (chest)"; *nuskaluk, nsiskuk,* etc., also "before (the eyes, face)"; *nute'k, kute'k, wute'k* or *npaqmk,* "behind me, you, him": *npaqmk etek, nusukwik,* "it is behind me, it follows me"; *newiskekipunqik kpaqminaq jel na'n pekisinkip aniapsuinu mekwaik ktininenaq,* "it is 45 years since the missionary priest came among us." Many other expressions are, like these, made of simple nouns in the locative case, thus including the English prepositions.

II. Conjunctions

It is not always easy to say whether a word is an adverb, preposition or conjunction; many are all three; in any case **conjunctions** are assumed to unite words and the elements of sentences, without modifying their inflections, unless they contain a negation or a prefix requiring contraction. Two of the main ones, "if" and "when," enter into the conjugation of verbs, and constitute two distinct modes. Here are a few others:

Aqq, "and": *aqq eskuiaq,* "and the rest," etc.

L'n, l'n ta na, l'n oquj, "for, indeed, in fact that": *l'n ta na mntu jipatk klujjiewey,* "for the devil fears the cross."

L'n tepituk or *tepituk,* "alone, only, except that, however": *l'n tepituk nesukuna'q minu'nsitew,* "but in three days he will rise again" (Par. II, 568).

Elp, "also, moreover."

E'sk or *ke'sk*, "while"; *e'sk mna'q* or *ke'sk*, "before"; takes the negative ending: *tapukuna'q ke'sk mna'q pa'kewimkek*, "two days before Easter."

Istike', *istike'j*, *istaqej*, *staqa*, "as, like."

We'kow, "then, next, in continuing."

Weji, "whence, wherefrom, because of"; requires contraction.

Oqu, *oquj*, "for, indeed"; is put in second position.

Wjiaj, *wjiej*, "in order to"; takes the subordinative.

Wjit, "for, because of."

Ula eym, "here I am" (Ex. 3, 4): *ula ni'n, ki'l, nekm*, "here I am, you are, he is."

Katu or *skatu*, "but, however."

Kenuk, "although"; *mu awan'ta'siw ntalasutman kenuk nketkien*, "I do not forget my prayer, although I am drinking" (Ms. 3, 192).

Ke'sik, ke'j, ke', "thus, and so"; *ke' ula*, "here is, there is"; also an interjection of encouragement: "let's go, try!" *ke' kilew*, "it's your turn"; *ke' ne'tata'sultinej*! "watch it, let's be careful!" (Ex. 1, 11).

Kisna, "or, or else"; neither ... nor is expressed by *mu, ma, moqwe, moqwa ... kisna*: "neither him nor me," *mu nekm kisna ni'n*; "either him or me," *nekm kisna ni'n*.

Kispn, "once, as soon as" (Gr. Ma. 39); "if once, if it happens thus": *kispn kjiju'lan kpunisape'wite'lsin, pa i'tes, sape'wit na*, "as soon as I know, (lit.) if it happens to me that I know, that you stop believing yourself wise, surely I will say, yes he is wise, this one" (Rem. gr. 14).

Kwlaman, "in order that, so that"; takes the future: *kwlaman wa'so'q l'ia's*, "in order that I may go, or so that I will go to heaven."

Klapis, "until, when."

Mita, "because, since"; originally composed of *mu* and *ta* or *tu*, and meaning: "isn't that right?" that is why it was construed with the negative form, which tends to disappear. M. Maillard gives both (Ms. 3, 176): *mu ta nekla metuipukwek tlisip weskijinuiwep?* "was I not born in the depth of winter?" *mu ta tele'nuk l'nuiktuk mu wnijanimmik mu welita'simmik*, "for that is how it is among the Indians, if one does not have a child, one is not content." *Tapusijik eykik l'nuipa'tlia'sk: mu ta Musiew Manako'q We'koqmikek eymukwa; katu ktika, Musiew Lutlo'q Lapuent Aposeulek eykaq; apj ktik we'ji'kipnaq Piktuk l'nuipa'tlia'saq* (ib. 184), "there are two missionaries of the Indians: for M. Manach is at Green Bay; but another, M. LeLoutre, is at Beausejour Point, I even found another one at Pictou."

Mu ta katu, "is it possible? not possible"; also, "nonetheless no."

Na wjit, "that is why": *na wjit, ke'! elkimul*, "go, therefore, I send you" (to Pharaoh, Exodus. 3, 10).

Nekla tlisip, "at that time."

Netna, "that is right, that is to say": *netna nekm kisitoqsipnl msit koqoe'l*, "it is He (God) who made all things."

Nike' to'q, "now"; lit.: "now then."

Ta'n, "when."

To'q, "therefore, then, well."

Toqu, "then"; *ntoqu*, "then"; *toqu tlisip, toqu tujiw*, "next, then."

Tlia', tlia'j, "although"; *tlia' skatu*, "however, nevertheless, yet."

Jel, "also, even, and (in numbers)"; *jel mu*, "than (in comparison)."

Jiptuk, "perhaps, than," in the Lord's prayer, *utinam*.

III. Interjections

The **interjections** are the exclamations, which do not relate to any other word and are complete by themselves.

A'a! (pron. aha), "ah!" interjection of agreement; "fine, all right" (see Leg. 90); accented *e'e*, "yes."

Aij, aiej, "such and such," is used as an interj. to express a hesitation: "what do you call it?" which is repeated while waiting for the word.

Ae (ahe), sigh from the *nskawaqn*; *awia*, final exclamation.

Aqai, "alas," written *akahie* (New Rel. 133 and 398).

Eyoq, "are you kidding?"

L'na pa, "sure, certainly; of course."

Oo (oho), lengthened oh! call, echo: *alasutmayikupp o o o*! "to prayer!"

O o o: *o Niskam*, "oh God!" *o wjit*, "oh! for ...."

Qasqew, qasqo, "wait, stop, listen, woa! take it easy!" M. Maillard (Pub. Gr. 32) translates "quietly," in speaking; that should rather be "slowly" (adv.); but that is not the meaning today; "to speak quietly" is *kimu'tuk, kimewistu.*

Ke'n, "thank you": *ke'n wela'lin!* "many thanks!"

Ke's, "go lie down"; said to a dog; to a person: *lisma'si.*

Ketl oqu, ketl etuk, "for sure, nothing truer."

Kwe'! "hey!" former call at the door of the hut; if the voice were recognized, the *ka'qn* (cloth door) was pushed aside and the master said: *piskwa',* "enter"; today one knocks on a wooden door, just like the rest of the population."

Koqoey ta wjit? "why not? of course, that goes without saying."

Kwastale! "ah! what a business"; expresses complete surprise; this is perhaps the *akastaleiei* of Rand (E.M. Dict. 283), which resembles "aghast." "O fine! Wonderful!" (M.E. p. 8).

Kujmuk, "outside, out of here."

L'nim ta na, "that is truly too much, goes too far, as hopeless, without remedy."

Lo'q etuk pa moqwe, moqwa, "God forbid!" *absit,* "far from it."

Me' katu! "what a mess (unpleasant, regrettable, tough), oh my!"

Meluij oqu! "What!"

Me'j oqu (swear word), it is stronger, "go to hell."

Mntu kjijaple'w! "hell!" vulgar swear word.

Nqwat, "you old devil"; said to a companion (cf. M.E. Dict. 82, 2).

Niskam! "oh God! my God!" in surprise.

Tale'k! "well!, what?" (Ms. 3, 196), "right?" (Ms. 2, 164).

Te' katu! "and how!"

Teken oqu? "what? what then?"

Tuoq? "how would I know?"

Joq! "curse of a man," says Mr. Rand, "resembles hellish"; "each class," says he, "had its own swear words, and did not use those of another"; ex.: *ketu'kwtmay,* "I want to smoke"; *ketu'joqtmay,* "I have a hellish, a furious desire to smoke"; *ketu'wkwai,* "I'm going to get mad"; *ketujoqkwai,* "I sure as hell am going to get mad."

It is notable that no real blasphemy is found in Mi'kmaw; the divine or holy names are always pronounced with respect; on the other hand, in anger, these are readily borrowed from other languages, more often than terms of piety or courtesy.

Kespia'tuksit

DEO GRATIAS

MI'KMAW WORDS

NA Noun, animate
NI Noun, inanimate
N Nominal element of no fixed gender
AI Animate Intransitive verb
II Inanimate Intransitive verb
TA Transitive Animate verb
TI Transitive Inanimate verb
PV Preverb
XP Particle or adverbial element

a'a	XP	yes, ah!; fine, all right
a'kwesn(l)	NI	headgear
a'lk	TI	swim here and there (fish)
a'maqnajl	TA	paint, stain
a'maqnsuti	NI	ointment
a'maqntm	TI	paint, stain
a'papi('k)	NA	thread(s), line(s)
a'pi('k)	NA	net(s)
a'qataik	XP	half, halfway
a'qatekiaq	II	the tide is halfway out
a'qati	PV	half, halfway
a'qatinstue'k	AI	half sensible
a'sk, asise, asisiw		XP overleaf, reverse (of a sheet of paper)
a'skk	TI	meet
a'skuajl	TA	meet
a'se'k, a'skuk	XP	on the other side (wall, etc.)
a'sisepuku'a'sit	AI	pass over, step over
a'sisepuku'et	AI	pass over, step over
a'sisepuku'eta'tuajl		TA pass over, step over
a'su'n	NI	outer garment, blanket
a'su'na'q	TI	be clothed
a't	XP	that one, that
ae	XP	sigh from the nskawaqn
aij, aiej, ayej	XP	such and such, soandso, expresses a hesitation
aja'sit	AI	progress, advance, make room
aji	PV	movement, more
aji amasek	XP	farther
ajiaq	II	advance, make room
ajiaq suliewey	II	interest
ajiet	AI	advance, progress, make room, increase, hour, time
ajioqjomin(k)	NA	blackberry(s), bramble(s)
ajipjulajl	TA	hope in, count on
ajipjutoq	TI	hope, wait for, count on
ajknewa'toq	TI	confuse, harm
Aklasie'w	NA	English
aklasie'wi'skw	NA	English woman
aklasie'wi'skwe'j	NA	English girl, not married
aklasie'wi'skwe'ji'j	NA	little English, Protestant girl
aklasie'wit	AI	be English
aknimuet	AI	proclaim, confess
aknutmaqn	NI	news
akoqmaw, akoqmekw	NA	herring (see also nme'ji'j)
al'kwilk	TI	search all over
al'kwiluajl	TA	look around for
al'tukwi'k	TI	run here and there
ala	XP	that one, that, there, over yonder
ala'q	TI	swim in every direction
ala'sit, alita'sit	AI	go from side to side, roam, walk around
alae'l	XP	over there, in that direction

alame's(l)	NI	Mass(es), log
alaqsin	AI	fly, flap around
alaqteket	AI	sail
alasumajl	TA	worship, honour, pray
alasutm	TI	worship, honour, pray
alasutmamkewe'l	NI	prayer book
alasutmamkwamkewe'l	NI	ceremonies
alasutmaq	II	that is Christian
alasutmaqn	NI	religion, prayer
alasutmaqnik	II	that is Christian
alasutmaqnji'j	NI	short prayer, an invocation
alasutmat	AI	pray (see also elasutmat, i'alasutmat)
alasutme'winu	NA	Catholic
alasutmelsewajl	TA	pray for someone
alasutmelsewatm	TI	pray for something
alasutmewajl	TA	make to pray, lead in prayer
alasutmo'kuom(l)	NI	church
alawey	NI	pea
ali, i'ali	PV	here and there
aliet	AI	go here and there, wander, roam
alikaw, alikew	NI	goods, linen, cloth, thing
alisma'sit	AI	stretch oneself out here and there
alispet	AI	be wet
alita'sit	AI	be distracted (see ala'sit)
alita'suaqn	NI	spirit, thought
alitk	II	it flows in different directions
aljaik	AI	be painted, stained
almaktk	TI	curse, swear
almi'ketek	AI	he curses
almimajl	TA	insult, curse
almitm	TI	insult, curse
alqatk	TI	remain here and there
alsipiskitat	AI	extend one's hands
alsumajl	TA	dominate, be the master
alsumkusit	AI	obey
alsusit	AI	be in command
alsutkl	NI	commands
alsutm	TI	dominate, be the master
alt	XP	there are some who, some
alt ... alt	XP	one ... the other, some ... others
alt wenik	XP	some people
altukuli'tijik	AI	they hunt everywhere
alu'sat	AI	be thin
alukwiaq	II	the sky becomes overcast
amali	PV	variety
amalika'taqn	NI	flowerbed
amalkat	AI	dance
amalkawaqn, amalkewaqn	NI	dance, prancing
amaloqwan	NI	embroidery
amase'ji'jk	XP	a bit far
amasek	XP	far
amasike'k	AI	be miserly, closefisted
amasikeimk	NI	avarice
amaskwiplnk	TI	torment
amaskwiplnajl	TA	torture, torment
amaskwiplnet	AI	suffer torture
amikska't	AI	almost lost (going into the wrong house)
amiamkuk	II	have passable appearance
amiamkusit	AI	have passable appearance
amiw	XP	partly, mediocre
amkwes	XP	firstly
amkwes elukutimkl	XP	Monday (first work day)
amlmekw	NA	mackerel
amskwes	XP	first, at first
amskwes elukutimkl	XP	Monday (first work day)
amskwesewa'j	NA	first
amskwesewey	NI	first (in time)
amskweseweyit	AI	be the first
amuiw	XP	almost
amuj, iamuj, miamuj	XP	certainly
anapow	XP	on one side
anapowey l'utaqn	NI	fence on one side
anate'lmajl	TA	hate, detest someone
anate'tk	TI	hate, detest something
anesk	XP	an odd number
ani, ana	PV	abhorrence
aniamajl	TA	look unfavorably upon, detest, regret
aniapsimk	NI	penance
aniapsimkewey	NI	penance
aniapsit	AI	do penance
aniapsuinu	NA	religious, penitent, missionary
aniaptk	TI	detest, look unfavourably upon, regret
ankamajl	TA	look at
ankamsit	AI	look at oneself

ankaptk	TI	look at
ankapteket	AI	look (at)
ankita'sit	AI	think, reflect
ankita'suinuit	AI	be a thinking, reflecting being
ankmiw, nankmiw	XP	immediately
anko'tasit	AI	be protected, looked after
anko'tk	TI	look after something
anko'tmuajl	TA	keep for someone
ankuj	XP	one by one, certain ones
ankujiw	XP	there are some
ankuna'jl	TA	cover
ankuna'toq	TI	cover a thing
ankwatkitk	TI	multiply
ankweiwajl	TA	look after someone
ankweyasit	AI	take care of oneself, protect oneself
ankwiskat	AI	his joints
anquna'jl	TA	cover, hide
ansale'wit	NA	angel
ansale'witji'j	NA	newly baptized child
ansma, assma	XP	just, exactly
ansue'k	II	that is unfortunate, it is strange
apaja'lajl	TA	bring back
apaja'sit	AI	return, after success
apaja'toq	TI	bring back, return
apaji	PV	anew, mental return
apajiet	AI	return, come back
apajipet, apijipet	AI	come back to life
apajita'sit, apatkwija'sit	AI	feel differently, convert
apanktawalsewajl	TA	pay for someone
apanktk	TI	pay
apanktuajl	TA	pay someone
apanktuowey	NI	payment, salary, recompense
apaqt	NI	sea
apaqtu'jk	XP	near the shore
apaqtu'jke'l	XP	some distance off
apaqtuiaq	NA	marsh bitterns
apaqtuk	XP	at sea, on the high seas
apaqtukewaq	NA	the Europeans
apatnmajl	TA	hand over
apatnmuet	AI	return
apatteluajl	TA	redeem
api	PV	to have just
api's	XP	especially, until, still more
api('k)	NA	bow(s)
apijipe't	AI	come back to life
apijipemk	NI	resurrection
apijipewey	NI	resurrection
apijipmkewey	NI	resurrection
apijipmkeweyi	AI	I am the resurrection
apiksiktuajl	TA	forgive, pardon
apistane'wj	NA	marten
apj	XP	afresh, again
apjkilk	AI	little (less large)
apje'ji'jk	II	quite little, very little
apje'jk	II	little, small
apji, iapji	PV	forever, eternal
apji'n	TA	thanks, you do good to me
apji'timk	AI	do good to each other
apji'timkewey	NA	Eucharist
apjiajl	TA	do good (to)
apjiw, iapjiw	XP	forever, eternal, always
(i)apjiw elmi'knik	XP	world without end
apkw	PV	deliverance, treachery
apkwa'l'ti'kw	AI	forgive one another
apkwa'l'timkewey	NI	absolution
apkwa'lajl	TA	deliver
apkwa'toq	TI	loosen, untie, deliver, put back
apkwalajl	TA	surrender someone
apkwatm	TI	deliver, betray
apkwepajl	TA	untie with the teeth
apkwetm	TI	untie with the teeth
apoqnma'sit	AI	help onesel
apoqnmuajl	TA	help
apoqnmuet	AI	aid
apoqoksit	NA	cauldron, boiler, kettle
app, apj	XP	again, yet again, once more, next
appusqa'q	TI	lock
apsatpay	AI	my small head
apskulapa'sit	AI	look back
apskwa'sit	AI	return unsuccessful
apskwapekitk	II	comes back (Jordan), flow back, ebb
apskwi	PV	return, recession, repetition
apskwipa'qapukuet	AI	return to confess
apsute'kan(k)	NA	doll(s)
aptsqa'q	TI	lock (up)

aptaqatk	TI	live there all the time
aptu'n	NI	cane
aptukopiso'tlajl	TA	crown
aptukopiso'tlk	TI	crown
apu'ajl	TA	send, make an envoy of someone
apu'kwetoq	TI	send
apune'k, epune'k	XP	downstairs, below
apuskapukuet	AI	he speaks badly, coarsely
apuski, apukji	PV	disorder
apustale'wit	NA	Apostle
aqai	XP	alas
aqay	XP	alas!
Aqlasie'w	NA	English(man)
aqm(k)	NA	snow shoe(s)
aqma'q	AI	have snowshoes
aqmi'k	TI	go in snowshoes
aqneiwajl	TA	look after someone
aqntie'wimk	XP	Sunday
aqntie'wimkl	NI	Sunday
aqntieuti	NI	week
aqoqme'kw	NA	herring (see also akoq maw, nme'ji'j)
aqq	XP	and
aqtapuk	XP	in the depth, middle of the winter
aqtatpa'q	II	at midnight, midnight
asitapukuemkewey	NI	a reply
asitapukuet	AI	answer
asite	PV	reply, permission
asite'tmajl	TA	permit
asiteklusit	AI	answer
asitemti'kw	AI	answer one another
asitemtimkewey	NI	response
askaiwajl	TA	disturb, do injury
asko'tk	TI	disturb a thing
asko'tmuajl	TA	disturb something of some one
asme'k, tett asme'k	XP	on this side, this way
asoqma'sit	AI	cross over
assma	XP	certainly (see ansma)
astaq	NI	heat (of the sun)
asukom	XP	six
asukom te'siska'q	X	sixty
asukom te'siskeksuti	NI	group of sixty
asukom te'suk(u)mu'kw	AI	go in sixes in a boat
asukom te'sunasik	XP	one fathom, span of the arms
asukomewey	NI	sixth
asukomikaqn	NI	bridge
atalmajl	TA	eat
ataluajl	TA	feed
atawtik	II	that is more expensive
atawtukwet	AI	raise the price
atel	XP	about to, from that moment
atelj oqo	XP	since
atelj oqo wlaku	XP	since yesterday
atelk(ik)	AI	more than
atelk(l)	II	more than
atiew, atiu	XP	goodbye
atiewiktuajl	TA	say goodbye to someone
atiewimkewey	NI	valedictory (speeches, songs, presents)
atiewit	AI	say goodbye
atkilk	AI	be bigger
atkitemit	AI	weep
atkna'jl	TA	do his share, make partici pate
atkne'waqn	NI	share
atkno'sit	AI	take one's share
atlasmit	AI	s/he rests
atlasmutikiskk	NI	the day of rest
atleka'timk	NI	pace, step
atu'tukwej	NA	squirrel
atuomkomin	NA	strawberry
aunaqaj, auna	XP	exception, to the contrary
awan'ta'sit	AI	forget
awanajl	TA	be unfamiliar with
awane'k	AI	forget
awani	PV	ignorance, forgetfulness
awanita'sit, awan'ta'sit	AI	forget
awanite'lmajl	TA	forget
awanite'tk	TI	forget
awanitoq	TI	be unfamiliar with
awase'ket	AI	spoil
awi	PV	around
awia	XP	sigh, final exclamation of song
awije'jit	AI	be rare
awije'jk	II	it is rare
awisi	PV	rarely
awisiw	XP	rarely

awiupqo'qosajl	TA	cense
awiupqo'qosk	TI	cense
awiw, awi, i'awi	XP	around, in a circle
awna	XP	on the contrary
awsami, wasami, ewsami	PV	too much (see also, wassami, wessami)
awsamiw, wasamiw	XP	too much
awti('l), awti'j(l)	NI	path(s), road(s)
awtiik	II	there is a road
awtikmat	AI	guide
ayej, aiej, aij	N	soandso
e'e	XP	yes
e'e pa'a	XP	yes, that is finished, that is all
e'e pa	XP	yes certainly
e'najl	TA	lose
e'pit	NA	woman
e'pite'ji'j	NA	little girl
e'pite's	NA	girl
e'pitji'j	NA	little woman, dear creature
e's	NA	clam
e'sk, ke'sk	XP	when, while, although
e'sk mna'q, ke'sk mna'q	XP	before
e'sku mnaq	XP	before
e't	AI	say
e'taqatiyoq	AI	follow one another
e'tas	XP	each one
e'tas wen	XP	each one in his turn
e'tasewey	XP	each, each one
e'tasit	AI	who is next
e'tasua'ti'kw	AI	walk two by two
e'tmaik	AI	come after
e'tmaiw	XP	next, next in line
e'tmapit	AI	in second place
e'tmasik	II	in second place
e'tmatek	II	in second place,
e'uk	TI	use
e'yoq, eyoq	XP	you don't say, are you kidding?
ejela'toq	TI	be unable to
ejele'k	AI	be feeble, unable
ejele'k	II	impossible
ejeleiwajl	TA	be incapable of helping
ejeli	PV	impotence
ejeliaq	II	it is impossible
ejelo'tk	TI	be incapable of helping
ejikla'lajl	TA	dismiss, reject
ejikla'sit	AI	withdraw, go away
ejikla'toq	TI	move it, remove
ejikla'tuajl	TA	remove from someone
ejikleket	AI	reject
ejikli	PV	sweep aside, reject
ejkujk	NA	cucumber, melon, pumpkin
ejkujkewey tepate	NI	pumpkin pie
ekel	XP	from time to time
ekiljet	AI	read, count
ekimajl	TA	count
ekitk	TI	read, count, recite
eksitpu'k, eskitpu'k	XP	morning
eksitpu'kwek	XP	yesterday morning
eksitpu'nuk	XP	tomorrow morning
eksuet	AI	tell a lie
eksuo'qn	NI	lie
ekuk	TI	pulverize
el'toq	TI	make
ela'kitteket	AI	file
ela'ko'jink	AI	incline the head to the front
ela'lajl	TA	carry
ela'lsit	AI	carry oneself
ela'luet	AI	lead, conduct, be carried
ela'q	TI	swim in one direction
ela'qatesk	II	the trap falls, closes
ela'toq	TI	take it
elajl	TA	say, say to
elapalajl	TA	sprinkle with water, baptise privately
elapatoq	TI	sprinkle with water, baptise privately
elaqamat	AI	braid the middle of the snowshoe
elasumajl	TA	worship, honour, pray
elasutk	TI	worship, honour, pray
elasutmat	AI	pray (see also, alasutmat, i'alasutmat)
elat	AI	resemble, look alike
eleke'wa'lajl	TA	make someone king
eleke'wi'skw	NA	queen
eleke'wi'skwe'j	NA	princess
eleke'wi'skwe'ji'j	NA	little princess

eleke'wit	NA	the chosen, king, he who is elected
eleke'witewit	AI	be a king
eleke'witji'j	NA	prince
eleket	AI	throw dice, vote, draw lots
elelmit	AI	laugh
eli	PV	go, go and do, thus, as
eli'koq	TI	serve soup, soak, drain, clear away
eli'sewet	AI	sew
elipkewietaq	AI	go down
eliwnaqietaq	AI	ascend
eliaq	II	go
eliet	AI	go
elipusit	AI	go to embark
elisink	AI	stay down, be lying down
elisma'sit	AI	go lie down, stretch out (slowly)
elistk	TI	refuse
elitk	II	it flows in one direction
elitoq	TI	make, shape, celebrate (the mass)
eliusit	AI	go to warm oneself
elkimajl	TA	appoint, send someone
elko'jink	AI	incline the head to one side
elkomiktuajl	TA	invite
elkusua't	AI	leap, go up by leaps and bounds
elkusualajl	TA	leap over
elkwiluajl	TA	go and look for
ellukwet	AI	go to work
elma'toq	TI	carry away
elmekiaq	II	tide ebbs
elmi'knik	XP	future, in the future
elmiet	AI	go home (one's own), go away
elmiknik	II	in the future
elo'lajl	TA	throw down, make a heap
elo'toq	TI	throw down, make a heap
elp, elk	XP	also, still, moreover
elqam'sipuk	XP	on this side of a river
elqamkuk	XP	on this side, of a sound, estuary
eltaqnewet	AI	spin
elu'lajl	TA	carry by water
elu'pk	TI	carry on one's back
elu'pajl	TA	carry on one's back
elu'toq	TI	carry by water
elue'wa'lajl	TA	pervert, make wicked
elue'wa'luksit	AI	be perverted, rendered wicked
elue'wa'toq	TI	turn something bad
elue'wiet	NA	madman
elue'wiet	AI	be mad, crazy
elue'winu	NA	a wicked person, a sinner
elue'wit	AI	be wicked, a sinner, be mad, crazy
elue'wit	NA	sinner
elue'wuti('l)	NI	sin(s)
elue'wutik	II	that is a sin
elui'tmasit	AI	swear
elukowajl	TA	work for someone
elukutimkl	NI	day of work
elukwalajl	TA	shape
elukwatk	TI	mold
elukwet	AI	work
elulajl	TA	send, command
elutmaqniket	AI	tell tales, spread gossip
elutoq	TI	send, command
emtklpukua'sit	AI	kneel down
emel'siktaq	TA	frighten
emel'siktmamkewey	NI	phantasmagoria
emel'siktmat	AI	dream, imagine strange things
emittukwalajl	TA	visit
emk	TI	say, one says
empie	XP	one foot (measure)
emqatui'ket	AI	borrow
emqatui'ketoq	TI	lend
emqatuiajl	TA	lend to someone
emqwan	NA	soup spoon
emqwanji'j	NA	spoon
emteskit	AI	be arrogant
emtoqwalajl	TA	praise
emtoqwatk	TI	praise
enqa'toq	TI	stop
entoq	TI	lose, lose something
epa'kwesajl	TA	put away, put aside
epa'kwesk	TI	put away, put aside
epa'qasajl	TA	warm (a stone, iron, hair)
epa'qasikn	NI	stove
epa'qask	TI	warm (a stone, iron, hair)

epa'sit	AI	sit down
epit	AI	be seated
epitkuiet	AI	make a genuflection
epmeko'jink	AI	have the head inclined
epmepikat	AI	his side
epmetuk awti	NI	sidewalk
epmetuk	XP	to the side
epsaqtej(k)	NA	stove(s)
epsit	AI	be warm, be hot, have a fever
eptaqn(k)	NA	dish(es), plate(s)
eptek	II	be hot
epune'k, apune'k	II	below
esa'jl	TA	chase someone, banish, hunt
eselajl	TA	give as food
eseleket	AI	give willingly
eselk	TI	give as food
esiputoq	TI	sharpen
esitk	II	it spills
eskpajl	TA	eat raw
esktk	TI	eat raw
eske'k	II	raw
eskipa'jl	TA	wait for
eskipe'sit	AI	wait for
eskipetoq	TI	wait for (a thing)
eskitpu'k, eksitpu'k	II	morning
eskitpu'nuk	XP	tomorrow morning
eskmalajl	TA	wait for, watch over
eskmatk	TI	wait for, watch over
Eskmaw	NA	Eskimo
eskwi	PV	left over, remaining
eskwipa'qapukuet	AI	make an incomplete confession
eskwiaq	II	be left over
eskwiet	AI	be left
eskwit	AI	sneeze
esmajl	TA	feed
esmuetoq	TI	furnish food, feed
eso'ksit	AI	be chased
espe'k	AI	be elevated, high, of high rank
eta	XP	affirmative particle, yes, indeed, that is so, that's it
etamajl	TA	ask for
etawalsewajl	TA	ask on behalf of another
etawalsewet	AI	intercede for someone
etawaqtmat	AI	beg
etawet	AI	beg, ask, seek
etek	II	be
etkwi'k, ketkwi'k	TI	run
etlaptaqatk	TI	reside permanently
etlaqatk, tetlaqatk	TI	remain, reside there, always
etlewistoq	TI	chat, blab, gossip
etlewo'kwet	AI	speak, chat
etli	PV	be doing, there
etlikwet	AI	grow
etltulit	AI	build a canoe
etoq	TI	he makes his nest
etu'kmkewe'k	NA	scapula
etu'kutewe'k	NA	scapula
etu'wi'kasik	II	written inside and outside
etui	PV	on both sides
etuipanue'k, etu'panue'k	II	open on both sides
etuiw	XP	on both sides
etuiw qami'kuom	NI	sideaisle (of a church)
etuiw sipuk	XP	both sides of a river
etuk	XP	probably, perhaps
etuk jel	XP	probably
etuk suel	XP	almost, maybe so
etulit	AI	build a canoe
eulamu'k	II	puny
eulamuksit	AI	appear miserable
eule'jit	AI	be poor, wretched
eule'jit	NA	a pauper
eule'jk	II	poor, wretched
eule'k	AI	be miserable, worthy of pity
euleiwajl	TA	treat badly
eulet	AI	lie
euli	PV	misery, pity
eulikwet	AI	grow badly
eulistmuajl	TA	hear kindly
eulite'lket	AI	have compassion
eulite'lmajl	TA	have pity, compassion
eulite'lmkusit	AI	be an object of pity, of compassion
eulite'lsit	AI	have pity on oneself
eulite'tk	TI	have pity, compassion
eulite'teket	AI	have compassion, be merciful
euljewe'jit	NA	poor little, puny little wretch
eunasi	PV	mental disorder

eunasiet	AI	crazy, deranged, *non com pos mentis*
eunasita'sit	AI	think self mentally disturbed
eunasite'lmajl	TA	think someone mentally disturbed
eupniaq	II	the sky is calm
ewa'qewa'sit	AI	be made flesh
ewa'qewa'toq	TI	change into flesh
ewait	AI	possess, have
ewask	II	the lightning before the storm
eweke'k	II	there is room
ewi'kk	TI	write, mark, photograph
ewi'kajl	TA	describe, paint someone
ewi'kasit	AI	be written, described, painted
ewi'kat	AI	build
ewi'katk	TI	build
ewi'kiket	AI	write
ewi'kikewajl	TA	write for someone
ewi'kmuajl	TA	write to
ewi'tk	TI	name
ewi'tajl	TA	name someone
ewikmawit	AI	have a relative, an ally, a friend
ewipk	II	the sea is calm
ewjimajl, wjimajl	TA	have a father
ewjisink	AI	be stretched out on
Ewjit Niskam	NA	God the son
ewjit	AI	have a father
ewsami	PV	too much
eyasit	AI	treat oneself well
eyk	AI	be, be somewhere
i'al'kwilajl	TA	seek
i'al'kwilk	TI	search around
i'ala'sit	AI	roam around
i'nkuj	XP	one by one
i'a	XP	oh dear
i'al'kwiluasit	AI	seek endlessly, be a researcher
i'alasutmat	AI	pray (see also, alasutmat, elasutmat)
i'paji	PV	humbly
i'pusit	AI	make many trips by water
iaj	XP	especially, still more
iamuj, amuj, miamuj	XP	yes, indeed
iap(aq)	NA	male(s)
iapji, apji	PV	always
iapjinmkewey	NI	eternal death
iapjiwskijinuuti	NI	eternal life
iapjiw, apjiw	XP	always
iapjiwowey	NI	eternal
ika'lajl	TA	put in place, wager, bet, vote for
ika'q	II	arrive
ika't	AI	arrive, bump into
ika'taqatimk	NI	offertory
ika'taqn	NI	garden, field
ika'taqoq	TI	be a farmer
ika'teket	AI	set down, make an offering
ika'toq	TI	put, place, wager
ika'tuajl	TA	place for, offer to someone
ika'tuewey	NI	stake (in a game), wager
ikalajl	TA	protect
ikatk	TI	protect
ikatne'wet	AI	race
iknmakwet	AI	be favoured by a gift
iknmasit	AI	appropriate for oneself
iknmuajl	TA	give, give to someone, at tribute
iknmuet	AI	give, make a gift
iknmuetoq	TI	give a thing, make a gift, renounce
iknmuksit	AI	be favored by a present
iktuk	XP	in, with, at, on (locative suffix)
il'jo'qwa'toq	TI	repair, rectify, set in order, ratify
ila'skukwet	AI	play cards
ila'skw	NA	card
ila'toq	TI	prepare, repair
ilitoq	TI	renew, remake
ilpilaqoq	TI	undo the strap of a burden
ilta'toq	TI	close
ilutk	TI	correct orally
inaqneke'l	XP	to the right, on the right side
ipajiet	AI	be humiliated
ipajikpmite'lmajl	TA	humbly honour
isop	NI	hyssop

isteke, istekej, istaqej	XP	as, like
jajika'sit	AI	follow the shore
jajike'k	AI	be in good health, be well, be vigorous
jajiki	PV	accurately, completely
jajikisqatmajl	TA	completely obey
jaqali	PV	quick, briskly, with zeal, energetically
jaqalikiskaja'toq	TI	get on with it
jaqalinpkaq	AI	soon dead
jel	XP	and even, also, and (in numbers)
jel me'	XP	still more
jel mu	XP	not even so many
jenu	NA	giant
ji'ka'w	NA	bass, achigan
ji'met	AI	row, paddle
ji'nm(uk)	NA	man, male(s)
ji'nmuit	AI	be a man
jijikwaqa, jijuaqa	XP	sometimes
jijkawikne'jk	NA	grapes
jijklue'wj(k)	NA	sheep
jijklue'wji'j(k)	NA	lamb(s)
jijuaqa, jijikwaqaj	XP	sometimes, at times, soon after
jikalukuk	TI	go alone in a boat
jikitqateket	AI	disturb, annoy by striking noisily
jiko'teket	AI	sulk
jikstoq	TI	listen to
jikstuajl	TA	listen to
jikuksuk(ul)	NI	tinder (sg. & pl.)
jile'k	AI	be wounded, by accident
jinpeknewet	AI	milk
jipalajl	TA	fear
jipalkuk	TI	be frightening, dreaded
jipaluet	AI	fear, be fearful, timorous
jipatk	TI	fear
jipji'j	NA	bird (see also, sisip)
jiptueke'l	XP	at times, sometimes
jiptuk	XP	probably, perhaps
jipu'ji'j	NI	stream
jitunajl	TA	protect
joq	XP	curse of a man, hellish
jqolj(ik)	NA	toad(s)
jqoljewiku's	NA	November
jujij	NA	lizard, reptile
kptaq	XP	up
kptaqe'l	XP	upwards, toward the heights
kplno'l(aq)	NA	governor(s)
ka'qn	NI	cloth door
ka't, kataq	NA	eel, eels
kaju('k)	NA	wild pepper(s)
kal (Fr.)	XP	one fourth
kalkie	XP	one fourth
kalkunewey	NI	biscuit
kaltie	XP	one quarter
kamlamimk	NI	respiration, breath
kamlamun	NI	heart
Kanipewa'j	NA	Abenaki
kaqai'sijik	AI	several times
kaqai'sk	XP	several times
kaqai'sukuna'q	II	several days
kaqamit	AI	stand up, stand
kaqaptkl	TI	see all
kaqi, kaq	PV	completely
kaqinenkl	TI	know everything
kaqiaq, kaqaiaq	II	finished
kaqiet	AI	finished, at an end
kaqkkl, kaqqakl	TI	he supports all
kaqkimajl	TA	recite them all
kaqkisitasik	II	it is finished
kaqkitmajl	TA	read, recite, count it all
kaqlukwet	AI	finish working
kaqmatawalsewajl	TA	take the place of another
kaqmatawalsewet	AI	be a reconciler
kaqmutat	AI	be patient, agreeable
kaqmutk	TI	endure
kaqoqtek	II	burned, consumed; be burnt out
kaqsk	TI	burn
kaqsajl	TA	burn
kaqsit	AI	burnt
kaqtukowik	II	it thunders
kaqtukwaq	NA	there is thunder, thunder
kas (Eng.)	NI	wagons, train
kasa'toq	TI	obliterate
kaskmtlnaqn	NI	one hundred

kaskmtlnaqnijik	NA	hundred
kaskmtlnaqnipuna't	AI	years old,
kataq	NA	eels
katu, skatu	XP	but
kawatkupi	NI	spruce beer
kawatkw	NA	spruce
kawi('k)	NA	porcupine quill(s)
kawiksa'w	NA	thorn
kawskusi('k)	NA	cedar (sg. & pl.)
ke', ke'j, ke'sk	XP	hey! try it, it's your turn; here is, there is
ke'kwakuk	XP	on the top of a hill
ke'kwakw	NI	the top of a hill
ke'kwe'k	XP	above, upstairs, on high
ke'kwe'ke'l	XP	from above
ke'kwi	PV	on high, above
ke'l	XP	towards
ke'n, wela'lin	TA	thanks, thank you
ke's	XP	go lie down (to a dog)
ke'sk, ke'j, ke'	XP	thus, and so; go ahead
ke'sa'lajl	TA	burn
ke'sa'toq	TI	burn, destroy
ke'sk, e'sk	XP	when, while
ke'sk mna'q	XP	before, until, when not yet
keji, kji	PV	very, many, large, great
keji'kusit	AI	be known
keji'sit	AI	know oneself
kejiajl	TA	know, be acquainted with
kejikawike'l	XP	quite recently
kejikew, kejikaw, kejiko	XP	lately, recently, not long ago
kejikewji'jk	XP	a brief moment ago
kejipilajl	TA	bind, attach
kejipilk	TI	attach, bind
kejitoq	TI	know
keket	XP	before long, nearly, about to
kekina'masit	AI	teach oneself, learn
kekina'masuti	NI	lesson
kekina'muajl	TA	teach
kekina'muet	AI	teach
kekinua'tuajl	TA	let know
kekntie'wimk	NI	Sunday
kelatkweta'jl	TA	nail
keljit	AI	frozen
kelnk	TI	hold
kelneket	AI	be a godfather or godmother
kelpilajl	TA	bind, attach
kelpilk	TI	bind, attach
keltk	II	frozen
kelu'lk	II	good, beautiful
kelu'siet	AI	become good
kelu'sit	AI	be good, beautiful
Kelu'sit	NA	God (Good, above all)
kelu'suti	NI	beauty
kelulajl	TA	speak to someone
kelusit	AI	speak,
keluskapewit	AI	he is a deceiver, liar
kelutk	TI	ask for
kelutmat	AI	make a request
kelutmelsewajl	TA	intercede
kelutmuajl	TA	ask someone for some thing
kemutmajl	TA	steal from someone
kemutnalajl	TA	steal
kemutnatk	TI	steal
kenuk, kenukuj, kenukej	XP	although, no doubt
kepetaq	XP	on high
kepijoqq	TI	plug up, obstruct
kepijoqtk	TI	block off
kepmi	PV	honour, respect
kepmite'lmajl	TA	honour
kepmite'tk	TI	esteem
kepsaqa'toq	TI	lock
keptin	NA	captain
kesalajl	TA	like, love ,
kesalkuk	TI	be likeable, be loved
kesalkusit	AI	be loved
kesalsit	AI	love oneself
kesaltimkewey	NI	charity
kesaluet	AI	love
kesamu'k	II	brilliant
kesamuksit	AI	be glorified, appear brilliant
kesatasit	AI	be loved
kesateket	AI	love
kesatk	TI	like, love
kese'k	AI	be careful
keseiwajl	TA	be careful of
keseulajl	TA	please
kesi, ksi	PV	very, many, large
kesiksaluet	AI	be very loving
kesiksinukwat	AI	be very sick
kesilue'wit	AI	crazy
kesipukweli	XP	excessively

kesiet	AI	be honoured
kesik	NI	winter, it is winter
kesikawamkitk	II	swift
kesikawiet	AI	go fast
kesinukuik	II	hurt
kesinukwa'jit	AI	be indisposed, a bit off-colour
kesinukwamk(l)	NI	sickness(es)
kesinukwat	AI	be sick
kesispa'lajl	TA	wash, purify
kesispa'toq	TI	wash
kesite'tasit	AI	be admired
kesite'tk	TI	admire, covet
keska'toq	TI	lose, demolish
keske'lmajl	TA	spare
keskmi	PV	promptly, before time
keskmi net, npk	NI	premature death
keskulk	AI	heavy
kesma'toq	TI	push (a button or a bell)
kesmi	PV	thrust, progress, advance, push on
kesmipukua'sit	AI	be sent on ahead, advance
kesmiet	AI	advance, progress
kesmnmatimkewey	NI	sacrifice
kesmnmuajl	TA	offer
kesptek	NI	Saturday
kespi	PV	the end
kespia'tuksit	NA	the end of the story
kespimima'ltimk	NI	Extreme Unction
kespiaq	II	that is the end
kespiaqeweyit	AI	be last
kespukwa'lajl	TA	deceive
kespukwa'teket	AI	deceive
kess	XP	(to a dog), go away
ketanajl	TA	collect, detest, pursue, hunt
ketanteket	AI	pursue, hate, hunt
ketantimkewey	NI	hostility
ketantoq	TI	detest, pursue, hunt
ketapa'q	II	flood
ketapa'sit	AI	sink (slowly)
ketapekiet	AI	sing
ketapetesink	AI	dive, plunge under the water
ketapo'lajl	TA	push into the water, drag under
ketapo'toq	TI	sink, make sink, drag under
ketaqamu'k	XP	rear part of hut, place of honour
ketatkwe'k	II	death threatens
ketkiet	AI	get intoxicated, be drunk
ketkio'ti	NI	drunkenness
ketkunit	AI	spend the night
ketkwi'k, etkwi'k	TI	run
ketl	XP	truly
ketl oqu, ketl etuk	XP	for sure, nothing truer
ketl pa	XP	yes truly, in truth
ketlamstasit	AI	believe (in oneself), to hold as true
ketlamstk	TI	believe
ketlamstuajl	TA	believe someone
ketleweiwaqn	NI	truth
ketlewey	NI	truth
ketmesajl	TA	burn completely
ketmesk	TI	burn completely
ketu'samuqwat	AI	be thirsty
ketuanajl	TA	want to kill
ketuapsit	AI	want to profit by it
ketui	PV	precede, wish, want
ketuiaqntie'wimk	XP	Saturday
ketuiliet	AI	want to go
ketuinpm	TI	I want to die, I will die
ketuipiskiaq	II	it will be dark, before dark
ketuk	II	toll, ring
ketuk	TI	cry, proclaim
ketuksit	AI	want to, need to sleep
ketukwl	XP	at the signal of the bell
ketupajl	TA	want to eat, crave food
ketutk	TI	want to eat, crave food
keuk	TI	fell trees
kewa'toq	TI	knock down, upset
kewiet	AI	get weak, fall slowly
kewisink	AI	be hungry
kewjit	AI	be cold
kewkunajl	TA	hold in the hands
kewkunewet	AI	hold, be a godfather or godmother
kewkuni('t)	NA	godfather, godmother
kewkunk	TI	have, hold in the hand
kewkusk(i')	NA	godfather, godmother
ki'k	NI	your house
ki'kajiw, ki'kaji, ki'kat	XP	resisting, obstinate
ki'katlue'ultijik	NA	obstinate sinners

ki'katmtoq	TI	insubordinate conduct	
ki'kk	II	sharp	
ki'kli'kwej	NA	chicken	
ki'kwesu	NA	muskrat	
ki'l	XP	you (sg.)	
ki'lewey	NI	yours	
ki's	XP	already	
ki's kisi	XP	previously	
ki's sa'q	XP	formerly	
ki'skisi	XP	already, after	
kia'skiw	XP	exactly	
kia'skiwowey	NI	exactitude	
kijka', kijka'j	XP	a little	
kijka'ji'jk	XP	a touch, a dash	
kiju'	NA	mother, Mom, you my mother	
kikamkun(k)	NA	perch (sg. & pl.)	
kikja'simajl	TA	approach	
kikjiw	XP	near	
kikpesaq	II	it is raining	
kikto'qwa'teket	AI	turn (the millstone)	
kikto'qwialasutmamk	NI	Way of the Cross	
kilew, kilow	XP	you (pl.)	
kilewowey	NI	yours (pl.)	
kimewistoq	TI	whisper	
kimi	PV	secretly	
kimipqa'luet	AI	bite secretly	
kimtuk	XP	in secret	
kimu'tuk	XP	in secret	
kina'matimk	NI	instruction	
kina'sit	AI	advance, continue, over strain onself	
kinap(aq)	NA	giant(s), hero(s), warrior(s)	
kinapewamuksit	AI	look like a giant	
kinapi'skw	NA	Amazon	
kinu	XP	we, us (inc.)	
kinuowey	NI	ours (inc.)	
kipitaik	XP	above, on high	
kipoqwa'sit	AI	(sun) goes down, be inclined	
kipoqwa'toq	TI	turn	
kiqqaji, koqqwaji	PV	correctly	
kiqqwa'toq	TI	seize, take, grab hold of	
kiqqwajiaq	II	be correct	
kiqqwajiet	AI	be appropriate, in order	
kiqqwajiw	XP	correctly	
kiqqwattek	II	straight	
kisa'lajl	TA	create, do, make of someone	
kisa'toq	TI	create, make (with effort)	
kisakisit	AI	become full	
kisatalk	AI	finish eating	
kisataluajl	TA	satisfy	
kisewistoq	TA	be able to talk	
kisi	PV	already, after; be able	
kisi'sit	AI	develop, be created oneself	
kisiatalultimk	XP	after the meal	
kisimiawla'kwek	NI	afternoon	
kisiajl	TA	make, create	
kisiku	NA	old man, gaffer, elder	
kisikue'pite's	NA	old maid	
kisikul'pa'tu's	NA	bachelor	
kisikui'skw(aq)	NA	old lady (ladies)	
kisikuiet	AI	grow old	
kisikuit	AI	be old	
kisita'sit	AI	make up one's mind	
kisitasik	II	be made	
kisitasit	AI	be made	
kisiteket	AI	make, create, develop	
kisitoq	TI	make a thing, create, carry out	
kisituajl	TA	make something for someone	
kiskaja'lajl	TA	accomplish, establish	
kiskaja'toq	TI	accomplish, prepare	
kiskaje'k	AI	be prepared	
kiskajiet	AI	be aware, finish	
kiskattek	II	be prepared	
kiskuk	NI	day, today	
kisna	XP	or, or else	
kispn	XP	as soon as, by means of, once	
Kisu'lkw	NA	God	
kitk	XP	each, both, both kinds	
kiwatqatk	TI	be bored (in one's house)	
kiwkw	NI	earthquake	
kiwnaqaj, kiwnaqa	XP	especially, principally	
kiwnik(ik)	NA	otter(s)	
kiwnikewey	NI	of the otter	
kiwtaw, kiwto'qwiw	XP	around	
kiwto'qiw	XP	around	
kiwto'qotesink	AI	leap around, whirl around	
kiwto'qotukwi'k	TI	run around, in a circle	
kiwto'qwa'jijit	AI	turn	
kiwto'qwi, kikto'qwi	PV	around	

kji	PV	big		knekk	XP	far
kjia'papi	NA	equator		knki'kwinaqa	NA	our first parents
kjialasutmaqn	NI	sacrament		ko'komin(k)	NA	sloe(s)
kjialasutmo'kuom	NI	cathedral		kopit(aq)	NA	beaver(s)
kjiansale'wit	NA	archangel		kopji'j(k)	NA	cup(s)
kjiapaqt	NI	ocean		kopsji'jk	NA	cups
kjieleke'wi'skw	NA	empress		koqoe'ji'j	NI	little something
kjieleke'wit	NA	great king, emperor		koqoe'juey	NI	trifle
kjikelu'sit	NA	God (Most Beautiful and Most Good), the holy, the good above all		koqoe'l wekla	II	what are these things?
				koqoey	NI	what?, thing, something
				koqoey wjit	II	why, because of what?
kjikmuatkw	NA	white pine		koqqwa'lajl	TA	catch, seize
kjil'ue'wuti'l	NI	deadly sins		koqqwa'toq	TI	seize, take, grab hold of
Kjiniskam	NA	great God		koqqwaji	PV	correctly
kjipa'tlia's	NA	bishop		koqqwajiaq	II	it is appropriate, suitable
kjipa'tlia'sji'j	NA	prelate		koqqwajiet	AI	be appropriate, in order
kjisape'wit	NA	the holy, the good above all		kpaqminaq	XP	at our back, behind us, ago
kjisape'wuti'l	NI	theological virtues		ksin	XP	last winter
kjisaqmaw	NA	great lord		ksinuk	XP	next winter
kjisipu	NI	great river		Ksispa'sue'kati	NI	Purgatory
kjiwinsit	AI	do great evil		ksu'sk(k)	NA	black spruce
kjiwlaqn	NA	great vase		ktk(ik)	NA	the other(s)
kjipituimtlnaqnijik	NA	million		ktk(l)	NI	other(s)
kjipituimtlnaqnl	NI	million (pl.)		ktki	PV	other
kjiwksuk	NA	one family		ktkinipn	XP	last summer
klapis	XP	until, as far as, so far, finally		ktkisapo'nuk	XP	day after tomorrow
klaptanek	XP	at the sorcerer's, at the blacksmith's		ktkisikun	XP	springtime before
				ktkiwla'kw	XP	evening before
klitaw(aq)	NA	raspberry		ktkiwlaku	XP	the day before yesterday
klopskiaq	NA	falcons		ktkipuk	XP	the past winter
kloqoej(k), kloqowej(k)	NA	star(s)		ktkitqoq	XP	autumn before
kloqoejuiaq	II	the stars appear		kta'nuk	XP	towards the open sea, the edge of the sea
klujjiewey	NI	cross				
klujjieweyktuk	XP	under the cross		kta'nuke'l	XP	at the edge of the ocean
klujjiewta'sit	NA	crucifix		ktaqmkuk	XP	on the other side (Newfoundland)
klujjiewtajl	TA	crucify				
klujjiewte'k	TI	crucify		ktaqmsipuk	XP	on the other side of a river
klujjiewtosit	AI	make the sign of the cross		ktlamstk	TI	believe
klusuaqn	NI	word		kujmuk	XP	outside, out of here, out!
kmeltaminiskamijinuaq	NA	our first ancestors		kul'piw	XP	forthwith, immediately
kmtn(k)	NA	mountain(s), hill		kulkwi's	NA	pig
kmu'j(k)	NA	tree(s) (standing)		kulkwi'suey	NI	bacon
kmu'jiktuk	XP	in the trees		kulkwi'suo'kuom	NI	pigsty
kmutnes	NA	thief		kulua'toq	TI	join, mix
kne'ji'jk	XP	a little later		kuluk	XP	also, with
knekji'jk	XP	a bit far		kulumkl	NI	wheat

kun'te'j	NI	little stone, pebble
kun'tew	NI	stone(s), rock(s)
kun'tewik	II	it is stony, there is stone
kun'tewit	AI	be a stone
kuow (pl. kuaq)	NA	pine (tree)
kuowa'qamitk	NI	grove of pine trees
kuowipkw	NI	turpentine, pine balm
kuta'sik	II	run, pour out
kuta'sit	AI	flow, pour
kuteket	AI	pour out, tip
kutputi('l)	NI	seat(s)
kwal'ti'kw	TA	cook for one another
kwanask	NI	driftwood
kwastale	XP	really!, ah!, what a business
kwe'	XP	greeting, hey
kwejaqmiet	AI	boil
kweltamit	AI	fast
kweltamultimk	XP	Friday (day of abstinence)
kweltamultimkewey	NI	fasting
kwesapskiaq	NI	point with the pebbled bottom
kwesawey	NI	point
kweseiwajl	TA	protect, look after, take care
kweso'tk	TI	protect, look after, take care
kwetaiwajl	TA	scare (children, animals)
kwetajikwet	AI	have a dreadful appearance
kwetapet	AI	endure, be punished
kwetapet	NA	ox
Kwetejk	NA	the Mohawks, Iroquois
kwetmat	AI	smoke
kwey	XP	hello!
kwilasik	II	be followed
kwilasit	AI	be followed
kwilk	TI	search for, look for
kwiluajl	TA	search, look for, inquire into
kwilutk	TI	seek
kwilutmajl	TA	ask
kwilutmuajl	TA	demand of someone
kwimu	NA	loon
kwis	NA	you my son
kwitn(l)	NI	canoe(s)
kwlaman	XP	in order that, so that
l'kusuaqn	NI	ladder, staircase
l'kusuaqnik	II	there is a ladder
l'kwetu	NA	cow, moose, caribou, ox, ram
l'mu'j	NA	dog
l'mu'si's	NA	puppy
l'n, l'n ta na, l'n oquj	XP	for, indeed, in fact that, because
l'nim	XP	too
l'no'qoqm(k)	NA	skate(s)
l'noqm	NI	green wood
l'nu	NA	man, person, Indian
l'nu'skw	NA	Indian woman
l'nu'skwe'j	NA	Indian girl
l'nu'tesink	AI	dance in the manner of the Indians
l'nua'lajl, elnua'lajl	TA	make him a man
l'nua'sit, elnua'sit a	AI	become a man, be made man (Indian)
l'nuey	NI	Indian
l'nuik, elnuik	II	there are people
l'nuit, elnuit	AI	be a person, Indian
l'nuoqta'w	NA	statue
l'pa, l'npa, l'na pa	XP	truly, really
l'pa'tu'skw(aq)	NA	girl(s)
l'pa'tu'stut	NA	my allies, my brothers
l'pa'tuj	NA	boy
l'ue'winu	NA	sinner, wicked person
l'ue'winu'skowit	AI	be a sinneress
l'ue'winuit	AI	be a sinner
l'ue'wuti	NI	sin
l'uiknek	XP	seven
l'uiknekewey	NI	seventh; Sunday
lsqe'kn, lsqeikn	NI	chest, casket
la'qn	NI	wound
la'taqsun(k)	NA	pail(s), bucket(s) (for carrying)
lakkla'ns	NI	barn
lakklem	NI	cream
lakko'l(k)	NA	cord(s) (of wood)
laklus(k)	NA	jug(s)
lamalqk	XP	interior of a cave, sepulchre
lame'k	XP	inside
lame'ke'l	XP	below
lami, lamu	PV	inside
lamikuomk, lamukuomk	XP	indoors, inside the hut
lamlutaqn	NI	court, enclosure

lampo'q	NI	spring water, pure water		malipqanj	NI	hazelnut
lamqamu'k	XP	underground, in limbo		malo'qn	NI	laziness, sloth
lamqwan	NI	undergarment		malqomajl	TA	eat, devour
lamso'q	XP	under a rock		malqotk	TI	eat, devour
lamua'w	XP	the inside of the egg		mals	NI	flint
lapa'y(k)	NA	tub(s), bucket(s), kettle(s)		malsan	NA	shopkeeper
lapaltinewey	NI	holy water		maqa'q	II	large
lape'ls	NA	yard		maqaj	XP	severely, hard
lapilask	NA	linen (plural)		maqamikew	NI	earth
laplusun	NI	prison		maqatkwik	II	the sea is bad, rough, high
lapolji'j(k)	NA	bowl(s), cup(s)		maqatpay	AI	my large head
lappels(k)	NA	yard(s) (measure)		maqmikek	XP	on earth
lapwel(k)	NA	hair (sg. & pl.)		maqmikew	NI	earth, land
laqatimkewey	NI	election		maqoqsit	AI	large
lasi'l	NA	sealing wax		maqtawekna'q	TI	be dressed in black
lassiet(k)	NA	plate(s)		maqtawekna'qawey	NI	of the Black Robes
latto'law	NA	bull (bovine)		maqtewe'k	AI	black
latusan	NI	dozen		maqtewi'tuat	AI	have a black beard
Lesui'p	NA	Jew		maskelmuksit	AI	accursed
letqa'mun(k)	NA	arrow(s)		maskwi	NI	bark (of a tree)
likpenikn	NI	basket		masqwa'toq	TI	put aside, hide
lipqatamun(k)	NA	lady's slipper(s) (plant)		matawe'k	NI	confluent
lipqomutaqn(k)	NA	top(s)		matawi	PV	encircle
lo'q	XP	very, many, much		matawiaq	II	be complete, whole
lu'sue'skw	NA	daughterinlaw		matawiet	AI	be complete
lukwe'k	XP	between		matew	XP	never, no more
				matnk	TI	wrestle against
				matnajl	TA	wrestle against
mta, muta	XP	for, because, since		matta'jl	TA	beat
ma'	XP	no, not (fut.)		mattaqa'teket	AI	ring (the bell)
ma' koqoey	XP	nothing		matto'ksit	AI	be beaten
ma' wen	XP	nobody, no one, not one		matues	NA	porcupine
ma'qey	NI	flesh		mawa'tmk	AI	all assembled, all counted
mail	NI	mile		mawi, maw	PV	much, (all) together, very
maja'sit	AI	move, stir, depart		mawialasutmamk	NI	public prayer, retreat
majulkwalajl	TA	follow		mawiespe'k	AI	most high
mal'tew	NI	blood		mawimskilk	AI	very big
mala	XP	over yonder, there		mawimtoqwa'lanej	TA	let us all adore him
malae'l	XP	that way, in that direction		mawiaq, mawiaj	II	come together
male'k	AI	be lazy		mawieyikw	AI	gather together
maleimk	NI	laziness, sloth		mawio'mi	NI	society, band, assembly
malike'w(k)	NA	quart(s), barrel(s)		mawkitasik	II	additional
malike'wji'j	NA	barrel		mawkitk	TI	add up
malikimajl	TA	poke fun at		mawkitmajl	TA	include
malikmsit	AI	poke fun at oneself		mawnmek	XP	whole
malikmuet	AI	poke fun at		mawnmuajl	TA	give all together

me', me'j	XP	more, still, yet
me' mna'q	XP	not yet
me' nalaiw	XP	later, farther on
me' tujiw	XP	at present
me'jeke'l	XP	at times, sometimes
me'si	PV	unable
me'si'wet	AI	be unshakable
me'sipkwansit	AI	cannot help self, unable to move
me'siajl	TA	be lacking to someone
me'su'tek	XP	uncovered
me'su'tuk	XP	bare, publicly
mejijk	XP	still
mejijk newt	XP	one more time
mekite'tk	TI	remember
meko'tik	II	expensive, dear
mekopa'q	NI	wine
mekwaik, miawe'k	XP	in the middle, among, amidst
meljekuiaq	NA	birds without feathers
melkpilajl	TA	attach strongly
melke'k	AI	be hard
melke'k	II	hard
melki	PV	strongly
melkiketlamstasit	AI	believe strongly
melkiketlamstk	TI	believe strongly
melkiknaq	II	strong
melkiknat	AI	strong
melkite'tk	TI	think hard about
melknk	TI	hold strongly
melknajl	TA	make strong, hold strongly
melmuapateket	AI	water
meltami	PV	in the beginning, at first
meltamipekaje'k	II	pure, immaculate
meltamikitamk	NA	firstborn
meltamtuk	XP	from, in the beginning, at first
meluia'kwek, miawla'kwek	NI	noon
meluij	XP	rather
mena'lajl	TA	remove, send back
mena'toq	TI	remove, tear out or off
mena'tuajl	TA	remove it from someone
menaqaj, menaqa	XP	with care
meniaq	II	be removed, detach
meniet	AI	move aside, withdraw
meniskk	TI	go and get, go look for
meniskuajl	TA	go look for
menkitk	TI	subtract
meno'lajl	TA	dig up (potatoes)
meno'tk	TI	dig up
meno'teket	AI	harvest
menueket	AI	need
menwi'kk	TI	copy, transcribe
mesa'lajl	TA	swallow
mesa'toq	TI	swallow
meselmajl	TA	beg, ask for something
meseltk	TI	ask for something
mesi	PV	entirely, all
meske'k	AI	regret, be sad
meski'k	II	be big, large
meskilk	AI	be big, large
mesnajl	TA	acquire, take, receive
mesnmuajl	TA	to get s.t. from s.o.
mesta	XP	all, whole
mestanajl	TA	have all
mestank	TI	have all
mestanmuajl	TA	give all
mesua'lajl	TA	show
mesue'k	XP	openly
mesui	PV	openly
meteskuaqn	NI	pride
metkwat	AI	have a bare head
metla's	XP	ten
metla'sipuna't	AI	years old
metla'sukmu'kw	AI	go as ten in a boat
metma't	AI	stroll, take a trip
metoqwa'lajl	TA	bring down from the woods
metu'na'q	II	bad weather
metue'k	AI	be hard, troublesome
metui	PV	difficult
metuinstasik	XP	arduous, difficult to understand
metuipuk	XP	hard winter
metukuna'q	II	bad weather
Mi'kmawa'j	NA	Mi'kmaw
mi'kmawi'skw	NA	Mi'kmaw woman
mi'kmawi'skwe'j	NA	young Mi'kmaw girl
mi'kmawit	AI	be a Mi'kmaw
mi'kmuesu	NA	the nymph of the forest
mi'mat	AI	be stocked for a trip
mi'soqo, mi'soquj	XP	until, as far as
mi'walajl	TA	thank (Restigouche)

mi'watk	TI	implore, thank (Restigouche; see also, mui'watk)	minua'lajl	TA	renew
			minua'lsit	AI	renew oneself
mia'wj(k)	NA	cat(s) (see also, qajue'wj(ik))	minua'teket	AI	be renewed, revived
miamuj, amuj, iamuj	XP	yes, indeed, certainly	minui	PV	anew, again
miaula'kwek	NI	noon (see also meluia'kwek)	minuiwskijinuit	AI	be reborn
miaw, miawe'k	XP	amidst, among	minuiwskijinuuti	NA	new life
miawikan	NI	middle of the hut	minuit	AI	be renewed
miawio'kuom	NI	nave	missemin(k)	NA	blackcurrant(s)
mijipjewey	NI	food	miti	NA	poplar
mijisit	AI	eat	mitiey	N	of a poplar tree
mijisotelajl	TA	take care of, feed, pasture (cattle)	mjijaqmij	NI	soul
			mjijaqmijueyek	NI	spiritual
mijjit	AI	eat (Restigouche)	mkkn	NI	fishhook
mijua'ji'j	NA	child	mksn(l)	NI	moccasin(s)
mikwite'lmajl	TA	remember (willingly)	mksna'q	TI	have footwear
mikwite'tk	TI	remember (willingly)	mkamlamun	NI	heart
mila'sit	AI	play, amuse oneself	ml'kiji'nm	NA	giant
milamu'kwl, milamu'kl	NI	various, diverse things	mlakej(k), molakej(k)	NA	milk, breast(s)
milesit	AI	be rich	mlakeju'mi	NI	butter
milesuti	NI	wealth, riches	mljoqm	NI	dry wood
mili	PV	number, quantity, variety, multiple	mna'q	XP	no, not yet
			mntu	NA	devil
mili'sit	AI	speak different languages	mntua'kik	NI	hell
milita'sit	AI	have various kinds of thoughts, daydream	mokasn(k)	NA	shoe(s) with a sole, boots
			moqopa'q	NI	wine
milkutat	AI	variously dressed	moqopa'qek	II	that is wine, there is some wine
miloqwet	NA	the chatterbox			
miltawemkewe'l	NI	various requests, invocations	moqwa	XP	no, not
			moqwa'j, moqwe'j	XP	no, not
milwikasit	NA	mottled; name for the parrot	moqwe	XP	no
mim'kwnajl	TA	anoint	mpitn	NI	hand, palm
mimajit	AI	live	mst, mst	XP	all
mimaju'najl	TA	give life	mst kaqikiskajiaq	II	used up
mimaju'nk	TI	endue with life	mst tami	XP	everywhere
mimaju'nsit	AI	give oneself life	mst te'skl	NI	all the individuals, all the objects
mimaju'nuet	AI	give life			
mimajuinu	NA	living being, person	mst te'sijik	NA	all the individuals, all the objects
mimey	NI	oil, grease			
mimi'l	NI	sugared almond, sugarcovered pill	mst wen	XP	each one
			msaqtaqt	NI	floor
mimn'tet	AI	spin	mtawekn	NI	flag
mimukwasit	AI	hide	mte'skm	NA	serpent
minijk	NI	fruit	mtesan	NA	baby, last child in a family
minit	NI	minute	mtia'qatestaqn	NI	collection
minu'nsit	AI	revive	mtijin	NI	thumb, inch
minu'nsit	AI	revive	mtln te'sijik	NA	ten

mtln	XP	ten
mtlnewey	NI	tenth
mtluikn	NI	finger
mtoqn	NI	garment
mtu'noqt	NI	storm, bad weather
mtukwape'kn	NI	chin
mtukwejan	NI	forehead
mtun	NI	mouth
mu	XP	no, not
mu koqoey	NI	nothing
mu l'nim	XP	not too bad
mu nkutey	XP	more than
mu pa	XP	certainly not
mui'walajl	TA	thank
mui'watk	TI	implore, thank (see also, mi'watk)
muiaq	NA	sea ducks
muin(aq)	NA	bear(s)
muine'skw	NA	female bear
mujajit	AI	love
mujkajewey	NI	well made, excellent, useful, pleasant
mulqatk	TI	dig
mun'ti('l)	NI	pocket(s), bag(s)
munsa, mujka, mujkaj	XP	very remarkable, extraordinary
munsaiwajl, munseiwajl	TA	beset, flatter, put pressure on
munsaptmuajl	TA	exactly observe someone's behaviour
munso'tk	TI	put pressure on, flatter
musapoqjat	AI	soft (soap)
musika'toq	TI	clean, clear, strip
muskatoq	TI	divulge
muskunikn	NI	cubit
musquiaq	II	the weather clears
musuatk	TI	lack, be bored, yearn
musuey	NI	handkerchief
mutputi	NI	chair, bench
n'kalaw	NA	gallon
n'katikn	NA	pound
na	XP	emphasis particle, and so, now, you see, therefore, this, that, there, then
na'koqteskk	TI	arrive by day
na'kowi	XP	by daylight
na'kowintukulit	AI	hunt in the daytime
na'kowiaq	II	there is daylight
na'kowiey	NI	daylight
na'ku'set	NA	sun, daystar
na'ku'setewey	NI	watch
na'kwek(l)	NI	day(s)
na'n	XP	five, five times
na'newey	NI	fifth
na'qaji'jk(e'l)(e'l)	XP	a little later, just now
na'qapukuet	AI	speak slowly
na'qek, na'qeke'le'l	XP	late
na'qeke'l	XP	further, later
na't koqoey	NI	something
na'tala'toq	TI	do something wrong, harmful
na'tami	XP	somewhere, nearly
na'tamutuk	XP	somewhere or other
na'te'l	XP	there
naji	PV	intend, be about to
nala	XP	those
nalaiw	XP	far, late, soon
nalko'n(k)	NA	comb(s)
nalsi'kuk	TI	scratch, scrape
nama'sit	AI	follow the wind
nan'temi, nan'tem	XP	always
nan'tunajl	TA	seek, feel, grope about
nan'tunk	TI	seek, feel, grope about
nanijik	NA	five (people)
nanipunqk	XP	five years
naniska'q	XP	fifty
naniska'qawey	NI	fiftieth
naniska'ql	NI	fifty (pl.)
naniskeksijik	NA	fifty
nankl	NI	five (things)
nankmi	PV	immediately, right away
nankmiw, ankmiw	XP	immediately
nanukumu'kw	AI	go as five in a boat
nanukuna'q	XP	four days
nape'kwik	NA	male otter, fox
nape'skw	NA	male bear
napeme'kw	NA	male fish
napesm	NA	male canine
napew(k)	NA	male bird(s)
napi	PV	trace, copy

napi'kikn(k)	NA	portrait(s), photograph(s)
napiaq	NA	male whale, male seal
napkk	TI	reproduce, copy
napkuajl	TA	replace, keep a place, be curate
napnk	TI	return
napnajl	TA	return
naptesink	AI	have the same fate
napui'kk	TI	copy, paint, photograph
napui'kajl	TA	copy
napui'kikn	NA	portrait, photograph
naqaji	PV	delay, negligence
naqaji'jke'le'l	XP	a little further on
naqajiket	AI	neglect, delay
naqajit	AI	delay
naqap	NA	servant
naqat	NA	these
naqatit	AI	shoot an arrow
naqla	NA	those
naqmaje'jk	II	easy
naqmasiaq	II	easy
naqsa'sit	AI	hurry
naqsi	PV	promptly, fast
naqsimijjit	AI	eat fast
nasaptk	TI	come and see
nasapteket	AI	come to see
nasawkwaw	NA	snow shoe
naskoplaw	NA	plank
naskwet	AI	be a virgin
naskwet	NA	virgin
nassamajl	TA	come to see
nata'	XP	capacity, ability
natqa'toq	TI	bring out, deliver
natqaspeka'toq	TI	withdraw
nattamajl, nassamajl	TA	go and ask
nattawaqtmat	AI	come to ask for, seek
natuaqnek	NI	Eel Ground
natuat	AI	harpoon
nawiaq	II	impossible
ne'a'toq	TI	show
ne'kaw	XP	straight ahead, continuing
ne'pa'jl	TA	he kills him
ne'patuajl	TA	kill, destroy something of another
ne's	XP	three
ne'sijik	NA	three, three people
ne'sisijik	NA	three
ne'siskl	NI	three things
ne'tata'suti	NI	intelligence, wisdom
ne'w	XP	four
ne'wowey	XP	fourth; Thursday
nekapikwa't	AI	be blind
neket	XP	these
nekla, wekla	XP	formerly, these past days, at that time
nekla tlisip	XP	at that time
nekm	NA	he, she
nekmewey	NI	his/hers
nekmewit	AI	it is him
nekmow	XP	they
nekmowewey	XP	theirs
nekmowey	NI	their
nekpa'q	II	flood in the house
nekuk	AI	bring game
nemi'ajl, nemiajl	TA	see
nemi'kusit	AI	be seen
nemi'sit	AI	see oneself
nemitasit	AI	be seen
nemiteket	AI	see
nemitoq	TI	see (a thing)
nemja'sit	AI	raise oneself
nemja'toq	TI	raise
nenaqi	PV	fast
nenaqikjijitoq	TI	learn fast
nenaqiet	AI	hurry
nenaqita'sit	AI	think quickly, in a hurry
nenaqitasit	AI	make an object for oneself quickly
nenaqiw	XP	fast
nenesatkitk	TI	divide
nenk	TI	know
nenqa'toq	TI	stop
nenuajl	TA	know (by sight)
nenuite'lmajl	TA	know it in the mind
nenuite'tk	TI	know it in the mind
nenustuajl	TA	know by the voice
nenwite'tk	TI	remember by reporting
nepat	AI	sleep
nepewisk	NI	moonlight
nepilajl	TA	take care of, give remedies to

nepitk	TI	take care of, give remedies to
nepk	AI	die
nepsa'toq	TI	raise
nepu'titkika	NA	the deceased
nepuajl	TA	put to sleep
nepuskwet	AI	go look for meat
nesamuqwat	AI	drink
nesat	AI	fear, mistrust
nesiska'q	XP	thirty
nesiska'qawey	NI	thirtieth
nesiska'ql	NI	thirty (pl.)
nesiskeksijik	AI	thirty
neskawet	AI	sing with gestures and responses
nespiet	AI	have with oneself
nespit	AI	remain
nestk	TI	understand
nestmalseuksit	AI	be interpreted
nestmalsewajl	TA	explain, interpret for someone
nestmalsewatk	TI	explain, interpret for a thing
nestmalsewet	AI	interpret
nestmalsewsit	AI	interpret oneself
nestmalsewti'kw	AI	interpret each other
nestmat	AI	understand
nestmuajl	TI	understand something for someone
nestuajl	TA	understand
nestuimajl	TA	recover, correct
nestuimsit	AI	recover oneself
nestuimuet	AI	recover
nesukumu'kw	AI	go as three in a boat
nesukuna'q	XP	three day
nesutk	TI	fear
net	XP	this, that, that one
net	AI	die
neta'tukulit	AI	be clever hunter
netaiwajl	TA	frighten
netawa'q	TI	know how to swim
netawe'k	NA	scout
netawet	AI	call out, sell at auction
netawi, natawi	PV	capacity, ability
netawselk	TI	give willingly
netna	XP	that is right, that's it
netuaik	AI	be a scout, spy
netui'ska'jl	TA	sell for someone
netui'sketoq	TI	sell
netukulit	AI	chase, hunt
netulajl	TA	be missed by someone
netutulit	AI	be capable, clever
neukumu'kw	AI	go as four in a boat
neukuna'q	II	four days
neukunit	AI	four days
newijik	NA	four (people)
newiska'q	XP	forty
newiska'qawey	NI	fortieth
newiska'ql	II	forty (pl.)
newiskekipunqk	XP	forty years
newiskeksijik	AI	forty
newkl	II	four (things)
newt	XP	one, once
newt ajiet	XP	one o'clock
newtanajl	TA	take one
newtaqik	NI	one dollar
newte'	NI	one thing
newte'j(k)	NA	person(s)
newte'jit	AI	one
newte'jk	NI	one
newtewistoq	TI	he speaks alone, soliloquy
newti, nkuti	PV	the same, only, the same thing
newtikiskk	XP	one day, a whole day
newtikit	NA	single progeny, an only son
newtipuk	XP	one winter
newtipuna't	AI	one year old
newtipunqk	XP	one year
newtiska'q	XP	ten
newtiska'qawey	NI	tenth
newtiska'ql	NI	ten
newtiskekipuna't	AI	years old
newtiskeksijik	AI	ten
newtite'lmajl	TA	think only of
newtitpa'q	XP	a, one night, all night
newtoqsit	AI	one (cylindrical object)
newtukuna'q	NI	one day
newtukunit	AI	one day old, the first of the month
newtukwa'lukwet	AI	be alone, a bachelor
newtunajl	TA	have (to hold) one of them
newtunk	TI	have (to hold) one of them

newtupistay	NA	my only (son), cherished one
ni'k	NI	my house, my cabin, my hut
ni'kji'j	NI	my little place
ni'mat	AI	be stocked for a trip
ni'n	XP	I, me
ni'newey	NI	mine
ni'newi	AI	it is me
nijkamij	NA	grandfather
nijkulajl	TA	cure
nikamu'tasit	AI	be fattened
nikani	PV	ahead, out front, before
nikanikjijitekewinu	NA	prophet
nikanintoq	NA	song master
nikaniw	XP	ahead, out front, before
nikantuk	XP	before, in front of, in advance
nikatne'wet	AI	win a race
nike', nike'j	XP	now
nike' to'q	XP	now; lit. now then
nike'jewey	NI	of the present
nikma'j	NA	my neighbor
Nikskam	NA	God (see also Niskam)
nilu	NI	my food
nimnoqn(k)	NA	birch (sg. & pl.)
ninasunajl	TA	choose
ninasunk	TI	choose
ninen	XP	we, us (exc.)
ninenewey	XP	ours (exclusive)
nipi	PV	at night
nipi('k)	NA	leaf(s)
nipi('l)	NI	cabbage(s)
nipisoqn	NI	shoot
nipisoqnta'jl	TA	whip
nipispaqn(l)	NI	poplar shoot(s)
nipitl	NI	my teeth
nipk	XP	summer
nipn	XP	last summer
nipnuk	XP	next summer
nipukt	NI	forest
nipuktuk	XP	in the woods
nisa'sit	AI	go down, descend
nisa'toq	TI	lower, go down
nisiw	XP	descending, downwards
Niskam	NA	God (see also, Nikskam)
niskameuti	NA	divinity
niskamewa'lajl	TA	make God
niskamewa'sit	AI	become God
niskamewa'toq	TI	make God
niskamewe'k	AI	be pious, holy
niskamewey	NI	divine
niskamewiwi'katikn	NI	Scripture
Niskamewikia	NA	Mother of God
niskamewit	AI	be God
niskamewita'sit	AI	believe in oneself, as a god
niskamewite'lmajl	TA	believe in someone, as a god
niskamewite'tk	TI	believe in something, as a god
niskamij	NA	grandfather, ancestor
niskamk wniskamual	NA	God of gods
nitap	NA	my comrade
nitapji'j	NA	my friend
nitu'l	NI	my beard
niwe'k	II	the tide is dried up
niwetek	II	the tide is out
njiknam	NA	my younger brother
njilj	NA	my fatherinlaw
njukwi'ji'j	NA	my motherinlaw
nkamlamun	NI	my heart
nkat	NI	my foot
nkij	NA	my mother
nklnikn	NA	(my) godchild
nkutapew	NA	bachelor
nkutapewi'skw	NA	old maid
nkutey	XP	once, one, too, also, the same, only, uniquely
nkuti	PV	the same, likewise, uniquely
nkutiskeksuti	NI	group of ten
nkutiw	XP	at once
nkutunemi'ksuk	NI	one single family of that sort
nkwe'ji'j	NA	my younger sister
nkwis	NA	my son
nme'j(ik)	NA	fish
nme'ji'j	NA	herring (see also, akoqmaw, aqoqme'kw)
nmis	NA	my elder sister
nmuksnk	NA	my footware, shoes
no'qoq	TI	cough
npaqmk etek	II	it is behind me
npisun	NI	remedy, cure

npitn	NI	my hand
nplaqnek, kplaqnek, etc.	XP	before me, you, etc. (chest, eyes, face)
npukum	NA	my gum, chewing gum, quid of tobacco
nqani	PV	old, worn out, useless
nqani'kuom	NI	old hut
nqani'psmun(k)	NA	chalice(s)
nqanie'pite's	NA	old maid
nqanil'pa'tu's	NA	bachelor
nqaniwen'ji'kuom	NI	an old house
nqano'pati	NI	well
nqanuisun	NI	family name
nqapaqsun(k)	NA	dipper(s)
nqasaiw, nqask	XP	immediately
nqasi	PV	immediately
nqosi	NA	my nail, claw
nqwat	XP	you old devil (to companion)
nstmalseuti	NI	interpretation
nstnaqn	NA	orphan
nsaqmam	NA	my lord
nsi	NI	my lip
nsis	NA	my elder brother
nsiskw	N	my face
nskawaqn	NI	Mi'kmaw song, this song
nsm	NA	my niece, cousin
nsptk	XP	at the same time
ntalikam, ntalikem	NI	my possession, property
ntaqo'qn	NI	shame (sense of), shameful
ntaqo'qney	NI	ashamed
ntaqo'qnl	NI	harmful things
nte'pitem	NA	my wife
ntepluk	NI	armed forces
nti	NA	my dog
ntinin	NI	my body, my person, myself
ntlamiluk	NI	my entrails
ntlu'suk	NA	my soninlaw
ntoqo, ntoqu	XP	then, next
ntue'm	NA	my work animal
ntui'sketoq	TI	sell a thing, of one's own
ntul	NI	my boat
ntus	NA	my daughter
nu'	XP	daddy
nu'kwa'q	II	burn
nu'kwa't	AI	burn
Nuel	NA	Christmas
nuji	PV	of the nature of, one who does
nujiapoqnmuet	NA	helper, assistant
nujikaqma'tawalsewet	NA	Intermediary
nujikina'muet	NA	teacher
nujikina'mueti'skw	NA	female teacher
nujikina'mueti'skwe'j	NA	young woman teacher
nujikjijiteket	NA	learned man
nujiktanit	NA	adversary
nujimaqatui'kti'tij	NA	bankers
nujinstmalsewet	NA	interpreter
NujiPkwatawalsewet	NA	Redeemer
nujitpi'ket	NA	Indian agent, distributor
Nujiwstawi'wet	NA	Saviour
nujiwsua'teket	NA	policeman
nujj	NA	my father
nujjinen	NA	our Father (priest)
nuku', nuku'j	XP	henceforth, from now on
nuku'jewij	II	let that be enough for now, stop
nukuk	TI	pulverise
nukwaltuko'n(k)	NA	comb(s)
nulmi	PV	by heart, from memory
nulmite'tk	TI	know by heart
nulmiw	XP	by heart, from memory
nuluks	NA	my nephew
nun'ji	NI	my head
nunat	AI	suckle, be at the breast
nunet	AI	suckle, be at the breast
nunuji	NI	my head
nuse'skw	NA	female animal
nuskaluk, nsiskuk	XP	before me (eyes, face)
nusukwat	AI	follow
nusukwik	II	it follows me
nusumskw	NA	female beaver
nuta'mat	AI	lack, not have enough
nuta'q	XP	lack, incomplete
nuta'q	II	lack, incomplete
nuta't	AI	lack something; it is missing
nutaiw	XP	finally, late; near, far
nutapteket	NA	an inspector, an overseer
nutawtikmuet	NA	shepherd, guide
nute'k, kute'k, wute'k	XP	behind me, you, him
nutk	TI	hear, hear it said
nutmu'kwl	T	we (incl.) hear them (inan.)

nutnk	TI	carry, be an acolyte
nutnajl	TA	carry, be an acolyte
nutnewet	AI	be a bearer, servant, acolyte
nutqwe'k	AI	be young, inexperienced
nutqwo'ltijik	NA	youths
nutuajl	TA	hear
o'pla'teket	AI	do evil, bad, harm
o'pla'toq	TI	offend, curse
oqnipkwa'toq	TI	hide, cache, inter, bury
oqoj	XP	for, indeed
oqomajl	TA	separate from
oqosi	NA	(finger)nail, claw
oqotey	NA	wife, husband, friend
oqoti	NA	friend
oqotkwetajl	TI	attach
oqu, oquj	XP	for, indeed
oqwa't	AI	to come ashore, land
oqwatk	XP	the north, wind from the north
oqwatke'l	XP	from the north side
oqwatn	XP	north
oqwatnuk	XP	from the north
ptewey	NI	tea
pteweyo'q	NI	teapot
pa	XP	certainly, indeed
pa'kewimkek	XP	Passover
pa'kewimk	XP	Easter
pa'kewimkek	XP	Easter,
pa'qalamajl	TA	view with admiration
pa'qapukuatk	TI	confess (one's sins)
pa'qapukuet	AI	confess one's sins
pa'qapukuo'ti	NI	confession
pa'qi	PV	completely
pa'qlaik	AI	be astonished, surprised, to admire
pa'tlia's	NA	priest
pa'tlia'sewit	AI	be a priest
pa'tlia'si'skw	NA	schoolmistress, nun
pa'tlia'si'skwe'j	NA	novice
pa'tlia'sji'j	NA	cleric
pajiji	PV	very, extremely, excess, above
pajijil'ue'wit	NI	excess of malice
pajijimlkita't	AI	the bravest among us
pajijiaq	II	that which surpasses
pajijiknat	AI	stronger
pajijiw	XP	above
pakusi('k)	NA	lily(s)
pana'toq	TI	open (in general)
pananqa'toq	TI	open (book)
panianuk	XP	next spring
paniaq	XP	spring
paniaqek	XP	last spring
panilja'sit	AI	open the hand
panilja'toq	TI	open another's hand
pansaqa'toq	TI	open with a key, as a chest
panta'toq	TI	open (a door)
papit	AI	play
papka'sit	AI	go down, downstream
papke'k	XP	downstream
papuaqn	NI	game
paqasiet	AI	he falls in the water
paqeket	AI	throw everything
paqtsajl	TA	fill with smoke
paqtsit	AI	be sick of it
paqtsk	TI	fill with smoke
pask	XP	only
paske'skmuatl	TA	crush
pata'sit	AI	commit a fault
pata'suti	NI	iniquity
pata'teket	AI	commit sin
pataluti	NI	table
patatujke'l	XP	on the left side
patekisk	II	the weather gets bad
pawe'k	AI	be slow, lazy
pawi	PV	slowly
pe'ikwi	PV	throughout, entirely
pe'ikwialsusit	NA	universal master
pe'ikwieleke'wit	NA	universal king
pe'ikwiw	XP	throughout, entirely
pe'l	XP	wait a minute!, listen
pe'l qasqew	XP	wait a little
pe'skk	TI	fire a gun at something
pe'sktek	II	a gun goes off
pe'skajl	TA	fire a gun at someone
pe'sketek	II	the gun goes off
pe'skewey	NI	gun
pejila'sit	AI	advance, go ahead

pejili	PV	most, more, very	pema'lajl	TA	carry
pejiliklu'lk	II	most beautiful	pema'q	TI	swim
pejiliksalkusit	NA	beloved, favourite	pema'toq	TI	carry
pejiliksaluet	NA	the most loving	pemape'k	II	hereditary
pejilimsiki'k	NI	biggest	pemapeksit	AI	come by generation
pejilinaskwenik	NA	most virginal	pemaqmi'k	TI	walk on snowshoes, move ahead
pejilipktaik	II	to the highest degree, in excelsis	pemi'k	II	last
pejilisape'wit	AI	most holy	pemi'pit	AI	trot
pejiliknat	AI	stronger	pemi	PV	along
pejiliw	XP	more	pemiankite'tk	TI	keep thinking about
pejilkilk	AI	larger	pemiaq	II	go, continue, move, flow (time)
pejipuk	XP	winter which is close			
pekaj, pejajiw	XP	entirely, from top to bottom	pemiet	AI	walk, move along, advance
pekaje'k	AI	be straight, pure, well preserved	pemipuk	XP	during the winter
			pemiteket	AI	make things grow
pekat	NI	last quarter, just finishing	pemitk	II	it flows
pekije'k	XP	long, a long time	pemlukwet	AI	continue to work
pekiji	PV	long, a long time	pemwi'kiket	AI	continue to write
pekilew(k)	NA	glass(es)	penoqite'lmajl	TA	scorn, think nasty things of
pekisink	AI	come	pepsite'lmajl	TA	scorn
pekisitoq	TI	bring, fetch, lead to	pepso'tasit	AI	be dominated, vanquished
pekisulajl	TA	bring to, lead to	pesaq	II	it is snowing
pekisulsit	AI	reach	pese'k	TA	feel, scent
pekisutajl	TA	bring it to someone	pesetoq	TI	feel, scent
pekitpit	AI	seated for a long time	pesi'kukwet	AI	drive the wood down the river
pekitqatk	TI	remain for a long time in one spot			
			pesi'kwet	AI	drive the wood down the river
peknetk	II	it gets dark			
pekwalajl	TA	procure, acquire, make, cause	pesikitk	II	it forks (Windsor)
			peska'lk	TA	I lead him off the trail
pekwanajl	TA	help, nurse (a patient), move	peskmkewey, pessmkewey NA object of piety, image, relic		
pekwank	TI	help, nurse (a patient), move	peskwesk	TI	mow, harvest, scythe, shear, reap
pekwatasit	AI	procure, make for oneself	pesoqopskatoq	TI	fail (one's duty)
pekwatawalsewajl	TA	procure on behalf of	pesoqwa'toq	TI	avoid, miss out, divert
pekwatawalsewet	AI	redeem	pesqa'lk	TA	I skin an animal
pekwateliket	AI	buy	pesqunatek	XP	nine
pekwatelk	TI	buy	pesqunatekewey	NI	ninth
pekwateluajl	TA	buy	pessmkewey, peskmkewey NA relic, medal		
pekwatoq	TI	make, cause, procure, acquire	pestie'walajl	TA	celebrate, keep as a holiday
			pestie'watk	TI	celebrate, keep as a holiday
pekwatuajl	TA	cause to have, procure	pestie'wimk	NI	feast
pela'toq	TI	miss	pestie'wit	AI	celebrate
peli	PV	fail to do	pestunk	TI	preach

pesu'kwet	AI	leap up, rush headlong
pesua'toq	TI	dry
petaqn	NI	tart
pettniaq	II	the wind rises
pewa'q	TI	sweep
pewalajl	TA	wish, desire, need
pewat	AI	dream
pewatk	TI	want, have need of, wish, desire
pewatmuajl	TA	want from
pewi'ket	AI	sweep
pewiajl	TA	dream about someone
pewitoq	TI	dream about something
pewituajl	TI	dream which concerns him
pi'kun	NI	feather
pi'taw	XP	up river, upstream
pi'tawa'q	TI	row, swim against the current
pi'tawa'sit	AI	ascend, go upstream
piamkilk	AI	be very large
pijoqosuti('k)	NA	pin(s), button(s)
pikweli, pukweli	PV	numerous, many
pikwelieulite'teket	AI	rich in mercy
pikwelk, pukwelk(ik)	AI	numerous, several
pikwelkl	II	several
pikwelukuna'q	II	a good many days
piley	XP	new
pili	PV	new
piljaqn	NA	glove
pilokwet	NA	parrot
pilsimajl	TA	bear false witness
piltu'kmnie'uti	NI	first communion
piltua'teket	AI	behave strangely
piltuey	XP	strange, new, unusual
piltui	PV	new, first, peculiar, strange, unusual
piltuk	NI	new rope
piluey	XP	other, different, another
piluey wen	NA	someone else
pilui	PV	other
pimat	AI	hunt birds
pipanuijkatk	TI	examine, scrutinize
pipnaqn	NI	bread
pipnaqne'ket	AI	go to look for, procure bread
pipnaqnik	II	there is some bread
pipnaqnit	AI	be bread
pipnaqnji'j	NI	roll, little bread
pipnaqsikn	NI	piece of bread, cake
pipnaqsiknu'j	NI	little piece of bread
pipnu'jaqmati	NI	mirror
piptoqopska'lajl	TA	form, shape in the round, mold
piptoqopska'toq	TI	form, shape in the round, mold
piptoqoqwa'toq	TI	make round
piptoqwa'toq	TI	make round
pipukwaqnl	NI	instruments
pis	NA	flea
pisit	AI	be inside, contained
piskiaq	II	late, dark
piskwa'q	II	enter
piskwa't	AI	enter
piskwa'toq	TI	bring in (a thing, quantity)
pisuiw	XP	freely, uselessly, in vain
pita'q	II	long
pita'qawe'l	NI	trousers
pitalqek	II	deep, high
pitapeka'toq	TI	pass something the length of
pitasuik	TI	walk in the snow
pitkmatk	TI	load (a ship, cart)
pitlika'sit	AI	take a long stride
pitlikat	AI	have a long stride
pitoqsit	AI	long
pitu'kun	NA	mantle
pitui	PV	lengthened, raised, beyond, at bottom
pitui laplusn, laplisun	NI	interior of the prison
pitui waqlusan	NI	the inner tower, inside the tower
pituimtlnaqn	NI	thousand
pituimtlnaqnijik	NA	thousand, (pl.)
pituimtlnaqnl	NI	thousand (pl.)
pituiniskamij	NA	greatgrandfather
pituiniskamijk	NA	ancestors
pituiwuji'ji	NA	great grandchildren
pjiliw	XP	especially
pkesikn	NI	silver coin
pketesnuk	XP	from the south
pkewe'k	XP	below
pkewe'ke'l	XP	down below
pkewiet	AI	descend, go down
pku('k)	NA	gum, resin, wax, incense

pkumaqn	NI	whip, weapon
pkuo'q(ok)	NA	incense box(es)
plamue'ket	AI	fish for salmon
plasulk	NI	schooner
plawej	NA	partridge
pleku	NI	nail
ples	NA	pigeon
plmskw	NA	male beaver
plos	NI	brush
pmtn(k)	NA	ridge(s), mountain chain(s)
pneknmuajl	TA	give from on high
pneskwit	NA	brood, litter
pnet	AI	lay (eggs)
pniaskwit	NA	litter (whales, seals)
poqji	PV	begin, beginning
poqjikit	AI	be conceived
poqjit	AI	flee
poqnitpa'q	NI	dark night, darkness, shadows, gloom
poqtkimajl	TA	ordain
poqtamka'sit	AI	start off, leave (by land)
poqtamkiaqeweyi	AI	I am the beginning
poqtamkiet	AI	leave (by water)
poqtlukwet	AI	begin to work
pqtaik, kptaik	XP	on high
pqan	NI	nut
pqanj	NI	hazelnuts
pqanji'j	NI	hazelnuts
pqaw	NA	spruce bark
pqawikan(l)	NI	cabin(s) covered with spruce bark
pqo'qt	NI	bump, bruise, lump
pqoju	NA	fugitive
pqotnanj	NA	bastard
pu'tay(k)	NA	bottle(s)
puaqn	NI	dream
puatk	TI	to want
puessu(aq)	NA	bushel(s)
pui'kn(k)	NA	broom(s)
puksuk(ul)	NI	fire log(s)
puktaqapteket	AI	look at only one object
puktaqi	PV	uniquely
puktaqita'simk	NI	fixed idea
puktew	NI	fire
puktewe'ji'j	NI	match
puktewey	NI	of fire
puktewijk	NI	intoxicating beverage (fire water)
puktewo'kuom	NI	(fiery) furnace
pukuales	NA	swallow
pukwelk(ik), pikwelk	AI	many, numerous
pukwelk(l)	II	many
pukwelukuna'q	II	a good many days
pukwey	NI	half
pun'jiko'teket	AI	stop sulking
puna'toq	TI	abandon, cease, renounce
punape'k	II	lack
puneket	AI	leave alone, stop doing
punewenk	TI	stop talking, crying
punewistoq	TI	stop talking, speaking
puni	PV	stop
puniaq	II	be finished
puniet	AI	be finished
punitoq	TI	stop making something
punkwilat	AI	stop barking
punmila'sit	AI	stop playing
puntemit	AI	stop crying
puntoqsit	AI	stop wailing
punulkwalajl	TA	stop following
puowin(aq)	NA	sorcerer(s), witch(es)
pusit	AI	set out in a boat, embark
puskatalmk	NI	greediness
puskatalmajl	TA	be greedy
puski, puksi	PV	subject to, inclined to
puskialita'sit	AI	be subject to distractions
puskiawan'ta'sit	AI	be very forgetful
puskiwe'kwata'sit	AI	be a real coward
puskiwkwaimk	NI	anger
pustemit	AI	weep a lot
pusu'l puna'ne	XP	happy New Year
pusu'l	XP	good day
pusue'l	XP	good evening
putp	NA	whale
putpe'skw	NA	female whale
putmat	AI	lack, omit, get out of doing
putu'suinu	NA	orator
qajue'wj(ik)	NA	cat (Restigouche; see also, mia'wj(k))
qalipu	NA	caribou
qaliputi	NI	shovel

qamawtik	XP	on the other side of the road or street
qame'k	XP	on the other side (river, valley, plain)
qamso'q	NI	rocks on the other side, Canso
qamu('k)	NA	suet pudding(s)
qasawo'q	NI	iron
qasawo'qapi	NA	iron wire
qasawo'qwey awti	NI	railroad
qasawo'qwey	NI	instrument of iron
qaskew, qasko	XP	wait!, stop!, listen!, whoa!
qasqe'k, kjikmuk	XP	on the shore
qosi('k)	NA	nails
qwaijk, qwaik, qwaikl	XP	in the middle, among, close to
sa'l	NI	shawl
sa'pk	TI	pierce
sa'pajl	TA	pierce
sa'q	XP	long ago
sa'qati('k)	NA	needle(s)
sa'qawe'jkik	NA	the ancients
sa'qawey	NI	old
sa'se'wa'toq	TI	change
salawey	NI	salt
sama'lajl	TA	touch
sama'toq	TI	touch
samuqwan	NI	water
samuqwanik	II	there is water
samuqwanji'j	NI	drop of water
sansu	NI	a dollar
santewi	PV	holy
santewit	AI	be holy
sape'wiet	AI	become wise or holy
sape'winu	NA	saint
sape'wit	AI	be wise, holy, virtuous
sape'wit kmu'j	NA	Christmas tree
sape'wuti	NI	grace, virtue, wisdom
sape'wuti	NI	grace, virtue, wisdom
sapetime'kw	NA	grampus
sapo'nuk	XP	tomorrow
sapteskuajl	TA	brush against
saqatuetesink	AI	fall, stretch out on the ground
saqma'j	NA	little chief, son of the chief
saqma'ji'j	NA	baby chief
saqma'skw	NA	chief's wife, a lady
saqma'skwe'j	NA	miss
saqma'skwe'ji'j	NA	miss
saqmaw	NA	chief, master, lord
saqmawa'ki	NI	chieftancy, district
saqmawit	AI	be a chief
saqntesk	II	fall lightly
saqpiku'n	NI	tear
saqsikwesk	TI	light (by rubbing)
saqsikwet	AI	fish by torch
saqtk	TI	obey, respond
saqtuajl	TA	obey
se'k	XP	in vain
se'kewe'l	NI	useless things
se'kewey	NI	a trifle
se'kewey mijua'ji'j	NA	found infant
se'sitk	II	it flows in all directions
se'skwet	AI	shout, cry out
sekepen(k)	NA	artichoke(s)
sekwiska'toq	TI	break, violate
semuimink	NA	rosary (see also, sunmink)
senkatikn	NI	raft
sent, sentl, sensl	NI	cent
senusaqtnuk	XP	from the southwest
sepaik	AI	hunt in the morning
sepanqa'toq	TI	close a book
sepey, sepay	XP	this morning
sepiljenajl	TA	hold in the hand (closed)
sepiljenk	TI	hold in the hand (closed)
sepiljo'tlajl	TA	put in the hand
sepiljo'tlk	TI	put in the hand
sesaki'k	TI	be barefoot
sesaki'kewey	NI	barefooted
sespapukuet	AI	talk stupidly
sespe'k	AI	dissipated, restless
sespena'q	NI	noise, racket
sespeta'sit	AI	be restless
sespi	PV	dissipated, restless
sesupa'lukwet	AI	glide, slide
sewiska'toq	TI	break, violate
sewk	II	sweet
sewkewey	NI	tid bit
si'ko'ku's	NA	March, Spring month
si'st	XP	three, three times

si'stewa'j	NA	third	
si'stewey	NI	third	
si'stewey	XP	Wednesday	
siawi	PV	often, continually	
siawiw	XP	continually	
sik, pasik	XP	only	
sikapun(k)	NA	artichoke(s)	
sikntasit	AI	be baptized	
sikntatimk	NI	baptism	
sikntuajl	TA	baptize	
sikun	XP	last spring	
sikunuk	XP	next spring	
sikw	XP	spring, springtime	
siniw	XP	suddenly, all together	
sinumkw(aq)	NA	wild goose, Canada goose	
sipeli	PV	in rank, in series	
sipeliw	XP	often	
sipelpukua'lajl	TA	arrange	
sipelpukua'toq	TI	arrange	
sipikk	II	it is hard, tough	
sipu'si's	NI	stream	
sipu('l)	NI	river(s)	
sipua'toq	TI	change into a river	
sisip	NA	bird (see also, jipji'j)	
sisku	NI	mud,	
sispanikn	NA	soap	
sitnikuk	AI	blow one's nose	
siwatqatk	TI	be bored (in one's house)	
siwe'k	AI	be tired, bored	
skmtuk, smtuk	XP	next, then, moreover; at once	
skatu, katu	XP	but, however	
skmnaqn	NI	observation post	
skmttuk, smttuk	XP	immediately	
sku	NA	leech	
skus(k)	NA	weasel(s)	
skwe'kwik	NA	female otter, fox	
skweme'kw	NA	female fish	
skwesm	NA	female canine (bitch)	
skwew	NA	female chicken (hen)	
skwewiaq	NA	female seal	
snawey	NA	maple	
snaweye'l puksukul	NI	maple wood (for burning)	
snaweyey	NI	of maple	
staqe, staqa	XP	like, as	
stoqn(k)	NA	fir (pl.), palm(s)	
su'n(l)	NI	berry(s)	
suel	XP	almost, nearly, as it were	
suklkaq	II	rotten	
sukwi'	NA	aunt	
suliewey	NI	silver, money	
sulieweye'ket	AI	go to look for, procure money	
sulieweyey	NI	of silver	
sulieweyiktuk	XP	with money	
sulieweyo'kuom	NI	bank	
sulnalji'j	NI	small journal	
sumalki	NI	one cent, piece of copper	
sunminji'jk	NA	rosary	
sunmink	NA	rosary, rosary beads (see also, semuimink)	
suppin(k)	NA	pint(s), cup(s), less than a litre	
suspanikn	NA	soap	
tptuk	XP	however, only	
ta	XP	question particle	
ta'n	XP	how, who, which, when, where, that, what	
ta'n nqasaiw	XP	as soon as	
ta'n pa ki'l	XP	as you wish	
ta'n pa tujiw	XP	whenever, anytime	
ta'n tami	XP	in those places where	
ta'n tlisip	XP	when	
ta'pu	XP	two, twice	
ta'puk	XP	two	
ta'puowa'j	NA	second	
ta'puowey	NI	second, Tuesday	
ta's	XP	how many times?	
ta's ajiet	AI	what time is it?	
ta'skl	NI	how many things	
ta'sa'q	NI	how big, what capacity?	
ta'sa'ql	NI	how many of these things?	
ta'sijik	AI	be how many, how many persons	
ta'sipuno'ltiyoq?	AI	how old are you?	
ta'sipunqk?	XP	how many years?	
ta'sukuna'q	XP	how many days?	
tal'pesuk	II	of what length?, how far?	
tal'pita'q	II	of what length?, how far?	
tal'pitoqsit	AI	of what length?, how far?	

tala'ljl	TA	treat in an unpleasant manner	te'pk	TI	deserve
tala'tu?	TI	what do I do with it?	te'pi'sewey	NI	pepper
talawtik	II	what price	te'pine'klewey	NI	vinegar
tale'k	XP	well!, what?, right?	te'plma'sewey	NI	cheese
tale'k	AI	how is he?	te's	XP	so many times
tali	PV	how	te'skl	NI	so many things
taliamasek	II	of what length?, how far?	te'skl	II	be so many
taliksukk	II	how heavy?	te'si	PV	each
taliwlein	AI	how are you?	te'si'kw	AI	be so many, we are such a number
taliaq	II	happen	te'sijik	NA	so many persons
talki'k	II	how big?	te'sikiskk	XP	each day
talkilk	AI	how big?	te'sinipk	XP	every summer
taluisit	AI	what is his name?	te'sipow	NA	horse
tami	XP	how, where?	te'sipowl'kwetu	NA	female horse
tami se'k	XP	elsewhere	te'sipunqk	NI	each year, every year
tami ta	XP	where ever?	te'sit	XP	each, each one
tami wejiaq	II	whence comes it, how come?	teke'ji'jk	II	a little cold
			teke'k	II	it is cold
tamie'l, tamieke'l	XP	toward what place, where to?	tekelukuna'q	NI	a few days
			teken	XP	what, who, whom, which
tapatan(k), tapatat(k)	NA	potato(es)	teki	PV	cold
tapatat(k), tapatan(k)	NA	potato(es)	tekieskitpu'k	NI	cold morning
tapi('k)	NA	bow(s)	tekikiskk	NI	cold day
tapu'kl	XP	two, two things	tekiwla'kw	NI	cold evening
tapu'kl tlantsu'l	NI	cents	tekik	II	it is cold
tapuinska'ql	NI	twenty (pl.)	tekinipk	XP	early summer
tapuiska'q	XP	twenty	tekipuk	XP	cold winter
tapuiska'qawey	NI	twentieth	tekitpa'q	II	cold night
tapuiskeksijik	NA	twenty	teklamsk	NI	cold wind
tapuiskeksuti	NI	score	teko'ti'kw	AI	be present together
tapukumu'kw	AI	go as two in a boat	teko'tk	TI	attend, be with (mass, assembly)
tapukuna'q	II	it is two days, two days			
tapuleyikw	AI	we are in two boats	teksk	NI	wind from the northwest
tapunaji	TA	he has two of them	tekweiwajl	TA	be with, assist
tapusijik	NA	two, two people	tel'pesuk	II	so far
taqmajl	TA	strike	tela'sit	AI	act thus
taqtk	TI	strike	tela'tasit	AI	treat self thus
taqtaqatimkewey	NI	telegram, a message	tela'tati'kw	AI	shake hands
taqte'k	TI	strike	tela'teket	AI	do this, do thus
taqteket	AI	hit, tap, telegraph	tela'tikl	II	they behave so
tatuji	PV	what extent, what age?	tela'toq	TI	do thus, treat thus, render thus
taultna'sit	AI	open the mouth			
te'j	XP	either	telakik	NI	flat round piece
te'ksek	XP	northwest	telamu'k	II	resemble, appear to be, such, like, similar
te'kseke'l	XP	from the northwest			

THE MI'KMAW GRAMMAR OF FATHER PACIFIQUE

telamuksit	AI	appear such	teluisit	AI	be so named, be named thus
telapukuet	AI	speak thus, promise			
telawtik	II	be worth so much	tema'kitteket	AI	saw
tele'k	AI	be such, in such a state	temik	II	it is deep
tele'k	II	be thus	temsk	TI	cut (a knife, a sickle, etc.)
teleiwajl	TA	treat someone so	temsajl	TA	cut (a knife, a sickle, etc.)
telewistoq	TI	speak thus	temsasik	II	be cut
teli	PV	thus, there	temte'ket	AI	work hard
teli'sit	AI	speak thus	teptuk	XP	alone, only, except that, however
teliamasek	II	so far			
telisqatajl	TA	obey	tepa'sit	AI	embark
teliaq	II	that is so, that is true	tepa'toq	TI	set down (an offering)
teliaqawey	NI	truth	tepate	NI	fish, meat pie
teliknat	AI	be so strong	tepaw	XP	near
telima't	AI	smell of	tepawe'l	XP	close enough, soon
telimajl	TA	say to someone, tell	tepe'k	TI	deserve
telintoq	TI	sing, sing thus	tepeket	AI	put into the collection, make a gift
telita'sit	AI	express though			
telita'suinuit	AI	be a thinking, reflecting being	tepesk	NI	an even number
			tepi	PV	enough
telitat	AI	be of such strength	tepi'ket	AI	divide, distribute
telite'lmajl	TA	think thus, believe, judge thus	tepiajl	TA	distribute to
			tepiaq	II	it, that is enough
telite'tk	TI	think of	tepite'tk	TI	find it enough, to be just right
telite'tasit	AI	be thought so			
telite'teket	AI	think so	tepkik(l)	NI	night(s)
telite'tk	TI	think thus, suppose so	tepknuset	NA	month, moon
telki'k	II	be of such a size, height	tepknusetewey	NI	calendar
telkilk	AI	be of such height	teplmajl	TA	judge
telkimajl	TA	command, order, tell thus	teplutk	TI	judge, rule
telkitasit	AI	prescribe, be counted	tepo'toq	TI	set down (a quantity)
tellukwet	AI	work thus	teppit	AI	be on board
telmtk	TI	behave	tepqatk	TI	be married
telmtoq	TI	behave thus	teptek, kettek	XP	inside a vessel, within
telnajl	TA	hold thus	tepu'lewey	NI	butter
telo'tk	TI	treat as such	tetapu	PV	exactly
telo'tasit	AI	be thus treated	tetapu'tesk	II	happen just right
telo'teket	AI	treat thus	tetapua'teket	AI	behave properly
telo'tmasit	AI	be treated as such	tetapua'toq	TI	do exactly, satisfy
teltamajl	TA	ask of	tetapuiaq	II	the time has come, just in time
telte'k	TI	cut, hack			
teluet	AI	speak, talk thus	tetlaqatk	TI	live here
telui'kasik	II	it is written	tetli	PV	in this place
telui'tk	TI	name thus	tetlimawieyikw	AI	assemble here
telui'tajl	TA	name thus	tetpaqa'q	II	what is, what happens
			tetpi	PV	equally

tetpiaq	II	it is time	tmkewa'j	NA	first
tetpikilk	AI	be of the same size	tmkewet	AI	be in first place
tett tleyawit	AI	be from	tmkewey	NI	first (in position), first of all
tett, ula tett	XP	here	tmoqta'w	NA	log, trunk of a tree
tette'l	XP	this way, in this direction	tmpuessu	NA	half bushel
tettoq	TI	have, owe	to'q	XP	however, then, therefore
tettuajl	TA	owe	tomawey	NI	tobacco
tettuet	AI	owe, be in debt	topaqn(l)	NI	toboggan(s), sleigh(s)
tettuo'qn	NI	debt	toqjua't	AI	go up
tetuje'k	AI	be that age, be so old	toqnasijik	AI	they live together
tetuji	PV	such extent, such age	toqnk	TI	have part of something
tewa'toq	TI	get something out	toqonasit	AI	live together
tewalqa'lajl	TA	take out	toqopukua'toq	TI	place together, unite
tewalqa'sit	AI	be rescued	toqu	XP	then, next
tewalqa'toq	TI	rip out	toqu tlisip, toqu tujiw	XP	next, then, after
tewaqa'toq	TI	take it outdoors	toqwa'q	XP	autumn
teweket	AI	throw out	toqwa'qek	XP	last autumn
tewiet	AI	go out	toqwanqa'toq	TI	join
tey	XP	wife, husband, companion	toqwatk	TI	join with another
tia'm(uk)	NA	moose	tpi	T	give him his share
tia'mue'ket	AI	go to look for, procure meat	tpi'i, tpi'	T	give me a share
tkpoq	NI	spring	tpu'nuk	XP	during this night
tkesnuk	XP	from the west	tpuk	XP	this morning
tkey	NI	cold	tqo'nuk	XP	next autumn
tkey matnik	TA	I have a cold	tqope'j	NA	twin
tku('k)	NA	wave(s)	tqoq	XP	last autumn
tkwik	II	there's a sea running	tu'aqn(k)	NA	ball(s) (for games)
tlako'pn(k)	NA	hellebore, hemlock, poisonous plant	tu's	XP	my daughter
			tuaqjikn	XP	ounce
tlantsu	NI	cents	tuey	NA	comrade
tlaqatik	NI	Tracadie, home settlement	tujiw	XP	then
tle'k	AI	be from, belong	tuksp	XP	perhaps
tle'l	XP	belonging to	tuli'jewe'l	NI	rice
tleyawit	AI	belong, be from there	tulkewey	NI	cannon
tlia', tlia'j	XP	although	tuoptia'toq	TI	frame
tliaj	II	amen	tuoq	XP	not known, how would I know?
tlisip	XP	when, then			
tma'qani(aq)	NA	shell bird(s)	tupi('k)	NA	spruce root(s)
tmaqn, tomaqn	NA	pipe	tutupi('k)	NA	spruce root(s)
tmawey	NI	tobacco			
tmelet(k)	NA	glass(es), tumbler(s)			
tmi'kn	NI	axe	u'j	NA	fly
tmi'kna'q	TA	have an axe	u'n	NI	fog
tmia	NI	half pint	u't	XP	who is this?; this one, this, that, here
tmipias	NI	fifty cents, halfdollar			
tmk	XP	firstly, at first	ukumuljin	XP	eight

ukumuljinewey	NI	eighth
ula	XP	this, this one, that one, here
ula tett	XP	right here, in this very place
ulae'l	XP	in this direction
upukj	XP	soon, before long
upukji	PV	soon, before long
usit	AI	warm oneself
utan	NI	village
utqotalajl	TA	inter, bury
utqotat	AI	have a funeral, take part in one
utqotatk	TI	inter, bury
wa'kw	NA	louse
wa'qaj	XP	hardly, almost impossible
wa'qewa'sit	AI	be made flesh
wa'qey	NI	flesh
wa'so'q	XP	heaven
wa'w(l)	NI	egg(s)
wa'we'ket	AI	gather eggs
wa'wey	NI	made of eggs
waij	NA	imp, sorcerer's doll
waijuey mun'ti	NI	medicine bag
waisis, wi'sis	NA	animal
waisisemo'kuom	NI	den, lair
waju'pet	AI	full
waju'pit	AI	be full
wala	NI	those things or persons, there
walae'l, waqelaik	XP	on this side
walamkew	NI	fishing hole
walney	NI	bay
walpo'q	NI	pond
waltes	NI	dice game
waltestaqn	NI	wooden dish for the game of dice
wanpit, wantaqpit	AI	sit still
wansit	NA	servant
wantaqa'lajl	TA	pacify
wantaqe'k	AI	be peaceful
wantaqi	PV	tranquillity
wantaqnajl	TA	keep quiet
wantaqpekitk	II	calm
wantaqpit, wanpit	AI	sit still
wape'k	AI	white
wapekna'q	AI	be dressed in white
wapiet	AI	whiten
wapk	II	it is daylight, dawn
wapkek	XP	at the break of day
wapn	NI	dawn
wapna'ki	NI	land of the dawn, of the Abenaki
wapniaq	II	daylight appears, it is dawn
wapnme'kw	NA	white porpoise
wapus	NA	hare, rabbit
waqasit	NA	wild animal
waqat	NI	those
waqla	XP	these, those
waqme'k	AI	be pure
waqmo'ti	NI	purity
waqntew	NI	bone
wasiantej(k)	NA	lamp(s) (glass)
wasitpa'q	II	clear night
wasoqnmaqn	NI	candle
wasoqotesk	NI	lightning
waspu	NA	seal
wassami, awsami, wessami	PV	too much
wastew	NI	snow
wat	NI	these
watapsit	AI	yellow
wataptek(l)	II	yellow
way	NI	his property
waywal	NI	their wealth
we'jiajl	TA	find
we'jitoq	TI	find
we'kaw, we'kow	XP	then, next, at once
we'kopekitk, we'kwapetkitk	II	the tide rises to there
we'kopekitk, we'kwapekitk	II	the stream runs right to the end
we'kwa'muet	AI	dispute, discuss
we'kwa'q	II	come at the end, that is the end
we'kwanmat	AI	be in need, at one's end
we'kwaptmk	XP	league, as far as the eye can see
we'kwata'sit	AI	be afraid
we'kwi	PV	the end, the completion
we'kwiklu'lk	NI	the most beautiful possible
weja'tekemk	XP	from

weji	PV	from, from there, because of
wejituiet	AI	he comes out
Wejiwli	PV	Paraclete
wejiaq	II	come from, result from
wejiet	AI	come from
wejikit	AI	descend
wejimanit	NA	fruit
wejipulkwet	AI	have convulsions
wejkiet	NA	leper
wejku'nk	TI	bring, pass
wejkuiaq	II	come
wejkuiet	AI	come
wejkunk	TI	give in return
wejkwa'lajl	TA	bring
wejkwa'toq	TI	bring
wejkwapa'q	II	rising tide
wejkwipuk	II	winter is coming
weju'sk	II	it is windy, the wind is blowing
wejuow	XP	near
wejuowa'sit	AI	approach, near
wejuowe'l	XP	nearby
wekaik	AI	get angry, be angry
wekaiwajl	TA	displease
wekaiwinamtpnik	TA	those who have offended us
wekamajl	TA	irritate, glare at
wekaptk	TI	irritate, glare at
weket	XP	these
wekla, nekla	XP	formerly, in that time
wekwijimajl	TA	have as a mother
wekwijit	AI	have a mother
wekwilat	AI	bark
wekwisimajl	TA	have as a son
Wekwisit Niskam	NA	God the Father
wekwisit	AI	have a son
wela'kowey	NI	supper
wela'kw	NI	evening
wela'kwek	XP	yesterday evening
wela'lti'kw	AI	do good to each other
wela'lajl	TA	do someone a good turn
wela'lsit	AI	do good for oneself, flatter oneself
wela'lue'k	AI	do good, do a favor, render a service
wela'luet	AI	develop, procure, look after
wela'luksit	AI	be a beneficiary
wela'sik	II	it is going well
wela'sit	AI	be well, act well
wela'tasit	AI	do good to oneself
wela'tat	AI	favour
wela'tati'kw	AI	do good mutually
wela'teket	AI	do well, do good, act good
wela'toq	TI	treat well, do good
wela'tuajl	TA	favour the interests of an other
wela'tuet	AI	favour others, in general
wela'tuksit	AI	be favoured in one's affairs
welamajl	TA	look kindly on
welamkusit	AI	good looking; be well considered
welamu'k	II	good looking, of a good kind
welapskiet	AI	get tips
welaptk	TI	look favourably on
welapukuet	AI	speak well
welataluksit	AI	well nourished
wele'k	II	good, that is good
wele'k	AI	be well, happy
weleiwajl	TA	do good to him
weleiwet	AI	be beneficient
welekisk	II	it is fine at sea
weleyasit	AI	treat oneself well
weleyati'kw	AI	act thus towards one another, each other
weleyuksit	AI	be well treated, blessed
weli	PV	well
weliketla'mstasit	AI	believe
welikiskk	II	good day
welipmiet	AI	move, walk well
weliusit	AI	warm oneself well
weliaq	II	all right, that is good
weliet	AI	become happy
welikisk	NI	beautiful weather
welikiskk	II	it is fine on land, beautiful day
welikwet	AI	grow well
welimajl	TA	bless
welintoq	TI	sing well
welipuk	XP	good winter
welita'sit	AI	be content, happy
welite'lsit	AI	be pleased with oneself

welite'lti'kw	AI	wish each other well
welite'lket	AI	be merry, be tipsy
welite'lmajl	TA	think well of
welite'lmuksit	AI	be the object of good thoughts
welite'lsit	AI	be happy with self
welite'tk	TI	approve, be willing
welite'tasit	AI	be wished well
welite'teket	AI	agree, be of that opinion
welite'tmakuet	AI	be wished well
welite'tmasit	AI	wish oneself well
welite'tmat	AI	agree
welite'tmati'kw	AI	wish each other well
welite'tmuajl	TA	be happy for someone
welite'tmuet	AI	wish well on behalf of others
welite'tmuksit	AI	be wished well
welitpa'q	NI	beautiful night
welkilk	AI	of good height
welkwija'sit	AI	to rejoice
welmtoq	TI	be good, behave well
welnmat	AI	be next
welo'tk	TI	treat a thing well, bless it
welo'tasit	AI	be blessed, be happy in one's affairs
welo'teket	AI	do well, profit
welo'tmakwet	AI	be blessed in one's affairs
welo'tmasit	AI	look after one's own interests
welo'tmat	AI	bless (in general), do favours
welo'tmati'kw	AI	do good for each other
welo'tmuajl	TA	treat something well for someone
welo'tmuet	AI	bless, do a favour
welo'tmuksit	AI	receive favours
welpekitk	II	flow well
welpit	AI	be well seated
welqwana'q	AI	be well clothed
welstk	TI	listen with pleasure
weltek	II	well placed
weltesink	AI	succeed, be lucky, meet success
welteskuajl	TA	meet
wemtkit	AI	have a native land
wen	XP	who, someone
wen'ji'kuom	NI	house
wen'ji'kuoma'q	TA	occupy a house
wen'ju'su'n(l)	NI	apple(s)
wen'ju'sukapun	NA	turnip
wen'ju'sun	NI	apple
wen'jui'skw	NA	French woman
wen'jui'skwe'j	NA	French girl
wen'juiko'komink	NA	plums, prunes
wen'juit	AI	be French
wen'juksnan(k)	NA	French footwear
wen'jutia'm	NA	cow (bovine)
wen'jutia'mu'j	NA	calf
wen'jutia'muey	NI	beef
wenaqa'sit	AI	get up, rise
wenaqi	PV	elevation
wenaqiet	AI	leap, jump, rise
wenaqkwija'sit	AI	raise one's thoughts
wenaskomit	AI	have a handmaid
wenijanit	AI	have children
weniskamijit	AI	have as a grandfather
weniskamit	AI	have as God
wenmaje'k	AI	suffer
wenmajeiwajl	TA	punish
wenmajeyasit	AI	torment oneself
wenmajit	AI	move painfully
wenmajo'teket	AI	torment
wenqaje'k	II	it is troublesome, hard, difficult
Wenuj	NA	Frenchman
wepskuninet	AI	be consumptive
weptnit	AI	have hands
wesamatesikuk	AI	be overburdened
wesaqmamit	AI	have as a lord, chief
wesimuktuajl	TA	flee someone
wesimukulajl	TA	carry away while fleeing
wesimukutoq	TI	carry away while fleeing
wesimukwat	AI	flee
weska'qelmajl	TA	kiss, embrace
weska'qelmsit	AI	be greeted
weska'qelmuet	AI	greet, embrace, kiss
weska'qeltk	TI	kiss, greet with a kiss, embrace
weskewe'k	AI	laugh
weskewkwija'sit	AI	have pleasures
weskiji	PV	on the outside
weskijinuit	AI	be born, live, appear
wesko'tk	TI	have, possess
weskukwat	AI	cook
weskumajl	TA	speak of

wessami, awsami, wassami	PV	too much
westat	AI	be saved, escape
Westau'lkw	NA	the Saviour
westawi'wet	AI	he saves
westawiajl	TA	save, save a person
westawitoq	TI	save a thing
westawituajl	TI	save what belongs to
wesua'latl	TA	take
wesua'toq	TI	take
wetewipnet	AI	complain
wetme'k	AI	be busy; disturb
wetmi	PV	occupation
wetmite'tk	TI	desire
wetmiwajl	TA	be busy with; disturb
wetmo'tk	TI	be busy with; disturb
wetqapatk	TI	put something to soak
wetqol'timkewey	NI	forbidden
wetqolajl	TA	forbid, prevent
wetqoluetoq	TI	forbid a thing
wetqotk	TI	forbid, prevent
wetsa'jl	TA	hunt because of that
wetsmajl	TA	feed with
wettk	II	the wind comes from
wettaqaiet	AI	belong to a party
wetusimajl	TA	have a daughter
wetusit	AI	have a daughter
wi'k	NI	his house, place
wi'katikn	NI	book
wi'kiknapu	NI	ink
wi'kmajl	TA	write to
wi'kue'k	II	that's strange
wi'kueit	AI	couldn't care less
wi'kui	PV	selfishness, egoism
wi'kupaljik	AI	feast together
wi'kupaltimk	NI	feast
wi'kwiat	AI	be dying
wi'n	NI	marrow
wi's	NI	den, beaver lodge
wi'sis, waisis	NA	animal (Restigouche)
wiaqa'toq	TI	mix, mingle
wiaqiw	XP	pellmell, mixed up, confused
wijk	NA	spruce partridge
wijki'skw	NA	female spruce partridge
wije'tijik	AI	go together
wije'wajl	TA	go with, accompany
wijey	XP	likewise, the same
wiji	PV	with
wijitkweiwajl	TA	be with
wijikti'kw	AI	be brothers
wijikmajl	TA	have as brothers, sisters, near kin
wikapu'k	II	taste good
wikapuksit	AI	taste good
wikew	NI	fat
wikewit	AI	be fat
wikk	II	tasty, sweet
wikpajl	TA	like (the taste)
wikpet	AI	like to drink
wiktk	TI	like to eat, like the taste of
wikuom	NI	house, hut
wikupj(ik), wipukji	XP	before long, soon
wikutk	TI	ask for, claim something
wikutmalsewajl	TA	ask for it for someone
wikwaje'jkl	NI	pleasures
wikwi	PV	extinction
wikwiet	AI	die
wilu	NI	his food
wina'toq	TI	dirty, spoil, do wrong
winapukuet	AI	speak bad
wine'jkl	NI	lewdness, evil, bad things
wini	PV	bad, wicked, dirty
winiktkio'ti	NI	disgusting drunkenness
winiaq	II	foul, bad, it is wicked
winiet	AI	be corrupted
winintoq	TI	sing badly
winita'sit	AI	sin
winjik	II	that is bad, evil
winjikl	NI	sins
winmtoq	TI	be bad, behave badly
wino'tasit	AI	be desecrated
wino'tk	TI	profane
winpasit	AI	try, make efforts
winpekitk	II	flow badly
winsuti'l	NI	evils, temptations
wip	NI	sap
wipemajl	TA	sleep with a companion
wipeti'kw	AI	we sleep together
wipetme'kw	NA	shark
wipiet	AI	be with, accompany
wipukj	XP	soon, before long
wipumajl	TA	eat with

wiputi'kw	AI	eat together
wisawey	NI	yellow
wisawisuliewey	NI	gold
wisku'pk	TI	cook for something
wisku'pajl	TA	cook for someone
wiskui	PV	astonishingly
wisqsit	AI	be sick
wisqsuaqn	NI	contagious disease
wisqsuaqnik	II	there is illness
wisqsuti	NI	contagious disease
wisqew	XP	suddenly, quickly
wisqi	PV	suddenly, quickly, promptly
wisqinpk	NI	sudden death
wisqiwkwaik	AI	quickly get angry
wisqoq	NA	ashtree
wisqwi	PV	surprisingly, astonishingly
wissukwalsit	AI	cook for oneself
wissukwet	AI	cook, do the cooking
wissukwo'l	TA	I cook for you
wisuiknetk	TI	conquer, surpass, tame
wisuiknetmuajl	TA	confound
wisun	NI	name
wisunkeuksit	AI	receive a name
wisunkewajl	TA	give a name
wisunkewatk	TI	give a name
witlukuti'kw	AI	work together
witpituajl	TA	be seated with
wituat, wituit	AI	have a beard
wius	NI	meat
wiusapu	NI	broth
wjiaj, wjiej	XP	in order to
wjijaqmijl	NA	his soul
wjipsk	NI	root
wjipnuk	XP	from the east
wjit	XP	for, because of
wksitqamu'k, wskitqamu'k	XP	on earth
wlaku	XP	yesterday
wlaqn	NA	vase, recipient
wlaqnji'j	NA	little vase
WliNi'mamkewey	NI	Extreme Unction
WliNkutiNe'susuti	NI	the Holy Trinity
wlita'suaqnik	II	there is rejoicing
wlita'suti	NI	happiness, joy
wlita'sutik	II	that is fun
wlo'nuk	XP	this evening, tonight
wlo'nukwe'l	XP	towards the evening
wlo'ti	NI	good fortune
wmtki	NI	his country
wnaqani'kn	NI	capital
wnaqapemka	NA	his disciples
wo'kejij	NA	spider
wo'kejija'pi	NA	spider's web, cobweb
wo'kejit	NA	spider
wow(k)	NA	pot(s), vase(s), vessel(s)
wowkwis	NA	fox
wpitney	NI	sleeve
wplaqnek, wpaqm	XP	before, behind him
wskijinu	NA	person
wskijinuik	II	there are people
wskijinuuti	NA	birth, life, nature
wskijipnekw	NA	host
wskitpaqtuk	XP	on the waves
wskitqamu	NI	earth
wskitqamu'k, wksitqamu'k	XP	on earth
wskitqamu'kewaq	NA	people
wskitqamu'kewey	NI	earthly
wskittuk	XP	over, outside of
wskittukewe'l	NI	the exterior things
wskittukwi'kmui	TA	write me the address
wsukuni	NI	his tail
wtejk	XP	the last time
wtejkewey	N	last
wuskaluaq	XP	before, behind him
wutapsun	NI	his belonging, possession

Father (Henri Buisson de Valigny) R. P. Pacifique (1863-1943)

Ordained in Spain in 1886 (L'Ordre des pères Capucins), Fr. Pacifique was sent to Canada in 1890 to further his studies. In 1894, Bishop André-Albert Blais asked the Capucin order to support a mission among the Mi'kmaq at Restigouche, NB. There, Pacifique set out to learn and support the spiritual and cultural well being of his parishioners, including learning the language.

He conducted services in Mi'kmaw, French and English and taught Mi'kmaw to the nuns of religieuses du Saint-Rosaire, in order that they teach catechism to local children. In the early 20th century, he devised a thirteen-letter orthographic system based on French. He wrote a regular column (between 1903 and 1908) in Mi'kmaw in the Saint John *New Freeman*, a weekly newspaper, and oversaw (1906-1936) the monthly *Micmac Messenger* out of Restigouche.

In 1906, he took part in conference in Québec, the "15th International Congress of Americanists," giving a paper on the characteristics of the Mi'kmaq. In 1910, he took advantage of the Montréal International Eucharistic Congress to report on the devotion of the Mi'maq to the Eucharist for three centuries.

In 1910, Pacfique organized a tercentenary celebration of the conversion of Grand Chief Membertou, including all the tribes of Mi'kma'ki.

He published a number of works, including (to name only a few) *Almanach micmac* (1902); *Le Catéchisme micmac* (1913); *Petite histoire de la religion en Micmac*; *Livret de Chants et de Prières en micmac*, 1913; and *Chroniques des plus anciennes églises de l'Acadie, L'Echo De Saint-Francois* (1944).

Father Pacifique of Restigouche, Big Peter Paul, Catherine Sack Maloney, Judge Christopher Paul (with formal top hat), Mary Jeremy Jadis (seated), Stephen John (in fashionable headress), and fellow Mi'kmaqs at St. Anne's Celebration, Shubenacadie, NS, ca. 1905. Nova Scotia Archives.

Referenecs

Creative Commons

Prins, Harald E. L. 1996. *The Mi'kmaq: Resistance, Accommodation, and Cultural Survival*. Fort Worth: Harcourt Brace College Publishers.

Wallis, Wilson D. and Ruth Sawtell Wallis. 1955. *The Micmac Indians of Eastern Canada*. Minneapolis: University of Minnesota Press.

About the Editors

BERNIE FRANCIS, DLitt, grew up on the Maupeltu (Membertou) First Nation community in Cape Breton, NS. From 1970-1974, he worked as the Director of the Court Worker Program for the federal court system.

After leaving the court system, he began training in linguistics with Doug Smith from the University of Toronto, developing a new orthography of the Mi'kmaw language with Smith, now officially recognized by the Mi'kmaw chiefs in Nova Scotia.

With Trudy Sable (Saint Mary's University), he published *The Language of This Land, Mi'kma'ki* (CBU Press 2012).

JOHN HEWSON, Professor Emeritus, Memorial University of Newfoundland, is a scholar of national and international reputation who has had a distinguished career in several branches of linguistics. His scholarly achievements in general linguistics, theoretical linguistics, historical linguistics, Amerindian and Romance linguistics are complemented by more than 14 completed books, 140-plus published papers and reviews and nearly 100 papers to learned societies.

www.ingramcontent.com/pod-product-compliance
Lightning Source LLC
Chambersburg PA
CBHW082112230426
43671CB00015B/2672